BARBARA LEIGH SMITH BODICHON

In memory of my father and mother

CLIFFORD AND JOYCE BLAKEMORE

BARBARA LEIGH SMITH BODICHON

1827–1891

Feminist, Artist and Rebel

PAM HIRSCH

Chatto & Windus

LONDON

First published 1998

1 3 5 7 9 10 8 6 4 2

First published in the United Kingdom in 1998 by Chatto & Windus
Random House, 20 Vauxhall Bridge Road, London SW1V 2SA

Random House Australia (Pty) Limited
20 Alfred Street, Milsons Point, Sydney,
New South Wales 2061, Australia

Random House New Zealand Limited
18 Poland Road, Glenfield,
Auckland 10, New Zealand

Random House South Africa (Pty) Limited
Endulini, 4A Jubilee Road, Parktown 2193, South Africa

Random House UK Limited Reg. No. 954009

A CIP catalogue record for this book is available from the British Library

Papers used by Random House UK Limited are natural,
recyclable products made from wood grown in sustainable forests.
The manufacturing processes conform to the environmental
regulations of the country of origin.

ISBN 0701 1 67971

Typeset by Deltatype Ltd, Birkenhead, Merseyside
Printed and bound in Great Britain
by Mackays of Chatham PLC

CONTENTS

PREFACE

Who was Barbara Bodichon? She was many things: artist, law reformer, pamphleteer, journalist, co-founder of Girton College, intrepid traveller, the red-haired charismatic leader of the Langham Place group, Florence Nightingale's first cousin and George Eliot's closest friend. She was born lucky, in the sense that she was born into a wealthy and cultured family on whom fortune had smiled. But, as a Unitarian, she also had a strong sense of having to *deserve* that fortune. Both her grandfather, William Smith, and her father, Benjamin Smith, served as reforming MPs so that Barbara grew up 'cradled in the traditions of the House', knowing as much about framing petitions as framing paintings.[1] It was her unusual political education and acumen that enabled her to assume the leadership role of the Langham Place group, the inspiration and focal point of feminist agitation in England for thirty years.[2] Barbara carried on the Smith political tradition, albeit obliquely, because as a woman she could neither vote nor enter Parliament.[3]

Aged twenty-one, Barbara committed herself to working for women. She wrote:

> Philosophers & Reformers have generally been afraid to say anything about the unjust laws both of society and country which crush women. There never was a tyranny so deeply felt yet borne so silently, that is the worst of it. But now I hope there are some who will brave ridicule for the sake of common justice to half the world.[4]

Her friend, the Pre-Raphaelite painter, Anna Mary Howitt, chose Barbara to model for her as Boadicea, brooding over the wrongs of her people.

But there was a shadowed side to Barbara's life. Although the Smith family was rich and powerful, her mother, Anne Longden, was a miller's daughter from Derbyshire whom Benjamin Smith had never married. Consequently, large sections of her father's family refused to recognise or acknowledge the Leigh Smith children. Mrs Gaskell wrote to a friend about Barbara:

> she is illegitimate cousin of Hilary Carter and F Nightingale, – has their nature in her; though some of the legitimate don't acknowledge her. She is – I think in consequence of her birth, a strong fighter against the established opinions of the world, – which always goes against my – what shall I call it? – *taste* (that is not the word,) but I can't help admiring her noble bravery, and respecting – while I don't personally like her.[5]

Barbara's rather ambiguous social position paradoxically allowed her an unusual social mobility. Although her father owned a great estate in Sussex, for example, her identification was not with the landed gentry, but with the disenfranchised seekers of liberty. She once wrote:

> I am one of the cracked people of the world, and I like to herd with the cracked such as ... queer Americans, democrats, socialists, artists, poor devils or angels; and am never happy in an English genteel family life. I try to do it like other people, but I long always to be off on some wild adventure, or long to lecture on a tub in St Giles, or go to see the Mormons, or ride off into the interior on horseback alone and leave the world for a month. I want to see what sort of world this God's world is.[6]

If Mrs Gaskell found Barbara's insouciant social style slightly hard to stomach, a younger, more bohemian group accepted her delightedly. After Barbara came into the orbit of the Pre-Raphaelites, Dante Gabriel Rossetti described Barbara to his sister Christina as a 'jolly fellow', and commented:

> Ah! If you were only like Miss Barbara Smith! A young lady I meet at the Howitts', blessed with large rations of tin, fat, enthusiasm, and golden hair, who thinks nothing of climbing up a mountain in breeches, or wading through a stream in none, in the sacred name of pigment.[7]

Barbara dreamed of a sisterhood in Art to match that of the Pre-Raphaelite Brethren. Her close friendships with Anna Mary Howitt, Eliza Fox Bridell, Gertrude Jekyll and Marianne North all form part of her story.

Choosing a lifetime partner was a difficult thing for her, as she wanted to retain the economic independence that allowed a sense of freedom and autonomy and the opportunities to travel and work in a rewarding career. Several men were attracted by her flashing beauty, but she chose for her husband a man as extraordinary as she was herself, a French philosopher, resident in Algiers. Shortly after her marriage to Eugène Bodichon she wrote to a friend: 'It is my duty to be an artist . . . I should like to give all I had to schools, and earn my own living by painting . . . There are so many people I love and want to see! I do wish I had three immortal lives. I would spend one only with my Eugène, and the other two for art and social life.'[8] In this trinity of desires, Eugène represents love, art represents work and social life represents, not tea parties, but her commitment to social reform. She remained true to all three.

Barbara Bodichon is much less well-known than one would expect from her achievements. Her friend Bessie Parkes wrote of her, 'except in art . . . she was absolutely devoid of personal ambition, but her memory remains with me as that of the most powerful woman I have ever known.'[9] She did *many* things, and historians seem to find it easier to understand and write about a man who pursued one 'great' goal. Women's lives and women's histories often look different, more diffuse and are (perhaps) harder to evaluate.

Nevertheless, the first significant account of the women's movement in Great Britain, Ray Strachey's *The Cause* (1928), immediately noted that 'there seems to have been something particularly vigorous and vivid about Barbara Leigh Smith'.[10] Olive Banks commented that 'perhaps the single most significant woman during the early days of the [women's] movement was . . . Barbara Bodichon . . . It was her ability to inspire others . . . which was perhaps her chief contribution.'[11] In 1983 when American scholars identified her as 'perhaps the most important unstudied figure of mid-century English feminism' Barbara's significance to the early women's movement at last began to be scrutinised.[12] Yet 'Bodichon' studies have been remarkably few, especially when compared with the enormous body of scholarship undertaken on her first cousin, Florence Nightingale.[13]

My contribution in telling her story is to remain faithful to those things the police call 'the facts' although empathising with her desires and frustrations. The biographer's craft is analogous to that of the mosaicist, who creates a picture out of tiny fragments of coloured enamel. In this story the letters to and from and about Barbara Bodichon are the most brilliantly coloured fragments. Census material, documents from public record offices and legal documents that have long lain in dusty boxes are the pieces with less lustre, though still necessary for overall effect. Sometimes fragments are missing altogether; if so, I have tried not to replace them with pasteboard, but simply to allow the cement ground of the narrative to remain exposed in an undecorated state. My mosaic picture is therefore not uniformly vivid, but the peculiar vibrancy and glamour of Barbara Bodichon herself may make up for those defects.

CHAPTER 1

The Smiths

In 1857 Barbara wrote, 'let me say a word about Barbara Smith . . . for I have earned a right to Barbara Smith'.[1] She was staking a claim to the name that the law of the land did not confer. Having studied English law she knew that 'an illegitimate child . . . may acquire a surname by reputation, but does not inherit one'.[2] This 'earning' of the name of her father (and grandfather) implied that she had taken up the political mantle of the Smiths.

The Smith story begins in the Isle of Wight, where seventeenth-century records show them in fairly humble surroundings, attending Independent chapels, and, generation by generation, achieving increasing commercial success and social status. Barbara's great-grandfather, Samuel Smith, born in 1727, was the founder of The Sugar Loaf, a successful wholesale grocery in London which imported sugar, teas and spices from all over the world.[3] After his marriage in 1754 to Martha Adams (from a wealthy Dissenting family), she bore four children in close succession and then died, aged only twenty-five, after complications set in following the birth of her last baby in 1759. Samuel was left a widower, with a booming business and a huge inheritance from his wife.

Of Martha's four infants, only William survived childhood. A picture by Zoffany shows Samuel giving his son a lesson in geometry; William has an exercise book and a pair of dividers on the table in front of him. Samuel is wearing a richly ornamented waistcoat trimmed with gold braid and a handsome coat with gilt buttons and his son is wearing a dark coat with a lace frill at the neck and cuffs. England at this time commanded the sea, which made her the storehouse of the world's goods. The richness of father and son's clothing establishes them as merchant princes, and the serious attention the two are giving to the matter in hand represents them as men (or man and apprentice) of business, not dissolute aristocrats.

William joined the family business and, on his father's side, was the sole heir to the Smith fortune; on his mother's side, he was the only surviving heir to the Adams fortune. In 1779, after inheriting money from Uncle Adams in the Isle of Wight, William withdrew to make room for his cousins Travers and Kemble. For this handsome young man with red hair and clear grey eyes, the world was his oyster. He was brimful of energy, high spirits and political ambition.

The Smiths lived at Clapham Common, and here William met Frances Coape, from an old and wealthy Nottingham Dissenting family. The important Dissenting families – Smiths, Coapes, Carters and Shores – formed a significant part of the liberal intelligentsia. The men were well educated and capable but, as Dissenters, were denied Oxbridge degrees, and therefore access to the professions. Thus men of the very highest ability put their talents to the service of commerce and industry. The greatest scientists and inventors of the period were not to be found in Oxford or Cambridge (where the classics were studied) but emerged from the Dissenting academies, where science served local industries. In the proliferating Philosophical Societies of Birmingham, Derby, Manchester and Sheffield, industrialists such as Boulton, Wedgwood and Watt met scientists such as Priestley, Galton and Erasmus Darwin. These men were creating the country's wealth and were at the forefront of the demand for the reform of Parliament which would allow them political influence.[4]

In 1781, when William and Frances married, their wedding was a stylish affair: the young couple departed for their honeymoon in a shell and four, with blue and silver liveries. They began their married life in Eagle House, a large handsome property on the west side of the Common, opposite the Windmill Inn, where William began to amass his celebrated collection of paintings.[5] They had ten children – Patty (1782), Benjamin (1783), Anne (1784), Fanny (1788), Adams (1789), Joanna (1791), Samuel (1794), Octavius (1796), Frederick (1798) and Julia (1799). In 1784 William Smith had the chance to stand for Sudbury, a rotten borough: it cost him £3,000 to be returned as Member of Parliament.

Once in Parliament, William Smith dedicated his political career to the achievement of three great changes – the abolition of slavery, the repeal of religious disabilities and the reform of Parliament. At Clapham Common, with Wilberforce and the other Clapham Saints, William joined the long abolitionist campaign.[6] The Smith family, like every mercantile family, was implicated in the slave trade, because the import of sugar was an important part of their business; yet William, against his own business interests, campaigned fiercely against it.[7] He joined the boycott of slave-produced sugar which Thomas Clarkson advocated. Some people switched to using honey, some insisted on sugar from the East Indies produced without slave labour, and others adopted maple syrup. In all, however, the boycott reduced the demand for sugar by roughly a third; not good business for the wholesale grocer.

More significantly politically was the fact that William Smith provided a bridge between the Saints, who supported conservative William Pitt, and the liberal supporters of Charles Fox. William's ability to win the confidence and to work productively with men of widely differing religious persuasions made him almost uniquely valuable. He belonged to the King of Clubs, the meeting place of the most liberal Whigs, including Lord Holland, Henry Brougham and Sydney Smith.[8] William was considered a valued colleague and friend by all, and this gift for friendship with widely differing people was a quality inherited both by his eldest son, Ben, and by his granddaughter, Barbara.

The Abolition Committee founded by the Clapham Saints struggled to abolish a trade that had largely underpinned the industrial revolution. William Smith subscribed to the *Anti-Slavery Reporter* which, month by month, published horrifying tales by former slaves which had a cumulative effect on public conscience. Josiah Wedgwood's company produced a design entitled 'Am I Not a Man and a Brother?' depicting an African slave in chains, kneeling in an attitude of supplication, to publicise the campaign. As well as being used as the seal of the Abolition Committee, the image and the slogan were reproduced on the top of snuffboxes, while women could wear the image on bracelets and hairpins. It was an unusual case, as Thomas Clarkson noted, of fashion promoting justice.[9] The mobilisation of British opinion against the slave trade was politically sophisticated and seems surprisingly modern, with its boycotts and carefully targeted propaganda, including the foundation of its own journal. The abolitionists gained massive popular support and persuaded vast numbers of people to sign petitions to Parliament. Undoubtedly, the example of all aspects of the abolition campaigns, passed down from her father and her Aunt Julia, formed a significant part of Barbara's political education.

Enormously powerful business interests, especially those in the ports of London, Liverpool and Bristol, were inevitably ranged against abolition. Despite the pressure in the House from Wilberforce and Smith, a decision to hear witnesses at the Bar of the House, and later before a select committee, proved to be more of a stalling device than a desire for resolution. The examination of witnesses continued intermittently from May 1789 until April 1790. Witnesses arguing for the continuance of the slave trade were by and large men of education and position – merchants, traders and shipowners – while ranged against them were men of humbler origin – carpenters, boatswains, ordinary

3

seamen. The powerful interests employed counsel to cross-examine the opposition; Wilberforce and Smith divided between them the *entire* examination of the hostile witnesses who supported the slave trade, an utterly exhausting business. It was financially demanding too: the Abolition Committee had to pay for witnesses to travel to London and for their lodgings in the capital. Sailors who spoke out against shipowners found it hard to get work again, and so needed a financial allowance from the committee to survive. This was an enormous drain even on those with deep pockets like William Smith.

The abolitionist movement ground to a halt with the onset of the French Revolution which was greeted by Unitarians with enthusiasm. Wilberforce pleaded with William Smith and Clarkson not to endorse it but, as he had feared, the relationship between the Abolition Committee and its French counterparts was seized upon by its enemies in order to discredit all of its members as Jacobins (revolutionary republicans). In July 1789 when the Revolution began in France, it was followed with keen interest and excitement by Dissenters, who expected it to serve as a model for further emancipation. Political societies sprang to life in London, Manchester, Sheffield, Birmingham and Norwich, all of which were filled with hopes of universal peace and freedom. Frances, in a letter to William dated 3 July 1790, referred to it as 'so great, so happy a revolution'.[10] Public expressions of approval, however, led to the risk of being accused of treason. One of the leading Dissenting intellectuals, Dr Richard Price, the leader of the Unitarian congregation at Newington Green, gave a sermon later published as *A Discourse on the Love of our Country* in which he welcomed the French Revolution as another manifestation of the growing spirit of liberty. In Birmingham a dinner was held on 14 July 1791 to commemorate the anniversary of the fall of the Bastille. These events gave a handle to the enemies of the Dissenters, who made 'Church and King' their cry to incite riots in which Dissenters' meeting houses and homes were broken into. William Smith immediately went to Birmingham with a barrister friend to enquire into the riots, and to find out why the local magistrates had not attempted to prevent damage to Dissenters' property. William's friend, Joseph Priestley, the Unitarian theologian and scientist who discovered oxygen, had his house burned down and his scientific instruments and books destroyed. His papers were ransacked and carried off in the hope that something might be found against him. For days the mob destroyed houses of other prominent Dissenters.[11]

Despite all the expenses of his political career, William lived in a grand style. He had a country estate, Parndon Hall, near Harlow in Essex, with about two hundred acres, good shooting and all available country house pursuits. The country estate was emblematic of the social position William Smith had achieved; it was in this ambience that his children grew up and no doubt it underpinned their expectations for their own lives. In 1794 William took an elegant town house in Westminster, number 6 Park Street (now 16 Queen Anne's Gate and home of Political and Economic Planning), overlooking Birdcage Walk and St James's Park.

William served as MP for Norwich from 1802 to 1830, except for a brief gap in 1806–7. Ironically, when Wilberforce's bill abolishing the trade in slaves finally succeeded on 23 February 1807, William was not a Member of Parliament. Nevertheless, he came up from Parndon and sat in the gallery to hear the debate, and so was able to join the crowd of friends who went over to Wilberforce's house in Palace Yard to celebrate their achievement, although he was always disappointed that he had been unable to vote on the day itself.

William was also the acknowledged leader of the Dissenting cause in Parliament. From 1805 to 1832 he served as chairman of the Dissenting Deputies, a committee of Presbyterians, Independents and Baptists, established in 1732 to take care of the civil affairs of Dissenters.[12] In this role he directed negotiations for the broadening of the Toleration Act in 1812, drew up and guided through Parliament the Unitarian Toleration Act of 1813 and presided over the successful campaign to repeal the Test and Corporation Acts in 1828. William himself was a Unitarian. Sometimes called 'free-thinking' Christians, because they insisted on the right to employ reason in interpreting the Scriptures, Unitarians fought against state persecution of any religious belief, not only their own, and stressed activity to improve society rather than religious ritual.

William's Achilles' heel was the assumption that he could invest energy in diverse social, intellectual and political activities and still maintain vigilance over his business affairs. In 1804, after his uncle, Benjamin Smith, had died leaving him £60,000, he entered into a partnership with Messrs Cooke and Tate in a whisky distillery and brewery at Millbank.[13] This was an unwise investment: the financial situation of the company was precarious. In 1806 a fire destroyed much of the distillery and William discovered he was under-insured.[14] His eldest son, Ben, responded to the emergency by taking charge of the business and giving it his wholehearted attention. The distillery was rebuilt, and this time business was under the tight control of Ben and his brother Octavius.[15] When Octavius married Jane, one of the Cooke daughters, in 1819, Mr

Cooke and Ben Smith were able to settle £10,000 on them.[16] By 1820 Cooke & Co. was producing 373,831 gallons of spirit a year, and making a handsome profit.[17]

Ben could rely on Octavius's sound business judgement, but Adams was incompetent and the cause of an acrimonious quarrel in another (Smith–Travers) family partnership. William set up yet another firm with Adams and his Kemble cousins in charge, in Philpot Lane. Between them they had brought the firm to the point of bankruptcy by 1819. Ben rescued the firm temporarily with money from the distillery business, but it had to be liquidated in 1823. From 1820, Ben Smith, not his father, was the financial head of the Smith family.

William's financial misadventures meant that he had to sell first his library, then his beloved painting collection and finally both his elegant houses. Ben leased a new town house, 5 Blandford Square, St Marylebone, then at the very edge of the city, with views of fields from the rear windows, and moved his father and mother into it. The house had mews for stabling horses and its front windows faced on to a garden with a lawn and young trees, the whole square being protected from intruders by an area gate. This house was to become Ben's political base and, later, that of his daughter, Barbara.

Ben took over financial responsibility for his two unmarried sisters – Patty, the eldest, and Julia, the youngest of his siblings – and for the hopeless Adams. Samuel went from Trinity to the Bar and Frederick, the youngest son, had a commission in the Indian army. In 1816 Ben's favourite sister, Joanna, married John (Bonham) Carter, a member of a wealthy Dissenting family in Portsmouth; for a wedding present Ben gave them his house and furniture at 16 Duke Street, Westminster. Fanny, considered the beauty of the Smith daughters, was persuaded by her father when she was nearly thirty to marry William (Shore) Nightingale.[18] Immediately after their marriage they set off on a three-year tour of Europe, during which their two daughters, Parthenope and Florence, were born, in Naples and Florence respectively.

Ben was typical of many wealthy Unitarians in that he interpreted it as his duty to improve society, and he saw education as the only 'charity' worth supporting. He was invited by Henry Brougham (later Lord Brougham) to participate in the management of the Infant School Society, a Whig group especially interested in educational innovations.[19] At New Lanark in Scotland, Robert Owen had set up an experimental infant school for the young children of his mill-workers. He employed as teacher an ex-weaver, James Buchanan, a Swedenborgian who believed that children were spiritual beings possessing earthly bodies (and therefore senses) who were engaged in a lifelong training of the soul to be ready for truth.[20] In 1818 Ben visited Owen's school with the Infant School Society committee and persuaded Buchanan to come to London, to become the teacher of an infant school they wished to set up in Brewer's Green, Westminster. But by 1826 the committee had decided Buchanan was too much of a Swedenborgian 'queer fish' and wanted to get rid of him.[21]

Ben could not stomach the idea that anyone should suffer for their religious beliefs, so took on the cost of a new school in Vincent Square, Carey Street, Westminster, where he financed the construction of a two-storey building, which served both as school and as a residence for Buchanan and his family. The whole bill came to 'above £1,000 on the buildings of the school – baths, gallery, playground etc'.[22] Vincent Square was quite a poor area; the parents of the children paid a penny a week to Buchanan, and Ben matched each penny with another. As well as education, food and warm baths were provided, and even the mending of clothes. Patty recalled her brother's experimental school as one of Ben's best deeds, writing in a letter to him: 'Do you remember the poor little things, flinging their arms about your legs in the streets of Westminster ... And the silent meetings for mending one another's rags, Buchanan praying in the midst ... it did good to Infant Thousands, though it wore out at length.'[23] The school continued until 1839.[24]

When the Infant Committee first turned against Buchanan, and before the new school was built, Ben sent him up to his sister Fanny who had returned to England in 1821, and now lived at Lea Hurst in Derbyshire. Buchanan stayed at Lea Hurst, opening and running an infant school in the small village of Crich.[25] There were some initial difficulties. Buchanan's ways were considered bizarre by the local people; they were astonished for instance to see him leading his troop of infants along the Crich road, playing on his flute.[26] He was so kind-hearted that he did not press the poor children for money and so lived wretchedly. After a year Ben rescued him from the miseries of Derbyshire and put him in charge of the new Vincent Square school in London. Buchanan was a remarkable man, and in her early years, one of the strongest influences on Barbara's life, second only to her father.

In Derbyshire, Fanny was dissatisfied. She had returned to England with high hopes of mixing in the best local society, with the addition of old friends and family. Despite the beauty of Lea Hurst's immediate surroundings, this was also an industrial landscape, scarred by lead mines, coal mines and ironworks; the soughs which drained the water from the mines in turn served and gave rise to the burgeoning cotton spinning mills. In 1785, Nightingale's Uncle Peter had sold his Cromford estate to Richard Arkwright, who had built the largest cotton spinning mill in the country. By 1816 there were 720 workers at Cromford, in a village of houses built for the workers.[27] This factory village was only two and a half miles from Lea Hurst, whereas the Smith country house at Little Parndon was suitably distant from 'trade' in London. Fanny complained that the local working people were 'ultra-savage'.

When Ben brought Buchanan up to Derbyshire, Fanny hoped to promote a match between him and her sister-in-law, Mai Shore. Ben stayed at Lea Hurst in March 1826 because his brother-in-law, William Nightingale, was helping him with negotiations for a coal pit, which Ben was considering buying, with a view to settling his brother Adams.[28] The Shores were delighted at the prospect of another marriage link between the two families, and became offended when Ben seemed reluctant to come to the point.

Ben hesitated because he had fallen in love with Anne Longden, a twenty-five-year-old milliner in Alfreton.[29] She was the daughter of John Longden, the Alfreton corn miller and his wife, Dorothy.[30] John and Dorothy had four children: Jane, born 1792; Dorothy, born in 1797; Anne, born 1801 and John, born 1806 (who lived only a month).[31] Whenever Ben visited Lea Hurst, he would arrive at Alfreton by stagecoach on the turnpike road and, from there, travel either by horse, or by carriage the six miles to Lea Hurst.[32] In 1826 Ben was making many visits.[33]

Anne lived in Alfreton Park with her father and her sister Dolly (her mother had died in 1819) at a water-powered corn mill dating back to the twelfth century. The mill and house stood at the foot of the park, on an island created between the brook and the mill-race. The Morewoods, the major landowners of those parts, whose family had occupied Alfreton Hall since 1629, owned the estate.[34] A footpath from the mill and the path from the Hall converged in a narrow lane leading to Alfreton Church where gentry and their tenants met on their way to Sunday service. In the evenings the narrowness of the lane made it a well-known courting spot.[35] Ben may well have spotted Anne when visiting the Morewoods with Nightingale to discuss the possible profits of local mining ventures. Perhaps the rich and handsome Ben Smith invited the two Longden sisters to Alfreton races, and it all started as an innocent flirtation. But when, by the end of 1826, Anne became pregnant, Ben chose not to abandon her: indeed, like the protagonist of Tennyson's poem, although his parents would certainly have felt that he 'might have look'd a little higher', he liked her better than all the suitable matches he might have made:

> It is the miller's daughter,
> And she is grown so dear, so dear,
> That I would be the jewel
> That trembles in her ear:
> For hid in ringlets day and night,
> I'd touch her neck so warm and white.
>
> And I would be the girdle
> About her dainty dainty waist,
> And her heart would beat against me,
> In sorrow and in rest:
> And I should know if it beat right,
> I'd clamp it round so close and tight.
>
> And I would be the necklace,
> And all day long to fall and rise
> Upon her balmy bosom,
> With her laughter or her sighs,
> And I would lie so light, so light,
> I scarce should be unclasp'd at night.[36]

There is a nice irony here, in that although William Smith's most prized painting was Rembrandt's *The Mill*, he would hardly have intended his favourite son to choose a miller's daughter for his partner.

Ben took the pregnant Anne down to East Sussex, where he was beginning to build up a country estate near Robertsbridge. He tucked her out of the sight of curious eyes in a rented lodge in Whatlington, a small parish two miles north of Battle (then) on the main road from London to Hastings.[37] Anne went under the pseudonym 'Mrs Leigh' (the name of Ben's relatives on the Isle of Wight).[38] Barbara was born safely at 11.30 a.m. on 8 April 1827. Ben's Smith blood was stirred by seeing that his little daughter's hair was the reddish-gold peculiar to his family.

No doubt William Smith would have been dismayed by Ben's romantic débâcle, especially as the Shores had been offended, but in the autumn of 1826 Ben's younger brother, Sam, married Mai and restored the dynastic connections between Smiths and Shores. William would not have been shocked. Although himself a devoted husband, in the course of his business and political life he had mixed with all sorts of people. He had worked closely with Charles Fox, for example, visiting him at his villa at St Anne's Hill, Surrey, where he lived openly with his mistress, Elizabeth Armistead (previously the mistress of the Prince of Wales). Although Fox had married her in 1795, Frances Smith avoided any meeting with her.[39] In Frances's eyes, if a women fell, she stayed fallen.

Ben was not banished from Blandford Square, but his mistress was condemned. Frances wrote to Fanny Nightingale: 'Oh! How it grieves me to think of his thraldom, for he is really as clever a man as can usually be met with, and think to what conversation he is confined.'[40] She saw her rich and clever son as the victim of a wicked woman, whereas, in reality, it was Anne who was in the vulnerable position, entirely dependent on Ben's continuing affection or sense of honour. None of the Smith women ever met Anne Longden. In her 'Reminiscences', Patty stated categorically: 'I never saw her', yet this did not stop her making harsh judgements.[41]

Exactly why Ben Smith did not *marry* Anne Longden remains a mystery. Even given Smith family (class-based) objections, Ben was clearly old enough and financially independent enough to have done as he pleased. It may well be that he had a Shelleyan objection to the contemporary marriage laws which made wives and children the property of men. The English law at that period stated that the mother of illegitimate children had the right of custody of any who were under seven years of age, while children of married women were the property of the father. Anne's family, the Longdens, and their cousins, the Grattons, were respectable people, primarily either corn millers or corn dealers. In terms of the complex stratifications of the Victorian class system, however, they were undoubtedly 'trade' whereas, although the Smiths' fortune had come directly from trade – first from the Sugar Loaf and subsequently from the distillery – by establishing themselves in country estates they had transformed themselves into 'gentry'.

From 1816 onwards, when Ben gave his Duke Street house to Joanna, he had been building up a sizeable estate. His first purchase was Brown's Farm in Robertsbridge, East Sussex, which included a modest but lovely house built around 1700.[42] In 1823 he bought a much grander house in the parish of Westfield. Crowham Manor was built on a slight rise in two hundred acres of parkland commanding a view of the sea, about five miles west-north-west of Hastings. Ben perhaps hoped that Crowham could replace Parndon as a summer retreat for his parents; presumably for sentimental reasons when the last of the Park Street furniture was sold by auction in 1823 Ben bought 'half the shabby sofas, crazy chairs, tumble down tables' and used them to furnish Brown's and Crowham.[43] In buying Crowham Manor, Ben's status had changed from the 'Mr Smith' who is recorded as having bought the property, to 'Benjamin Smith, Esq., Lord of the Manor of Crowham'.[44] Owning a country property carried with it a social cachet which money itself could not provide.

When Ben went down to Sussex he stayed at Brown's house, which was some little distance even from its own farm buildings. He could ride over to Whatlington, along wooded bridle paths, without being observed. When Barbara was eleven months old, she was joined by a baby brother, Ben.

Perhaps believing that his common-law partnership with Anne Longden would be more acceptable there, towards the end of 1828 Ben decided to go to America. In a letter to his sister Joanna, he had speculated on the possibility of forming a colony on the Moravian plan in America, to which he would invite all his nieces and nephews.[45] Although it was a throwaway line, Ben may well have been seriously attracted by a different kind of community, one based less on wealth and power. Idealistic men whom Ben knew, such as Morris Birkbeck, who had emigrated to America in 1817, were publishing pro-emigration pamphlets which influenced a whole new generation of radical Unitarians.[46] From the turn of the century onwards, the idea of emigrating to America was one which appealed to many who felt that the old country would never accept their new ideals.[47] Ben made the necessary legal arrangements to retire from the distillery. Patty's letter to her sister Fanny Nightingale, dated 1 October 1828, says:

> Ben was here from Sunday till Tuesday. He came to sign a Dissolution of Partnership – and he is now out of the business. There is much in such a resolution to make him very thoughtful. After twenty years exertion of so much done for other people, to find himself in his present situation.[48]

Ben and Anne went to America with their two young children, Barbara and little Ben, and stayed there for nearly two years.[49] When they disembarked at Liverpool in July 1830 Ben was ill with a fever and Anne was so close to term that she gave birth to their third child, Isabella, at Crosby. Ben and Anne's last two children, Anne and William, were born in 1831 and 1833 at Brown's.

By 1833 Anne was suffering from the disease which was to kill her, and Ben took rooms at Pelham Place in Hastings, where the climate was recommended as beneficial for consumptives. Anne underwent a regime of warm baths, alternated with cold plunges, followed by airings in an invalid chair along the promenade. After the return from America, Ben made no attempt to hide Anne away. Agitated letters flew between Patty and Fanny Nightingale about Ben's shameless behaviour, and the terrible predicament were Ben to be left with five illegitimate offspring. Patty could not even bring herself to refer to Ben's beloved by name and so leaves a blank: 'The – is dying if not dead – at Pelham Place Hastings. What in your judgement should be done with the Children? I do not think he will part from them unless he gets tired of them. Could he marry, do you think & own them & educate them at home. Pray think about it. For myself I have little hope that he will marry so as to be happy, & none at all that he will be happy without.'[50]

Patty's letters remained agitated, partly because their youngest brother Fred had also hooked up with an unsuitable woman (from their point of view). She informed Fanny:

And now about Ben – I expect he will act without much plan & without telling me any more about it – But if the mother there dies, then I think the children *might* be placed in a better situation than Fred's – & in one less injurious to the next generation of this family – & this must be thought of, because nobody can cast off Ben and Ben will never cast off his children – He would indeed be a villain if he could – after living with them and for them exclusively to a degree no people in the world have opportunity for, till the eldest is now 7 or 8 years old – but think of the actual state of the case. The Mother *I am told* is a married woman – at least someone used to come after her & it is supposed in order to be paid off – the Sister vulgar & cunning & dependent even for her Clothes, then lived with them! The Upper nurse has had 3 natural children – Judge of the thrall & the mire in which Ben has lived & into which the children will sink deeper if he does not take some decided steps of separation from the relations & old servants when the Mother is dead – indeed whether she dies or not, I expect to find he is gone abroad – in order to educate & separate the children from this mess, altho' to hear him speak no one would think there was anything to detach them from, except the Sussex dialect. The bent of his thoughts, he would else be too miserable, seems to be to the innocency of the life he has led . . . I cannot think that with all his sophistry – that even he, can look back thro' the last 25 years, & consent to see his sons & daughters do likewise – with all the hideous environment of other sins & crimes that accompany this way of going on but it is from the total forfeiture of all appearances hitherto that I hope a little now. It would become too bad to last. He will give them all his money unless he marries I don't doubt & provide well for them if he does marry & has another family – but this money & the style they have lived in (travelling with 2 or 3 carriages & 6 or 7 servants gamekeepers &

hounds – & with everything that is called handsome about them at Brighton) joined to the morals around them, there will be ruin, the lowest & most degrading, if they are put among low people. I see nothing for it but for him to take them to some part of Switzerland & isolate them among honest pious educated instructors to give them new habits & above all to save them from the cruelty of cutting those whom they have been taught to love . . .[51]

I can find no evidence in Derbyshire records that Anne Longden was ever married to anyone else. It is possible that the male caller was her perfectly respectable cousin, Jo Gratton, a substantial corn dealer in Shoreditch, coming to ascertain that his two kinswomen were safe and well. Clearly Patty thought the only hope of rehabilitating the children would be to sever them from their 'low' maternal relations, and to get them out of the country.

Increasingly desperate, in November 1833 Ben took Anne to Ryde on the Isle of Wight. Like Hastings, Ryde was considered a favourable climate for consumptives. The nurse employed to look after the children was a Hastings woman, Hannah Walker, and she and Ben wheeled Anne along the promenade in an invalid chair hoping against hope during her last weeks. But all attempts were in vain; she died on 30 August aged just thirty-two. Barbara was seven and Anne's last baby, Willie, only a year old. The record of her burial, in the name of 'Anne Smith', states only that she 'died at Ryde'.[52] This is an odd entry, because no home address is entered under the column marked 'abode'. Sadly, this confirms her dispossessed and 'outlaw' status.

After Anne's burial, Ben returned to Brown's in a terrible state of mind, accompanied only by Adams. Patty was aghast to learn that Ben was considering bringing his children up in England. She wrote to Fanny:

Nothing for the present seems to touch him but marks of regard towards the deceased. He says for instance he shall have friends in travelling that this Old Woman [Hannah Walker] made friends with on the promenade at Ryde . . . Do you think Ben in better days would have allowed a Woman of such a character to be forward on the public walk . . . It does but prove into what blindness he has fallen. Adams left him very undecided abt. going abroad. He thinks that if anybody was compassionate as [William] Nightingale he might carry his points in England. In short he is quite tempest-tossed. I still think kindness is the only way with him . . . kindness might still win him to a path which Julia could act with him & for him. She is the person. If not – you may

be sure this Old Woman will throw some new attraction in his way, &
the last business will be worse than the first . . .[53]

Initially, out of all his siblings, Ben could only count on the sympathy of
Julia. His brother-in-law, William Nightingale, was kinder to him than
the rest of his kin. Ben wrote to tell him on 15 September that 'the
service was performed by Jervis in a manner which I can never forget to
feel grateful for . . . I must return to the Island, having some necessary
arrangements to make there. I would, if I could, devolve the task upon
some other person, but the task is properly my own & I must do it – She
who is gone, was the least selfish being I ever saw.'[54] This view of Anne
strikes a very different note from Patty's representation of her as some
kind of professional courtesan. Ben went to the Isle of Wight and, at St
Edmund's Church, Wootton, where Anne was buried, he ordered a white
memorial urn. It reads 'Anne Smith died August 30th 1834, aged 32'. In
death at least, Anne was honoured as Ben's wife.

Still grieving Anne's death Ben was startled to hear that his father's
health had declined suddenly. He rushed up to Blandford Square
towards the end of May 1835. Joanna reported to Fanny: 'the sight of
another sick bed seems to affect him very much, and his spirits fluctuate
with the view he takes of the symptoms – Poor fellow, independent of his
natural tenderness of disposition, no doubt he dreads all the recollections
that another death will recall to him.'[55] Joanna's long-standing love for
her favourite brother was clearly moving her towards compassion.

William Smith died on 31 May 1835, three years after the triumph of
parliamentary reform and one year after Parliament had committed itself
to the abolition of slavery throughout the empire.[56] He was buried at the
new St James's Church, Bermondsey, close to the wharves where the
whisky distillery stood, and where the smell of imported spices made the
air pungent. This was an apt place to bury a member of the merchant
class, whose wealth had been built up from those very wharves.[57] William
Smith, whatever his failings in matters of business, had provided a
pattern of commitment to public service which was echoed by Ben and,
in the next generation, by his granddaughter, Barbara.

Ben hoped that the Smiths would come to recognise his children, with
'Aunt Ju' as their champion. Joanna was widowed in 1838, but she and
her seven children stayed on at Ditcham Grove, their house on the downs
above Buriton in Hampshire. The Nightingales spent most of the year at
their new house, Embley Park in Hampshire, Anne and husband George
Nicholson lived at Waverley Abbey near Farnham, Samuel Smith

and Mai lived at Combe Hurst in Surrey. All these 'Smith' families visited each other, but they did not visit the tabooed family.

CHAPTER 2

The Early Years

At Brown's Ben had planted five fir trees, one for each of his five children, possibly from seeds he and Anne had brought back from their American journey. He said that fir trees were always 'aspiring' to grow up straight and true, and that is what he hoped for his children. Hannah Walker, usually called 'Nursie', adored her 'good master' and cared for his children lovingly, singing them to sleep with old Sussex songs such as 'Nicholas Wood'. From her they picked up the Sussex dialect, calling woodpeckers 'gellie-birds' and blindworms 'deaf-adders'. Barbara was the leader of the high-spirited little gang of five, always adventurous. Despite frequent warnings from Nursie to keep away from a muddy pond, she inevitably fell in and returned home cross and covered in mud. Hannah was horrified but the Pater, as the children called him, just laughed. He liked his bold girl.

In 1836 the Pater moved the children out of Brown's and into Pelham Crescent, right on the sea front at Hastings with bay windows looking straight out to sea. It was one of the most elegant examples of Regency architecture anywhere in Britain.[1] From a simple fishing village, Hastings had become a fashionable watering place, an echo of Brighton, although it was both smaller and more picturesque. A daily stagecoach ferried passengers to and from London, although, in winter, the diligence was 'frequently impeded by the overflow of the Rother at Robertsbridge, and sometimes it floated'.[2] To Barbara, Hastings was the next-best thing to paradise, with never-ending entertainments: going down on the beach to see the fishing boats land, watching the heaps of glittering silvery fish sold by Dutch auction at the bustling market, walking or riding over the downs, or taking picnics along to Bohemia.

In 1837 Ben's friend, the MP William Ewart, encouraged Ben to stand for his father's old constituency of Norwich.[3] In July, Barbara, aged ten, joined the hustings 'clad in a dress and sash of her father's colours and paraded herself boldly before his constituents'.[4] Ben pledged moderate reforms and, invoking his father's name, he assured the electorate that if he became their representative he would aim 'to merit a renewal of the confidence formerly placed in him, who, after a life dedicated to his country's service, is gone to render an account of his stewardship'.[5] Although Ben did not have such a long or illustrious career as his father, he faithfully attended Parliament when it was in session and supported liberal causes.[6] Barbara at ten, was already learning what being a 'Smith' involved.

After 1837, when Parliament was in session, Ben needed to be in London, but he could call on Aunt Dolly (Longden) or Aunt Ju to go down to Hastings. Even Patty's heart eventually softened towards Ben's children although Barbara never loved her as much as Aunt Ju. When Barbara was seven, Patty was fifty-two and suffered from 'nerves' and gout, whereas Julia was only thirty-five. Julia loved Ben's children, both for his sake and for their own. Julia never cared for grown people who made light of children's cries because they didn't bother to imagine what the children were feeling. The Leigh Smith children were in no danger of this misfortune in the company of the Pater, Aunt Ju, Aunt Dolly, or Mr Buchanan – the four key adult figures of their childhood, apart from their nurse.

Barbara adored Mr Buchanan; she remembered the first time she had been taken to Westminster Infant School, purportedly to help. She wrote that poor children were 'clustring on him like hiving bees, all trying to caress him'.[7] Sometimes, Barbara recalled, he had fits when 'he would do no work at all [but] would study or dream away his time and my father used to have patience with these fits and send him from London down to Robertsbridge or Hastings', supposedly to teach the young Leigh Smiths to read. This principally took the form of his 'reading aloud to us from the three sacred books – the Bible, The Arabian Nights and Swedenborg'. The Leigh Smith children might have tried the patience of another man. Barbara recalled that:

> We were all five of us very tyrannical towards him but he never resisted our tyranny *never*! . . . I remember often, we made him read to us at meal times, & would not let him eat anything. Our nurse would say 'Oh Mr B do come to dinner' 'No Nursie, I will read to the dear children & explain as long as they will listen' & never did I see him out of patience in my life. We used to make him carry us upstairs & I believe if he were in the house I never walked up three flights of stairs even when I was nine years old unless I was frisky enough to run up. He was very peculiar in his manners, perfectly childlike & without self feeling – for instance, he was never ashamed to stop people in the streets to exhort them if he thought they were doing anything wrong! He was harder on grown up people than children & used to lecture my

father considerably. To animals he was tender as to children, never killed any living thing.[8]

Anyone involved with the Smith children had to cope with their tireless energy. Harry Porter was employed by Ben as a daily (afternoon) tutor of Latin and history. Porter had lost a civil service appointment in the West Indies and trailed back to England with a Creole wife, of whom his father disapproved. After the death of his wife, Porter was reconciled with his father and gave up the daily tutoring of the young Leigh Smiths, no doubt with a huge sigh of relief, because they used to tease the poor man unmercifully.[9] Similarly, the girls' governess, a Miss Catherine Spooner, was dragged hither and thither on expeditions by her pitiless charges. Barbara's journal recorded: 'it was excellent fun helping Miss Spooner across rivers and up hills and down hills and over walls and through hedges . . . [she] surprised us all by getting to the very top [of Plynlimmon], and that too without any damage but a sprained ankle.'[10]

All five children were taught to ride by the best local riding master, Mr Willetts. In 1842 Ben ordered a family 'omnibus' to be built by a renowned firm of Hastings coachbuilders. It was a magnificent eight-person carriage, drawn by four horses, driven by their coachman, Stephen Elliott. The bill from Rock & Baxter of £215 detailed such delicious and luxurious items as 'the Body & Carvings painted a rich Lake relieved with Ultramarine Blue & highly Varnished, the inside handsomely lined with drab Cloth Silk Tabaret & figured Lace and filled up so as to form a double sofa with pillows and cushions stuffed with the best horsehair and springing'.[11] In this carriage the whole family went on tours, and Barbara followed Smith tradition by keeping journals of the tours, which give glimpses of the family at play. In one she refers to a visit to Hereford Cathedral, when the verger forbade her to sketch one of the tombs: 'Papa, as usual when he thinks people's just rights are invaded, got angry and went to the Dean.'[12]

Barbara, Bella and presumably Anne (or 'Nannie'), in her turn, were educated at a Unitarian secondary school run by the Misses Wood in Upper Clapton in London, from about 1838 to at least 1841.[13] After the freedom of her life in Hastings, and her unusual teachers, Barbara found the school rather trying. A description by Elizabeth Whitehead (who was later to become principal of Barbara's Portman Hall School) of the Misses Woods' school which she attended in 1842 makes it clear why this should have been so. Although the Misses Wood were 'kind and good women who tried to make their pupils happy', unfortunately 'teaching as an art was then and there so little understood':

Learning by rote from poor text books was the method employed; there
was no explanation, no illustration, no attempt to awaken the mental
faculties. Sums were given out to be done mechanically, not the most
elementary principle was laid down. You puzzled over them, the
answers were looked out by the teacher in a book, if wrong you were
sent back to your desk to puzzle again![14]

It seems no wonder that Barbara went off to school clutching her beloved
copy of *The Arabian Nights* as a touchstone of all she believed about
imagination being at the heart of education.[15]

Ben sent his boys to Bruce Castle, at Tottenham, an offshoot of
Hazelwood, an experimental school which Thomas Wright Hill had
started with a strong emphasis on producing cultured, self-reliant men of
affairs.[16] Willie's report at the end of his junior school in 1842 showed no
great distinction, with the exceptions of 'perusal' [private reading] and
'elocution', both of which were regarded by his masters as 'very
satisfactory'.[17] Both boys went in their turn as weekly boarders to Mr
Mahew's Unitarian school at Brede, about six miles from Hastings.

All the children had drawing lessons; and all five showed some talent.
The cultivation of art and music in their daughters had become a
commonplace of the middle classes and the precise point at which a
woman's artistic talent crossed that mysterious line from an accomplishment to professional ambition is never quite clear. With Bella, one feels
that it remained a ladylike accomplishment, but both Barbara and Nannie
were more ambitious, and went on to exhibit their paintings and to sell
them. Hastings attracted many painters, both amateur and professional,
who appreciated its beach scenes and craggy Castle Hill with its romantic
ruins at the top. Cox, Linnell, Prout, Turner and Hunt had all painted
there. Of these artists Barbara knew William Hunt the best. From 1809
onwards he had passed his winters in a small house at the foot of the East
Cliff.[18] Hunt had studied with John Varley and mastered the classic
Girtinesque method of using coloured washes almost calligraphically.[19]
Around 1825 he began to evolve a new system in which he worked a
mixture of transparent and body colour over a ground of Chinese white
to give his luminosity. The technique was one Barbara often used in her
paintings, and it seems likely she learned it from its originator, as we
know Hunt advised Barbara on her paintings.[20]

Barbara had lessons from Cornelius Varley,[21] and from W. Colling-
wood Smith (a cousin of the landscape painter William Collingwood).[22]
Collingwood Smith took Barbara to John Hornby Maw's house on West
Hill with its oak-panelled studio, a reproduction of an Elizabethan room,

filled with Elizabethan furniture and costumes used at the famous Eglinton tournament. Maw was a retired pharmaceuticals businessman and a good amateur painter, who allowed local artists, including William Hunt, William Collingwood and his cousin, to use his studio and props. He owned a fine collection of Turner watercolours displayed in a thirty-foot-long drawing room.[23] Through the Collingwood Smith connection, the Maws were at first intimate with the Smiths; indeed they shared their tutor Mr Porter, who went to the Maws in the mornings and the Leigh Smiths in the afternoons. Maw's daughter remembered spending an evening with them and being struck by 'their wit and their beauty'. She was disappointed when the intimacy between the two families came to an abrupt halt 'after cautions from my mother's friend Mrs Hardman'.[24] The only cause one can imagine for this sudden withdrawal must have been gossip that the children were illegitimate, and this snub gives us a concrete example of the slightly anomalous situation of the Leigh Smith children. They were the beloved children of their rich, handsome and popular father, yet they were illegitimate, and therefore not entirely respectable. Barbara, presumably, would initially have been puzzled by the nature of these rebuffs, but must have come to recognise that it was the status of her dead mother which was at issue.

Barbara adored her Pater, but part of her growing up included having to accommodate difficult information about her father's unorthodox relationship with her mother, and its implications for her own position. There are several indications that this process was a painful one to her. In February 1847, for example, Barbara's friend Bessie Parkes wrote a letter to her commenting: 'What a pity English women do not do anything but be governesses & milliners, I mean the tolerably educated; milliners!'[25] Bessie's disparaging comment about milliners presumably means that she knew nothing about Barbara's mother. Barbara's response was to 'cut' Bessie. Bessie never forgot this experience and in all her dealings with Barbara thereafter was extremely tactful and circumspect. As late as 1855, after a firm friendship of nearly ten years, when Bessie went on holiday to the Isle of Wight she made a private pilgrimage to Anne Longden's grave. Bessie wrote to Aunt Dolly (Longden), telling her Barbara thought about the grave but had never visited it. Bessie indicated in her letter that she hoped Aunt Dolly 'would pass the letter on to Barbara, but [Bessie was] shrinking from writing directly to her'.[26]

Generally Barbara was sheltered from such social snubs by a select group of tried and trusted friends in Hastings. These friends were liberal in politics and intellectual and artistic in their interests. They included the family of Frederick North, who had become the Liberal MP for

Hastings in 1830; his daughter, Marianne North, three years older than Barbara, was to become one of her closest friends in later years.[27] Another friend, Miss Bayley, had two houses, at 2 Halloway Place, Hastings and in Wimbledon, interested herself in the welfare of the motherless Leigh Smith girls and willingly chaperoned them when Aunt Ju was not available. Through Miss Bayley, the Leigh Smiths came to know her dear friend George Scharf, an antiquarian, scholar and artist, who in 1859 was to become the first director of the National Portrait Gallery. A confirmed bachelor, highly gregarious and good-hearted, he was one of the earliest mentors of Barbara's artistic aspirations.

Mrs Ann Samworth, a widow who lived at Bruckland Cottage, Hastings, with her children John, Annie, Elizabeth and Joanna, also befriended the Leigh Smiths. The three Samworth girls and the three Leigh Smith girls frequently went on painting expeditions; one of their favourite walks was along the cliffs to Fairlight and then down into the winding paths which led to the Dripping Well. From Fairlight Glen the stream dropped precipitously through large rocks and heavy forest before falling into the sea. In the other direction, above the spring, was a path up a steep cliff to Lovers' Seat. Joanna Samworth took lessons with Barbara from Collingwood Smith. In 1851, Joanna went to study in Paris in Henri Scheffer's studio and subsequently enjoyed a quiet success with landscapes and flower studies in watercolour.[28]

Other lifelong friends made initially in Hastings were William and Mary Howitt and their children, whom Barbara first met in 1845. Mary wrote to her sister describing her first impressions:

> Thou inquirest . . . who our friends the Smiths are, who contributed so much to make our Hastings sojourn agreeable. The father is MP for Norwich, a good radical and partisan of Free Trade and the abolition of the Corn Laws . . . the young people are left very much to pursue their own course of study. The result is good; and as to affection and amiability, I never saw more beautiful evidences of it. There are five children . . . their buoyant frames and bright clear complexions show how sound is their health.[29]

The Howitts had four children, Anna Mary, Alfred, Herbert and Margaret. In 1844, the year before they met the Leigh Smiths, their youngest son Claude died from a complication which had set in after a knee injury. They were still in a state of shock and depression over this death, and no doubt the infectious good spirits of the Leigh Smiths were especially timely. Although the Howitt family was very hardworking, their finances were always somewhat precarious. Ben Smith was generous, without being patronising, and when the two families were together Ben simply footed the bill. Anna Mary's letters are peppered with thanks for Christmas gifts of hampers which included pheasants and partridges shot on Ben's estate and toys for the younger children to which the Howitt tight budget could not stretch.

This is not to imply that the advantages of the friendship between the two families were all one way. Bessie Parkes wrote to a friend about Mary Howitt: 'You cannot think the intense pleasure it is to sit close to this noble woman and hear her talk in her low measured Quaker tones . . .'[30] In Mary Howitt, the Leigh Smith children gained a loving 'aunt' at a time when not all of their 'real' aunts acknowledged them. Mary was to write to Nannie many years later, 'I have always felt toward Barbara, Ben, and you as to none of our friends, as if in some mysterious way you were kindred to us.'[31] Mary's love and respect was a vital element in Barbara's ability to come to terms with her slightly anomalous social position.

In 1847 the Howitts resigned their membership of the Religious Society of Friends and allied themselves with Unitarianism, which is a significant date, considering their friendship with the Leigh Smiths. Shortly after meeting them, William Howitt found himself in an awkward financial situation. He had joined the staff of John Saunders' *People's Journal* in 1846, a journal which published 'popular' articles from working-class writers, paying £800 for one share.[32] This journal was not financially successful and so William had set up *Howitt's Journal of Literature and Popular Progress* in December 1846, thereby entering into competition with Saunders' journal, in which he was a shareholder. As well as this piece of business folly, William does not seem to have understood that, as a shareholder, he could be held liable for Saunders' debts, and he ended up bankrupt in 1848. Ben Smith clearly did not feel moved to rescue the journal; he was an astute businessman himself so no doubt felt that Howitt had got himself into an extraordinary financial pickle by the kind of naivety which is rarely cured. Nevertheless, the wide-ranging causes the *Howitt's Journal* espoused – peace, free trade and civil liberties – were precisely the values which generations of Smiths had struggled for, and Ben remained a generous friend to the family, but not to the business. Ben's view that business and friendship made bad bedfellows (learned from his father's experience) was no doubt strengthened by the fall-out from the Howitt–Saunders débâcle. The Howitts lost some dear friends at this period, such as the Ashursts, and so, correspondingly, their ties to the Smiths intensified.

As a result of their literary endeavours the Howitts knew many literati and provided exciting introductions for Barbara and Bessie. Through the

Howitts, they met Elizabeth Barrett Browning, Anna Jameson, the poet 'Barry Cornwall' and his daughter, Adelaide Procter, who was also a poet. Other introductions were to William Johnson Fox, who had been the Unitarian minister of South Place Chapel until a scandal broke out about his relation with his ward, Eliza Flower. As MP for Oldham, he was the first man to introduce a bill for national education.[33] They also met John Chapman, a bookseller and publisher who aimed to publish 'liberal' thought and had reprinted William Howitt's *History of Priestcraft* in 1846.[34]

Anna Mary Howitt was training to become a professional painter at Sass's art school in London where students usually studied for two years and then took the entrance examination for the Royal Academy schools.[35] Although Francis Cary was himself willing to teach women students, very few women trained there because they were excluded from the RA schools. Anna Mary attended Sass's at the same time as Tottie Fox,[36] whom Bessie described as having 'a lovely expressive dark face, such eyes, & a low broad Grecian brow'.[37] At Sass's Anna Mary met a band of young male painters: the tall, dark Thomas Woolner, Holman Hunt with golden beard and piercing blue eyes, and, her favourite, Dante Gabriel Rossetti. These young men had decided to exhibit under the collective name PRB (Pre-Raphaelite Brethren), supposedly to mark their turn away from the classical and towards the close observation of nature. The Howitts' financial crisis meant that they could no longer afford to pay for Anna Mary's lessons at Sass's, although Cary continued to teach her, kindly saying she could pay him once her career was established.[38]

Anna Mary introduced Barbara to the world of aspiring women artists. As well as Tottie Fox, she knew Margaret Gillies, an artist who made her living by portrait miniatures, usually watercolour on ivory.[39] She and her sister Mary lived with their friend, Dr Southwood Smith, a Unitarian preacher turned physician, and helped him bring up his granddaughter, Gertrude Hill. In 1842 Southwood Smith had published a report for the Royal Commission on Children's Employment (Mines), with compelling illustrations by Margaret Gillies. Ben Smith promptly commissioned Margaret to paint a portrait of Bella, partly because he wanted one, of course, but the timing of his request was at a point when her finances were especially stretched, which suggests Ben's usual generous and tactful impulse.

Anna Jameson was another motherly figure in Barbara's life, and, like Mary Howitt, was a woman whom Barbara admired because she 'earned her own bread'.[40] Born in Dublin, the eldest of five daughters of an Irish miniature painter and his English wife, she had made a living as a governess from the age of sixteen until her marriage in 1825. The marriage had been a disaster, her husband turning out a drunk, but after separating from him in 1829 she had made a living as a writer, mainly as an art critic. She was a great traveller, interested in everything and everyone, and as a consequence was extremely good company. Her conversation was enhanced by 'one especial charm which no picture could ever give or perpetuate. It was her voice. Gentle, low and sweet'.[41] Anna's devoted 'philosophical friend', Robert Noel, moved swiftly from 'Mr Noel' to 'Uncle Robert' in the affections of the young Leigh Smiths.[42] Robert was cultivated, much travelled, and extremely attractive to women. In 1835 he had married a German *baronin*, and lived in Bohemia, painting a little, translating, writing on history, geology, art and phrenology.[43] He frequently visited England on publishing and other matters, and when in town was always a welcome and lively guest at dinner parties in Blandford Square or Pelham Crescent.

The lively spirits of the Smith children were remarked on by all their visitors. Barbara, in particular, was full of energy and the acknowledged leader of her little gang of five. As her doting Pater once wrote: 'Dear Barbara, your cheerful spirit/Never needs a stick to stir it.'[44] Charades, acting and writing ballads were a favourite part of their self-made entertainments at Pelham Crescent. Barbara wrote a ballad dedicated to Aunt Dolly about a 'Lady Beda' who was threatened with death if she would not marry the bounder, Sir Burleycock.[45] He is drawn with curling moustaches in one of Barbara's earliest scrapbooks.[46] Other drawings show Barbara, Nannie and William all dressed up with false moustaches and acting out an unidentified theatrical scene at the 'Theatre Royal, Pelham Crescent'. Another picture in the same scrapbook shows Barbara and probably the same two siblings acting out a scene from *Twelfth Night*.[47] Barbara's delight in dressing up and in the acting of characters from *The Arabian Nights* is revealed in a teasing letter to Aunt Ju in which she admits that she had been to Greenwich Fair. Greenwich Fair was then considered far too rowdy a place for ladies to attend, so if they went at all, they hoped no one respectable would see them there. Barbara sent Aunt Ju a picaresque tale about how she dressed in 'a pair of Shakrajah Turkish trousers' to disguise herself as an orange seller. When the thrill of listening to the 'natural humour rather wise satire . . . evil humour & satire equally that which Shakespeare & Swift give to the common people' wore off she went on to act out a 'Turkish solo drama in a bright yellow caravan'. The letter becomes more and more fantastic, but probably indicates that Barbara had really visited Greenwich Fair, although she knew it was not quite respectable, and that she knew quite well that Aunt Ju had been there too. It is highly likely that Barbara went there safely accompanied by her brother Ben, although she does not say so directly, only that she saw there 'a fellow of Jesus'.[48]

Ben continued to buy land around Robertsbridge so that, as well as Crowham Manor and Brown's Farm, by 1841 he owned a third farm, Scalands.[49] A few years later he bought Glottenham Manor, which included the ruins of a fourteenth-century fortified house, surrounded by a moat, by that stage declined into romantic ruins. This parcel of land also included Mountfield Park Farm. Ben was now lord of two manors, thereby more than regaining the social high ground that William Smith had lost when forced to sell Parndon Hall.

Barbara continued to take a close interest in her father's political career. Ben was an intellectual disciple of David Ricardo and his professor, Nassau Senior, the political economists who led the arguments against protectionism and for free trade. Their argument was that unless you regulated the wages of labour it was unjust to regulate the price of food by unnaturally raising the cost of corn. An anti-Corn Law association was formed in London in 1836, an association in Manchester started in autumn 1838, and other cities followed suit until a nationwide Anti-Corn Law League was established in 1839. Ben was a member of the council of the Anti-Corn Law League, which consisted of all who had subscribed over £50 or more, ultimately more than 500. William Cobden and John Bright were the leaders of a highly effective campaign which petitioned Parliament, ran bazaars to raise money, wrote and circulated pamphlets, tracts, handbills and ballads, which were delivered free to every library, mechanics' institute, every individual and firm listed in Pigott's Directory of tradesmen. Although the League insisted that the repeal of the laws was not a party-political question, this assertion was more rhetorical than accurate. A change in the law could be achieved only by votes in the House of Commons. As Cobden wrote: 'the country's salvation must be worked out at the hustings and in the polling-booths'.[50] When seats became vacant the League put up a free trade candidate. For this reason Ben was called on to propose Robert Moore, an Irishman, for the borough of Hastings in 1844. Robert Moore was a barrister, engaged by the League as one of their twenty-five lecturers, who toured the country giving speeches on free trade. By a strange coincidence his son was to come into Barbara's life many years later.

In 1845 Ben took his family to Ireland, at a time when the blight of the potato crop had caused famine and fever. It was this 'great hunger' and destitution in Ireland which, more than anything else, finally brought about the repeal of the Corn Laws. Perhaps he was visiting Ireland at this time with a view to reporting back to the Anti-Corn Law League. The visit made a powerful impression on Barbara, as can be seen in her watercolour *Ireland 1846* showing a ruined cottage with a mourning girl in the foreground, and a corn ship, possibly more dreamed of than real, in the background. Almost certainly, Barbara would have read Elizabeth Barrett Browning's poem 'The Cry of the Human' published in 1844, which includes the verse:

> The curse of gold upon the land
> The lack of bread enforces;
> The rail-cars snort from strand to strand,
> Like more of Death's white horses!
> The rich preach 'rights' and 'future days'
> and hear no angel scoffing, –
> The poor die mute – with starving gaze
> On corn-ships in the offing.
> Be pitiful, O God!

In 1846 a series of measures effectively peeled back the Corn Laws. By one of the strangest quirks of parliamentary history Sir Robert Peel's three-and-a-half-hour explanation was received in stony silence by his own Conservative benches and by cheers from the Opposition side. He pointed out that the earlier extension of free trade had not harmed agriculture, and that true Conservatism required taxing those best able to bear the burden, not the poor. In particular, the crisis in Ireland, following two years of blighted potato harvests, made delay impossible.[51] On 26 June 1846 the Act to Amend the Laws Relating to the Importation of Corn finally reached the statute book. The League, a body formed for a single purpose, met on 2 July to congratulate each other and to wind up the organisation they had created.

Barbara's journals during Ben's years in Parliament usefully serve as her gloss on her father's political thinking. For instance in the journal covering a trip to Scotland in the summer of 1847 she commented: 'Whiskey. Whiskey. Whiskey. I don't believe the devil lies in brimstone but in whiskey. It is the bane of Scotland, worse I think than Ireland, for here in spite of education and all that, they are idiots and madmen when they drink. Everybody seems to drink the abominable stuff. The other night there was a great noise of fighting outside my door, and in the morning I learnt that a whiskey drinker was going to bed! An old woman came here on Sunday, drank whiskey and behaved in a most outrageous way . . .'[52] Although he had made his money from the distilling of whisky, Ben very much disliked public drunkenness, and voted against an attempt to reduce the term of imprisonment for being drunk in the streets from fourteen days to seven. On the other hand, he disliked hypocrisy and so voted against the Lord's Day Observance Bill on the grounds that it stopped working men from drinking in public houses whilst 'gentlemen' could drink wine in their clubs.

Ben did not stay in Parliament after 1847. Perhaps he felt that the repeal of the Corn Laws was the fruitful end of a major campaign and that a steady trend towards reform was safely established. He was, in any case sixty-five – a suitable age to retire from Parliament. In his retirement Ben became a magistrate in Hastings, and he never lost his interest in political questions. A letter written by Barbara in October 1848 to her old friend and teacher, James Buchanan, now out in Natal, commented:

[The Pater] is quite well, and looks so, and is in very good spirits, but thinks the prospects of Europe dark. As politics form a great part of our existence here, the bloody scenes which are going on over the water often make him and all of us very melancholy, though we all believe in the progress of the people, yet the democrats are acting savagely, brutally. It is a great struggle between kings and people, between the Old Ways and New. We are always saying, 'What strange times!' For there is nothing to compare in strangeness, nothing by which one can guess what will come next. Papa reads the newspapers and gives us his opinions and the benefit of his experience upon all the great questions at home and abroad.[53]

1848 was the year in which revolutions overthrew Louis Philippe in France and Metternich in Austria, and led to a general movement against Austrian domination in Italy. Ben, like his father before him, was a 'friend of peace'. Exiled political refugees, such as Freiligrath, Kinkel, Mazzini, Ledru Rollin and Kossuth could count on his untiring hospitality and generosity.[54] Ben naturally enough looked to his eldest son to follow him into the political arena. However, it proved to be Barbara who took up the dynastic role for this third generation of Smiths.

But it would give a false picture to suggest that Barbara learned about politics only from her father. Anna Jameson, Mary Howitt and especially Barbara's beloved Aunt Ju all introduced her to specifically female modes of participation in political events. The campaign to repeal the Corn Laws had a particular influence on Barbara's political development because middle-class women played a larger and more public role in it than they had in any previous political organisation. Women's formal involvement in the League's work began in October 1840 with a tea party on a huge scale in the Corn Exchange in Manchester. Mrs Richard

Cobden organised a women's committee in September 1841 to consider how women could best assist the League. This original Manchester committee of women soon swelled to a network of about 360 'Ladies' Local Committees' distributed throughout the country. They organised the Free Trade Bazaar in the Theatre Royal, Manchester, in January 1842. The sum of £10,000 was raised by donations, and from entrance charges and a sale of the goods the women had made, including such items as Anti-Corn-Law pincushions, with 'Let me come free' carefully embroidered round a sheaf of corn. This kind of propaganda had been used to good effect in mobilising opinion in the anti-slavery campaign, and this emblem was to appeal to the conscience of the well-to-do concerning those who were below the bread line. Such was the success of the Manchester bazaar that another was organised, to be held in the Theatre Royal, Covent Garden, London, in May 1845. The council of the League clearly recognised the importance of the women's work and sent out an appeal:

TO THE WOMEN OF GREAT BRITAIN

LADIES. By a majority of the other sex you are excluded from direct interference in political matters . . . By this same majority and by universal consent you are invited to interpose in matters of charity . . . The proposed Bazaar . . . affords a most unquestionable mode in which your aid may be as efficient as it is welcome. What *mere* charity can be compared with the great and sacred cause of justice, which you are thus invited to advance? . . . how much you achieved towards the abolition of the slave trade? And how much you may achieve towards the abolition of the starvation trade.[55]

This is inspired campaigning; it invokes the example of housewives giving up sugar as a material way of objecting to slavery in the colonies. It invites them to be part of a political campaign but in a way which stresses the feminine quality of concern that underpins the principles of justice. Aunt Ju took both Barbara and her youngest sister, Nannie, aged respectively eighteen and fourteen, to the London Bazaar, where they met Rebecca Moore (the estranged wife of Ben's friend, Robert Moore), who was full of 'ideas, and very clever ones too upon policies, morals and literature and education and homeopathy, – all alive and full of intellect'.[56] In Manchester Rebecca Moore earned her living by running a Froebelian school attended by the children of nonconformist manufacturers and by her own son, Norman. Like Anna Jameson she was one of the feminists of the 1840s who redefined notions of where the public and private spheres intersected for women and acted as role models for Barbara and her generation. This was a first-hand opportunity for Barbara to see women take an active part in a political campaign.

Julia's closest women friends tended to be Unitarians whose desire for women to be respected as rational creatures inclined them towards the drive for more rational education for girls, women such as Harriet Martineau and Elizabeth Reid (née Sturch). Elizabeth Sturch, a member of the Essex Street Unitarian Chapel, was one of Julia's very closest friends. In 1821 she had married Dr John Reid, who had died after only thirteen months of marriage. After his death and the death of her father, a wealthy ironmonger, she was both well-to-do and free to follow her charitable and reforming instincts. After the death of her mother, Elizabeth Reid moved into 21 York Terrace with her unmarried sister, Mary Sturch, and this address then became a centre for those involved in the anti-slavery movement. With the passage of the Emancipation Act in 1833, the next stage of the battle was to petition Parliament to end the apprenticeship system in the West Indies (which was slavery by another name). A petition containing 500,000 signatures supported its overthrow in 1839. Having achieved this object, many of the women became auxiliaries of the British and Foreign Anti-Slavery Society dedicated to overthrowing slavery throughout the world.

Aunt Ju, Elizabeth Reid and Mary Howitt were all involved with this phase of the anti-slavery movement. In 1840 William Lloyd Garrison arrived from America with women delegates to the World's Anti-Slavery Convention in London, an Anglo-American gathering to celebrate the end of the apprenticeship system and to focus on slavery elsewhere. Thomas Clarkson, now eighty years old, made the opening speech in which he paid tribute to his dead friends, Wilberforce and William Smith.[57] The British and Foreign Society, however, which was hosting the convention, refused to allow the women delegates on to the floor; they had to adjourn to a gallery where they were joined by Garrison and other male supporters. One of the women delegates, Lucretia Mott, the head of the Philadelphia Anti-Slavery Society, was befriended by Aunt Ju and Elizabeth Reid.[58] Mary Howitt was also involved in the anti-slavery movement, specifically in raising money to ransom a fugitive slave, Frederick Douglass, who, after escaping from the South, had joined the American abolitionist movement as a full-time lecturer. In 1845 he published an account of his years in bondage, *Narrative of the Life of Frederick Douglass, an American Slave, Written by Himself*, which had an enormous impact but exposed him to the attention of slave catchers. Consequently, Douglass removed himself from harm's way by going on a lecture tour of England. In 1846 Barbara sent £2 from her father to Mary Howitt for the Frederick Douglass fund.[59] Subsequently, Douglass established a newspaper as a forum for black writers, where they could address the issue of racism in the North, as well as the issue of slavery itself. Barbara and Bessie may well have considered at this point what a journal run entirely by women for women might achieve.

Even in Barbara's early years then, the seeds of a feminist political education were being sown. As well as learning from her father's parliamentary career, she had witnessed two campaigns within which women had carved out significant roles for themselves – running committees, raising funds and petitioning Parliament. She had seen the historical moment when women crossed the line from 'privately' supporting organisations run by men to asserting their own authority and their right to have a voice in the formation of laws. Ironically, had her own mother lived, Barbara might have had a shadowed life, never fully able to enter the public domain. This very uncomfortable thought could not have escaped Barbara's astute mind when, in 1854, she herself entered the political fray.

CHAPTER 3

The Apprenticeship Years

In October 1848 Ben Leigh Smith entered Jesus College, Cambridge, as a pensioner. For Barbara, who was as intellectual in her interests as her brother, this must have been a moment of conflicting emotions. Her brother was off to university, whilst she, simply because she had been born female, had no such option. As she wrote to Helen Taylor much later, 'ever since my brother went to Cambridge I have always intended to aim at the establishment of a college where women could have the same education as men if they wished it.'[1]

The Pater had recognised that Benjamin was academically gifted, but considered that Willie's talents lay in a different direction. At nearby Battle Abbey Estate, the erstwhile manager, John Scales, had recently been appointed principal of a new agricultural college, founded in Cirencester in 1845.[2] Its aim was to import the ideas of Liebig on agricultural chemistry and so to establish a truly scientific approach to farming, and this was to be Willie's university.[3] Barbara wrote to Mr Buchanan, 'Willy is grown into a young gentleman with a coat with tail! He shoots and rides and loves the country. He is very handsome, and witty and merry, and the life of the house . . . At Christmas he will leave Mr Mahew's and go to some agricultural college to learn farming.'[4] Over the Christmas vacation Pater had arranged for an examiner from the College of Preceptors in London, Philip Kingsford, to tutor Willie in political economy.[5] William Ewart, who was on the council of the college had hinted that Kingsford, who was suffering from ill health and overwork, would benefit from a semi-convalescence in Hastings.[6]

When Kingsford arrived at Pelham Crescent he found Barbara, then twenty-one, the more eager student for some formal teaching. He was an exceptionally gifted teacher; in a letter to Bessie at this time Barbara said '[PK] can teach well. He is so precise and clear.'[7] Kingsford's definition of a scholar covered exactly the broad scope which she herself desired:

it is the scholar alone who knows how, in the fullest measure, to grasp and to comprehend [the power of beauty]. In the soul of the scholar, the perception of beauty, at first vague and indistinct, and apparently purposeless except for immediate enjoyment, gradually acquires significance, and at last expands into an habitual admiration and love for all that is lofty and excellent . . . The aspiration must have assumed some definite form; the energies must be capable of being concentrated, and brought to bear upon some high purpose. The whole being, physical, intellectual, and moral, must have been trained to some work of a dignified character – the very existence must be an instrument for attaining some further purpose.[8]

In the 1851 census of Hastings, Barbara recorded her occupation as 'scholar at home'.

Kingsford was thirty-four years old, and close proximity with Barbara led first to mutual fondness, and on his side to a passionate love. He was the first man to be seriously attracted to her; Barbara admired him, and was desperately sorry for his broken-down health, but she was not in love with him. Bessie wrote in 1854, immediately after Kingsford's death, that he was 'dearer than a brother to her, yet not of sufficient power to attract so powerful a nature as her in the nearest relationship. The tie between them was very strong; she sustained & blessed him & comforted him through life in a marvellous way'.[9]

But much of Barbara's education came from her habit of forming reading groups with like-minded young women. As well as Anna Mary Howitt, Barbara formed a fast friendship with Bessie Parkes, who came from a Unitarian family whose radical credentials were equivalent to those of the Smiths. Bessie's mother, Elizabeth Rayner, was a granddaughter of Joseph Priestley, and her father, Joseph Parkes, was a radical lawyer who, like Ben Smith, was an advanced liberal. After the death of his legal partner in 1845 Parkes slowly withdrew from political activities, and took rooms at 6 Pelham Crescent, because Bessie's brother Priestley was suffering from consumption. The dependence of the Unitarian faith on science and rationality, which had previously seemed to Bessie so superior to 'superstitious' forms of faith, now presented itself to her as a weakness. From the time of Priestley's last illness, Bessie felt the need for some new ground of faith that the Unitarianism of her upbringing could not offer. Writing to an old school friend Bessie commented:

Unitarians say 'Be good & you will go to Heaven' [but] the cause of every great change [must depend on] feeling and not intellect alone . . . To conclude my irreverent speeches on many Unitarians of the modern school, they crush their Religion between eleven and half past twelve on a Sunday morning & make common sense do the rest of its work.[10]

As a young woman brought up in Sussex, which was especially hostile to 'Priestcraft' (William Howitt's term) Barbara feared that Bessie would turn to Catholicism. Barbara regarded herself as simultaneously a free thinker and profoundly religious, which was a position it was possible to hold within Unitarianism. She was the unwilling witness of the first unshacklings of Bessie's childhood faith during the late 1840s, and Bessie's inevitable movement towards a different spiritual home. Unitarianism was often regarded by cynics as a net to catch a falling Christian; in Bessie's case it was a net tested and found wanting.

Barbara and Bessie recommended books to each other and critically discussed, either face to face or by letter, everything they had been reading. Bessie was the ideal partner for Barbara in this educative enterprise. Their ambitions – Barbara to be an artist and Bessie to be a poet – plus their desire to serve the world in some way, formed the linchpin of their friendship. Unlike Barbara, Bessie had been educated at a remarkably good school for girls run by the Field family at Leam, near Warwick. At school, Bessie's teacher, Lucy Field, had inspired in her an intense love, which had, in fact, been rejected rather brusquely by Miss Field. When she left Leam aged sixteen, Bessie needed a new intellectual and spiritual mentor. Barbara identified and described this need in Bessie as 'awful love', meaning a love full of awe, a kind of idolatry.[11] Although Barbara was only two years Bessie's senior, she had enjoyed a peculiarly free intellectual life within her family, and was in some ways a good deal more sophisticated than Bessie. She replaced Lucy Field as Bessie's heroine; Bessie referred to herself as 'Ganymede', implying that Barbara was the Goddess, and she, only the messenger. Bessie was just as ardent as Barbara in her quest for knowledge, but acknowledged in her diary that: 'Barbara has a queer way of going to the point which I have not'.[12] This had a great deal to do with the Smith family habit of discussing all political and social affairs openly; the Pater did not censor reading and discussion on gender lines.

Bessie found the contrast between her own family life and the louche Smith family style enchanting; she never forgot seeing the Pater kneeling down to put Barbara's boots on, something she could never imagine her own father doing.[13] She loved to escape from her more conventional family to join the glamorous Smiths. From 1846 onwards, when trains linked London and Hastings, even the journeys down to the Sussex coast seemed to spell freedom:

To Hastings; mad in the train, singing, shouting, yelling, laughing. Oh how happy I was, thinking of the glorious winter to come, all the books

33

to read, all the lovely rides, all the reading and talk with Barbara, all the acting and music, & the seaweeds & the ferns; Ecclesbourne Fairlight & all the jolly places. Then came Heaven down upon earth to my fancy, & I felt so intensely happy that I could scarcely contain myself. Oh those free wild spirits the Smiths always seem to have, how glorious to feel their rush into one's own heart.[14]

Alongside Barbara's high spirits, which Bessie found so intoxicating, she was just as serious as Bessie in her efforts to learn. Having read George Combe's *Moral Philosophy* when she was seventeen, Barbara had taken his dictum for her own, that 'gaining knowledge is a moral duty'. Perhaps to mark the start of an ambitious reading programme, in 1846 the Pater gave her his own father's copy of Francis Bacon's *Essays*. A scrutiny of their letters reveals a wide-ranging programme of reading between 1846 and 1849. In January 1847, for example, they were reading and discussing poetry by Tennyson and Byron, *The Taming of the Shrew* and *All's Well That Ends Well*. The next month they were studying *Measure for Measure* and Bacon's *Advancement of Learning*. Bacon was much invoked by Unitarian philosophers such as Joseph Priestley because he represented knowledge as power, but the power was to be acquired in order to serve the community, thus rendering the scientist the paradigm of the 'good citizen and [a] useful member of society'.[15] It would be exhausting to rehearse their reading programme month by month – suffice it to say that over a three-year period, letters reveal their critical responses to works by Bacon, Frederika Bremer, Charlotte Brontë, Butler, Carlyle, Chaucer, Diana Craik, Maria Edgeworth, Fielding, Goethe, Mary Howitt, Keats, Locke, Harriet Martineau, Hannah More, Tom Paine, Richardson, Shelley, George Sand, Shakespeare, Eugène Sue, Tennyson and Wordsworth.

At Christmas 1847 Bessie sent Barbara a copy of Tennyson's *The Princess* with a letter saying: 'I think you would marry the Prince: were there such a creature he would satisfy even your romance.'[16] Barbara had obviously responded to the poem with great enthusiasm. Bessie's next letter, in January 1848, comments: 'You are a quick scholar compared to me . . . You say you see nothing absurd in Ida; now tho' I thought her a magnificent creature, I thoroughly agreed with Tennyson's moral. I think she set the laws of God aside in attempting the cure of our great social evils.'[17] Anna Mary wrote to Barbara: 'I think all *true* women must like it, and for the sake of the beautiful noble conclusion henceforth enthrone Tennyson on a golden throne in their hearts. It is [a] poem on women's education, women's rights, woman's true being – and according to our notions noble and true . . . I wonder whether the Princess herself, Ida, will remind you of yourself? She strongly reminded me of you throughout.'[18]

In May 1848 there was some alarm about Barbara's eyesight, which seems to have suffered from painting outdoors in hot, glaring sunshine. Aunt Patty was sent for by Pater to take charge of the household for six weeks, and, in particular, she was supposed to stop Barbara from reading or painting too much and damaging her eyes still further. This duty hardly endeared her to her niece, who found six weeks of Aunt Patty, unrelieved by her usual pursuits, almost more than she could bear. Ultimately, Barbara borrowed a pair of blue-tinted spectacles from Anna Mary, which subsequently Anna Mary invited her to keep, as she herself could borrow her mother's violet-tinted glasses. The spectacles seem to have served the purpose, and no doubt Aunt Patty, having done her duty by her brother, was relieved to get away from the exuberant Leigh Smith young. Poor Aunt Patty tended to be the butt of Barbara's jokes: she liked to dine out on stories of *le malade imaginaire*. Marian Lewes (George Eliot) once wrote in her journal that Barbara's description of a conversation with her Aunt Patty was 'a scene beyond the conception of Molière'.[19]

One of the crucial moments in Barbara's development was her reading of Frederika Bremer's *Hertha*, which Mary Howitt had translated in 1846. In it the eponymous feminist heroine tells her sister, Alma that she wanted to found a

' . . . higher school, where they shall not learn French or German, or music or drawing – all these can be learned elsewhere – but where young girls, out of whatever class of society they may be, which have awoke [*sic*] to a consciousness of a higher want, and for whom the true knowledge of themselves and of their vocation, as members of society; may teach themselves to reflect and to answer the questions: "What am I ? What can I do? What ought I to do?" . . . [Jesus] lived and died for a great purpose; and many beside us, seem merely to live and to pine away slowly and die, without any object!'

'Yes', said Alma sadly, 'that is the worst of it.'[20]

Barbara's excitement is replicated in the urgent tone of her letter to Bessie: 'I have a great deal to say to you about work and life and the necessity of your fixing early on a train of action, you I mean, what is so sad so utterly black as a wasted life, and how common! – I believe that there are thousands and tens of thousands who like you and I intend doing, – intend working but live and die, only intending.'[21] They particularly considered the position of women in society. Bessie wrote:

> We have some brains among our Sex, our own. . .
> You cannot need another word to show it;
> I need but name a Martineau and Howitt.[22]

What is clear from all this is that the apparently private activity of women reading at home had potential social implications.[23]

Barbara's first opportunity for expressing her opinions more publicly was given to her in 1848 by William Ransom, a remarkable young man of twenty-six who was editor of the *Hastings and St Leonards News*.[24] Liberal in politics, a supporter of free trade, he was the great champion of Frederick North, who he judged to be an honest politician when such a person was relatively rare. By the time he died Ransom was considered, even by rival newspapers, as the father of the local press. He was another of the friends Barbara made in young adulthood, who was to be a friend for life. Bessie generally honed her skills by writing pieces for the *Birmingham Journal*, because of the Parkes's Birmingham connections, but Barbara naturally looked to this newly founded liberal organ in Hastings to place her early articles. Her very first article, 'An Appeal to the Inhabitants of Hastings' in June 1848 indicates why she had adopted the *nom de plume*, 'Esculapius' (the God of Healing): it was the name associated by the press with Chadwick and Southwood Smith. In her appeal Barbara wishes that reformers would put the same energy into health and environmental issues as the Church of England was putting into distributing bibles. Referring (by implication) to her reading of Wollaston's 'natural laws' she praises the work of Lord Ashley, Southwood Smith 'and several others [who] have within the last twenty years greatly enlightened the upper classes as to the laws under which it has pleased God to place our health. People, instead of considering their diseases as the hand of a special providence, begin to attribute them to the infringement by themselves of the Almighty Parent's injunctions.' She urges reformers to 'Spread physiological and scientific truth wide as the winds, wide as the ashes of Wickliffe [Wyclif] the Reformer, and you will reap reward in the increased vitality of that religious spirit in society which you at present labour *solely* to encourage.'

In August she wrote a piece called 'Conformity to Custom' which restated Mary Wollstonecraft's argument that the enforced feminine 'innocence', which was really 'ignorance', effectively denied women citizenship.[25] The tone of the article echoes Wollstonecraft's argument and rhetorical style:

> The dependent and environed life of women of rank is not innocent. The creature, never stirring without a footman, seeing only the stuccoed and carriage thronged streets, never coming into contact with vice and crime, those mournful facts which all should know in order that they be better stimulated to ameliorate – this woman forfeits her rights and duties as a human being, and the conscientious seeker after good should not conform.

This was followed by an attack on the foolishness of fashion, especially on the injurious habit of tight-lacing stays. Conforming to fashion's dictates, she argues, victimises women, and is in defiance of natural and moral rules. Barbara practised what she preached, refusing to wear corsets, and choosing clothes and boots suitable for an active life. Another of her articles, 'The Education of Women', pleaded that parents should let 'your "blue" [stocking] daughter, your political wife, your artistic sister, and eccentric cousin, pursue *their* paths unmolested, – you will never make ideals of them; you will only make your home the scene of suppressed energies and useless powers.'[26]

Part of Barbara's desire for a healthy life, physically, intellectually and spiritually, was grounded in her conviction of human need for connection with nature. She was always angry when Sussex landowners prevented people from walking over their land. She urged Bessie:

> Please to write for the H news [*Hastings . . . News*] about the beauty of the green fields and the necessity for people to see and love and study nature for their health of body and mind and of the vile wickedness and baseness and selfishness of men who shut up footpaths, which are the only right which millions hold in their native land. Write, write a stirring poem, a battle cry against the oppression of the selfish Squires.[27]

Barbara, herself, probably about the same time, drew a satirical sketch of a tree on the way to London forbidding the way to travellers.[28]

Bessie was always struck by Barbara's quick response to political events; Barbara drew a picture of herself weeping over the Paris Revolution of 1848.[29] The bad cereal and potato harvests of 1845 and 1846, rising grain prices and consequently rising bread prices, had caused hunger, widespread disorder and severe government repression in France. This must have reminded Barbara of the situation in Ireland, which had so appalled her on her 1845 visit. Liberal demands for free trade in France, as in England, had made it necessary to open the markets (temporarily) to foreign grain, but the young generation emerging from the *polytechniques* were beginning to see liberalism as an inadequate response to the needs of society: it had succeeded only in gaining some hard-won liberties for a small wealthy minority. Reading Michelet and Lamartine they were pressing for liberty and equality for all. Louis Blanc and the Fourierists, in particular, were promoting the notions of organisation of work and the 'right to work' among some segments of the public. In February 1848 Louis-Philippe was forced to abdicate and flee to England disguised rather absurdly with false whiskers and travelling as 'Mr Smith'. Although Barbara believed in the progress of the people, she feared that, as with the Terror following the French Revolution, a bloodbath might result from the flight of the monarch from France. Bessie responded robustly to Barbara's fears:

> I quite agree with you that whatever becomes of France, Germany & Italy will have great reason to rejoice in the times. Indeed I think it is in those two countries alone that real progress will be made. Yet France is a great Mirror, the only thing is that it is better she should educate herself in freedom than under Louis Philippe. It is just like your duck in the pond when you were a child. She may get into bloodshed and trouble as you did into mud, by having your own way, but she is more likely to gain experience & self government in the end, than if she were cramped.[30]

On 22 April 1848 the *Birmingham Journal* published Bessie's optimistic poem 'Progression' in response to the situation in France and Barbara wrote to tell Bessie of the Pater's approval.[31]

Everything that she read inspired Barbara to commit herself to action; the problem was where to start. After reading Goethe's *Wilhelm Meister* she was once more full of the conviction that thought must be translated into action, and felt the pressing need for a sense of direction for her energies. Writing to Bessie from London in 1849 she said:

> I feel a mass of ideas & thoughts in my head and long for some expression, some letting out of, the restless spirit, in work for those who are ignorant. I feel quite oppressed sometimes with so much enjoyment of intellect (for I was all day yesterday seeing painting & pictures) & so I have been ever since I came up, I love & take keen delight in all this intellectual world but I feel still as if I had no right to enjoy so much while there is so much ignorance in the world & so many eyes shut up. Oh! When one really knows & understands a little

of the misery in the world & its ignorance, is it not wicked to sit still & look at it? Ought one not to go out & help to fight it, even if ever so humbly. This is what is ever ringing in my head sometime loud & sometime soft but it is always there. But what is the use of talking. I am always thinking and talking, never acting.[32]

One immediate consequence was her decision, in 1849, to study drawing at Bedford College with Francis Cary, the same master who had taught Anna Mary at Sass's Academy, who had been appointed Professor of Drawing at the new Ladies' College, in Bedford Square, Bloomsbury.

This college was the brainchild of Aunt Ju's close friend in the anti-slavery campaign, Elizabeth Reid. Indeed she used the rhetoric of that movement to express her view that the work of the college was only the first stage of the struggle for women's political emancipation. 'My dearest wish is that the whole proceeding may be as an Underground Railway, differing in this from the American UR that no one shall ever know of its existence.'[33] The Underground Railway referred to the secret routes through which abolitionists assisted fugitive slaves to Canada and freedom and the image suggests that these female reformers saw improved female education as the key to women's entering the professions, training other women and girls, and, ultimately, proving their worthiness to vote. Although the Reverend F.D. Maurice and the Governesses' Benevolent Institution had already founded Queen's College in 1848 to provide training so that governesses could obtain better salaries, this was an Anglican establishment helped by several of the lecturers at King's College. Elizabeth Reid, however, because she was a Unitarian, was keen to set up a non-sectarian 'college' and so she looked for her support mainly to lecturers at University College in London, which had itself been founded to award degrees to Dissenters.

In the nineteenth century the word 'college' did not imply 'tertiary' or 'higher' education. Education was stratified not so much in terms of age but of class. The three main categories of Victorian education were those of 'elementary', 'secondary' and 'higher'. Elementary schools were for working-class children up to the age of fourteen. The teaching at mechanics' institutes and night schools for adults was also considered 'elementary'. Secondary schools were for the children of the middle class, whose ages could be anywhere between seven and twenty.[34] When Mrs Reid set up the Ladies' College in Bedford Square (Bedford College) it was non-residential and largely concentrated on making up for deficiencies in earlier education. Some of the students, however, were attending a full-time four-year course to obtain certificates of general proficiency teaching and this sense of considering teaching as an art for which training was needed was quite a new thing. There were also 'ladies' attending courses for brief periods, the income from whom kept the college afloat in the precarious early years. Julia Smith was just such a student and she brought with her the three Leigh Smith nieces, Barbara, Bella and Nannie. Julia also supported Bedford College by serving as a member of the council for one year and as a lady visitor for five.[35] For Barbara, as well as the drawing instruction itself, several important things came out of the Bedford College experience.

Firstly, the Leigh Smith sisters made friends who helped them with future feminist enterprises and Nannie met the woman who was to become her life companion, Isabella Blythe. Despite Bedford College's cramped premises, and the fact that it could not provide the intellectual community that a residential college would offer, her experience there was nevertheless undoubtedly an important first step in Barbara's career as an educationist. On the one hand she met women who were being trained to teach, and on the other hand, the possibility of providing a separate environment for women, offering full-time study and independence from family duties, began to flicker in her imagination. The *limitations* of Bedford College as well as its opportunities under-pinned her grand ideal of achieving for women the same kind of college which it was assumed provided the best possible education for young men.

From April 1848, when Barbara reached the age of twenty-one, she became financially independent because, at their majority, Ben gave each of his children, a portfolio of stocks and shares.[36] These yielded between £250 and £300 a year according to the market, so Barbara was able to plan a future and decide on strategies, using her own money. This placed her in an almost unique position for a young unmarried woman of that period, and the years between 1848 and 1854 were not fallow years, but apprenticeship years. Barbara's rather bohemian home, although it occasionally gave rise to difficulties in polite society, also meant that she was unusually free to pursue her studies. As Bessie said about Barbara in her diary, 'What a glorious thing it must be to care as I see she cares with regard to all social questions. Unlike most people, she carries the feeling through the minute ramifications of all her social life in a manner I feel beautiful to see'.[37]

Of course, no nineteenth-century woman escaped entirely from family claims, nor did Barbara want to. But in November 1849, when Barbara and Bella went up to Alfreton to see Aunt Dolly, who was ill, Barbara was shocked to find some of her Alfreton relatives woefully uneducated.

Bessie replied to one letter: 'Are all the Alfreton folk Devils Incarnate? You write as if they were'[38] She gently criticised Barbara, for being 'too fastidious in feeling. Dearest between educated and uneducated people there is some difference but a vast similitude. We have the advantage in a few years of culture, we are fellow in feeling; perhaps not even fellows in goodness.'[39] There is in Bessie's careful letter one of the few shreds of evidence of Barbara's psychological difficulties in accommodating the two strands of her family life. She had been brought up by her father in a highly cultured upper-middle-class environment, and her father was rich and powerful. Anne Longden's family, though perfectly respectable people, in class terms were of about the same rank as the Smith and Leigh forebears four generations back on the Isle of Wight. Bessie, acutely aware of Barbara's sensitivity about her mother, delicately reminds her that 'culture' is merely the polish which comes *after* the previous generations have made the money. In this fraught area, Bessie clearly offered consistent calm, tactful support. It was a good return on Barbara's fund of high spirits, which helped guard Bessie from depression during the difficult period of her brother's decline and death.

Barbara's closest artist friend was that 'little fragile spiritual creature', Anna Mary Howitt.[40] Barbara felt a dilettante compared with her and, following her example, determined to take her art more seriously. In one letter she explained to Bessie the radical step she had taken to effect an improvement in her draughtsmanship:

> I must explain what I have done, that is given up *coloring* (my dear color box is locked up for 6 months) 'some natural tears I shed' or very nearly but I was so convinced of my inability to draw that it was not so difficult to as I expected. It was wretched work! Coloring without form & so see me sticking to outlines & light & shadow. Mr. Scharf, Aunt Julia & some other artists said '*you may be an artist*, for you *love nature & color well*, but you have never learned to draw'.[41]

Barbara's self-dramatisation as Eve locked out of paradise is comical but also an indication of her sensuous enjoyment of colour and a determination to hone her skills. Bessie replied: 'I am glad you are going to study form because I always thought your colouring much the best of the two' and commented: 'I think you generalise too much in your drawings; give too much the suggestions of nature without a sufficient exactitude. This will narrow your public too much, to the people who sympathise with your view of the poetry of things.'[42]

While Barbara read eclectically, many of the books in her library (and the particular pages noted) reveal a musing consideration of the appropriate relationship of humankind with nature, one that might result in restorative harmony. The political radicalism of Blake and of the young Wordsworth and Shelley attracted her, but also their emphasis on the poet's transforming subjectivity. In July 1849 she sent Bessie a fiction called 'A Parable. Filia', which construed emblematically the relationship between (female) artist, nature and culture:

> She saw that every tree had its leaves written over with beautiful hymns and poems, and every flower had a song written on its open petals, and every stone was engraved with tales of wonder. On the mountain cliffs were written histories of deepest wisdom, and on the sand under her feet were traced tales of the old world – Filia saw all this and still stood in wonder – here were more volumes than all the libraries contained which she had ever seen. She tried to read these poems and these histories. The hymns and songs she could easily read, they were in her own language, but alas there were very few of the histories of which she could read anything. Then she saw the depth and wonder of nature, and felt her own ignorance and wished for books that she might learn the languages of Nature. 'Now that you understand Nature and Life to be *the books* and all others but aids to them you are worthy to be trusted with Men's works' said the friend; and Filia had her books and her drawing and her music, and she went back to the city with new bloom on her cheeks, and a bright lustre in her eyes.[43]

This fable bears witness to Barbara's close reading of William Wollaston's *The Religion of Nature Delineated* (1738) which argued that the seeds of knowledge are given us by nature, but not knowledge itself. It also suggests her study of *The Prelude* (1805) in which Wordsworth explores his own development from an original symbiosis with maternal nature, through intellectual self-consciousness and finally to the harmony of nature and culture achieved by his own imagination. Wordsworth effectively produces a self as Romantic hero in the figure of Mother Nature's favourite son. As 'Filia' means daughter, Barbara seems to be putting forward a similarly privileged female heroine, a model explored by the women writers Barbara most admired, George Sand and Charlotte Brontë.

Barbara's apprenticeship as a painter was spent in studying and copying the techniques of the English landscape masters – David Cox, Derwent, Girtin, Prout and Turner. Her paintings were Romantic in the sense that they sought to capture the 'clouds and chasing shadows' of a particular moment, but, more significantly, they represented the mood of a landscape or, arguably, her own mood.[44] She constantly carried sketchbooks in quest of her visions and was known to work outdoors for twelve hours at a stretch. In 1850 she went on painting expeditions in the Lake District and in Wales. In the Lake District she visited Wordsworth's grave and sketched it; inscribing in the front and back covers of her sketch cum commonplace book two cantos from Shelley's 'Queen Mab' (1821), in which Mab is the personification of an all-pervasive 'Spirit of Nature', and 'mother of the world', co-eternal with the universe.[45] Shelley's model replaces an authoritarian patriarchal God with some kind of female immanence. Mankind, in Shelley's view, must commit itself to serve the cause of justice and freedom.[46] For Barbara, 1850 marked the first move from painting privately towards entry into the public domain. She had two Welsh landscapes accepted by the Royal Academy – *View near Tremadoc, N. Wales* and *Dawn – near Maentwrog, N. Wales*. Barbara's paintings never simply reproduced a view; she always sought to capture that Shelleyan 'Spirit of Nature', a spirit which was appreciated by some of her critics more than others. Anna Jameson wrote to Bessie: 'Barbara's pictures are full of that fresh feeling for nature, that absence of the conventional in treatment which delights me.'[47]

The year 1850 was also crucial one for Anna Mary. She was not able to attend the Royal Academy schools, for no women were admitted. After attending a public lecture at the Academy, she wrote ruefully to Barbara that 'it seemed after all the Royal Academy were greater and more to be desired than the Academy of Nature'.[48] This is no doubt a reference to Barbara's parable 'Filia', which had been passed round among the friends in 1849, although Barbara, typically, had been staking a claim for nature *and* culture. As she could not train in London, Anna Mary decided to continue her studies with Kaulbach in Munich.[49] Barbara, now having her own money, planned an unchaperoned trip and persuaded Bessie's parents to let her come too. Priestley Parkes had died on 26 June 1850, aged twenty-five, after two agonising last weeks. The Parkes parents thought it would be good for Bessie to get away, so agreed to let her travel with her beloved Barbara, arranging, however, to meet them in Munich and bring them safely home.

In great excitement Barbara wrote a poem called 'Ode on the Cash Clothes Club,' dedicated to her father, 'that well known patron of all liberal institutions' of 'Liberty Hall, Blandford Square':

> Oh! Isn't it jolly
> To cast away folly

And cut all one's clothes a peg shorter
(A good many pegs)
And rejoice in one's legs
Like a free-minded Albion's daughter.[50]

Their trip took them through Belgium, Germany, Austria and Switzerland, both wearing short black boots with coloured laces and skirts lopped off four inches above the ankle for ease of walking.[51] Barbara, equipped with her blue-tinted spectacles, noted everything. Her letters home were a typical mixture of the picturesque and the political. She described the scenery near the Danube as 'hills covered with woods and in places the fine bones of the world coming through'. Switzerland was 'the land of houses with overhanging roofs, like Ben's eyebrows; the expression of the windows looking out of the dark are just like his eyes'. She felt so oppressed in Austria that she could hardly wait to leave: 'I did not know before, how intense, how completely a part of my soul were all feelings about freedom and justice in politics and government. I did not think, when I was so glad to go in Austria, how the sight of people ruled by the sword in place of law, would stir up my heart, and make me feel as miserable as those who live under it.'[52] Barbara's words are reminiscent of Shelley's 'Lines Written among the Euganean Hills', whose closing lines: 'And the Easter Alpine snow/Under the mighty Austrian' symbolised the disruption of nature by political repression.

Anna Mary had gone to Munich with another artist, Jane Benham, who earned her living as a book illustrator.[53] When Anna Mary and Jane arrived at Munich they found that Kaulbach had kindly given them a small room to sleep in and the use of his studio for the winter. Until 25 October, when he was to return from Berlin, they had only to pay for their food and for the cost of fuel, which was an enormous help to these not very well off young women. The excitement of being able to live as independently as young male art students is largely recounted in Anna Mary Howitt's *An Art-Student in Munich* (1853), published after her return to England. In it Barbara, described as 'my beloved friend . . . the sister of my heart', is represented as 'Justina', whose heroic dimensions reminds the reader of Anna Mary's earlier identification of Barbara with Tennyson's Princess Ida:

When we entered the Ludwig Kirche, I saw [Justina's] form dilate with emotion. She seemed to grow taller and grander; a rich flush came over her face; and her eyes filled with tears: 'I do not feel this,' said she, 'to be the work of man, but of nature. The arched roof produces upon me the same thrill as the sky itself!' Then we walked through the light and shadow of the English Garden – and I pointed out to her those particular spots that had always reminded me of her landscapes ... Justina looked grandly beautiful, with that golden hair of hers crowning her with a halo of glory, and her whole soul looking through her eyes, and quivering on her lips ... She had a large scheme of what she calls the Outer and Inner Sisterhood. The Inner, to consist of the Art-sisters bound together by their one object, and which she fears may never number many in their band; the Outer Sisterhood to consist of women, all workers, and all striving after a pure moral life, but belonging to any profession, any pursuit. All should be bound to help each other in such ways as were most accordant with their natures and characters.[54]

It is clear from this narrative that Anna Mary has invested Barbara with enormous significance; Mary Howitt was busy translating Norse myths and both mother and daughter regarded Barbara as 'a modern Valkyria'.[55] In the English Garden in Munich Anna Mary confessed to Barbara that she regarded her as a mediator who revealed God's grace. Anna Mary had painted Barbara in 1849 and was to use her as a model on several further occasions, as Boadicea (the warrior queen) and as Beatrice (she who makes blessed). Barbara's physical presence was in some sense inspirational to Anna Mary: she was both heroine and muse.

At the time of the Munich trip, Anna Mary was engaged to Edward Bateman, a friend of the PRB and a decorative designer and illustrator who worked with Owen Jones.[56] She was committed to studying with Kaulbach for at least two years, before marrying, after which she intended to continue in her career as an artist.[57] Anna Mary assured Barbara that their close relationship would not be altered when she married Bateman; her anxiety to explain suggests that she had a particular fixation on Barbara's role in her life. In a letter of 10 February 1851, Anna Mary wrote:

I have written him worlds about you – and he knows my devoted love to you – I have told him what a joy it is to me to feel that my love of him had if anything only increased my love for you and that this proves to me that both [are] affectionate and genuine – that my love of you is not the weak silly affection which girls are accused of feeling towards each other until love usurps its place – no, that must be no true friendship it seems to me which is not rather strengthened than shaken by love – don't you think so?[58]

She continued to stress all the things which the women had planned in Munich; Anna Mary, now imagined as 'Mrs Bateman', would be giving lectures to girl students: 'very beautiful lectures especially addressed to women-artists – their Art must be of so different a character, of such a much more spiritual character than ordinary Art'.

Barbara and Bessie attracted the attention of several young German men, although, according to the letters sent home, these same young men seemed hardly to know what to make of such singular young women. Writing to Bella and Nannie, Bessie gave an account of a potentially romantic encounter with a young German, whose growing ardour was suddenly transformed to mirth when he caught sight of her Balmoral boots. The amorous tale ends 'Believe as much as you like', and is in the same genre as Barbara's account of the visit to Greenwich Fair, a story grounded in a real incident but quickly moving into fantasy. Barbara's letter to her sisters cautions them not to 'believe a word Bessie says. She tells most dreadful stories . . . If I have my spectacles, she has her boots, which make sentimental Germans laugh, and with which she vows to stump out every bit of love from every heart which warms to her.'[59] Bessie and Barbara were clearly having lots of fun in each other's company, at the expense of would-be wooers. Both Anna Mary and Jane Benham, whom they had left behind in Munich, were 'deep in love' with their fiancés left at home, but Barbara and Bessie were fancy free.[60]

Barbara's apprenticeship years were also strongly influenced by her father's constant desire to give his children both pleasure and education in its broadest sense. Like most Unitarians, he believed that technological and scientific progress would create wealth, which could then be used to improve the lot of all sections of society. When Prince Albert's brainchild of an international exhibition to display the skill of engineers and the prowess of British manufacturers opened on 1 May 1851 the Pater took his five 'Leigh Smith' children to its opening day. The Crystal Palace in Hyde Park was designed to be constructed of iron and glass as a 'symbol both of the practical skill and the romance of industrialisation'.[61] Barbara saw the young Queen Victoria in pink silk and diamonds, her husband, Prince Albert, and the royal children all in their kilts.[62] Various of their friends had taken part in the exhibition. Owen Jones, as superintendent of works at the exhibition with Edward Bateman as his assistant, saw it as an opportunity to regenerate taste in the decorative arts. Charles Bray's factory had sent examples of ribbons with a pattern of flowers entwined with wild grasses, especially designed by Coventry School of Design. Anna Mary, who returned to England briefly that spring to see the exhibition, called it 'the grand Poem of the present day – an embodiment of the nineteenth century'.[63]

One of the industrial revolution's most significant inventions, the application of steam power to transportation, afforded Barbara another memorable day. In 1851 the Pater generously took a party of twenty-one friends for a day out in Cambridge, for which he paid all the expenses. The day began at 6 a.m. with breakfast at Blandford Square, then carriages took the guests to Shoreditch station, and they travelled in reserved compartments of the train. The party was led by 'Mr Smith, who seemed as happy as a boy' and included Mrs Parkes and Mrs Howitt, plus several German and Hungarian refugees. After the failed revolutions of 1848 there had been another large influx of escapees from repressive states – Hungarian nationalists like Kossuth and Pulszky and French socialists such as Ledru-Rollin and Louis Blanc had arrived in London, where they were befriended and championed by English radicals such as John Chapman, the Howitts, George Henry Lewes, Peter Alfred Taylor (a grandson of Samuel Courtauld, who was chairman of the Friends of Italy) and Ben Smith himself. His party that day included the exiled German professor, Gottfried Kinkel, the Hungarian, Pulszky, and should have included the German poet, Freiligrath, but he missed the meeting place.

Once the large, noisy, multilingual group arrived at Cambridge, their party was augmented by Benjamin Leigh Smith and six hungry undergraduate friends, all of whom were included in the Pater's invitation to dinner at the Bull:

> Everyone was full of fun, and what roars of laughter there were! When full justice had been done to the pickled salmon, ducks, fowls, tongue, and pigeon-pie we joined the party at King's and went the round of every college; each being alike, yet different; all beautiful, all rich; a union of architectural grandeur and picturesque effect with the verdure of lawns, meadows, and lovely trees.[64]

Barbara enjoyed the fun as much as anyone that day, dispensing soda-water and ginger-beer from her brother's well-stocked cupboards in his rooms at Jesus College, and laughing at the chaff of her brother's friends. But she must have had a strong sense that the experience of college life for these young men was very different from her experience at humble Bedford 'College', which was neither 'beautiful' nor 'rich'.

In this same year of 1851, the first discovery of gold was made in Victoria, Australia. It was unusual in that the ore was relatively accessible and did not require deep mining or large capital investment. Diggers poured into Victoria from many parts of the world, notably from Cornwall where the tin mines were pretty well exhausted. Edward

Bateman's cousin was Governor of the recently established colony, so perhaps it was he who told William Howitt of the fortunes to be made there. In June 1852 William Howitt, then aged sixty, went with his sons to Australia hoping to recoup money lost in his unfortunate involvement with the *People's Journal*. The Pater had no faith in William Howitt's practical or business faculties, despite sympathy for his popular politics. In a discreet attempt to dissuade William from undertaking such a hazardous journey, he offered to finance a trip to Iceland for the Howitts so that they could write a money-making book.[65] But William set off hopefully with Charlton and Alfred and their miners' tools. Bateman and Thomas Woolner (the PRB sculptor) went out to join them in July.[66] Before leaving for Australia, Bateman offered Mary Howitt the lease of a strange little house on West Hill, Highgate, called the Hermitage, which included a studio, and she looked forward to the men's safe return.

In 1853 Ben Smith gave up the lease on 9 Pelham Crescent. Willie had finished his stint at agricultural college at Cirencester and Ben appointed him as Glottenham estates manager. Benjamin had finished his studies at Cambridge (although he, like his father before him, could not be awarded a degree because he was a Dissenter) and was training as a barrister at the Inns of Court. Bessie saw the end of Pelham Crescent as the end of an era:

> Mr Smith was walking about in his nightcap, much to Annie's distress who thought, I suppose, that the said audacious headdress, which is just like the helmet of Horatius, was a deadly insult to me – Belle looked pale, but when you get her on horseback I am sure she will improve . . .
>
> I feel your leaving no 9 very much, personally, I loved the house and the memory of our long evenings together, and the parties & charades & country walks. But of all this my little book is to me a lasting fragment . . .[67]

The 'little book' referred to was *Poems*, published in 1852 with a dedication to Barbara.[68] Blandford Square was now their principal home. Barbara was a frequent visitor to the Hermitage where she tried to cheer Anna Mary, who was saddened because Bateman's letters slowly dropped away and finally ceased in March 1853. Fortunately, that spring was enlivened by visits to the Hermitage from members of the Pre-Raphaelite circle. Here Barbara met William Allingham, a gentle and talented Irishman, who wanted to be a poet. Born in 1824 into a Protestant family at Ballyshannon, Donegal, he desperately longed for a literary career, but had had to leave school early when his father fell ill. In the early 1850s he arrived in London to make a living as a journalist, whilst hoping for success with his poetry. At the Hermitage he would read the women his latest efforts; he finally gained some popular recognition with *Day and Night Songs* in 1854.

Barbara wrote to Bessie that 'Dante Rossetti is my favourite of these young men [the PRB]. I like the poetic narrow minded thorough artis [*sic*] Italian nature.'[69] It is interesting that Barbara referred to him as 'Dante', whereas friends and family generally called him 'Gabriel', implying that he seemed a romantic figure to her. Indeed Gabriel seemed effortlessly to cast a spell over all women who came into contact with him, despite not being especially handsome. A description by Anna Mary's cousin, Mary Harris, noted a kind of duality in his face:

> the upper part of his face intellectual even spiritual, contrast with the lower part of his face; the sensuous lips and mouth and heavy Italian jaw which, however, had the beautiful keel-shaped curve of genius. His eyes were very remarkable; they had a sort of lazy lustre when he was speaking under the influence of thought; they glowed and melted like a carbuncle, such glow as is seen at times in the eye of an animal.[70]

Barbara particularly loved to listen to his soft, rich voice when he read his poetry aloud. But it was his easy acceptance of Anna Mary and Barbara as fellow travellers searching for truth and beauty in art that especially endeared him to their hearts.

In the late 1840s Gabriel had set up a Cyclographic Society with Millais and Collinson: this involved circulating a portfolio, into which each artist inserted their offering for criticism by the others of the group.[71] As the collective energy of the original PRB had dispersed, Anna Mary, Barbara and Gabriel started a new group. Barbara bought a magnificent Russian leather portfolio for this new club, called the 'Folio'. They aimed to circulate the portfolio monthly for contributions based on a chosen theme. In July 1854, for example, the Folio theme was 'Desolation'. Barbara's contribution was a 'wild and desolate and strong' landscape called 'Quarry by the Sea', which was admired by Gabriel and William Rossetti.[72] Millais contributed a pen and ink sketch of the Romans leaving Britain, focusing on a Roman soldier leaving a British girl utterly wretched. Anna Mary was at that time planning a series of paintings to be called 'The Castaway'. She put in a preliminary sketch for one of these, an illustration of a 'miserable flower-girl and her sheaf of despised lilies' with a motto adapted from Job 30:19: 'He cast me into the mire, and I become as dust and ashes.' Gabriel referred to Anna Mary's contribution as 'a rather strong-minded subject, involving a dejected female, mud with lilies lying in it, a dust-heap, and other details'.[73] Gabriel's own sketch, 'Found', showed a streetwalker discovered at dawn by her former sweetheart, bringing a calf to market. Gabriel's sweetheart, Lizzie Siddal, drew on an incident from Browning's dramatic poem 'Pippa Passes' for the same 'Folio' theme.

Given her mother's history, Lizzie's anomalous social and romantic position exerted a kind of fascination on Barbara. Like Lizzie, Anne Longden had not been accepted by Ben's mother or sisters. Barbara wrote to Bessie:

> Private now my dear, I have got a strong interest in a young girl formerly model to Millais and Dante Rossetti, now Rossetti's love and pupil, she is a genius and will (if she lives) be a great artist, her gift discovered by a strange accident such as rarely befall woman. Alas! her life has been hard and full of trials, her home unhappy and her whole fate hard. Rossetti has been an honourable friend to her and I do not doubt if circumstances were favourable would marry her. She is of course under a ban having been a model (tho' only to 2 PRB's) ergo do not mention it to anyone.[74]

A second letter confirms her sense that if 'Ladies' do not acknowledge her, she is in danger of being a 'Castaway' in Anna Mary's sense of the word, a woman who, in losing her chastity, would be expelled from polite society:

> I wrote in a great hurry as Dante Rossetti only came as the post was going out ... I think Miss S. is a genius and very beautiful and although she is not a lady her mind is poetic and that D. Rossetti sympathises with and does not much consider the 1st. He wishes her to see Ladies and it seems to me the only way to keep her self esteem from sinking. I do not think she will recover and perhaps this prevents one from thinking much about the future for them. The present is all we have – do not let us or them cast it away.[75]

Barbara seems to have been sure that Lizzie was doomed to die; indeed this seems almost a built-in feature of the romance of Dante Rossetti and his 'Beatrice'.

In April 1854 Barbara helped to organise a convalescent stay for Lizzie at Mrs Elphick's at 5 High Street, Hastings, in a room big enough for 'eating and drawing and sleeping'. Gabriel took Lizzie down to Hastings where Bessie met them, noting in her journal for 21 April:

Dante Rossetti brought Miss Siddal down on Saturday. Together they form the most touching group I ever saw in my life. He is a slim Italian; English born & bred, but a son of Italy on both sides of the house – short dark hair, lighter eyes, a little moustache & a beard; very gentlemanly, even tender in manner; with a sweet mellow voice – she the tallest, slenderest creature, habited in pale lilac; with masses of red auburn hair looped up in a wild picturesque fashion – every line of her is spiritual grace, but I fear there is no hope for her, she seems to me in an early but hopeless stage of consumption . . .[76]

In May Anna Mary and Barbara went down to stay at Scalands Farm on a painting expedition, where Anna Mary gave Barbara instruction in oil painting. Barbara told Bessie that 'AMH says my little oils are very good for 1st productions from nature. My landscape is very PRB . . . My head is full of pictures and I shall be a selfish cove all summer for I must work out a grand picture landscape and one figure which is in my head distinct'.[77] She goes on to say that she cannot 'see exactly why DGR should not have a room at Mrs Elphick's', which presumably is a comment on Bessie's wondering whether this would be a respectable arrangement. Writing to his mother Gabriel said:

> Barbara Smith and Anna Mary came down to see Lizzie yesterday from Robertsbridge, some miles from here, where they are staying; and we all took a walk together, which did not seem to fatigue Lizzie much. There are several other ladies who have been most attentive to Lizzie, and every one adores the dear. No one thinks it's at all odd my going into Gug's [Lizzie's] room to sit there; and Barbara Smith said to the landlady how unadvisable it would be for her to sit with me in a room without a fire.[78]

Gabriel's letter to his mother seems reminiscent of Ben Smith's letters pleading the 'ladylike' qualities of Anne Longden. Gabriel seems to feel that Barbara's approval of Lizzie will persuade the Rossetti women in her favour, while Barbara appears to have fallen into the role of simultaneously playing Cupid and drawing a veil over any possible irregularities. The postscript to Barbara's letter asks Bessie what she thinks William Holman Hunt's picture *The Awakened Conscience* means. Perhaps, after all, despite Barbara's championing of the Gabriel and Lizzie romance, Barbara feared that Gabriel might cast Lizzie off like an old glove, were she to lose the glamour of imminent death.

Writing to Bessie once more, Barbara commented that:

Miss R. and Miss S. were sitting on the top of the East Cliff so happy and cheerful that one could hardly believe anything of gloom or any form of death could be near yet I still believe she is going fast – Rossetti is like a child, he cannot believe she is in danger.[79]

On 8 May Gabriel and Lizzie visited Scalands Farm, where Gabriel, Anna Mary and Barbara all painted Lizzie with irises in her hair.[80] Iris, the messenger of the Gods, was 'fleet of foot' because 'the bloom of the flower is short', sadly prophetic of her short life.[81] For Barbara, there must have been some sense of *déjà vu*, a re-running of history. The apparently casual reference to Hunt's painting in Barbara's previous letter now seems more charged. Although Barbara had been only seven when her mother died, she had pictures in her mind of her beautiful but sickly mother, who was 'not a lady' yet was adored by her gentleman father. But this romantic version of the story, like that of Gabriel and Lizzie, was to come under increasing stress.

CHAPTER 4

The Pioneers

Barbara's circle of friends were all remarkable women, but two of her closest friends, whom she met in the early 1850s, were remarkable even in this company. Bessie's cousin Elizabeth Blackwell was the first woman to qualify and register as a doctor.[1] Born in Bristol, she emigrated with her family to America, and, on the death of her father in 1838, with her mother and two of her sisters she ran a small private school to keep the family afloat. When she was twenty-three a family friend who was dying of uterine cancer told Elizabeth that the embarrassment and distress of her treatment would have been lessened if only she could have been attended by a woman doctor. Elizabeth managed to gain admission to an obscure medical college at Geneva, in New York State, as the only female student among 150 men. She graduated as MD in 1849 at the head of her class, with top honours in every subject.

While continuing her studies at the leading school for midwives in France she contracted ophthalmia and lost the sight of one eye. She had then to give up her hope of training as an obstetric surgeon and turn to general medicine instead. Sir James Paget at St Bartholomew's Hospital in London agreed to let her enter for a year's postgraduate training, although, as she recorded in her book *Pioneer Work* 'every department was cordially opened to me, *except the department for female diseases'.*[2] This was deeply ironical, as Elizabeth was excluded from the very area where she felt the presence of women doctors would help women patients, and that the presence of a woman doctor might help ensure a more respectful attitude to women patients in the male medical students.

In October 1850 she arrived in London and took rooms within walking distance of Bart's Hospital. No doubt informed of Elizabeth's arrival in London by her Dudley cousins, Kenyon and Sam Blackwell, Bessie called on her and found a tiny woman, barely over five feet tall with wispy blonde hair and with the disfiguring marks of ophthalmia on her blind eye. Bessie wrote to tell Barbara about her:

Dearly beloved Barbarosse,

... Such a tale! Of energy, & hope; of repulses from men, & scorn of her own countrywomen. (During her 2 years residence in Geneva, the college town, not a Geneva lady would call, or speak to her) –

Of the glorious day when in a church crowded from ceiling to floor the chief Professor after giving the Diplomas to the young men, called her up alone, & *rising from his seat & lifting his cap* gave her the title of Dr Blackwell.[3]

Elizabeth's impression of Bessie, when she wrote to her sister Emily, was more mixed: 'She will not wear corsets, she won't embroider, she reads every heretic book she can get hold of, talks of following a profession, & has been known to go to an evening party, without gloves! ... she is really a very noble girl, but chaotic & without definite aim.'[4]

Barbara, immediately befriending Elizabeth, used her network to introduce her to women who might be financial backers for a women's hospital in Britain. She arranged introductions to the Countess de Noailles, Lady Noel Byron and Emilia Gurney.[5] One introduction Barbara could not effect was to her cousin, Florence Nightingale, so this was arranged by Aunt Ju, and Elizabeth was invited to Embley Park. Initially, each woman admired the other's qualities; Elizabeth wrote that Florence considered that 'she should be perfectly happy working with me, she should want no other husband'.[6] This seems a complete misunderstanding of the character of Florence, who would never work in a subaltern position.

On Elizabeth's return to America she kept them informed of her doings in letters addressed to the 'Reform Firm'. In May 1857 Elizabeth established the New York Infirmary for Women and Children staffed entirely by women, with herself as director and her sister Emily as surgeon.[7] Barbara saw in Elizabeth a pioneer capable of opening up the medical profession to women in England. On her honeymoon, she made a point of visiting Elizabeth, and persuaded her to return to England, promising to arrange a lecture tour in order to raise funds with the hope of establishing a women's hospital.

On 18 August 1858 Elizabeth sailed for England, with her adopted daughter Kitty, and was presented at Liverpool with a letter of welcome signed by Barbara, Lady Byron and fifty other people, asking Elizabeth to give a course of lectures on the principles of health and disease prevention, as well as the means of opening up the medical profession to women. In January 1859 Elizabeth was summoned to an interview with Florence Nightingale, who had returned covered with glory from the Crimea, and now wished to establish a training school for nurses. She asked Elizabeth to supervise it, but was refused. Elizabeth explained to

Barbara, in a letter of 29 January 1859, 'I could not carry out her plans, as they stand at present in her own mind, because it would entirely sacrifice my medical life.'[8] Florence's letter to Elizabeth on 10 February indicated her disappointment: 'I remember my impression . . . that you and I are on different roads . . . you to educate a few highly cultivated ones . . . I to diffuse as much knowledge as possible.'[9] Although Florence herself was antagonistic to women aspiring to be doctors, the reverence with which Nightingale's lady nurses were held following the Crimean War acted as useful leverage for young women interested in a medical career. Fathers who considered that for a lady to go in for 'doctoring' was disgusting found this position harder to maintain in face of the public gratitude and adulation which ladies who had nursed in the Crimea received. Logically, if nursing was no longer considered fit only for working-class women, but could be undertaken by ladies, then 'doctoring' by ladies could not be considered disgusting either.

Barbara secured Marylebone Hall, near to Blandford Square, for the first of a series of three lectures on the subject of 'Medicine as a Profession for the Ladies'. Although Elizabeth had succeeded in getting her name placed on the New Medical Register instituted by Act of Parliament in 1858, the Medical Council, alarmed by this, resolved to exclude all other holders of foreign diplomas, so that, in future, if women qualified abroad they would have no status in Britain. The newspapers were interested in this issue and referred to 'Doctrix Blackwell' in either jocular or hostile tones. Lizzie Garrett, a young woman from Aldeburgh, noticed these newspaper articles and asked her father Newton Garrett, a grain malter and partner in a brewery, to make contact with Valentine Smith (Octavius's son), whom he knew through business, to arrange an introduction for her to Barbara.[10] Barbara and her sisters decorated Marylebone Hall with 'primroses and other lovely flowers and green wreaths' brought up from Sussex.[11] Elizabeth's first lecture was given on 2 March 1859 to an audience of about fifty women. Lizzie Garrett was impressed on hearing about the contribution women physicians could make to their own sex in sickness and to the education of wives and mothers in healthy living.[12] Elizabeth noted that the 'most important listener was the bright, intelligent lady whose interest in the study of medicine was then aroused – Miss Elizabeth Garrett – who became the pioneer of the medical movement in England . . .'[13] After the lecture Barbara gave a party at Blandford Square where she introduced the two women. This was to prove the founding moment of Lizzie's own prestigious career in medicine.

Elizabeth Blackwell went on to repeat her lectures in Manchester,

Birmingham and Liverpool, whilst poor Kitty was placed in a boarding school in Surrey, which Barbara had recommended, but which Kitty hated. A letter to Barbara dated 16 March 1859 reported on Elizabeth's progress:

> I repeat my lectures in all the principal points in England, condensing them into two, and revising so that gentlemen as well as ladies may be admitted, and wherever interest is excited forming a local committee to work with the London centre. In this way we give a pretty fair test to English sentiment, and if the matter is fully responded to, I think we shall be justified in considering that we commence a great work in England. If not, then it must grow up gradually from private practice, for no one can do the same work twice in a life-time, and I do not think it is for me to settle in London & work up a private practice.[14]

As it turned out, the lectures in the cities other than London were not sufficiently publicised, so that the numbers who attended were disappointingly few.

Elizabeth reported to Barbara in the same letter that Florence Nightingale had made a renewed attempt to

> absorb me in the general nursing plan, which would simply kill me, if it did not accomplish any medical plan, and I am desirous of committing myself to the education of physicians, before taking part in her schemes. This I see she is very desirous I shall not do, but I consider it rather the turning point of my being able to help her . . .[15]

By July 1859, having failed to attract any substantial financial support from elsewhere, Elizabeth decided to return to America, and use the Countess de Noailles's money to establish a rural sanatorium. She reported to Barbara that once she had made it clear that she would not be involved in schemes for training nurses, Florence had sneered at her ideas of a women's hospital. There seems to have been a real difference of character between the two cousins. Barbara, like her father, gave unstintingly of her money and time to aid any good effort; Florence required anyone who worked with her to submit absolutely to her vision and supremacy.

Barbara continued to work towards her hopes of establishing Elizabeth in England. Around Christmas 1859 she persuaded her father to give £500 towards the establishment of a women's hospital. Elizabeth responded: 'For a certain paternal offer, dear Barbara, in your letter I send my warm recognition.'[16] But a letter of 2 March 1860, returning Ben

Smith's £500, shows that Elizabeth did not herself feel that the time was ripe in England. A month later, when Ben died, Elizabeth's letter was one of the many letters of condolence which Barbara received, appreciating his generosity.[17]

In 1868 Barbara again urged Elizabeth to 'Come to England. You know you always planned to settle here sometime. And we need you desperately. Come and help us do for the women of England what you have done for the women of America.'[18] It took until July 1869 for Barbara to persuade Elizabeth to come to England and to use Blandford Square as her base for as long as she chose. An almost immediate example of her 'unique' status as a woman doctor was demonstrated at the 1869 meeting of the National Association for the Promotion of Social Science at Bristol. The Association had been founded by Lord Brougham in 1856, and met annually for a week in a different city each time, inviting women to participate in discussions. However, when a session was set up to discuss the repeal of the Contagious Diseases Acts, the only woman allowed to remain was Dr Blackwell. These Acts embodied a hypocritical double standard, in that women suspected of prostitution could be subjected to compulsory examination but not the men who consorted with them.[19] At Bristol the national campaign against the Acts was launched, for which Elizabeth campaigned until the Acts were repealed in 1886.

Barbara, Bessie and Anna Mary had privately discussed the trade in female bodies although ladies were not supposed to know of their existence despite the evidence of their own eyes. In 1854, when writing the *Brief Summary of the Most Important Laws Concerning Women*, Barbara had excluded the laws to do with prostitution and brothels, in case her intended middle-class readers should throw the pamphlet aside.[20] This was a pragmatic decision; it was not that she was afraid of tackling the subject. She wrote two letters to the 'Open Council' of the *Leader* (a liberal journal founded and edited by George Lewes and Thornton Hunt) on the subject of 'the Domestic Moloch'. They appeared on 19 August and 2 September 1854, under the *nom de guerre* 'BB'. In them, she repudiated the notion that one social class of women should be sacrificed (as though to Moloch) in order to protect the supposed innocence of ladies. Typically, Barbara attempted to analyse underlying causes, rather than simply dealing with the symptoms. As a result of this analysis, she argued that:

> Magdalen hospitals and refuges are not to be trusted [to cure prostitution]. We must go deeper, and find out what causes place

women under the sore temptation of adopting such a life, and what causes produce men so degraded as to take advantage of such misfortune. Women are generally driven to degradation from ignorance and the difficulty of getting respectable employment, compared with the great demand and temporary high wages of this accursed trade. Also by that public opinion which condemns them as lost characters after the birth of one child out of wedlock, and forces them down to a lower and lower depth. Men are debased by bad training in youth, and by the wretchedly low theory and hypocritical bearing of society on the subject of prostitution. Most women will forgive vice in men before marriage, and the best do not dream of bringing public opinion to bear openly and efficiently on sinners. The absurd difficulties placed in the way of marriage from the number of superfluities deemed necessary in life, and the inaccessibility of respectable young women who are needlessly shut out from intercourse with young men, joined to the impossibility of divorce for the middle classes are some of the evils that lie at the root of the matter.[21]

Barbara went on to wish that 'some explicit teaching of right and wrong upon the subject, some distinct warning of the penalties of transgression on both sexes, ought to be given to all boys and youths'. She had discovered from her conversations with Elizabeth that many women who had entered marriage happy and healthy and whose subsequent poor health went undiagnosed were suffering from 'gonorrhoeal infection derived from husbands of former loose life'.[22]

In 1870 Elizabeth set up her first private practice in London and helped Lizzie Garrett in the dispensary she had opened, which was run on similar lines to Elizabeth's New York model. In 1874, when the London School of Medicine for Women was opened, Elizabeth Blackwell was lecturer in midwifery, sharing the appointment with Lizzie Garrett. Through Barbara, Elizabeth met Frances Power Cobbe, writer and feminist campaigner, who was equally energetic in the promotion of animal welfare. She had founded the National Anti-Vivisection Society, which Elizabeth then joined, advocating the use of humane methods of research. She withdrew her support from any hospital which subjected animals to painful experiments.

Increasingly Elizabeth felt that medicine was preoccupied with bacteriology at the expense of hygiene. On 12 May 1871 Elizabeth, Barbara, George Hastings, Anna Goldsmid and Ernest Hart founded the National Health Society as an adjunct of the Social Science Association. Its motto was 'Prevention is better than cure'. The records of the society are missing before 1873, but Barbara was certainly a member of the

General Committee in 1875–76 and 1879–80, and Nannie was a corresponding member from Algiers where she now lived.[23] The National Health Society published pamphlets giving advice on diet and hygiene, lobbied the government over the provision of clean drinking water and secured the opening of school playgrounds during evenings and school holidays. It also set up the first training programme for health visitors. It was, in effect, the prototype and forerunner of the National Health Service, which finally took over the work of the society in 1948. Barbara frequently described herself as a 'sanitarian', in reference to this area of her work.

In 1879 Elizabeth felt that her health was suffering and decided to leave London. She took a lease on Rock House, Hastings, wishing to live near Barbara's Sussex home. From 1881 she became increasingly interested in issues of moral reform and she joined the Social Purity Alliance and the National Vigilance Society. Ideologically Barbara and Elizabeth drew apart, although remaining friends. But Barbara had no time for Elizabeth's notion of reclaimable and unreclaimable prostitutes, rather similar to the notion of deserving or undeserving poor.[24] She continued to regard women's prostitution as essentially an *economic* matter, and was never interested in quasi-spiritual cant about 'purity'. In 1854 she had written:

> We must apply more energetically to the education of women of the lower classes, to open out the avenues to employment in every possible direction both to them and to that portion of the middle class, who, from want of subsistence, are constantly dragged into this most miserable and suicidal life ... We wish that all workers and well-wishers *would think before they act*; it is not sufficient that we do something – we ought *to do the best.*[25]

Barbara's position remained constant on this point. She always considered better education and wider employment opportunities as the keys to social improvement, and that is where she directed her own reforming energies throughout her life.

A different kind of pioneer, who was also to become one of Barbara's closest friends, was Marian Evans, soon to be known as the writer George Eliot, whom Barbara came to know through Bessie.[26] Bessie's father, Joseph Parkes, like other well-to-do Unitarians, was committed to promoting efforts in biblical criticism (sometimes called 'Higher' criticism as a direct translation of Eichhorn's phrase 'die hohere Kritik') as part of a political campaign against the Anglican establishment. When

Parkes offered to pay for a translation of *Das Leben Jesu*, written by the German theologian, David Friedrich Strauss, he asked his friend, Charles Bray, the Coventry ribbon manufacturer, to suggest a translator. Bray asked his sister-in-law, Sara Hennell, but she was too busy because she had taken a job as governess to the Bonham Carter children. Then he turned to the young woman who had recently become part of their circle at Rosehill, Marian Evans, the intellectual daughter of the estate manager of Arbury Hall, Warwickshire.

Strauss's work was a survey of the whole history of myth, starting from the earliest Greek sources, using the Hegelian notion of *mythus* – the subjective transformation of objective facts into literature. By the time Marian had translated it she had lost the Anglican faith of her childhood, which upset her in so far as it had led to a 'holy' war with her father when she refused to accompany him to church. After her father's death Marian started to work for John Chapman, a publisher and editor of the *Westminster Review*. In 1851 she went to live as a paying guest at 142 Strand in London, where Chapman conducted his publishing and bookselling business on the ground floor and his wife had lodgers on the floors above. Chapman was married to Susanna Brewitt, fourteen years his senior. They had two children, Beatrice and Ernest, and a governess, Elizabeth Tilley, who was also Chapman's mistress. Marian fell in love with Chapman, but probably did not understand the complications of the household she had joined until Elizabeth displayed violent jealousy of Chapman's attentions to the new inmate. Chapman had that particular brand of *faux-naïveté* whereby he pretended he could not understand why women became angry with him. Bessie's daughter, the writer Marie Belloc Lowndes, was later moved to comment on Chapman:

> Such men are to be found in every generation & in every class but they are fewer than are generally supposed. A distinguished Victorian lady had a generic name for such men. She called them the charmers, but she once admitted to me that she had only known three in her long life. Among famous men of the preceding hundred years, we agreed that we could only recall Palmerston, who when asked why he made love to so many replied: 'I like to give every woman a chance.'[27]

Chapman certainly liked to give every woman a chance, and it seems more likely than not that he succeeded in seducing the naive Marian.[28]

When Marian came to live in London Joseph Parkes frequently invited her to dinner at the Parkes house at 2 Savile Row, where he rather liked to show her off as his personal intellectual 'discovery'. In March 1852 Bessie wrote to Barbara saying:

> Dearest Fellow . . . I dont know whether you will like Miss Evans. At least I know you will like her for her large unprejudiced mind, her complete superiority to most women. But whether you or I should ever love her, as a friend, I dont at all know. There is as yet no very high moral purpose in the impression she makes, & it is that alone which commands love, every day I feel it more. I think she will alter. Large angels take a long time unfolding their wings; but when they do they soar out of sight. Miss Evans either has no wings, or, which I think is the case, they are coming, budding – when people have large minds, and a capacity of warm affection, must not their souls grow?[29]

There is a clear sense here that Bessie is considering whether Marian meets the criteria of the sisterhood first dreamed of in Munich.

When Marian met Barbara in June 1852 she was immediately attracted to her.[30] Bessie wrote later that George Eliot's eponymous heroine of her novel *Romola* was a portrait of the young Barbara.[31] Assuming this to be right, then Marian's first sight of Barbara was of a young woman with hair of a 'reddish gold colour' with a 'refinement of brow and nostril counterbalanced by a full though firm mouth and powerful chin, which gave an expression of proud tenacity and latent impetuousness; an expression carried out in the backward poise of the girl's head, and the grand line of her neck and shoulders.'[32] Marian would undoubtedly have known from her friend Sara Hennell about the complicated relations between the Smith and Leigh Smith families, because of Sara's role as governess to the Bonham Carter family.[33] In July 1852, Hilary Bonham Carter (at Sara's request) visited the Strand with her Aunt Mai Smith, and her cousin, Florence Nightingale, in order to call on Marian. Marian was not favourably impressed; as she wrote to Sara:

> My talk the evening Miss Carter was at Mr Chapman's was chiefly with Miss Nightingale and Mrs S. Smith. I have so profound a faith in your likings, if not in your dislikings, that I am quite sure any unfavourable impression about your Hilary is the sign of a want in me rather than in her. Had she been a person whom you had not prepared me to respect, I should have thought her rather affected and the least bit snobbish – that is thinking of her conventional rank and afraid lest you should overlook it . . . I am far more agreeably impressed with Barbara Smith – one of the tabooed family – who is Bessie Parkes's intimate friend.[34]

Barbara invited her to Blandford Square to meet the intimates of the Leigh Smith circle, some of whom she already knew from Rosehill, such as Richard Cobden and Robert Noel.

By the beginning of 1853 Marian was secretly involved with George Lewes, at that time editor of the *Leader*, a liberal journal he had begun in 1850 with his friend Thornton Hunt and with the financial backing of the wealthy incumbent of a Lincolnshire parish, Edmund Larken.[35] Lewes's domestic situation was confused; his wife Agnes's first three children were fathered by Lewes, but her next two by Thornton Hunt and Lewes had left the marital home some time in 1852.[36] As Lewes had not sued for divorce it meant in legal terms that he had condoned his wife's adultery, and therefore was ineligible for divorce.

In October 1853 Marian moved out of the Chapmans' house and into a ground-floor flat at 21 Cambridge Street, Hyde Park Square. Barbara sent some of her paintings to brighten up Marian's rather dark rooms. Increasingly, Marian distanced herself from Chapman's messy financial affairs, resigning from the *Westminster* in order to pursue a free-lance career. By June 1854 Chapman was facing bankruptcy and was only saved by loans from Harriet Martineau, Sam Courtauld and Barbara's uncle, Octavius Smith, who had at his disposal the fortune from the distillery which the Pater had established, and which Octavius had successfully augmented. The Chapmans moved out of the Strand and into 43 Blandford Square, perhaps feeling that proximity with Barbara and her 'large rations of tin' might be fortuitous.

That year, Marian was translating Ludwig Feuerbach's work, *Das Wesen des Christenthums*, a work to which she had been introduced in July 1851 by Robert Noel, when he was visiting the Brays.[37] Lewes was familiar with Feuerbach from his work on the *Biographical History of Philosophy* (1846) and consequently took a deep interest in Marian's translation. Their discussions served as Cupid; Feuerbach's definition of marriage (akin to Shakespeare's definition of a marriage of true minds) was to underpin their future relationship. Feuerbach wrote: 'But marriage – we mean, of course, marriage as the free bond of love – is sacred in itself, by the very nature of the union which is therein effected. That alone is a religious marriage, which is a true marriage, which corresponds to the essence of marriage – of love.'[38] This formulation appealed strongly to Marian; Lewes's marriage to Agnes could no longer be regarded as 'sacred'; it allowed her to imagine a public commitment between herself and George.

Marian discussed these ideas in a rather abstract fashion with Bessie, without however having made it entirely clear that she herself was considering acting on such a plan. On 20 July 1854, the die was cast: Marian accompanied George to Germany, where he was going to research the life of Goethe he was planning to write. By chance, on the steamer, they met Robert Noel, who had been visiting the Brays and was now returning to his wife, the *baronin* Louise de Henniger at his estate at Teschen, Bohemia. A man of the world, he saw at a glance what the relationship between them was, and, no doubt, when writing to his English friends, the Brays, the Leigh Smiths and Anna Jameson, he would have said so.

Barbara's first feelings about Marian's involvement with Lewes were heavily influenced by Joseph Parkes's hostile account. Parkes had himself been influenced by Mrs Gaskell, who had told him some gossip along the lines that Lewes had seduced a young woman who had been employed by him in some kind of literary work, and the resulting illegitimate child had been farmed out to a foster mother.[39] There seems no evidence to support Mrs Gaskell's story; it may well be a scrambled version of the truth – that Lewes himself was illegitimate, his father having deserted first a legitimate family and then his illegitimate one.

Assuming that Barbara believed the blackest versions of the tales told against Lewes, she would have been distressed by stories of seduced women abandoned, and must have been immediately repelled by the notion of a father leaving his 'five' children. Joseph Parkes certainly 'cut' Lewes, and it seems likely that Lewes, in turn, 'cut' Bessie. Barbara, writing to Bessie, reported on a mutual acquaintance saying,

'Oh Lewes! Yes, I think I've seen him – a flippant conceited superficial little man but clever, he has taken all the ideas he possesses from Comte but he cannot in the least comprehend Comte's philosophy, what he writes concerning it is worthless' . . . I wish you could have heard it, and his utter contempt for Lewes' moral character was very rich, you would not have felt any mortification at Lewes' cutting you. I really think I ought to be ashamed of his speaking to me, the cutting was a compliment to your moral nature, which he did not pay to mine.[40]

The 'Mr Williamson' who had sneered at Lewes's ideas may have been speaking out of envy, because Lewes's first published book, the *Biographical History of Philosophy*, unashamedly addressed to the layman rather than to the professional philosopher, had sold well. It was a useful overview of philosophical thought from Descartes to Comte, and established Lewes as one of the new class of intellectuals, journalists and writers emerging in the metropolis. A contemporary once remarked, in a way that acknowledged his talent and versatility, but with perhaps a little sting in the tail: 'Lewes can do everything in the world but paint: and he could do that, too, after a week's study.'[41] Lewes had not, because of poverty, been able to attend Oxbridge, so *ipso facto*, he was considered neither a scholar nor a gentleman.

Joseph Parkes's view of the 'elopement' was that Marian's part in it was 'folly' and Lewes's part 'vice'. Parkes felt that Marian's almost exclusively male bohemian set had cut her off from the moral values of her past. Bessie received a letter from her father – she was staying with Barbara in Wales – saying that he considered Lewes's 'concubinage with Miss Evans (not his first amour of this kind) an infamous seduction'.[42] Bessie's reply was a model of good sense and also of loyalty to her friend:

> My dearest Father . . .
> [Marian] never was fitted for our English social life, and such a character must work out its own teaching, amidst storm and disciplines of which the world that is now talking of her cannot judge. There are some truly valuable elements of her character; eminently one – sincerity, for which this generation will yet find use. I always knew that she was capable of taking the step she has taken, but I thought that social reputation meant more to her than it seems to have done – and that she would never actually burst the bounds. I thank you for speaking with the degree of kindness you do. It is yet possible that her power may retain Mr. Lewes, and give him great responsibility of life.[43]

As neither Barbara nor Bessie felt able to fit into conventional English life, Bessie was perhaps taking the opportunity to give warning, however politely, that she intended to form her own judgements. Elizabeth Parkes viewed Marian's reputation as irrevocably stained and wished Bessie to have nothing to do with her; both father and mother were adamantly against Bessie visiting Marian where she lived with Lewes. In general, after George and Marian returned from Germany in March 1855, the double standard operated: for example, Thomas Carlyle and his wife Jane continued to invite Lewes to their house, but Marian was not invited.[44]

Barbara and Bessie had, before this test of their principles, a series of very intense conversations about the issue of what chastity meant in a woman's case and had come to the conclusion that what mattered was commitment, not the marriage sacrament itself. This was a formula which would accommodate the behaviour of Barbara's mother, as well as that of Marian Evans. Whatever either of them privately thought about Lewes, they accepted Marian's commitment implicitly and simply prayed for her sake that Lewes's commitment would equal hers. Marian and George set up home in East Sheen, Surrey, where Bessie went to visit on 30 April 1855, against her parents' wishes. Barbara wrote to Marian pledging her continued friendship in July. Marian was so pleased with the letter that she sent it on to her Coventry friend, Sara Hennell, saying that it was 'a manifestation of [Barbara's] strong noble nature. Burn it when you have read it.'[45] Barbara acknowledged Marian's acceptance and return of friendship 'granted under your hand and seal August 1855' as a semi-sacred commitment.[46] Bessie stayed faithful to Marian, but she never entirely got over her father's account of Lewes as a sensual man, whereas Barbara quite quickly became converted in his favour. After spending a few days with the Leweses at Tenby in July 1856 she wrote to Bessie explaining her conviction that George was entirely different from what they had been told:

> I do wish, my dear, that you would revise your view of Lewes. I have quite revised mine. Like you, I thought him an extremely sensual man. Marian tells me that in their intimate marital relationship he is unsensual, extremely considerate. His manner to her is delightful. It is plain to me that he makes her extremely happy.[47]

The same letter indicated that the Leweses practised some form of birth control, as they intended to have no children. Aside from any social considerations, almost certainly the new couple could not afford to have any. They were both free-lance writers, whose living was inevitably precarious. Lewes gave Agnes an annual allowance of approximately £100 and paid for his three sons' schooling separately; he also chased up Thornton Hunt on Agnes's behalf, to pay for the upkeep of his children by Agnes and, in short, he and Marian regarded Agnes's welfare as their responsibility throughout their lives. Probably, it was on this visit to Tenby that Barbara gained a clear sense that Lewes, although he may have acted unwisely as a young man, had abandoned his responsibility neither to Agnes nor to his children. Lewes, in his turn, appreciated Barbara's honesty and energy and came to love her more than any other of Marian's women friends. She became the trusted friend of both, for as long as they lived.

In one of their many intimate conversations, Barbara told Marian of James Buchanan's method of reading *The Arabian Nights* to them as parables when they were children. Barbara wrote: 'I never forgot some of the stories and Marian Lewes felt them through me.'[48] A shared philosophy based on *The Arabian Nights* seems to have given rise to a kind of shorthand between the two women. Barbara's recounting of

Scheherazade, whose only resource to protect her own life and her sister's was the power of her story-telling, must have been a powerful icon for Marian, then an aspiring writer. But it also emphasised that the women – Scheherazade and her sister Dinarzade – were acting together, in the bid for liberty. It was emblematic therefore of the importance of women's friendship. There were other, more painful, reasons, perhaps, why *The Arabian Nights* came to have a special significance to the two women. Barbara told Marian her favourite tale, the story of Perie-zadeh, in which the heroine set out on a quest to find the three things she had been told of by a devout old woman. Barbara wrote, 'That story of Perizade [*sic*], the princess who did find the black stones when she was bent on getting the living water, the talking bird, and the singing tree, has made an impression on my life. Wasn't I glad she got to the top of the hill! Wasn't I glad she could do it though her brothers had failed.'[49] This tale of 'Perizade' or 'Parizade', as the two women variously spelt it, by which a daughter's triumph recuperated the honour of her disgraced mother, became a kind of talisman for Barbara and Marian, a myth which not only ratified female ambition but also suggested that this ambition served other women, rather than betrayed them. As Barbara and her siblings were tabooed by some parts of the Smith family because of their illegitimacy, the honour of the mother had a particular significance for her. Marian Evans, after her elopement with Lewes, had become the 'tabooed' member of her own family, and would be a dishonoured woman in the eyes of society unless the success of her own stories, her 'children', could recuperate her position.

As so many women repudiated her, including erstwhile champions such as Harriet Martineau, Anna Jameson and even Aunt Ju, Marian was at this stage in her life dependent for female friendship on a tiny handful of other exceptional women, women who were sufficiently insouciant about Victorian notions of respectability to be able to continue their visits to her. Bessie's and Barbara's continuing commitment was precious. In particular, one of Barbara's greatest gifts was a deep-seated desire to validate other women's intellectual ambitions, and a generosity of spirit which made her as exultant about her friends' achievements as she was about her own.

In the autumn of 1856 Marian began to write three short stories, which later appeared in *Blackwood's Magazine* anonymously, as did all its articles. In 1858 they were reprinted as *Scenes of Clerical Life* under the pen-name George Eliot and enthusiastically reviewed. Enormous anxiety attended Marian's move from writing anonymous articles to writing fiction which must bear some name, if only a pen-name. A major concern was whether she had the ability to produce something first-rate, because, as she wrote to Barbara much later, 'the deepest disgrace is to insist on doing work for which we are unfit'.[50] By the time of the birth of 'George Eliot' Barbara had married and was living in Algiers, where she had the English papers sent out to her. On 26 April 1859, she sent an ecstatic letter to Marian:

> I have just got the 'Times' of April 12th. with the glorious review of 'Adam Bede' and a few days ago I read the 'Westminster Review' article. I can't tell you how I triumphed in the triumph you have made. It is so great a one. Now you see I have not yet got the book but I *know* that it is you. There are some weeks passed since in an obscure paper I saw the 1st review and read one long extract which instantly made me internally exclaim that is written by Marian Evans, there is her great big head and her wise wide views.
>
> Now the more I get of the book the more certain I am, not because it is like what you have written before but because it is like what I see in you. 'It is an opinion which fire cannot melt out of me. I would die in it at the stake.' I have not breathed a word to a soul except to the Doctor [Barbara's husband] who is like the tomb for a secret.
>
> Here an Archdeacon of the Church of England, one of our friends, is eloquent in the praise of the Scenes of Clerical Life and sent me all the 'Times' notice of A.B. I can't tell you, my dear George Eliot how enchanted I am. Very few things could have given me such pleasure.
>
> 1st. That a woman should write a wise and *humorous* book which should take a place by Thackeray.
>
> 2nd. That you *that you* whom they spit at should do it!
>
> I am so enchanted so glad with the good and bad of me! Both glad – angel and devil both triumph!
>
> Everybody (but Bessie and my Doctor) have bullied me for saying 'My friend Marian' so you will see I may take a little pet bit of delight to myself that you will be what all will wish to claim as 'my friend Marian'![51]

It is clear that Barbara, like Bessie, had come under pressure to repudiate Marian after her elopement and she now felt thoroughly vindicated. Her comment 'you whom they spit at' is a reference to the tale of Perie-zadeh. The mother who had produced 'monsters' had been punished by exile and ritual humiliation. Her husband, the Emperor, had decreed:

> Let a wooden shed be built for her at the gate of the principal mosque, with iron bars to the windows, and let her be put into it, in the coarsest

habit; and every Mosselman that shall go into the mosque to prayers shall spit in her face.[52]

Marian's books, or her 'children' as Barbara always called them, acted as the guarantors of their mother/creator's integrity. (Barbara always remonstrated when Marian's books were sent out by her publishers in 'bad clothes', bindings she thought ugly.) Marian's return letter indicates her joy in the vital flow of understanding between the two women and her gratitude for Barbara's act of recognition:

> God bless you, dearest Barbara, for your love and sympathy. You are the first friend who has given any symptom of knowing me – the first heart that has recognised me in a book which has come from my heart of hearts. But keep the secret solemnly till I give you leave to tell it, and give way to no impulses of triumphant affection. You have sense enough to know how important the incognito has been, and we are anxious to keep it up a few months longer.[53]

George Lewes added a postscript saying: 'You're a darling, and I have always said so! I don't know that I ever said it to you – my modesty may have held me back, as usual; but I say it now. You are *the* person on whose sympathy we both counted; and only just escaped having the secret confided to you before you went; but we are glad you found it out for yourself.'

On 28 June Barbara warned Marian in a letter that 'Almost all the women are jealous of you. From this feeling I fear a yell mixed with the men's hypocritical yowl.'[54] Marian shows her confidence that Barbara will rejoice in her success:

> The 4th edition of 'Adam Bede' (5000) sold in a fortnight! These are the results that give fortitude to endure one's enemies – even to endure one's friends. I will not call you a friend – I will rather call you by some name that I am not obliged to associate with evaporated professions and petty egoism. I will call you only Barbara, the name I must always associate with a true, large heart.[55]

On 30 June she received George Lewes's permission in a postscript to a letter of Marian's to tell anyone she liked of Marian's authorship:

> You may tell it openly to all who care to hear it that the object of the anonymity was to get the book judged on its own merits, and not prejudged as the work of a woman, or of a particular woman. It is quite

clear that people would have sniffed at it if they had known the writer to be a woman but they can't now unsay their admiration . . . p.p.s. *Entre nous.* Please don't write or tell Marian anything *unpleasant* that you hear unless it is important for her to hear it. She is so very sensitive, and has such a tendency to dwell on and believe in unpleasant ideas that I always keep them from her. What other people would disregard or despise sinks into her mind. She knows nothing of this second postscript, of course.[56]

George clearly trusted Barbara to take his hint. All the reactions she reported thereafter were positive ones. In a letter of 1 July she told Marian of the reactions of Aunt Ju and Bella:

> Both enchanted! Heartily glad and congratulations to you. Aunt Ju is profoundly moved by Adam Bede and it carries her over her little narrow ideas. She kissed me for having such a friend! Oh Marian you ought to be a happy woman! With such power to sway the people. Here is Aunt Ju who has read your book in Derbyshire with Derbyshire people and not only feels the human part as perfectly true but the local colouring. Here is old Joe Gratton crying over Hetty and my Aunt Dolly (both Derbyshire people) swearing that it was written there and must all be true and crying too as she speaks of Lisbeth whom she knows quite well – you don't know her as well – Lisbeth lives at Alfreton where my aunt was born and my aunt knows her and her house quite well and won't believe you did not draw exactly after nature . . . As for Mr Gratton he is $\frac{1}{2}$ an hour over every page and though no novel reader and has *no imagination* he just lives with your Adam and Seth &c . . . I told [Nannie] the dead secret. She was so enchanted! She congratulated me with tears in her eyes – that a woman had done it – a friend – you. I wish you had seen her![57]

Barbara must have also felt a particular satisfaction in writing to Aunt Patty, who disapproved of Barbara's bohemian friends, that she had known Marian for seven years and had 'a kind of delight in her presence which could only be explained by a sonnet. I never knew she had written fiction only philosophy and criticism and yet I knew Adam Bede was by her – for in it I saw her peculiar and surpassing tenderness and wisdom. I know no one so learned, and so delicate and tender.'[58]

In June Nannie had sent Marian a picture of Perie-zadeh, the day after Barbara told her the author of *Adam Bede* was Marian.[59] Writing to thank her, Marian said: 'The picture . . . turns out to have a symbolism perfectly fitted for my case, for after it came yesterday I had reason to foresee the great need I should have of Princess Parizade's cotton wool in my ears, lest certain noises should distract me from going steadily along my way.'[60] In *The Arabian Nights* tale, Perie-zadeh had to push cotton in her ears to prevent herself from hearing 'a great many affronting speeches and raillery very disagreeable to a woman'.[61] George Lewes had been sadly prescient in suggesting that once Marian was unmasked, it would be difficult for her to get a fair critical hearing. Later on that year, when Marian had started to write *The Mill on the Floss*, she wrote to Barbara: 'it happens, quite curiously, [that Nannie's] Perizade has a mysterious resemblance for me, to the heroine of the book I am writing. It is not a formal outward resemblance, but an inward affinity felt through the attitude of Perizade and the expression of her face.'[62] Barbara sent Marian a country hamper from Mountfield filled, as Marian described it, with 'beautiful things – the butter, such as Mrs Poyser (who ran a perfect dairy in *Adam Bede*) would not have scorned, the ferns, the cresses, the fruits, the mushrooms! I took it as a hamper full of love, expressed in all those sweet country things'.[63] Nannie had put in ferns and had meant to put in blackberry jam, but by an oversight it was left out. After Barbara had left for Algiers, Nannie sent Marian the jam, commenting, 'I hope you will like to think that the greatest pleasure I have had in my life – out of work *done*, has been from the thought that an idea of mine has been found worthy to hang over the writing desk of George Eliot, whose most devoted & loving reader will ever be Nannie Leigh Smith.'[64] With Perie-zadeh presiding over her desk Marian had a constant reminder that Barbara and Nannie were with her in spirit.

Barbara's encouragement and loyalty while Marian set about closing the gap between her own ambitions and her achievements was experienced as a great blessing. Although Marian was not a member of the 'Reform Firm', in the sense of being directly involved with their projects, she admired their energy and commitment. In her novels she created a whole sisterhood of heroines who fitted uneasily into the roles which society prescribed for them. Barbara regarded Marian's works of fiction as the best possible contribution she could make to the Cause, and identified herself as Dinarzade to Marian's Scheherazade.

CHAPTER 5

Portrait of a School

When Barbara was studying with Kingsford, they had discussed the purposes of education.[1] Kingsford, as a founder member of the College of Preceptors, was at the leading edge of the movement towards the professionalisation of (nonconformist) teachers. In a lecture at the college, given in 1848, he defined education as including 'the most important wants of the time, and its best aspirations . . . our anticipations of the future are bright only in proportion as we recognise its presiding influence'.[2] While studying Mill's *Political Economy* with Kingsford, Barbara glossed Mill's opinion that 'No remedy for poverty can succeed which has not in mind to raise the standard of learning' with her own comment, 'In a word – to improve the people, to give them some intellectual necessaries, indeed *education* seems to me to be the only remedy.'[3]

In 1848, when Barbara reached twenty-one, the Pater had given her the title-deeds to his own educational experiment, Westminster Infant School in Vincent Square. But she felt that the spirit of her father's old school had departed with Buchanan, and that she would do better to start afresh with a new name in new surroundings. In Hastings she visited the British Schools (for Dissenters), sometimes going in to teach, but more often recognising the poor education of the teachers, 'cultivating the teachers, and trying to help them'.[4] In London she visited National (Anglican), Catholic, ragged and industrial schools, studying their methods and noting with concern the poor quality of the teachers.[5] Writing to Bessie in 1847 she despaired of schools which relied for books on 'Bible, Testament, Testament, Bible, and so on. Is it not miserable and heartbreaking that they will only just teach what is comprehensible and nothing more.'[6]

The school she envisaged was to be 'the child of Robert Owen's child of James Buchanan'.[7] She wanted her school, and more specifically the teachers in it, to have the same or similar influence on the *imagination* of its pupils that Buchanan had had on hers. Writing to a Buchanan family member she commented:

I think the daily religious conversation with him in all our games together had an effect in making me wish to do some good in the world, and in making me see the beauty of the natural objects he used to Swedenborgise up. Nature and schools are now the two greatest loves and objects of my life. Education seems to me now to be of more importance than Politics; the first is of eternal interest, the second temporary.[8]

As a result of experiencing the teaching of Buchanan, whose methodology was so intimately bound up with his whole personality, Barbara had an overwhelming sense that the most important thing was to find the right person to lead the school. She was also influenced by Kingsford's claims that 'competent preceptors [provide] a medicine for the mind as well as for the body; and that this medicine, when it has been properly exhibited by the Educator, will, by promoting a sanitary habit of common sense, form a tolerably safe antidote against quackery of all kinds'.[9] Barbara, when asked to define her creed, often described herself as a sanitarian. It was a joke, but it implied not only a commitment to physical health (in the style of Southwood Smith and Chadwick), but also a kind of mental health or 'sanity'. The term 'sanitarian', to Barbara, incorporated the notion of disinterested pursuit of Goodness, Truth and Beauty, the three graces which Kingsford regarded as attending 'successful' education.

As well as influencing Barbara's broad philosophical position, Kingsford had also pointed out to her the importance of an appropriate relationship between the principal of a school and its master. He lamented that often 'Instead of being, as it ought to be, a relation of friendship and of co-operation in the noblest work upon earth, the training of the youthful mind for usefulness, for earthly happiness, and for heaven, this relation is degraded to the same level as that between master and servant.'[10] Barbara intended to establish an ideal relationship between herself as principal and her chief mistress so she spread the word throughout her large network of Unitarian friends that she was looking for a suitable mistress.[11] In 1853 a promising letter of enquiry was delivered to Blandford Square from Elizabeth Whitehead, the eldest daughter of a Chelsea solicitor whose fortunes had unfortunately gone downhill to the extent that the bailiffs had been sent in to confiscate their furniture.[12] One after another her brothers had left for the colonies and Elizabeth herself set about earning her own living and trying to help her younger sisters do the same. Her first job, as governess to the Hon. Henry Fitzroy's spoilt daughter, frequently reduced her to despair.[13] At this low point in her fortunes, she was befriended by Mentia Taylor (who had herself been a governess) and encouraged to write to Barbara about her projected school.

Elizabeth, like Barbara, had been educated at the Misses Woods' Unitarian School in Clapton, and she shared with her an acute dislike of its dull rote learning methods. Barbara liked Elizabeth immediately and set her on a path to become her 'chief mistress'. Elizabeth gave notice to the Fitzroys, who were astonished that she should wish to give up teaching their little darling in order to join such a doubtful venture. Yet the designation 'chief mistress' bespoke something significant. Barbara had explained that, as principal, she would provide the financial resources for the school (and indeed it cost her a 'small fortune') but that Elizabeth would have day to day responsibility. She could rely on Barbara to support her, but not to countermand her authority within the school. As Elizabeth wrote, 'having settled together the principles which should underlie our work, Barbara left me with utmost freedom to carry it out.'[14] It was a great incentive to her that her younger sisters would be able to attend the school.

Barbara set Elizabeth the task of training herself for the great experiment, firstly by recommending the writings of educational innovators. Secondly she asked her to visit and observe the best 'elementary' schools in London, making notes of which theories produced the best results. The most influential educator of the mid-nineteenth century was William Ellis, who was the founder of a series of remarkable schools which demolished the twin pillars of the orthodox curriculum, classical languages and denominational religion, and replaced them with science and political economy. The first 'Birkbeck School' was opened in 1848 in the theatre of the Mechanics' Institute in Southampton Buildings, Chancery Lane, followed by schools in Finsbury, Westminster, Bethnal Green, Peckham, Kingsland and Gospel Oak.[15] The Birkbeck schools were accused by Anglican churchmen of godlessness, of having 'entire indifference to all preparation for the *next*' world.[16] Dickens satirised these utilitarian schools in the fictive shape of Gradgrind's school in *Hard Times*, although their aim was to make their pupils intelligent, self-reliant, thrifty, future citizens.[17]

Ellis trained his own teachers, giving weekly instruction to a class of about fifty at a time in Southampton Buildings. Elizabeth attended his lectures and for six months went five days a week to the Birkbeck school in Peckham, opened in 1852 under the headship of William Shields. This was a hard grind; she observed teaching, took classes herself and had her classes criticised. She endured a wearisome journey every day on insufficient food and she found some of the young men and women who were training there quite shocking in 'manner and tone'.[18]

The year 1854 was an auspicious time for Barbara to open her school as it was the year that the Royal Society of Arts organised the first national Education Exhibition ever to be held in Britain. Patronised by many public figures, including Prince Albert, it aimed to be a showcase for new ideas and experiments in education. Children's work from many schools was displayed and prominent educationists gave public lectures.[19] Madame Ronge, for example, gave a lecture and demonstration of Friedrich Froebel's system stressing the harmonious development of children's abilities through play, which was strikingly similar to Buchanan's methods. Elizabeth attended a lecture by the University College Professor of Mathematics, Augustus De Morgan, which delighted her, although, as she wrote to Barbara on 20 July 1854, she thought it would have been 'rather startling to the Peckham people – for he urged upon teachers the necessity of training the imaginative, equally with the reasoning powers of the child & reminded them that the nations most famed among the ancients for mathematical inventions had likewise produced the finest poetry &c'.[20]

The two women studied the prospectus which the Peckham school sent out before working up their own. Barbara's first draft advertising the projected 'model day school on unconventional and advanced lines' did not entirely meet with Elizabeth's approval: 'The prospectus you send me is strictly business-like, & nothing more. I am not satisfied with it. I shd. like allusion made to the "founder's intentions" – if done with all simplicity & delicacy, I think it wd. be likely to win us support. Disinterested action must sooner or later touch minds & hearts – & you shd. let the knowledge of yr. disinterestedness do its legitimate work.'[21] Elizabeth uses 'disinterestedness' in this context to mean that the school was not tied to any religious organisation: 'We are known to be ungodly people attending no church in the parish, but I hope this will not stand in my way.'[22] Notwithstanding their ungodliness, Barbara managed to hire rooms in Carlisle Street, a rather poor neighbourhood near the Edgware Road, not far from Blandford Square. It had been used for meetings of temperance societies, and the largely Christian Committee took some persuading to let the rooms to such heterodox persons as Barbara and Elizabeth.

A letter of 25 July from Elizabeth sent the 'dear golden-haired lady' an example of the revised version of the prospectus and suggests issuing 2,000 of them in the neighbourhood. Judging from a letter from Anna Mary to Barbara, the second version included some more personal touches than the first: 'How capital is your prospectus of the school – and to me how affecting to see how you have thought of all the "cutting out" and "mending".'[23] No doubt this detail was inspired by Barbara's memory of Westminster Infant School and Mrs Buchanan's practice of using part of the school day as a time for teaching, not fancy stitch work, but good plain sewing that the children could put to the immediate practical use of mending their own clothes.

Elizabeth also sent Barbara an account of one of her training observations:

> I have been to the Professor of 'Rational Gymnastics' since I wrote to you – seen some of the exercises & practised a few – much to the amusement of 2 of my sisters, who caught me, they say, making unaccountable movements without any apparent cause. The worthy Professor teaching gymnastics, & nothing else, urges very properly the importance of what he teaches but declares scholars should practise these movements for at least 2 half hours every day. We cannot find this possible, I fear, but I shd. think the gymnastics might soon become popular 'plays'. How charming it would be to organise a regiment of stay-less, free-breathing, free-stepping girls! I must stop! My imagination runs on, & pictures school-girls like Grecian water-carriers – but I check it – I fear the sins of the mothers will permit no great amount of grace in English girls of this generation? If we make them abjure stays, it will be doing much for the next at least! . . . By the bye – the Professor of Gymnastics agrees with you in thinking it essential the children shd. have backs to their seats.[24]

The main room at Portman Hall in Carlisle Street, had a raised platform at one end of the room with a swing-slate and music-board. On the sides of the hall Barbara and Elizabeth displayed maps, pictures and diagrams, 'of the best kind'. Elizabeth's letters are peppered with questions asking for Barbara's expert advice on these matters:

> By the way do you know whether the physiological diagrams are being prepared with body-colour – one of the gentlemen at a Conversational meeting at the [Royal Academy's Educational] Ex. the other day regretted that any diagrams should be varnished – because they could not be seen clearly by a class at a little distance . . . I don't clearly understand the distinction – but of course you will.[25]

Portman Hall School, which opened on 6 November 1854, was progressive in the sense that it educated young boys and girls together, which, although common for working-class children, was not generally considered acceptable by the middle classes. Barbara specifically aimed to mix social classes. Children of professional parents, children of tradesmen and children of artisans all attended the school. An international or cosmopolitan atmosphere was encouraged; children of various nationalities were welcomed as pupils.

Barbara considered that the teaching of religion in schools was 'generally utterly useless' and should in any case be left to churches, chapels, synagogues or mosques.[26] The great importance of secular schools, in her view, was that 'children of different denominations being together, they learn toleration, forbearance, and charity'.[27] At morning assembly, therefore, she asked that there should be a reading of a poem, a parable from the Bible, or a story of some heroic deed. The ethos of the school was to develop intellectual skills by stimulating curiosity rather than inculcating feats of rote learning. Great emphasis was placed on developing the children's aesthetic sensibility. Armed with Barbara's money, Elizabeth spent a lot of time hunting for suitable art objects; sometimes finding the best value for money in 'Catholic shops'. In a letter of 1 September 1855 Elizabeth told Barbara of her plan to purchase a statue of the Virgin Mary found in one such shop:

> a sweet young figure with simple flowing drapery falling from the shoulder – a fine lovely face – the serpent lies at her feet but it is not disagreeably prominent . . . I should like to have this very much. It wd. be one type of womanhood – very beautiful for our girls and boys to love . . . Some day I should like to have a Michael Angelo type of woman in the school – as a contrast to the lady of grace.[28]

Barbara herself was especially involved in taking the children on trips out of school, visiting museums and art galleries to widen their range of cultural experiences, and to 'reward' the children for their efforts.

Barbara took on a Miss Watson to help with the 'junior' department of the school. She had high hopes of her, because she had been trained at Combe's school in Edinburgh.[29] The first winter of the school's life Barbara was suffering from congestion of the lungs, and had been sent away from London fogs to spend the winter abroad. Writing from Sorrento to James Buchanan's daughter, Annie, Barbara said:

> It was a great trial to me to leave the school, about which I have thought so much, just as it was beginning to flourish. But I have had great satisfaction in it even so far off. Everything about it has prospered, and I have heard nothing but good accounts from my sister Bell, who has been most indefatigable in attending to it, and from

Elizabeth Whitehead, who is the teacher, and who loves and is loved by the school. Our numbers, I heard yesterday, were 113.[30]

By August 1855 it was decided that Miss Watson was unsuitable and Barbara found a governess called Ellen Allen, to replace her. Elizabeth reported to Barbara on 1 September that she had 'taken to her work splendidly [though] she finds our children very different' from the well-behaved French children she had been governessing. She was quite strict with her monitors, the older girls who instructed younger children in reading, writing and arithmetic, having, Elizabeth reported, 'no toleration for slovenly teaching in those things she has taught'.[31] It seems slightly surprising that they used a monitorial system at all, as it had been one of Owen's radical moves to abolish that system in his school. Presumably it was a pragmatic decision to keep costs down, and perhaps good teachers were so hard to find that it was deemed better to have a cascade effect from the excellent chief mistress via the monitors, rather than employ inadequate mistresses. One of Elizabeth's sisters, Alice, was a monitor in the infant section of the school. Like Elizabeth she professionalised herself by attending Saturday classes at Johannes Ronge's kindergarten in Hampstead. Ronge and his wife, Bertha, were German refugees who had come to London in 1849 and set up the first English kindergarten in 1851.[32] Elizabeth proudly reported to Barbara that:

Alice is a delight with her little children – & I think she has succeeded well so far. The children enjoy themselves exceedingly in the room upstairs all to themselves. A is full of the right feeling & spirit about them. We have long talks night and morning in our walks, about her charges, & she is undertaking it with so much zeal and anxiety to fulfil it in the very best way . . . [Mr Ronge] said he wished he cd. educate a thousand such as Alice as teachers.[33]

As well as the paid mistress and her assistants, the school had help from lady volunteers who came to give lessons. This aspect of the school was considered by Barbara to be extremely important. When asked to make a submission on her experience to the Commission on Popular Education (1861), she wrote:

I believe that much good can be done by ladies of culture giving a few hours a week to teaching in schools, and I most earnestly recommend the commissioners to open an examination and give certificates to volunteer lady teachers . . . The corps of volunteer teachers at Portman Hall School is unique, and the most successful part of the school. Some children come many miles to school, and when asked why their parents sent them so far (from Tottenham Court Road to Paddington), answered because the parents thought the lessons on physiology and laws of health so good. These lessons are taught by a volunteer. The same might be said of many other lessons . . .

The volunteer who taught 'physiology and the laws of health' was Jessie White, whom Barbara had met in Rome in the winter of 1854 and had recognised as a kindred spirit, someone to whom liberal politics were part of the air she breathed. As a result of this meeting, when Jessie brought one of Garibaldi's children, Ricciotti, for treatment in a London hospital, he attended Portman Hall. Although crippled, he was more active on his crutches than most children with two good legs, and frightened the little children by leap-frogging wildly around the room.[34] Jessie was devoted to the cause of the Risorgimento and had tried (unsuccessfully) to train as a doctor in order to serve the Italian cause.[35] Jessie went on to become embroiled in one of Mazzini's unsuccessful attempted coups. Although she claimed that she was a political reporter not an actor, it seems likely that she acted as a courier, bearing documents to an Italian underground group. In 1857 she was imprisoned in Genoa for four months with another 'conspirator', Alberto Mario, whom she married after their release in December of that year. When the war of independence against Austria began, Jessie was involved in nursing Garibaldi's Redshirts in makeshift battle hospitals. She spent the rest of her life reporting national developments in Italy for various Italian and foreign periodicals. Benjamin Leigh Smith regarded Jessie as 'wild' and disapproved of his sisters' admiration of her.

Another volunteer was a friend of the Howitts, Octavia Hill, who gave French and drawing lessons at Portman Hall.[36] Her parents had run a pioneering infant school in Wisbech, Cambridgeshire, based on similar Pestalozzian principles to Owen's school in New Lanark. Severe financial problems had led to one of her sisters, Gertrude, being brought up by her maternal grandfather, Dr Southwood Smith, and by the Gillies sisters who lived with him. Margaret Gillies trained Octavia as an artist and she later earned her living as a copyist for John Ruskin.[37] Two years before Portman Hall started, Caroline Hill, Octavia's mother, had founded a co-operative crafts workshop for unskilled women and girls.[38] Aged only fourteen, Octavia had been in charge of the 'toymakers', a group of girls from a ragged school whom she trained to make dolls' furniture out of wire and chintz.

Octavia and her sister Miranda (Andy) had left the Unitarian faith of their family and had become Christian Socialists. A letter from Octavia to Andy in August 1860 asks whether her sister would be interested in a teaching job, pointing out that the school was insistently secular:

> I do not know how you think or feel about the Portman Hall school. You know I do not think the omission of all religious teaching a sufficient reason for disapproval to counterbalance the immense good which I think they are doing there, especially as the teacher there and three of the monitors are earnest believers ... You will wonder why I write all this. It is because they are trying to find a lady to help there; and I have mentioned you to them ... they first wanted a person's entire time for £100; but now they have resolved to divide their fund, and would probably like to have you for about two or three hours daily except Saturday. I do think that a permanent work of this sort, and among that class of children, would be deeply interesting; that it would make a nice change from private pupils; that you would find Mme Bodichon and Mrs Malleson [Elizabeth Whitehead's married name] delightful people to work under.[39]

In the event F. D. Maurice leader of the Christian Socialists, advised Miranda not to work in a school where she would not be allowed 'to speak to the children in any way that seemed best to you'.[40]

The volunteers at Portman Hall were all remarkable and unconventional women, who must have lent some excitement and glamour. Barbara, Bella, Nannie and Tottie Fox all gave drawing lessons. Inevitably, however, the major responsibility fell on the chief mistress, Elizabeth Whitehead, who, despite her enthusiasm for the great experiment and attempts by Barbara and her family to give her refreshing holidays, suffered a breakdown in her health. Looking back on this time, she commented:

> Excessive walking, insufficient rest and food, and a building in nearly every way unfit for school-keeping, brought me by mid-summer to a state of sleeplessness. Miss Julia Smith insisted upon carrying me away to Germany to Konigstein, where we went with Belle Smith. I returned after the holidays and went on again working until the winter, when I became so seriously out of health that I was compelled to give up teaching, though I tried again, and was again convinced I could not continue such work, though I retained the inspectorship of the school for some years after my marriage.[41]

One of the things that had exhausted her was the inconvenience of not having a purpose-built school, but having to operate in a rented building, which was still used for temperance meetings in the evenings, so that all the furniture and equipment had to be stacked away at the end of each day.

Barbara, writing to Marian Lewes about Elizabeth on 14 January 1856 said:

> [the School] has had a severe blow in the illness of my dearly beloved teacher Elizabeth Whitehead who is laid on the sofa for 3 months to come from pain and weakness in the back. We have 2 teachers who work well but alas! young women have such bad health that one cannot depend upon them. If I could find a trusty man and true, a good teacher to boot, I would give the school to him – girls learn best of men – but there is not one to be found in the wide world. I used to think women were ill because they were idle but these last 3 years have quite changed my opinions . . .[42]

Fortunately, Elizabeth's health recovered, and on 26 May 1857 she married Frank Malleson, who was related to the Courtauld and Taylor families. He was a partner in Fearon & Co., whisky and gin retailers and wholesalers of Holborn, and had the typical Unitarian interest in educational reform. Barbara was delighted to hear of the marriage of 'my dearest saint', being convinced Frank held his wife in high esteem, and noting that he had willingly agreed to leave the word 'obey' out of the marriage service.

Following her marriage, Barbara appointed Elizabeth as inspector to the school and Ellen Allen took over as chief mistress. Barbara hoped to forestall a breakdown in the health of her new mistress by inviting her on holiday to Algiers (where she spent the winters after her marriage). Aunt Ju gave her a present of two gowns to take with her on her first visit, a muslin one for the day, and a heavier one for dinner in the evenings.[43]

Inevitably, there were some disappointments. A Miss Carmichael was taken on, but she proved entirely unwilling to undergo the same training as Elizabeth. Barbara was disappointed that some of the women she appointed seemed to have no desire to professionalise themselves. Teaching, especially that of young children, was often seen as an extension of maternal nurturing. It was therefore one of the few activities 'ladies', which is to say women of the middle class, could engage in without significant loss of caste; and for working–class women it offered modest upward social mobility. Bessie passed on to Barbara the information that 'Miss Carmichael won't be trained, refuses to be under obligation, the Goose! So it must all be as it is till you return to decide what is to be done.'[44] The final blow was her disappointment in the loss of

Ellen Allen, who was soon to be married, both for what the school would lose and because Barbara was concerned for her future happiness. She gave Ellen a wedding party at Blandford Square, but in a letter of 2 August 1863 confessed to William Allingham:

> as she has been eight years working with me I must see her safely into her new life: this marriage is what the world calls good because she, a penniless lass, marries a man with £2000 a year: for me, I *hope* it will be good, but he is a Roman Catholic and very *devout;* and already he bullies her, and calls her a pagan! because she is about where you are in belief. This marriage is a great up-rooting of one of my interests in life because it has made me give up the school; I know no-one I can trust to carry it on and so it is wiser to stop. It is the individual that makes the work and I have no faith in Schools, institutions, &c., unless there is a soul in them. It is absurd of people to say they will do good and establish this and that, the great thing is to find a good worker with good head, good heart, and sound health, and then just be contented to help them to do what they best can without any fixed plans of your own which only shackles the real worker.[45]

Barbara needed to let Elizabeth know immediately of her decision to close the school because of her role as inspector. Elizabeth was saddened, although she concurred in her opinion that, with Ellen Allen's departure, none of the other existing staff were capable of the task of leadership. In her letter of 21 August 1863 she commented:

> The more I think of the school passing away from us – of there being no Madame Bodichon's school with all that it implies – with no results that man can estimate (though deep down in many a heart are results wh. one can estimate) – it seems more & more heart breaking . . . It is true that no school can depend on any one labourer other than its teacher or teachers – no committee could make a fine school with a Miss Carmichael, or only a Miss Croyden as its head – a school is the incarnation of its teacher – & no one outside can help or save if the spirit is wanting within . . . I do uphold that tho' I have not been able to teach in the school for at least 2 years – I have been able to give all that was needed while Ellen was teacher – I've been able, as it seemed, to comfort her on dark winter days – to rejoice with her on bright days – to hold in your absence that slender thread necessary to hold things together . . .[46]

Elizabeth accepted the demise of the school, however, and turned her thoughts to another educational enterprise, which she saw as the logical successor to her work at Portman Hall. What was wanted now, she felt, was 'a place where the children taught in good elementary schools (such as Portman Hall and the Birkbeck Schools) could get more knowledge'.[47] Naturally enough, Elizabeth's thoughts turned to the model of the Working Men's College.

The Working Men's College had been founded in 1844 by R.D. Litchfield and F.D. Maurice, the leader of the Christian Socialists, and was supported by several of Barbara's friends, including Gabriel Rossetti, who was on the committee, and the Revd Llewelyn Davies, whose sister, Emily Davies, was to become Barbara's partner in another educational experiment. Other supporters whom Barbara met included J.M. Ludlow, Vernon Lushington, his twin brother Godfrey (who married her cousin, Beatrice Shore Smith)[48] and John Westlake. The college relied on the services of volunteers; Rossetti, for example, taught the advanced art class there from 1855 to 1861, and Ruskin gave lectures on art. Elizabeth now wanted to turn her energy and experience into establishing a Working Women's College, intended as a sister institution to the Working Men's College. Elizabeth wrote to Barbara asking her if she would be its principal, but received a somewhat discouraging reply in December 1863.

In response to Barbara's obvious reluctance Elizabeth wrote again on 13 January 1864 trying to persuade her:

> You gave me a heart's blow in yr. letter about the Working Women's College ... For years, remember, the students of the Men's College have longed for education of the women belonging to them ... You know how necessary & precious yr. sympathy is to me – & how as you first set me to work educationally & my proudest thought for public work, is to work with you, it pains me to the heart that you shd. not be quite with & for this really great idea – wh. you once bade me carry out – & for which I believe the time is quite ripe.[49]

Elizabeth wanted to provide (secondary) education for teachers, shopgirls and servant maids. Barbara was not willing to be directly involved with Maurice, as he was too evangelical for her liking. Elizabeth's report of Maurice's comments probably did not help her cause:

> [Maurice] feels very strongly the need of such a means of education for women, tho' he certainly has not the same idea of what education for women shd. be. He is very desirous the 'intuitive wisdom of women' shd. not be overlaid & injured by a 'hard intellectualism'. I hope I had the power of convincing him we were not desirous of educating the women in the ugly notion of 'strongmindedism' – but in humility, love

and knowledge & beauty – & in dutifulness. 8 elder girls of the [Portman Hall] school have sent their names as pupils of classes . . . we hope to have first rate MA's [to teach] some of our advanced classes.[50]

This troublesome term 'strong-minded', which in the late eighteenth century was applied in admiration of men who had a vigorous or determined mind, from about the mid-nineteenth century began to be applied in a disparaging way to women. It implied that women who desired knowledge somehow risked losing 'femininity'. Sometimes it also operated as a covert term for 'lesbian' by that twisted logic which concludes that the only explanation which can account for women being more interested in learning than in flirting is that they are men *manqué*. For example, when Bessie Parkes published *Remarks on the Education of Girls* in 1854, in which she called for various reforms, a large section of the press greeted her book with derision as the work of a 'strong minded female', as though this was a criticism well understood.[51] Barbara, needless to say, was wholly in support of strong-mindedness for women, in its original eighteenth-century sense. She was not desirous of its denial; nor is it likely that she would have wished to have a close institutional connection with Maurice's particular brand of Christianity.

Elizabeth, although disappointed that Barbara would not join her, gamely continued in this enterprise. As Barbara had declined the role of principal she chose instead to have a council of teachers, which included Octavia and Miranda Hill, with Elizabeth herself as honorary secretary and her husband as treasurer. Barbara offered them any of the equipment from Portman Hall that would be useful and also gave some money, following her father's motto: *bis dat qui cito dat* (he gives twice who gives promptly). Elizabeth sought and received help from other 'leaders of liberal thought' including John Stuart Mill, Marian Lewes, Harriet Martineau and the Lushington brothers.[52] Elizabeth, with the confidence which her training and experience had given her, succeeded in opening the College for Working Women in 1864. Barbara had refused her commitment to this enterprise because, like Princess Ida of Tennyson's poem, she was starting to dream of a university college for women.

CHAPTER 6

'One Round of a Long Ladder'

In the winter of 1848–49 when Barbara had been studying with Kingsford he had defined political philosophy as 'that branch of *Moral Philosophy* which treats of the *laws* intended to regulate the conduct of mankind considered as members of political society'. He taught her that 'the laws in actual operation at any period, must necessarily be so many indications of the civilisation of that period'.[1] Consequently, when Barbara made an abstract of Mill's *Political Economy,* she made an accurate précis of the main points of Mill's argument, and then commented on what she felt to be missing:

> tho' I cannot criticise the book, yet there is something with which I can find fault or rather regret, for it is not a fault, I mean that Mill touching so often on unsettled questions of the greatest importance, and interest, has not gone away from Pol. Ec. dilated and given us his valuable opinion upon them. The Contract of Marriage to which he first alludes is one of the Laws concerning women and there are many more.
>
> As far as he has let one see his views he thinks nobly, rightly and liberally. And I wish with my whole soul that one who carries so much weight would put these things before men and I do not doubt that they would see the injustice of their laws to women and the absurdity of the present laws of marriage and divorce.
>
> Philosophers & Reformers have generally been afraid to say anything about the unjust laws both of society and country which crush women. There never was a tyranny so deeply felt yet borne so silently, that is the worst of it. But now I hope there are some who will brave ridicule for the sake of common justice to half the people of the world.

Barbara was brave, and she had been encouraged by her Pater to fight for what she believed in. After his death she commented: 'My father used to say to me "Salt of the earth ye virtuous few" &c as an encouragement to stand up against the crowd of worldlings.'[2]

The Pater also influenced Barbara to think 'politically' rather than to think 'charitably', at a time when most well-to-do women were willing to be called philanthropists, but usually unwilling to engage in anything approaching the political process. Barbara, on the other hand, regarded anyone who ignored political affairs as an 'idiot', in the sense derived from the Greek origin of the word, meaning a person who fails to assume the responsibilities of a citizen. Barbara's potential as a leader of a political movement was substantial.[3] She was a descendant of the powerful politically minded Smith dynasty. She was highly intelligent, and for a woman of her time, well educated. She had independent money, which she regarded without embarrassment as a power to do good, and she had also, in Blandford Square, a base for political operations in London. Finally, she possessed that crucial, although indefinable skill of being able to inspire others. It is unsurprising that Anna Mary Howitt chose Barbara as the model for her illustration of Tennyson's 'Boadicea', 'the lover of liberty' who 'roved about the forest, long and bitterly meditating' on the wrongs suffered by her people.[4]

During her apprenticeship years, as part of her Unitarian inheritance, Barbara had studied Mary Wollstonecraft's *Vindication of the Rights of Woman*, and recommended it to any woman she ever met who, unaccountably, had failed to read it.[5] Wollstonecraft, perhaps more than any woman previously, had pushed the demand for women's emancipation into the mainstream of British political life. In *The Wrongs of Woman* (published posthumously in 1798) she had demonstrated that 'women are the outlaws of the world'; neither they nor their children were protected by the law, were they to come into dispute with their husbands. Wollstonecraft's theorisation made clear that the presumed distinction between the public world of politics (where the laws were made) and the private world of the family, had served to exempt family relations from the rules of justice. The sentimental idealisation of the family by conservative writers and politicians, according to Wollstonecraft, merely disguised the 'outlawed' position of women.

As well as the knowledge Barbara accrued in scholarly activity, she also knew women who had suffered directly. Anna Jameson, for example, had separated from her husband in 1838, and although he became Attorney-General of Canada and was financially well off, he made her only a very small yearly allowance. When he died in 1854 he left her nothing in his will. Anna Jameson had made a virtue of necessity, and from 1838 until her death she supported herself and her sisters from her writing. Even more notorious was the case of Caroline Norton who had quarrelled with her husband in 1836.[6] He had then removed their three children to an undisclosed location, and sued Lord Melbourne, the Prime Minister, for 'criminal conversation' with Caroline. This kind of legal action could only be initiated by men, and, if the defendant was found guilty, the husband was awarded 'damages'. In such actions, the wife was prohibited from testifying in her own defence; it was a legal contest *between men* for alleged damage to a husband's 'property'. The clear implication of such a law was that a husband had a right to his wife's sexual services, and if these were enjoyed by another man her husband had to be reimbursed. In the event, although Lord Melbourne was found 'not guilty', Caroline's reputation was blackened: it was as if by dragging her name into the public space of a law court she had become polluted. Caroline discovered that fathers had absolute right, under common law, to custody of their children and she could only gain access to her three children with her husband's permission. Patently, she had not got that, so she set about getting the law changed. She published a pamphlet, *Observations on the Natural Claim of the Mother to the Custody of her Infant Children, as affected by the Common Law Right of the Father* (1837) and circulated 500 copies to MPs and other influential figures.

In Parliament the cause of reform was taken up by her friends and a reform in common law was brought about. Following an Act of Parliament in 1839, the Court of Chancery could award mothers custody of their children under the age of seven and access to their children under the age of sixteen, *if* the mother was of good character. Like a ghastly chess game, George Norton responded to this by removing the three children to Scotland, which was outside the Lord Chancellor's jurisdiction. Tragically, Caroline's youngest son, William, aged eight, died after a fall from his horse.

In 1854 Caroline Norton produced another pamphlet, *English Laws for Women in the Nineteenth Century*, in which she reviewed her own case, disclaiming any strong-minded motive, but arguing that, 'failing her natural protector, the law should be able to protect [women] and the LAW exercise remedial control'. This pamphlet, and the consequent publicity, inspired Barbara, who knew that in political campaigning timing was crucial. She felt moved to enter the fray. Her aim was to lay out a clear and concise description of the existing laws. Being frankly strong-minded, she regarded it as unreasonable that women should have to rely on the good feeling of men, when what was required was simple justice.

She studied Wharton's *Exposition of the Laws relating to the Women of England*, a 550-page tome published at the beginning of 1853.[7] Deeming it a splendidly lucid account, but doubting whether many women would wade through such a huge volume, Barbara produced a summary, abstracting its main points in the way Kingsford had taught her. Wharton had divided his work into seven sections, a scheme which Barbara largely adopted, although she changed the order and emphasis. Whereas Wharton began with a section on 'Infancy', Barbara began *A Brief Summary, in Plain Language, of the Most Important Laws concerning Women* (1854) with a section on 'Legal Conditions of Unmarried Women or Spinsters'. The purpose of this shift was to establish the fact that the single woman (or feme sole in legal terminology) was the 'best case scenario' of a woman's legal position at that time. Barbara's opening sentences announced that 'a single woman has the same rights to property, to protection from the law, and has to pay the same taxes to the State, as a man. Yet a woman of the age of twenty-one, having the requisite property qualifications, cannot vote in elections for members of Parliament'. Her very first sentence, therefore, gave notice of her understanding that to be recognised as having a legal personality was the necessary first step towards being recognised as a citizen.

Yet, even for the single woman, there were elements of current law which defied logic. For example, she drew into her first section the issue of 'seduction', pointing out that 'if a woman is seduced, she has no remedy against the seducer; nor has her father, excepting as he is considered in law as being her master and she his servant, and the seducer having deprived him of her services'. This reveals, once again, that it is not the woman herself who is represented as having a grievance: she exists legally only as the 'property' of her father, from whom another man has stolen the woman's 'services'.

Barbara divided the rest of the material into easily readable sections with the titles 'Laws concerning Married Women', 'Usual Precautions against the Laws concerning the Property of Married Women', 'Separation and Divorce', 'Laws concerning a Widow', 'Laws concerning Women in Other Relationships', 'Laws concerning Illegitimate Children and Their Mothers'. This is all very businesslike, but Barbara (like Caroline Norton) did have a personal interest: the status of her own mother, and the issues of illegitimacy. It is to be noted that Wharton's two sections on 'Concubinage and Harlotry' and 'Trustship' were replaced in Barbara's *Summary* by one section only: 'Laws concerning Women in Other Relationships'. Wharton begins his section with the statement that:

> The unwedded relationship between paramour and mistress, is not recognised in any way by our national jurisprudence, as it was by the civil law (a) of Rome, and the municipal regulations of the ancients. Nevertheless, it cannot be denied that such free and unchained

endearments are very frequently concluded, and preserved with something more than temporary caprice and alterable attachment . . .

(a) A concubine did not mean in the civil law, a harlot; the concubine was a person taken to cohabit in the manner, and under the character, of a wife, but without being authorised thereto by a legal marriage.

Yet Barbara reduced the whole of Wharton's long section on 'Concubinage and Harlotry' to a single sentence, the last of her section on 'Women in Other Relationships'. Barbara's version said only that 'if a man place a woman in his house, and treat her as his wife, he is responsible for her debts'. She must have experienced no small degree of discomfort at discovering that, in legal terms, her father was a 'paramour' and her mother his 'concubine'. Her complete avoidance of either of these terms may suggest either prudence or dismay.

Wharton's first section, 'Infancy', considers the issue of legitimacy, pointing out that the legal rights of an infant and 'frequently the chaste reputation of its mother' depend on this question. A child is defined as illegitimate, according to Wharton, if the child is born out of wedlock, 'and no act or proceeding of the parents, afterwards can legitimate it in this country'. Barbara devoted a whole section to the 'Laws concerning Illegitimate Children and Their Mothers'. One of her comments seems peculiarly personal:

> The rights of an illegitimate child are only such as he can acquire; he can inherit nothing, being in law looked upon as nobody's son, but he may acquire property by devise or bequest. He may acquire a surname by reputation, but does not inherit one.

The Pater's careful naming of the five children as 'Leigh Smith' seems suddenly to have an added pathos. If the Smiths denied them (and some of them did), the 'Leighs' of the Isle of Wight were too humble in class terms to protest at the appropriation of their name. One is reminded of Mrs Gaskell's response to meeting Barbara: 'She is – I think in consequence of her birth, a strong fighter against the established opinion of the world – which always goes against my – what shall I call it? – taste (that is not the word) but I can't help admiring her noble bravery, and respecting – whilst I don't personally like her.'[8] Barbara, as one of the third generation of the Smiths, was imbued with concepts of natural justice (hence Anna Mary's characterisation of her as Justina) but she was also enjoined to battle by a personal identification with the wrongs women suffered. These entwined elements were twin aspects of her role as a political leader.

Barbara's *Summary* was designed to be read and digested at a single sitting. In the last and more discursive section, 'Remarks', she pointed out that the position of a married woman in the mid-nineteenth century was not significantly different from that of the seventeenth century, quoting Judge Harlbut's *The Lawe's Resolutions of Women's Rights* (1682):

The next thing that I will show you is this particularitie of law; in this consolidation which we call wedlock is a locking together; it is true that man and wife are one person, but understand in what manner. When a small brooke or little river incorporateth with Rhadanus, Humber, or the Thames, the poore rivulet loseth her name, it is carried and recarried with the new associate, it beareth no sway, it possesseth nothing during coverture. A woman as soon as she is married is called covert, in Latin nupta, that is vailed, as it were clouded and overshadowed she has lost her streame . . .

Barbara's next description of the state of the married woman is to say that 'she is absorbed' by her husband. It was surely no coincidence that when Marian Lewes came to write *Middlemarch*, her heroine, 'Miss Brooke', represented as a single woman of independent means and reforming tendencies, was described as being a diminished figure after her (second) marriage: 'Many who knew her, thought it a pity that so substantive and rare a creature should have been absorbed into the life of another, and can only be known as a wife and mother.'[9] Both Barbara's pamphlet and George Eliot's fiction are examples of writing *as* representation, the only available form of female representation in the nineteenth century.[10]

Barbara sent her draft manuscript to her friend Florence Davenport Hill at Bristol, hoping that her father would scrutinise it for legal mistakes. Florence was one of the daughters of Matthew Davenport Hill, an advanced Liberal MP and reformer of criminal law, and from 1851 to 1869 the commissioner for bankrupts in Bristol.[11] Davenport Hill's father, Thomas Wright Hill, had founded Hill Top School in Birmingham, and Barbara's brother, Ben, had attended its offshoot, Bruce Castle School in Tottenham. Letters from Florence to Barbara between 1852 and 1874, not surprisingly, given their similar backgrounds, show a shared interest in various social reforms. Florence set up reading rooms for poor people in Bristol and, with her twin sister Joanna, became increasingly active in Poor Law reform. Her elder sister Rosamund did sterling work as a member of the London School Board, but was not sympathetic to feminist issues. A letter from Florence, dated 6 August 1854, pledges her own support but warns Barbara not to expect too much from Rosamund:

I am very glad that you intend calling the attention of our passive sisters to some of the injustice from which we suffer, and shall rejoice to help you if I can – Rose too will be happy to be of any use to you in the object you have in view. Had you proposed the reform of any other of the hard laws concerning us poor women I believe she could not conscientiously have entered into your project, for she is quite a tory respecting them and thinks there is no need to amend.[12]

Davenport Hill looked over Barbara's manuscript and drew attention to a small legal point. Florence's cover note had a slightly apologetic air: 'I hope you will not mind that he laughs at us a little – some of us do deserve a little ridicule – and he is a staunch friend at heart.'[13] Barbara, it seems, had to bear a 'little ridicule' even from those men broadly in sympathy with her aims. In another letter, of 13 August 1854, Florence offers Barbara the benefit of her own critical reading:

Your summary of the Laws so far as I have read seems very clear. I am not however quite sure that we are by Law excluded from the professions – that is by any special laws directed to our exclusion. Is there more than the ignoring of feminine existence in all laws regulating entrance to the professions?[14]

Barbara noted this caveat, altering her comment on women's access to the professions to read: 'The professions of law and medicine, whether or not closed by law, are closed in fact.' Florence also passed on a hint to Barbara:

My father thinks it very desirable that no more than absolutely necessary should be said upon subjects which are considered as forbidden to women. He fears that the subject may call forth attacks upon your little works which would greatly injure the cause you are labouring for . . . long experience has convinced him that if we wish to reform the world we must be tender of its prejudices or we shall never gain a hearing.[15]

Barbara largely accepted this advice. Wharton had discussed prostitution under the term 'harlotry', and his section was primarily involved with laws concerning brothels. Barbara restricted herself to commenting on what Wollstonecraft had defined as prostitution *within* marriage; in 'Laws concerning Married Women' she wrote that 'A woman's body belongs to her husband; she is in his custody, and he can enforce his right by a writ of *habeas corpus*.'

As a consequence of the knowledge she had gained, when she wrote *Women and Work* in 1857, she commented: 'Fathers have no right to cast the burden of the support of their daughters on other men. It lowers the dignity of women; and tends to prostitution, whether legal or in the streets.'[16] Barbara did not feel she was ducking the issue of prostitution in her *Summary*, because she believed that it was not so much legislation as far-reaching social reforms of women's education and employment opportunities that were necessary to remedy this evil.

Davenport Hill wrote to Barbara advising her not to deal with the machinery of the law but to stick to giving a clear statement of the principle of the law. He also made the suggestion that she should compare English law 'with other and better laws in force in foreign parts'.[17] Barbara took this advice and quoted examples of French, Turkish, Hungarian and American laws which she regarded as 'improvements on ours'.[18] The advantage to Barbara of being able to consult expert witnesses was important, and yet another example of Unitarian networking. Nevertheless, it is worth stressing that the publication of the *Summary* was her own idea, and was largely the result of her own study and her determination to make available to the general public the clearest account possible of the laws affecting women. It was published anonymously in October 1854 by John Chapman. Florence wrote on 8 October: 'I think it will astonish some of our sisters considerably, for I have myself met with perfect incredulity when setting forth some of the laws under which we live.'[19]

The *Summary* was widely circulated and read, in part because both Harriet Martineau and William Fox drew attention to it in the press. Early in 1856 Chapman published a second edition and Davenport Hill brought the *Summary* to the attention of the Law Amendment Society (LAS), of which he was a member. The LAS was the brainchild of Henry, Lord Brougham. Founded in 1844, it was dedicated to reforming outdated laws. As well as Lord Brougham, its members included other friends of the Leigh Smiths, including Mr Serjeant Manning and George Hastings (a barrister), who was its secretary. The LAS was interested in reforming the anomalies caused by the existence of what amounted to two quite separate legal systems – a common law which was frequently anachronistic and a Court of Chancery acting in equity, which only protected the interests of men and women of the wealthier classes. For example, many fathers, alarmed by the lack of protection which common law afforded their daughters after marriage, made use of the Court of Chancery to ensure that a prospective husband would consent to a settlement of property on his wife. A trustee, or trustees, was then appointed to act on behalf of, and protect the interests of, the wife. However, as this safeguard was available only where a wife's property was £200 and over, or produced dividends of £10 a year and above, it was a recourse not available to poorer women.

Barbara regarded the interest of the LAS as a sufficient signal to form a committee of women, all of whom were dedicated to the reform of laws which affected women. In short, she rounded up her friends; of the older generation Mary Howitt was asked to act as secretary, and Anna Jameson, Elizabeth Reid and Mary Sturch all joined; the friends of her own generation were Bessie, Anna Mary and Tottie and a new friend, Maria Rye, the daughter of a London solicitor (who took over as secretary). Using the drawing room at 5 Blandford Square as their headquarters, the committee organised a country-wide campaign collecting evidence from women who had suffered under the existing laws. They heard such harrowing tales that Barbara believed she could never put herself into a man's power by marrying.

She drafted a petition which was circulated with a request for signatures. This was a very successful campaign. In the space of only a few months seventy petitions with over 26,000 signatures were gathered in. In London alone the petition had more than 3,000 signatures. Anna Mary reported to her sister Meg various poignant moments during the campaign, telling her, for instance, about 'a very old lady on her death-bed, who asked to be allowed to put her name to the petition, and thus wrote her signature for the last time'.[20] The petition also gained signatures by the mechanism of a series of chain letters of friendship. For example, Barbara wrote to Marian Lewes from the Isle of Wight on 14 January 1856, where she was on a painting expedition with Anna Mary:

> I send you a copy of a Petition which I have set going and which has already been signed by H. Martineau, Mrs Gaskell, Mrs Howitt, Mrs Jameson etc. etc. Will you sign if I send a sheet and will you tell me any ladies to whom I can send sheets, perhaps among Mr Lewes' friends there may be some ... On second thoughts I send the sheet for signatures – return it if you have no one who will like to get it filled – before the 1st of March it must come back to me.[21]

Marian Lewes promptly signed it and sent it on to Sara Hennell in Coventry.[22] Sara Hennell signed and sent it on to Eleanor Cash, the sister of John and Joseph Cash, Quakers, in whose Coventry factory silk ribbons for the fashion industry were produced. A letter from Marian, dated 28 January, thanked Sara for her efforts:

I am glad you have taken up the cause, for I do think that, with proper provisos and safeguards, the proposed law would help to raise the position and character of women. It is one round [rung] of a long ladder stretching far beyond our lives.[23]

This is perhaps the first time that the aims of the women's movement were called 'the cause'.

Mary Howitt personally collected hundreds of signatures, and spent many hours, with the help of Octavia Hill, then aged eighteen, pasting the sheets of the petition together.[24] Nevertheless, Mary had disappointments with some of the friends she asked. At the head of the petition Barbara had shrewdly placed the names of some respectably married women – for example Elizabeth Barrett Browning, Jane Carlyle, Elizabeth Gaskell and Mary Howitt herself. This was to counter anti-feminist suggestions that it was only women with some special grievance who would sign such a petition. Out of the twenty-four names there were fourteen writers, two women involved with the theatre, three artists, two women who had been active in the anti-slavery campaign, and three who were merely 'relational', in the sense that it was their connection with a famous man or a noble family which was their claim to 'fame'. The writers (other than those mentioned above) were Anna Blackwell, Isa Blagden, Mary Cowden Clarke, Amelia B. Edwards, Matilda Hays, Anna Jameson, Geraldine Jewsbury, Mrs Loudon, Harriet Martineau, Mary Mohl and Bessie Parkes. The artists were Eliza Fox, Anna Mary Howitt and Barbara herself. Mrs Reid and her sister, Miss Sturch, had been involved in anti-slavery campaigning and in the foundation of Bedford College. In the final category, Jane was notable only in that she was married to Thomas Carlyle, Sarianna only for being the sister of Robert Browning, and the Hon. Julia Maynard because she was the only scion of a noble family.

Despite Barbara's attempts to give a strong impression of respectability, when Mary Howitt approached her friend, the philanthropist and founder of a magdalen home, Angela Coutts, she demurred at two names high on the lists because she regarded them as having free opinions with regard to marriage. One of the women she objected to was Anna Jameson, who was separated from her husband. Her other objection is not known, but it could have been to Matilda Hays or Anna Blackwell, both of whom had translated works by George Sand, then widely assumed to write books attacking marriage. Mary Howitt also met with a refusal from Agnes Strickland, the author of *Lives of the Queens*, whose refusal was based on her opinion that 'the disabilities of women were part of the condemnation of Eve'.[25]

On 14 March 1856 the petition was presented in Parliament, by Lord Brougham, in the House of Lords, who 'made a capital little speech . . . paying Mrs Jameson and [Mary Howitt] each a very nice compliment, to which there was a "hear, hear". When Sir Erskine Perry unrolled the petition in the Commons it reached the whole length of the House'.[26] To keep up public interest, the LAS sponsored a large public meeting in London on 31 May. The society's journal records that 'a large number of ladies were . . . present, including Mrs Jameson, Mrs Howitt, and many other lady authors'.[27] Sir Erskine Perry moved a resolution that 'the conflict between law and equity on the subject ought to be terminated by a general law based on the principle of equity which should apply to all classes'. The resolution was seconded by Davenport Hill and carried unanimously. Barbara asked John Chapman, editor of the *Westminster Review*, to publicise evidence they had collected of the hardships suffered by women because of 'faulty' laws. This he did in October 1856, referring to the petition 'from the pen of a lady already known as the author of "A Brief Summary of the Most Important Laws concerning Women" '.[28]

Organising support in the sympathetic press was as far as Barbara and her committee could go. They now had to rely on the LAS to continue the battle in Parliament. In February 1857 Lord Brougham introduced a bill which aimed to establish a married woman in the same position as an unmarried woman with respect to property. Lord Brougham frankly admitted that this would be a long campaign, but as a veteran politician he believed that, as with the battle to abolish slavery, success would come at last. In the event, Brougham's bill was read a first time, but proceeded no further, for soon afterwards Palmerston was defeated in a vote on his foreign policy and the government resigned. The summary of its provisions, as reported in *The Times* on 18 February 1857, indicates that it would have treated a married woman's property as her 'separate estate', and this was the course which the reforms actually took in 1870 and 1882.[29]

Barbara, like Mary Wollstonecraft, was politically ahead of her time. Much later, in July 1869, when the *Westminster Review* praised John Stuart Mill's *Subjection of Women* as being full of 'stern revolutionary purpose', it went on to link it with Barbara's *Summary:*

A very courageous and well-advised step towards carrying out the principles of Mr Mill's work has been made by Madame Bodichon, who is well known to the enlightened English public for her unresting and single-minded energy and benevolence in carrying forward important social objects, especially those concerned with the amelioration of the position of her own sex. Madame Bodichon rightly holds that, with a view to making new laws, the first stage is to apprehend clearly and compendiously what are the old ones. For this purpose she does what professional lawyers have no mind or heart to do, that is she 'codifies' the part of the English law which specially concerns women. There are some cases where the proverb may fairly be reversed, and 'angels step in where fools fear to tread'.

The review makes it sound as though 'Madame Bodichon' had only just produced the *Summary*, whereas Barbara had produced it well before her marriage. The connection with Mill holds, however, in that it was, in part, her regret that Mill had not said more on the subjection of women that had urged her to make her own study. This was in fact the third edition of the *Summary*, this time published by Trubner. It took many years and many fresh attempts to move from the *Summary* of 1854 and the petition of 1855 to the final enactment of all its aims in 1882. Nevertheless, the significance of this first campaign to reform the Married Women's Property Act would be difficult to overvalue. The whole experience had served as a training ground in political education for the women closely involved with it. Barbara had discovered that she had the ability to inspire others to take action, she had learned to utilise sections of the press sympathetic to her cause(s) and finally, as Bessie Parkes commented later, 'In the effort to obtain signatures people interested in the question were brought into communication in all parts of the kingdom, and the germs of an effective movement were scattered far and wide.'[30] Many of the names first encountered on Barbara's petition became important figures in other feminist campaigns – for women's education, for women's work in general and entry into the professions in particular – having learned some of their strategies on this first round of the long ladder.

CHAPTER 7

Wild Desires

In March 1852, the Pater had a violent quarrel with Ben over his career. Ben was interested in becoming a mining engineer but the Pater wanted him to train as a lawyer, with a view to a parliamentary career.[1] There is a desperate gendered irony here. Ben was being pressed into training for a career he had no aptitude for, because he was the firstborn son. Barbara, who had all the desires and personal attributes of a political leader, as a daughter, was ineligible.

Ben had been pronounced a 'wrangler' in mathematics at Jesus College, Cambridge, and was admitted to the Inner Temple on 18 November 1852.[2] Although he was called to the Bar he never practised: he was very shy and had no talent for any kind of public declaiming, in either court or senate. With his background of shooting on the Glottenham estate he was a good shot and became an enthusiastic member of the Inns of Court Volunteers, competing in the Queen's Hundred. This seems to have been the only aspect of law life he enjoyed; his other great pleasure was sailing.

At some point in the fierce quarrel with the Pater, Barbara learned something which undermined her hero worship of her father. In 1848 Barbara had put her signature to a second codicil on the Pater's will, but had not read its contents.[3] This codicil arranged to leave £2,000 each (in addition to £2,000 each left to them in an earlier codicil), to three children named Bentley Smith when they reached their majority. The Pater had three children tucked away in Fulham, just as the young Leigh Smith children had once been tucked away at Brown's with Anne Longden. Ben Smith had sired three children born to a Jane Buss: Jane born in 1837, Alexander born in 1838 and Henry born in 1839. The dates suggest that Ben had taken a mistress two years after Anne Longden's death. All three children were being educated, no doubt at Ben's expense, at schools in Hampshire and Kent, under the name Bentley Smith. There is no obvious reason for the name Bentley, unless Jane Buss had the pseudonym Mrs Bentley, rather as Anne Longden's pseudonym was Mrs Leigh.

In the terms of his will, Ben Smith's money was to be divided up in equal parts between his Leigh Smith children excepting £4,000 each to the Bentley Smith children.[4] Catherine Spooner was left the sum of £50 with a request for 'her care and attention to the above mentioned children during their respective minorities'. Although this was a substantial amount of money, the Bentley Smiths were not left any of Ben Smith's *property*. This was divided up between his Leigh Smith children before his death. Benjamin Leigh Smith received the Glottenham estate, Willie Leigh Smith received Crowham Manor, Barbara was given Blandford Square and Nannie was given property Ben owned in Bath Street, London. Bella had £5,000 in lieu of property on her marriage, as her husband had his own property.[5]

Just as the Nightingales seemed reluctant ever to acknowledge the Leigh Smiths as their cousins, the Leigh Smiths made no public acknowledgement of their half-siblings, the Bentley Smiths. As a Jane Buss was born in 1802 to a family of agricultural labourers in Froxfield, close to Joanna Bonham Carter's house, Ditcham Grove, in Hampshire, it looks as though there is a pattern to Ben's amours.[6] Ben used to visit his sister Fanny Nightingale at Lea Hurst, Derbyshire, and, bored with drawing room conversation, he found a pretty young woman near by (Anne Longden). It seems as though Ben may have repeated this procedure when he visited Ditcham Grove. It is not certain, but seems likely, that by the time of the 1848 codicil Jane Buss was dead, as the only address given for the children at this stage is that of the schools. His three Bentley Smith children, having had a fairly decent education, and £4,000 each from Ben Smith's estate when he died in 1860, effectively moved up a social class from that of their mother. The 1881 census shows Jane Bentley Smith living in Hammersmith married to John Cross, a surveyor of taxes, with their nine children and one general servant. With her lived her younger brother, Henry, who is described as a master mariner. Given Ben Smith and Benjamin Leigh Smith's love of sailing, this is suggestive. Did Ben Smith teach this son to sail, or was *all* the care of the Bentley Smiths devolved to others?[7] The Bentley Smiths were not, of course, of the class which described themselves as 'ladies' and 'gentlemen'; Jane had only one live-in servant despite her large brood of children. The Bentley Smiths ended up in a quite different sphere of life to the Leigh Smiths. It appears that, perhaps after the family outrage over his relationship with Anne Longden, this time Ben kept his liaison absolutely private.

The revelation burst upon Barbara as an enormous psychological shock. She had built up a fantasy of her parents' romance, but now the

Bentley Smith children stood as a kind of ghostly Other to the Leigh Smith siblings. It raised the question of how the Leigh Smith children would have been placed, had their mother *not* died. The knowledge that Catherine Spooner was privy to all the Pater's affairs was also offensive to Barbara. She was so distressed that all her creative drive was stymied. Bessie sent her a comforting letter towards the end of March:

> Dearest Bar . . . I dare say you cannot paint at all now you are in pain & grief, darling, but you will find this afterwards . . . I don't know how I could bear a great wrong doing in anyone I loved, because, never having had that sacred love in an instructive relation, I have chosen love associated with conscience, and never was pained by seeing sin where I loved; but I know that if I had loved anyone as long as I could remember, and found out gradually that they did very wrong it would be very bad. But Barbara, even then is it not better to be linked to those whose noble natures make you feel the fall with such bitterness, than to those of whom you would always take a calm & gentle view because there seemed no high nature to make the contrast black? Dearest Bar, your father has that something immortal about him, which so many men are apparently without, something that will rise, that must rise, something that I feel vividly when I am with him, & I know you do too, something that won't die . . .[8]

In December Ben had another passionate quarrel with the Pater, and he left Blandford Square to stay at the Athenaeum Club; Barbara tried to mediate between her father and brother. She wrote to Ben: 'remember you have duties & ties to others besides him. Living away from home will be better for you no doubt feeling as you do – but you cannot throw up responsibilities any more than any of us.'[9] During these strained times, a solicitor friend of Ben's, John Thornely, fell in love with Bella and wrote a note to his friend in July 1854, asking for his advice and hoping for his blessing. John pointed out that his property was small, bringing him in only about £100 a year, and that his professional earnings amounted to no more than about £50 a year at that stage in his career. Ben replied immediately: 'I am more pleased than surprised by your letter for if I had to choose a brother in law you would be the man . . . My father I am sure will not object to any thing Bell may wish. Of our history I need say nothing as you know that already.'[10] This letter makes it clear that John, as a trusted family friend, was privy to insider knowledge of the tangled family politics. But the marriage was not to be. Bella declined his proposal, although he remained a trusted friend of all the family.[11]

Because Ben Smith ran 'Liberty Hall', in the sense that he allowed young men and women to meet freely, without oppressive chaperonage, Bella knew John well and refused him on the straightforward grounds that although she liked him she was not in love with him. Bessie, however, in her parental home, was not allowed the free intercourse with young men which the Leigh Smith sisters enjoyed. Consequently, she was utterly astonished when a young man called Robert Lacey proposed marriage after meeting her only a couple of times, in public situations.[12] Bessie refused him immediately but engaged in a correspondence explaining her reasons for refusing, and also wrote telling her father what had happened. In her diary she notes how impossible she found the thought of getting married and being dependent on him 'for intellectual nutriment after living with BLS, with her flashing beauty'.[13] Subsequently, when Bessie's cousin Sam Blackwell, a Dudley ironmaster and widower, wished to become engaged to her, Bessie found it difficult to know her own feelings and said as much from the outset, although their mutual cousin Elizabeth Blackwell was influential in promoting the match.[14] The tender-hearted Bessie was moved to compassionate love for Sam largely by Elizabeth's representations, but was baffled as to how she could get to know him intimately enough to form a judgement of his character. Bessie's parents would only allow her free social intercourse with Sam *after* she became engaged to him.

At the beginning of August 1854 Barbara and Bessie retreated into a cottage called Pen-y-lan in Maentwrog, near Port Madoc, for a working holiday. The two 'solitary thinkers' were busy editing proofs, Barbara checking her *Brief Summary* and Bessie her *Remarks on the Education of Girls*.[15] When they were together, away from family pressures, they were in high spirits, as a letter from Bessie to 'Belos' (Bella) describing one of their expeditions indicates:

If a pen could paint the Lake of Landewin yesterday evening! Up we went early in the afternoon, I thought I had never seen water before in my life; so perfectly limpid, and of a green color under the blue sky. What did we do? Why we sent the car on some way & then bathed alternately under the free air of heaven, in the most utterly crazy Diana-like way with no Actaeon save a mountain mutton or two who came and stared and thought we were literally two very odd fishes. One sheep distinctly ejaculated 'Bar', thereby putting her into an agony of alarm, as she thought it was your Father, summoned magically from Glottenham, and standing sternly like some white tressed druid on a heathery rock about to continue, 'Bar, I'm ashamed of you'.

It was a state of things! Fancy us going on like Grecian nymphs who had never had any sense of propriety. I felt positively an ennobled human creature, – that I was akin to the ferns and the water; and I sang a great many songs to Echo, who sang them back to me.[16]

Barbara's painting *View of Snowdon with a Stormy Sky* inscribed 'Frantic remains of a Sunday walk never to be forgotten' may well be a record of this day.[17]

In Wales Bessie heard her father's account of Marian's 'elopement'. In setting up home with George Lewes and 'living in sin' Marian had done no more than Barbara's father had done with Anne Longden (not to mention the more discreet liaison with Jane Buss). Ben Smith, however, would not pay the price of society's ostracism, any more than George Lewes would. At first Barbara displaced her ambivalent feelings towards her father on to Lewes. Lewes was the sensualist and the seducer. Although she made up her mind never to desert Marian, she intended to ignore Lewes as far as possible.

After the Robert Lacey 'affair', and the more serious Marian Evans/ George Lewes affair, it seems as though the Parkes parents began to feel alarmed that Bessie's involvement with the bohemian intellectual and artistic group might lead her to do something rash, especially as during the course of Barbara's work in exposing the anomalies of British law as it affected women, they had heard some harrowing tales of women's subjection within marriage. They were stories that married women did not usually tell unmarried women, in that conspiracy of silence about some of the less appealing aspects of male sexuality. Bessie's mother, especially, seemed to think that only in an immediate engagement and early marriage to her cousin Sam Blackwell would Bessie find 'some kind of safety'.[18]

Sam and Bessie managed to see each other in Wales but their 'intercourse . . . was of the scantiest & most uncomfortable kind, before strangers, & in such small intervals of private conversation as I could snatch for the discussion of subjects involving the happiness of a life . . . the confessed attraction that he possesses for me does not make me easy to jump into a connection involving so much responsibility & many of whose laws & customs you are well aware I regard with no favour'.[19] Barbara was largely in favour of Bessie accepting Sam's proposal, because she thought Bessie's marriage to a rich industrialist would allow her to do the useful social work of setting up a school for the children of Sam's Dudley factory workers. Bessie ended up having a ten-year engagement, which may have suited her, as it protected her from other suitors. Bessie, in a letter of 17 March 1855 to Elizabeth Blackwell's sister, Emily, tried to explain her strong reservations about her own fitness for marriage:

I never was made for domestic life. *I hate it.* The near prospect of it has made me rise up with every faculty in utter disgust and affliction at it ... I never saw any Man equal to [Barbara] in breadth of mind & firmness, & I never had for Sam the feeling I have for her.[20]

Bessie's strongest attachments were to women – to Lucy Field (her teacher at school), to Barbara, to Matilda Hays, to Mary Merryweather and to Adelaide Procter – they seemed far more significant than her engagement to Sam Blackwell.

While Barbara and Bessie were still in Wales, they received grave news of Barbara's erstwhile tutor, Philip Kingsford who was in the last stages of consumption. Barbara had written guiltily to Bessie, 'I am so sorry about PK and I think the Devil possesses me entire, I cannot write long and interesting letters to him.'[21] Aunt Ju went to visit him and wrote to warn them he was dying: 'His state is a very sad and suffering one. He talked like himself though one felt it was with effort & that he had better talk very little. Yet when an invalid is haunted with painful images & can neither write nor walk nor move, if he does not talk them off he is devoured quite.'[22] Barbara fell into an anguished state, guilty that she had been unable to return his feelings. Bessie wrote to Sam that the waiting for news of his death had made Barbara 'pale and ill ... she would hardly eat any dinner yesterday'.[23] There was a tragic irony in the situation; as Barbara proof-read her *Summary*, compiled by using the analytical methods Kingsford had taught her, he lay dying. He died aged forty on 3 September 1854.

Hardly had Barbara got over the sad death of her first suitor when on 21 November she received a proposal of marriage from a man she had only recently met, James Joseph Sylvester, then aged forty, an eccentric but brilliant man, once the professor of natural philosophy and astronomy at London University.[24] He had gone to Virginia as professor of mathematics, but had suffered such offensive anti-Semitism that he had resigned the post. Returning to England in 1842, he studied for the Bar, tutoring students to keep himself going. Some time in 1854 he met the Howitts, who introduced him to the Leigh Smiths. Such prejudice as Sylvester had suffered would have assured him of a sympathetic reception in the Leigh Smith household. He soon became a regular visitor at Blandford Square, and his admiration of Barbara led him to hope for something more than friendship from her. He wrote:

Dear Miss Smith,
Let me hope that you may not be offended at what I venture to

express in this note, however surprised you may be at its tenor. I fear that the avowal may on many grounds appear to you to be most presumptuous – still it is true that I am conscious of an ever increasing charm in your society and conversation and that I should regard myself as most favoured by Providence were it possible for me to believe that you could accept the offer of my attachment and earnest and lifelong devotion. I could not bring myself under any inducement to say what I do not think and feel; no one can know you without being made better by the influence of your example and to love you is to love goodness of heart generosity and all that ennobles our nature. Let me hope that whatever other ill effect this note may produce it may not occasion me the loss of your friendship which I know how to prize at its full worth.[25]

Barbara liked Sylvester enormously as one of her group of intellectual friends, but she was not at all in love with him. She turned down his offer of marriage tactfully and the friendship which he so prized lasted all their lives.[26]

Nannie had gone to Rome that winter to study painting. Florence Davenport Hill had advised Barbara to warn Nannie of certain 'Roman' dangers:

> I think she may find it necessary to give up some of the usual Roman amusements, expeditions & so forth for unhappily a party of ladies among whom was Miss Cushman and Miss Matilda Hayes [sic], who were at Rome the winter before last brought great discredit on the plans of young ladies being independent of chaperones, by the very extraordinary manner in which they conducted themselves . . . Your pretty young sister might perhaps find herself in a painful position if she be not aware of the states of feeling which the ladies I have alluded to created in the artistic circles in Rome, among which I believe they chiefly lived.[27]

Matilda, or 'Max', Hays belonged to a bohemian set which included the painter Samuel Laurence as well as George Lewes. She had written her first novel, *Helen Stanley*, in 1846, in which she made a plea for a woman's right to earn a living rather than prostitute herself in a marriage and had translated many of George Sand's books. She had persuaded the Boston actress, Charlotte Cushman, famous for her theatrical portrayals of male roles like Romeo and Cardinal Wolsey, to train her as an actress, playing Juliet to Cushman's Romeo to good reviews. Elizabeth Barrett Browning described Charlotte and Max as having a 'female marriage' in which they had 'made vows of celibacy and eternal attachment to each other – they live together, dress alike'.[28]

Charlotte was also a patron of a young American neo-classical sculptor, Harriet Hosmer, whom she had persuaded to go to Rome for further study; she provided her with rent-free lodging there for seven years. Hatty became the centre of an Anglo-American community in Rome, which included artists, sculptors and literati such as the Brownings and Isa Blagden. Hatty believed that for a woman artist, marriage and career simply would not go together, and she waged an 'eternal feud with the consolidating knot'.[29] Rather like the Munich group in 1850, Hatty referred to the women artists with whom she lived and worked as a 'sisterhood' and referred to her sculptures as 'children'. Although the nineteenth century tolerated a much wider latitude of emotional responses between women, this group was infamous, not so much over the issue of the ardent nature of their romantic friendships, as because the group were gender outlaws, publicly wearing male jackets and waistcoats, rather as George Sand had done. This cross-dressing, which signified their taking up of a man's place in the world, and their utter disregard of male approval for their 'feminine' charms was considered scandalous.

In December Barbara had been diagnosed as suffering from congestion of the lungs and decided to go out to Rome with Aunt Ju to join Nannie. They visited many artists' studios although Barbara was not impressed with the large formal historical or religious scenes she saw: 'Oh the waste of time in studios here! I wish I could turn all the artists out into the country. I am quite disgusted and feel that for an artist Rome is a dangerous place. They nearly all get into the old tracks instead of trying new ones!'[30] She herself hired a horse and rode most days in the Campagna. 'My most vivid ideas for pictures are all horseback views, wild and dashy,' she wrote to Aunt Dolly.[31]

Despite Florence's coded warning, Barbara went to visit Hatty Hosmer, who thought Rome a good place for a woman artist: 'Here every woman has a chance if she is bold enough to avail herself of it, and I am proud of every woman who is bold enough . . . Therefore I say honor all those who step boldly forward, and in spite of ridicule and criticism, pave a broader way for women of the next generation.'[32] Barbara approved of Hatty's stance and attitude, writing home enthusiastically to the Pater:

> You should see Hatty Hosmer. She is the queerest little creature! Very sturdy, bright and vigorous. The most tomboyish little woman ever I saw. She looks more like a jolly little stone-cutter than a lady, and yet she is very fascinating, being so uncommonly clever and lively. She does exactly what is most agreeable to herself and best for her work, and does not care what anyone says in the very least. She looks the very

picture of happiness, and her radiant round face and broad square forehead are tokens and prophecies of success. Bessie would see her in a poetical light, though she smokes and wears a coat like a man.[33]

Although Hatty broke all the rules of ladylike behaviour – she would meet young male sculptors for breakfast in cafés and ride her horse *astride* through the streets of Rome – she managed to get away with it because, physically tiny, she projected the image of a playful tomboy. Barbara had also been accepted unequivocally as a 'jolly fellow' by the Pre-Raphaelite Brethren and understood it to be a persona which allowed a kind of androgynous professionalism.

With regard to Max Hays, however, Barbara seems to have missed Florence's hint. Unlike Barbara's close and loving friendships with several women, the passionate relationships Max sought were exclusive and marked by dependency, jealousy and turbulence. When Max felt that Charlotte was tiring of their 'eternal attachment' she made a play to become Hatty's beloved instead, which led to a quarrel with Cushman. There was a brief reconciliation in London, but the knot had been loosened. In London, Max started to look for another protector. Bessie admired Max for daring to translate George Sand, since she had risked her reputation in having her name associated with the scandalous French woman writer. By June 1855 Bessie had become very involved with her, referring to her in letters as 'my Matthew'.[34] Bessie's feeling for Max must be seen in the context of her pleasure in the company of all the talented women in their circle, and to Bessie there was no absolute boundary between love and friendship. Writing to Barbara in August 1855, she said:

> It pleases me to see of women that they be downright like Jessie, or big & artistic like Miss Cushman (geniusful I ought to say) or moral and tender like your St. Elizabeth [Blackwell] or travelled & [?] like Miss Blagdon, or daft upon missions like Bessie & Bar, or deep & dainty like my Matthew, they are all bent on doing the right.[35]

Both Max and Jessie White (whom Barbara met in Rome in spring 1855) became part of Barbara's circle of friends and their activities in London. Both these women were distrusted by Ben Leigh Smith, who disapproved of his sisters' 'wild' friends.

In spring 1855 the Leigh Smith party moved down to Naples and were electrified by the sight of an eruption of Vesuvius, the worst for five years. Barbara wrote to Aunt Dolly:

It is really a grand and awful sight to see it even as I have seen it, from the shores of the bay, looking across the water to the dark mountain at night, and watching its crown of fiery vapour, and the long lines of the rivers of lava running down its sides . . . To think there is a hole right down into the red-hot centre of the earth, to the very place where the devil is! That is strange! Strange, very strange, it is, to find hot water and hot steam and hot air everywhere about here. One feels terribly close to hell![36]

The vastness, the strangeness and the darkness contrasted with intensely bright colours and the steam-blurred outlines, all speak of an imaginative response to her reading of Milton's *Paradise Lost*. As always, foreign travel restored Barbara's health and vigour, but by mid-May she was ready to go home. Writing to Annie Buchanan on the 17th she said:

My Father has never been so long without me and I feel very homesick. I feel too that my work is in England, and all the beautiful things in these southern countries would never make me willing to reside away from my own Island.[37]

At this stage of her life Barbara could not imagine living out of England; ironically, only two years later she would face a decision which would mean just that.

The summer of 1855 was to be a crucial one for Barbara, for two men were laying siege to her. One of these men was perfectly eligible, another Jewish intellectual, like Sylvester. Joseph Neuberg was a businessman, raised in Germany, and now living in Nottingham. In 1854 he had come to London to act as Carlyle's unpaid research assistant for his work on Frederick the Great.[38] In London Neuberg boarded for long periods at the Chapmans', where he met Barbara. During the summer of 1855 he paid her serious attentions, until at last she fled to Hastings; her affections had already been captured by another man, who may have been intellectually Neuberg's equal, but who was certainly not eligible as a suitor.

By the summer of 1855 Barbara was deeply in love with the ubiquitous John Chapman, then aged thirty-four.[39] At the age of twenty-two he had married Susanna, the daughter of Thomas Brewitt, a lace manufacturer, against the wishes of the bride's family, who considered him a financial adventurer. Susanna was fourteen years older than Chapman and they were described as an odd couple by Elizabeth Whitehead Malleson:

I saw Dr Chapman first when I was fourteen and was at school at Miss Woods'. He came to an evening party with his wife. I remember at this distance of time the strange contrast of the two. He, tall with a fine expressive face, full of alert intellectual power, and absorbed in ideas; she, short, stout and unattractive.[40]

Chapman's early nickname of 'Byron' was a reference to his good looks and mop of wavy hair, and also to his way with the ladies. Like Palmerston, he believed in giving them 'all a chance'.

In his struggle to keep the *Westminster Review* afloat Chapman continued his long career of shifts and manoeuvres for getting money. He had borrowed £600 from Samuel Courtauld in January 1853 and Octavius Smith, Julia Smith and Barbara herself all became involved in helping to keep the journal solvent. Joseph Parkes told Bessie in 1854 that Chapman's debts were about £9,000: 'the £2500 he managed to extract from his wife's trustees I call the worst . . . His talents and activities I respect, but he is not a man I would trust. He is also so self-opinionated and wilful that no one can be of real use to him in aid of his own judgement.'[41] It seems impossible to avoid the suspicion that Chapman was just as interested in Barbara's 'tin' as he was in her beauty, intellectual or otherwise.

In June 1854 the Chapmans rented a house at 43 Blandford Square, and Elizabeth Tilley, Chapman's mistress, did not go with them. Perhaps Chapman had high hopes of his propinquity to the glamorous (and rich) Leigh Smith sisters. Barbara was now twenty-seven and had come into close contact with Chapman during the publication of the *Summary*. Chapman no doubt felt that Barbara's understanding of the terrible dangers of marriage was a factor strongly in his favour, when he tried to persuade her to enter a free union with him during the course of 1855. One of his letters said specifically, 'knowing what your feelings are I would not allow you to surrender yourself legally into my hands by means of an English marriage even if there were no legal impediments to our legal union'.[42] There is a terrible irony in that it was precisely Barbara's feminism that made her vulnerable to his sophisms. Chapman was a man women liked, but he was an opportunist in the sexual arena second to none. Exactly when shared commitment slipped into a love affair is not entirely clear, but a series of letters from 8 August until 22 September 1855 reveals the denouement of a rather bizarre seduction attempt by Chapman and an indication at least of Barbara's temptations and vacillations. As we do not have Barbara's side of the correspondence, we can only infer what she said from *his* letters, although as he sometimes quotes them back to her, one can guess reasonably accurately.

The extant correspondence begins with Chapman's letter of 8 August indicating that Barbara has attempted to put an end to the entanglement. She had returned Chapman's portrait and had written to him that she must cut out of her nature 'the strong necessity of loving'. Chapman did not immediately give up. He presented a quasi-scientific argument about 'natural laws', a transparently male-defined concept of sexuality as a compulsive urge or instinct which must have an outlet. Chapman's pseudo-feminist pose was to argue that this necessity applied to women too, and that 'the deepest passion of our common nature must be so grounded in good and for such good ends that we ought to welcome its development'. The first prong of his argument is that sexual relations between men and women are part of nature and therefore holy in a Feuerbachian sense. Referring to the portrait of him which Barbara had returned as that of a younger more idealistic self, he argues that he could only look like that again if he could live 'fully' in Barbara's love. The second temptation is that with Barbara he can be a better man than he could ever be without her. She is asked to redeem him, to save his better self. He pleads for a portrait of her: 'You need not fear: you will always excel every picture of you, so that I shall look upon you each time with renewed admiration.' Blatant flattery seems to be the third element of the heady concoction.

Chapman clearly thought he might still be able to persuade her to be his mistress. Apologising for something which had upset her, he wrote:

> It was very painful to me to grieve and excite you by a foolish word on Monday, but I confess to have been surprised by a new joy and even an intense feeling of admiration and love when casting in my arms you burst into sobs and tears ... I feel more and more anxious to be liberated from the cares of the business; I shall never do either the Review or myself justice until I am thus emancipated; oh, this £.s.d. problem is very difficult to solve.

Chapman's view of Barbara as his 'beloved angel' seems to include the idea of her winging down to solve all his money problems.

Barbara, deep in the throes of a doubtful love affair, and wondering how it would end, was also concerned about the health and nerves of Anna Mary, who was still feeling 'used up'. Following the breaking off of her engagement with Edward Bateman in August 1853, she had become quite severely depressed, swinging between bouts of hopelessness and bouts of frenetic excitement when ideas came so thick and fast that she found it hard to stick with one painting at a time. At the beginning of August 1855 Barbara determined to get away from the tempting physical presence of Chapman, so took Anna Mary down to Sussex. Anna Mary had been commissioned by Angela Burdett Coutts, a rich philanthropist whose chosen work was the 'redemption' of prostitutes, to produce a painting of Beatrice and Dante.[43] Barbara was to be the model for Beatrice.

Before leaving London, Barbara had been suffering from a sore throat and feeling rather unwell. She had consulted Dr Williams of 49 Upper Brook Street, Physician-Extraordinary to Queen Victoria.[44] It is very noticeable in Victorian medical mythology that any ailment of a woman was somehow related to her reproductive system. Why Dr Williams should consider that a sore throat had any connection with irregular menstruation is hard to say, but it seems that he did. In medical textbooks of the time the vagina was often represented as having a 'mouth', the womb a 'neck' and a 'throat', and the cervix as being like the 'tonsils'. Some of the wilder reaches of Freudian theory may well derive from this 'medical' discourse of displacement. The sceptical Elizabeth Blackwell regarded this kind of theorisation as little more than an excuse for male practitioners to examine female patients' genitalia.

Chapman made his own somewhat doubtful claims to be a doctor. He was the son of a druggist and although originally apprenticed to a watchmaker, had run away to Australia and then Paris, where he maintained that in 1842 he had undertaken medical studies with the chemist Gay-Lussac. When he married he described himself in the register as 'surgeon', although he was certainly not licensed. In his letters to Barbara, however, he adopts the authoritative tone of a medical man. A letter of 13 August advises her of the absolute importance of regular menstruation: the 'flow' was to be produced by sitting in a 'hipbath of water at 96 or 98 of temperature rendered pungent with mustard' for an hour at a time each day. He advises horsehair socks by day and 'loose-fitting lambs-wool socks to sleep in'. He pronounces as a fact that her heart is weak and therefore she must not wear tight boots which would impede the circulation. The idea that Barbara had a weak heart is especially puzzling as she was rather fond of rejoicing in her own 'animal spirits' and pitied anyone, like Anna Mary, who lacked these. Chapman seems to believe (or says he does) that if Barbara's periods were to become regular, this would avert any danger to her lungs. Anxiety about Barbara's lungs is not so surprising because of her mother's death; the fixation on menstruation *is* odd. It appears that Chapman was also taking an interest in Anna Mary's menstrual cycle, as he cannot resist prescribing 'Olei juniperi Sabine' for her, as though he were an expert in menstrual dysfunction.

Barbara and Anna Mary stayed at Clive Vale, Mrs Samworth's farm at Hastings. Holman Hunt had previously stayed there in 1852, painting *Our English Coasts* with cliffs sloping down to the sea and sheep resting on the top; he had in fact painted the sheep in the farmyard. As Anna Mary wrote to her mother on 10 August, 'We were very much amused by finding the traces of Holman Hunt's painting in great spots of green, blue, and red, and traces of oil and turpentine upon a picturesque, little, stout oak table, which we had chosen also for our work; and thus quite unintentionally we have trodden in his steps.'[45] Barbara exhibited paintings from this expedition both at the Royal Academy and at the Crystal Palace in May 1856 which were praised by William Rossetti as being 'full of real Pre-Raphaelitism, that is to say, full of character and naturalism in the detail, as well as multiplicity of it'.[46] Her picture of Mrs Samworth's cornfield with all the shocks tossed over by a gale was singled out for particular praise by Ruskin.[47]

At this stage of her life Anna Mary was having mixed success. She was, perhaps, taking more risks than Barbara, as many of her paintings made explicit social comments on the double standard of morality. *The Lady*, for example, showed 'a hollow eyed pale woman . . . in her arms a baby whose heavy sleepy head hangs innocently over her shoulder [confronting] the man [who] stands between his secret crimes and his honourable respectability'. It had been shown at the Portland Gallery in March 1855 to rather poor reviews.[48] In June 1855 the *Athenaeum* commented on seeing her painting *The Castaway* at the Royal Academy: 'We hope Miss Howitt will not confine herself to these heart-broken, tear-stained subjects, but get out into the sunshine, and show us of what healthy joy the earth is capable. Why will she stand sounding the depths of this salt sea of human tears?'[49] The model who had served Anna Mary for 'the castaway' was a 'poor girl who has a baby and no wedding ring', so at the time of this particular painting expedition the price women might pay for 'free' sexual expression must have been a subject of earnest discussion between them.[50]

Chapman was urgently pleading with Barbara that celibacy was unnatural and inherently damaging.

Sex is certainly not a barrier to the most perfect intercourse of the soul; on the contrary it ensures the fullest intercourse of all and reveals depths in our being which without it are never fathomed. Only because the sexual feeling presses its claims with supreme imperiousness so long as they are unsatisfied do the other parts of our nature shrink for the time from the full operation of themselves in its presence.

But Barbara had a 'horror' of the 'Master Passion' of sexual desire dragging her down; she was trying to resist the attraction and refers on another occasion to her 'accursed love'. Chapman wrote: 'if you often "hate" me, and always wonder why you "should care a straw for me", I shall begin to fear that you will soon cease to love me'.

In between trying to run his business, sort out his family and his debts, Chapman nevertheless found time to consult Ashwell, 'a man who devotes himself to the diseases *peculiar* to women'. Chapman was clearly extremely pleased with himself, reporting to Barbara that Ashwell

> was delighted with the clearness and minuteness of my exposition of your case. He stopped me in the course of it to express his admiration of the discrimination and appreciation I displayed in mentioning all important and characteristic points and only those . . . he inclines to think the womb is distended with blood in which case iron would not be good.

There seems something bizarre about these two men discussing an absent woman's body in supposedly 'expert' mode, and more than a hint of prurience. Ashwell advised several glasses of good claret a day as efficacious, and forbade any outdoor drawing. He also urgently recommended the purchase of a 'Chamber Horse', although as Chapman said, unless Barbara stayed in one place, it could not be all that useful:

> It is a sort of chair elastic with air in which you move up and down and which he says has a more direct mechanical action on the womb than has any other exercise. This seems impracticable unless you were fixed in one place. I consulted him on the effect of marriage; he eagerly jumped at the idea, exclaiming: 'best thing in the world! Best thing in the world!'

Again, the sense of collusion in the two men's decision that 'marriage', here clearly a euphemism for penetrative sexual intercourse, would solve all of a woman's health problems at a stroke, so to speak, would be laughable were it not so irritating. Right at the end of August, Barbara finally achieved a menstrual flow and dutifully let Chapman know. His reply of the 30th was ecstatic and full of further instruction:

> Four days after it is *over* resume the iron as prescribed by *Dr Williams* and continue Dr Ashwell's general directions, and mine . . . I mean you to traverse your orbit regularly in 31 days before I have finished your education. Oh my darling I am full of joy.

Chapman's intention seems to have been to get shot of his wife, although supporting her and the children financially, but Barbara's insistence on secrecy meant that he would have to maintain a 'nominal home' somewhere in the country for his family while taking 'London rooms' for himself and Barbara. By 29 August Chapman is telling Barbara that he is sure Bell 'knows I love you' and that as the Pater had heard through some grapevine that Chapman had visited them at Clive Vale twice, surely it would be best for Barbara to tell her family of their plan to be together. His argument is that openness to her family 'would enable us to be far more effectually secret as regards the world. You would then maintain your right and equal relation towards them, and would be able without fear and undue anxiety and without the knowledge of the world to be really united with me and to look forward with joyous anticipation to becoming a Mother'. This argument suggests, I think, that Chapman not only knows that the Leigh Smiths are illegitimate, but may well be aware of the Pater's Bentley Smith family in Fulham. Chapman pressed her to tell her father, although admitting that 'it will be a terrible trial' for her. Barbara wanted to make him wait for a year, presumably as a test of his fidelity, and Chapman responds:

> My own darling loved one I do believe we shall in due time be fitted physically to have a glorious little creature uniting us both in one . . . But darling, do you not think you could spare me that lock of golden hair now, instead of making me wait a year?

But Chapman's mask slips when he reveals his disappointment that Barbara's income amounts to less than £250 a year from her investments. As Susanna has only £60 a year, and he will need £250 to maintain her and the children, he is at a loss to figure out how he can run two households. Presumably the idea of two separate households arose because he found that trying to keep Susanna, a mistress and Marian Evans all happy in the same household had been beyond even his wit, ingenuity and energy. But Chapman's most fatal error of judgement was in expressing a desire that Barbara should not work. His poor wife had always worked hard taking in boarders, but presumably he hoped to keep Barbara a fresh and blooming mistress. Barbara was horrified, writing, 'I see how the old falsehood still clings to you. You think I shall lose something womanly by struggling for money.'

Barbara determined to test Chapman by making him wait for 'union' until 1857. Interestingly, at this point she started to make claims about loving nature best, perhaps invoking her heroine Jane Eyre, who had turned to Mother Nature to strengthen her resolve against seduction by the married Rochester.[51] But Chapman had formulated his own version of nature's laws and protested vigorously against deferring their sexual union:

> Such a delay will involve the loss of nearly 2 years of the most precious part of our lives: but the strongest reason with me is derived from a consideration of your health, and from the conviction of the re-invigorating effects on your system of a fulfilment of love's physical desires . . . These feelings in both sexes, when developed and enjoyed as the expression of real perfect love, enrich, ennoble and indeed *perfect* the being physically, intellectually, morally; but if when nature makes her demands, she is denied, she generally contrives to punish her disobedient children.

On 14 September Chapman sent Barbara an account of how much it would cost him to train as a doctor; clearly all this amateur doctoring had encouraged him to fancy the status of MD, not to mention the income that becoming an MD would generate. Once again he pressed his claims that sexual union would confer benefits:

> Your physical system would not *directly* feel the change so great and marked as it would were you to conceive; but *indirectly* it would profit immensely from the fulfilment of mutual wishes, the cessation of exciting anticipations, anxieties, feelings of suspense, perplexity &c &c, also from the positive repose you would experience from at length freely resting and sleeping in my arms . . . I think it would be desirable that you should not conceive just now and we might avail ourselves of Riciborski's law for a time . . . We ought to enjoy each other speedily because your unwell *time* will soon come again, and if we do not before then, we must wait according to Riciborski until about 12 days after it is over.

In common with Riciborski, Chapman believed – quite erroneously – that conception was most likely to take place around the time of menstruation.

Finally Barbara told the Pater about her plans to set up a 'free union' with Chapman. He was predictably furious. Chapman's letter of 22 September indicates that he has heard the bad news:

> he must appreciate the real state of your health; what you have suffered; what you will suffer, and how your mind is destroying your body by this terrible contest . . . if his parental love be really deep and pure ought he not to be thankful that across all the difficulties and

untoward chances of this strange world his favourite daughter has the love and devotion of a man the very elect of her own soul, and who, *reason*, as well as feeling, assures her will ever be her real mate . . . What are houses and lands, worldly position, and the respectabilities, compared with this?

He then urged Barbara to come to his rooms in Hastings; it was his last chance, but she refused. The Pater must have had some bitter thoughts. He was hardly in a position to take the moral high ground, and perhaps he feared that the money he had given Barbara to put 'wind in her sails' had only succeeded in making her a target for adventurers.

It seems likely that Ben Smith made some enquiries into Chapman's finances at this point and would have easily been able to demonstrate to Barbara that Chapman was as unreliable with money as he was with women; indeed the two tended to be strangely entwined. His debts were enormous. It seems likely that Ben also had some words with his friend Sam Courtauld, because in 1855 Courtauld shifted his ground from feeling that Chapman was an honourable liberal intellectual who had the bad luck to be not very capable in business matters, to regarding *all* his business affairs with deep suspicion. He refused suddenly to have any personal dealings with Chapman and in a letter to Harriet Martineau in 1858 suggested that there were many 'exhausted sufferers from Dr Chapman's parasitical life'.[52] Octavius Smith, however, continued to bankroll the *Westminster* 'in the general interest of a free theological press'.[53] This may suggest that Ben was less frank with Octavius about the reasons behind his personal antipathy to Chapman than he was to Sam Courtauld. Octavius might well have queried whether Ben's own example was part of the problem. In any event, Chapman had made himself two powerful enemies in the Pater and in Barbara's brother, Ben.

No doubt on this occasion her father saved her from real harm, and Anna Mary and Bessie tended her lovingly while she got over her heartbreak. Interestingly, Chapman does not seem to have entirely forfeited the good will of the circle of women. Anna Mary wrote to him on 1 October to tell him that Barbara was 'dreadfully distressed in mind – but seems really pretty well in body . . . I am thankful to say that, in a long conversation with Ben I have found him much tenderer in feeling towards her than I dared to hope and he entirely agrees that she shall be left quite *unworried* by him – poor fellow! – and by her Father – and shall go away with her friends for the present. I go with her till Bessie can come'.[54] Such an upset in the family must have touched all of them to some degree, and caused tensions and silences. Bella had also been fond of Chapman, and, once again, he had taken it upon himself to advise on her health.[55] It raises the horrible possibility that Chapman was laying siege to two Leigh Smith sisters simultaneously, so that if one slipped his net, another might be caught.

Shortly after this romantic crisis in Barbara's life, in February 1856 Dr Williams diagnosed Bella as suffering from 'incipient' phthisis, which might prove fatal. Barbara shook off her own cares and took her to the Royal Hotel, Undercliff at Ventnor on the Isle of Wight. Establishing Bella under the immediate care of Max and Bessie, Barbara asked a local physician, Dr Martin, to attend her sister. She reported back to Ben on 6 February:

> Bell is not better – she is in better spirits because she loves Miss Hayes [sic] & is happy to have her here. She has not inflammation as I had with spitting of blood & incapacity to breathe going up stairs [winter 1854] . . . A voyage to the West Indies might even now be recommended. I hear of cases worse than hers in which a long voyage has cured. Bell has not the spirit up in her to resist disease, & any change to a new place would be of the greatest benefit . . . Miss Hays has had many relations who have died of consumption & thinks Bell very ill. She, Miss H, is a capital person to be with Bell, gentle & yet decided, so that Bell is ruled by her to be careful even when she does not see the necessity. I was as you know prejudiced against Miss Hays but I think Bell & Bessie know her best . . . [56]

A second letter from Barbara to Ben, on 10 February, sheds a little more light on the picture. It seems as though Bella was suffering from unrequited love for some unnamed person. Ben clearly disliked Max, so Barbara was at pains to tell him that Miss Hays was the only one who could restrain her. Barbara described a recent occasion when Bella had gone

> out for a walk with Miss Hays. After a little while she seemed ill & breathed hard going up the hill at the top she suddenly threw herself into Miss Hays arms fainting. Miss Hays took her into the Hotel & brought her home in a fly (this was about 2 o clock) she lay down & had a violent hysterical fit palpitation gasping & shivering by turns . . . Miss Hays is Bell's good angel. There is a mental cause for Bell's illness. I have done everything which it is possible for human creature to do – you can do nothing but be kind to her & respect her affections. She complained to me that you disliked her friends & did not behave respectfully to her & them. Miss Hays loves Bell & has a tender power over her which may save Bell's life. Dr Martin thinks the mind has so

much to do with her disease that her having her friend with her is of greatest importance, so you must not go against her but forward in every way her love for Miss Hays and Miss Cushman. Bell has never had from any friends of her own choosing such love & tenderness as she has fr. these 2 & has had now for a year . . . Her unhappiness is of years standing, she told me of it, I cannot tell you as no end would be answered. I hoped she had got over it but it is not so, the less she is in B. Sqre the better. It was bad for her to be with me, but now, I think, it is good for her. It is not family unhappiness. B & I are quite right to be together now but one out of her own family like Miss Hays can do her more good than all of our care . . . *You must not tell anyone there is a mental cause. The Pater must not know.* Nanny I have told today.[57]

Ben remained deeply suspicious of the sexually dubious cross-dressing 'Max' Hays and Charlotte Cushman, and did not want to be involved with them. Nevertheless, Barbara asked him to swallow his antipathy and come to the Isle of Wight.

Bell has never recovered [from] the Hysterical attack of Friday. Her brain has been disordered ever since. Her mind runs on the subject of love & marriage & all the force of her long pent up passionate nature has burst forth. Miss Hays is like an angel to her but will soon be worn out by constant watching & anxiety. Bell is sometimes happy & gentle as a child then wild & frantic. She was always stronger than me & now is very much stronger. Twice she has seized me & hurt me – today she tried to throw herself out of the window. I caught hold of & pulled her back after she had broken the glass & cut herself. She screamed & Miss Hays who had only left to wash & dress herself came again to her & she became happy & quiet. I do not fear permanent affliction of the brain for we will do all we can to give her thought new channels *thro' Miss Hays*, but of this I am quite sure, she will never be well unless she marries. All Doctors & all who know what women & men suffer from going against the imperative laws of nature agree . . . As soon as possible she must travel about with Miss Hays who solemnly assures me she will not forsake her poor child.[58]

Barbara still seems to believe Chapman's pseudo-scientific nonsense about the consequences of repressing sexual desire. Another undated letter followed, urgently requiring Ben's assistance. Barbara had certainly come to the conclusion that Bella's lung condition had been aggravated by hysteria and was no longer, in itself, the major problem. It was Bella's mental state that was now her main concern: 'Bell is worse . . . her cough is better & she is altogether better but this awful madness . . . We shall probably move soon as the place where she had an attack is the worst for her & I must not be with her or anyone of her family'.[59]

Clearly, Bella was terrified that she was dying of tuberculosis, but there seems to be a second element: that of a disappointed love affair. Barbara was emotionally drained by her own troubles and then by Bella's. She remained sad and depressed by the loss of love. Bessie, always a friend in need, wrote to her:

> Darling, everything is so sad just now; but we have got to live. Don't forget that. Sometimes I think you forget it. I can't bear to hear you speak of all of us as you do sometimes. Yes, I feel at last, as vehemently as any human being can, the cry in my nature for an engrossing love & sympathy. Nay, perhaps I feel nothing you have never felt, that to be out of harmony with the strongest affection in your nature, is to be at jar with the very universe. It gives me as an artist a terrible sense of incapacity. Nevertheless we must determine to live & do our work, come what may to our love. Then, to those who can live without it, it comes.
>
> No one does more work than you do; but your action seems pervaded by a sense that we must all come to a stop. We must not. As for me, I have a nature which sways about like a reed, I don't feel to have any bones, any firmness, any principle, any anything. Only a conviction that it won't do to give in. That if one is ill one must get better; if one cries one must smile after; if one does wrong one must accept the consequences and repent; if one is a fool one must rest on the knowledge that God is wise – that the time demands us in many ways, & if we give in, because this our youth is sad & lonely, we shall be wretched cowards.[60]

Barbara also wrote to Marian Lewes some time at the beginning of June, confiding all her troubles. Marian replied from Ilfracombe on 13 June in a delicately phrased letter: 'Dear Friend ... I wish I could drink in the sight of you among other pleasant things; and perhaps if the weather will have the goodness to clear up, you can make a little expedition [to join them] ... I shall say nothing of sorrows and renunciations, but I understand and feel what you must have had to do and bear'.[61] Barbara joined them at Tenby on 12 July and stayed with them for four days, during which she entirely revised her earlier (hearsay) opinion of George Lewes. They were the best of friends thereafter. Marian recorded in her journal: 'We enjoyed her society very much, but were deeply touched to see that three years had made her so much older and sadder. Her activity for great objects is admirable, and contact with her is a fresh inspiration to work while it is day.'[62] It was three years since Barbara had discovered the existence of her father's other family, a shock which had jarred her profoundly.

Max bravely wrote to Ben Leigh Smith expressing her conviction that Barbara was in need of care quite as much as Bella:

> You know that I am very anxious about the coming winter for dear Bar. She has quite made up her mind that Nannie must go with Belle, thinking it almost as necessary for Nannie's health, as Belle's . . . The medical men all say she cannot pass a winter in London without great risk – & they judge only from her physical condition. You and I know there are moral reasons why, this winter especially, she should not be in London, and above all, in Blandford Square . . . I feel it so important for Bar to be away from London this winter, for all reasons, that I shall not think of it, if she has to remain. But she ought not, must not remain – health & Happiness are both at stake & these must be cared for . . .[63]

This view of things must have impressed Ben, and in turn the Pater, who decided to take all three of his daughters to a better climate for the winter of 1856. Perhaps he had read the words of a certain French physician called Dr Bodichon, who, writing in 1838, had commented that 'a residence in Algeria can ameliorate and even cure consumptive patients'.[64] With high hopes of curing bad lungs and broken hearts, Ben set off with all three daughters on a trip which was to change the course of Barbara's life in particular, and Nannie's too. Barbara had said to Bessie after the fiasco with Chapman that she wanted 'to find someone worthy to take what is almost a necessity to me to give, it will be a dreadful waste of my life if I can't find anyone. You don't understand the feeling at all nor the desire for children which is a growing passion in me. Where are the men who are good? I do not see them'.[65] In Algeria, Barbara fancied that she had found one.

CHAPTER 8

Barbary

After the break-up of the Hastings home in 1853, the whole family seemed unsettled. Willie accompanied his sister Bella to Paris for the winter and considered joining Uncle Adams in Rome. The Pater had reluctantly accepted that his dream of Ben taking up his (Smith) place in Parliament was never going to happen. During the spring and summer of 1853 Ben had been keenly watching the international situation which brewed up into the Crimean War. The immediate cause of the war was a dispute between the Roman Catholic and Orthodox Churches in Palestine, then part of the crumbling Ottoman empire. The Czar claimed a right to protect the Christian subjects of the decaying Turkish empire, and used a riot in Jerusalem as the pretext for invading the Ottoman provinces of Wallachia and Moldavia. Britain was alarmed by the growth of Russian naval power based on the great naval dockyard in the Crimea, fearing that Russia could threaten not only Britain's trade in the Mediterranean, but also Britain's Near Eastern routes to India.

The Cabinet preferred to preserve peace, but dispatched the Mediterranean fleet to Besika Bay, off the Dardanelles. At the end of October 1853 the Sultan declared war on Russia, and on 30 November the Russians destroyed the Turkish fleet at Sinope. At this point British public opinion, aroused by the thundering of *The Times*, turned in favour of war. The fleet was ordered into the Black Sea in a final attempt to intimidate the Russians. When this strategy failed, war was declared on Russia on 27 March 1854.

Ben, then aged twenty-five, wandering around Europe, was strongly encouraged by Uncle Adams to join 'the grand theatre' of war, and he was picking up letters of introduction to various military personnel.[1] It seems possible that he was distracted from this aim by Mr Gratton, because, in November 1853, while waiting for a boat to take him from Marseilles to Constantinople, Uncle Jo asked Ben to reconnoitre for him in Algeria where he was considering putting some money into a mining project.[2] Uncle Jo's timely intervention may well have saved Ben's life, as

Frances Coape Smith holding
her eldest son, Ben

Barbara's paternal grandfather,
William Smith, abolitionist and Unitarian
spokesman in Parliament

Barbara's beloved Pater, Ben Smith

Ben Smith's and
Anne Longden's grave
and memorial at
St. Edmund's church,
Wootton, Isle of Wight

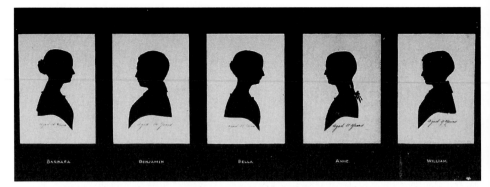

Silhouettes of the five Leigh Smith children:
Barbara aged 15, Ben aged 14, Bella aged 12, Anne aged 11, Willie aged 9

Pelham Crescent, Hastings, where the Leigh Smith children grew up

Barbara and her siblings liked to put on plays in what they called 'The Theatre Royal' at their home, 9 Pelham Crescent. Here, Barbara plays Olivia, with Bella as Maria and Ben as Malvolio in *Twelfth Night*

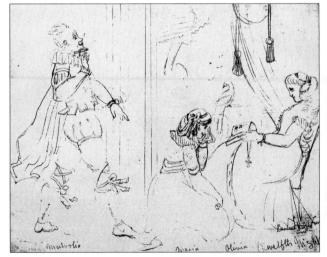

Barbara's beloved 'Aunt Ju', the favourite
of all the 'Smith' nieces and nephews

James Buchanan, Barbara's first teacher

William and Mary Howitt who were
kinder than kin to the young Leigh Smiths

Anna Brownell Jameson, art historian, who
encouraged Barbara in her artistic ambitions

Barbara's painting *Ireland – 1846* refers to the Great Hunger in Ireland which she witnessed on a visit with her father. She has written the word 'hungery' [sic] on the back

Trieste – Vienna Road (1850) painted by Barbara on her trip with Bessie Parkes to Munich to visit Anna Mary Howitt and Jane Benham (Hay)

Barbara's cartoon of Bessie Parkes with her skirts cut short and wearing Balmoral boots for ease of walking

Barbara's cartoon Ye Newe Generation shows four women – three holding artists' equipment and one a writer's notebook (surely Barbara herself, Bessie Parkes, Jane Benham and Anna Mary Howitt)

Her self-deprecating cartoon of herself 'in the Pursuit of Art, unconscious of small humanity'

Barbara's drawing of Lizzie Siddal with iris in her hair, dated 8 May 1854 at Scalands Farm. Anna Mary Howitt and Dante Gabriel Rossetti drew Lizzie on the same occasion

Vesuvius erupting, painted in May 1855 and sent to 'Mr Gratton with Barbara's love'

Barbara on her marriage tour, in New York in 1857

Barbara's picture of a Louisiana swamp was reproduced in the *Illustrated London News*, 23 October 1858

Bessie Parkes, journalist, poet and editor
of the *English Woman's Journal*

Elizabeth Blackwell, the first woman
doctor in America, whom Barbara
persuaded to come to England to open
up the medical profession for women

George Eliot, who regarded Barbara
as her 'first friend'

Jessie White (Mario), who was one of the
'Lady Volunteers' in Barbara's Portman
Hall School. Having failed to get enrolled
in medical school she later became implicated in Mazzini's unsuccessful republican
plots. She married an Italian and became
the Italian correspondent of *The Nation*.

Adelaide Procter, who was the most popular woman poet of her day and one of the principal poets of the *English Woman's Journal*. She was the dear friend of Nannie Leigh Smith's youth, although Nannie was dismayed by her conversion to Catholicism in 1851.

Florence Davenport-Hill, part of the Unitarian network, who encouraged Barbara in her work on the *Brief Summary of the Most Important Laws Concerning Women* (1854)

Jessie Boucherett, a member of the Langham Place group, especially involved with the Society for the Promotion of the Employment of Women (SPEW)

'Max' Hays, novelist, translator and co-editor of the *English Woman's Journal*. Her passionate friendships with women caused tensions within the Langham Place group.

Barbara's husband, Eugène Bodichon, was a French physician long resident in Algiers, whom few of her friends or family appreciated

Campagne du Pavillon, the house Barbara bought for herself and her husband in 1859, on Mustapha Supérieure, Algiers

Barbara's drawing of Arab draught players accompanied by an article by Bessie Parkes in the *Illustrated Times* 14 March 1857, after their first visit to Algiers

Barbara in the courtyard of her Algerian home, receiving the post from Hamet, her young Arab servant

Uncle Adams had been egging him on to join the war, as though it were something out of a *Boy's Own* adventure story.

The reality was very different. From the beginning of October 1854 *The Times*, which had supported England's entry into the war, was alerting its readers to the fact that the medical arrangements of the army were a good deal less than satisfactory. A harrowing report on 13 October denounced the horrors of the hospital at Scutari and the suffering aboard the ships at Constantinople. Describing conditions on board one ship, the *Columbo*, it said, 'the worst cases were placed on the upper deck, which in a day or two became a mass of putridity. The neglected gunshot wounds bred maggots, which crawled in every direction, infecting the food of the unhappy beings on board. The putrid animal matter caused such a stench that the officers and crew were nearly overcome.'[3] Liberal opinion in England was roused to indignation and a surge of philanthropists rushed to offer their services. Florence Nightingale was now superintendent of the Hospital for Invalid Gentlewomen in Harley Street, where one of the committee, Elizabeth Herbert, was married to the Secretary of War. Two days after the harrowing account in *The Times* had outraged public opinion Sidney Herbert asked Florence to head up a band of nurses sponsored by the government. She therefore arrived at Scutari in November 1854 with an official sanction never before granted to a woman, and her reforms of military nursing in the Crimea quickly assumed mythical proportions. The Smith extended family knew all about her successes, partly because she was an indefatigable letter writer, and also because Aunt Mai and Uncle Sam were also drawn in as her subalterns in differing ways.[4] Writing to Annie Buchanan of Aunt Patty, Barbara said:

> She is much interested in all public affairs, and reads with intense pleasure everything concerning her niece Florence Nightingale's good mission in the East. She, Florence, is the real hero of the fight. You will be glad to hear that she has been very successful in all her undertakings, and has been in good health. Uncle Adams is at Balaklava, and is, I believe, very well, but it is very long since we heard of him.[5]

As Florence never acknowledged any of the Leigh Smiths, Barbara rather awkwardly refers to her as Patty's niece, rather than 'my cousin'.

At the beginning of 1856, on a painting expedition with Anna Mary on the Isle of Wight, Barbara, restless for a new aesthetic stimulus, had written to Marian, 'I must go to some wilder country to paint – because I believe I shall paint well.'[6] Ben's letters and drawings home describing the 'savage grandeur' of Algeria had excited Barbara's interest, so long whetted by *The Arabian Nights*.[7] In October 1856 the Pater set off with his three daughters for Algiers, arriving in November. Barbara's first letter to Bessie from Algiers was full of excitement at its new and exotic scenes. On their arrival the hotels had been full and they had rented a room with mattresses on the floor:

> A sudden thought strikes us; of course we must take a bath. So away we go – Pater, Bell, Nanny and I along the covered Bazaar dimly lighted into a street where we see a white mosque dimly against blue evening, here a fountain, there a clump of red and white Arabs huddled together round the low arch door of a coffee shop. We pass some Sinbads and oh so many one eyed Calenders [members of a Mohammedan fraternity, professing poverty], more than seven. This really is an Arabian night! Now we dive into a dark arched [building] with mysterious doors leading into darker passages. Now we turn into one and suddenly we find ourselves in a real Arabian Court open to blue sky, Moorish arches, 2 tiers, white alabaster, but of course dimly lighted, a fountain in the middle with [?] and some creeping plants trained from the centre by strings to the upper gallery. This is a delicious place after all our trials by sea and land, quite enchanting! Here a crimson chair on which the Pater sinks and says that it is the most comfortable place he has seen to pass the night and there he means to stay.[8]

After this slightly disorganised beginning, the family took a house for the winter, where Bessie came to join them.

Algeria is a long strip of country bounded on the north by the Mediterranean and cut off from the south by the Sahara desert and from the Valley of the Nile by the great eastern desert Barbary, as it was called in the Middle Ages, had been invaded and re-invaded over the centuries.[9] The Romans and the Carthaginian empires had come and gone, Jews arrived after the first Diaspora, invaders from Arabia had converted the country to Islam in the seventh century, bringing with them black slaves across the Sahara. More recently the Ottoman empire had established a 'Regency of Algiers' where the Dey had levied taxes and ensured order, but his authority was limited to the city and its suburbs. The rest of the territory had been divided into three beylics: Medea, Oran (western Algeria) and Constantine (eastern Algeria).

By 1830 the indigenous population of about three million consisted of very diverse elements: Berbers, (who spoke the old Kabyle language), semi-nomadic Arab tribes, Turks, Kouloughis (the offspring of Turks and North African women), Andalusians (descendants of the Moors exiled from Spain), blacks (mainly soldiers emancipated slaves and slaves) and Jews. With the decline in piracy, economic relations had been established with the Italian states, with Spain (which had held Oran until 1794) and with France, which had obtained coral-fishing concessions at La Calle and Bone. Marseilles enjoyed a lively trade with Algiers until a squabble over payments for a shipment of grain broke out, in which the Dey believed that the French were trying to cheat him. This led rapidly to an exchange of insults, a French blockade of Algiers and French occupation. After the Dey's departure in 1830 a rapidly growing European population had poured into the former Regency. More than half the immigrants remained in the cities of Algiers and Oran. Algiers itself was a half-military and half-civilian society of speculators, hucksters and adventurers, although there were also more high-minded *colons* who aimed to promote philanthropic, Saint-Simonian and Fourierist experiments in the new French territory.[10]

Barbara's initial response was excitement: there was a certain Otherness about this landscape, which made it quite unlike any in Europe:

I have seen Swiss mountains and Lombard plains, Scotch lochs and Welsh mountains, but never anything so unearthly, so delicate, so aerial, as the long stretches of blue mountains and shining sea; the dark cypresses, relieved against a background of a thousand dainty tints, and the massive white Moorish houses gleaming out from the grey mysterious green of olive trees.[11]

While Bella rested, Barbara and Nannie went out on sketching expeditions, bringing back asphodels, bamboo, cyclamen, heliotrope and violets to paint which Barbara described as 'African flowers such as Dido might have culled to deck the banquet for the pious Aeneas'.[12] Barbara's reference is to Virgil's story of the great love of the Queen of Carthage for the Prince of Troy.[13] Barbara's letters from Africa, full of the romance of the place, so different from Ben's letters discussing Algeria's mining prospects or its attributes as a colony, show her to be ready for love. Possibly the abortive affair with Chapman, which had not been physically consummated, had awakened her desire for a sexual relationship.

On 21 November 1856 Barbara wrote to Marian, giving the first hint that she had met someone who intrigued her: 'It is ravishingly beautiful and you and Mr Lewes would be very happy here . . . No one ought to go south without a dearly beloved of some sort or other . . .' The letter continued: '. . . now for the Frenchmen. I have got into a jolly set of queer liberals, prisoners (who live like Princes), scientific men and other very interesting creatures and shall see a bit of life very interesting to me, of which more when we meet some day.'[14] The prisoners Barbara refers to were *détenus*, military personnel who were not allowed back into France because they would not swear an oath of allegiance to Napoleon III. The man to whom Barbara was becoming attracted had a politically mixed background. Eugène Bodichon had been born in 1810 at Mauves, near Nantes in Brittany. His grandfather, René Bodichon, a cordage manufacturer in Nantes, had been decorated and personally ennobled for fulfilling a large government contract. René had made the family fortune, rather as Samuel Smith had made the Smith family fortune. Eugène's father, Charles Theodore Bodichon had been an officer in the republican army, retiring in 1796. On the other side, Eugène's mother, Antoinette Le Grand de la Pommeraye, had been born in St Domingo, and came from an old Catholic family with royalist sympathies, all of whom had suffered under the Revolution, some losing their lives.[15] At this point, Eugène was at this point the last of the Bodichon line.[16]

When training as a doctor in Paris Eugène had come under the political influence of Louis Blanc and Ledru Rollin, becoming a member of the Société des Amis du Peuple, founded by Cavaignac and largely composed of law and medical students. Comte, the founder of positivist philosophy, had close connections with the Ecole de Médecine de Paris, which Eugène attended.[17] At the Ecole there was a focus on 'social pathology' or what we would now call public health issues. The emerging students were encouraged to see themselves as social leaders in a drive to improve the hygiene of the poor (in France) or of subject races in the colonies.[18] Most graduates went straight into military service, many as officers in the medical corps in Algeria. Eugène had arrived in Algiers in 1836 as an army surgeon but had also 'held an official post, analogous to that of Coroner, under the administration of the Orleans family, previous to 1848'.[19]

He was violently anti-Bonapartist, considering the very idea of hereditary emperors a betrayal of the republican principles in which he believed. In 1848 Bodichon was elected corresponding member of the Chamber of Deputies for Algeria, and in this role he appears to have been instrumental in helping to bring about the abolition of slavery in the colony. His election address expressed his 'espérances pour l'avenir [que] le genre humain ne formera plus qu'une seule famille', a sentiment which must have seemed to Barbara very similar to the core political view of her grandfather and father.[20] The 1848 upheaval had seemed briefly to offer a renewed promise of social justice, but Louis Napoleon's 1851 *coup d'état*, effectively driving an imperial coach and horses between the struggling ranks of republicans and monarchists, had reinforced all Eugène's anti-Bonapartist views. After 2 December 1852 when universal (male) suffrage conferred the title of Emperor Napoleon III on Louis, it became apparent that his claims to preserve the principles of the 1848 revolution had been a sham. 'Universal' suffrage was in fact supervised and controlled by means of official candidature. The press was subjected to a system of *cautionnements* (caution money), which had to be deposited as a guarantee of good behaviour, and also to *avertissements*, which were requests by the authorities to cease publication of certain articles and books. Censorship prevented the circulation of oppositional arguments. Eugène had written a two-volume book, *De l'Humanité*, in 1851 and 1852; the first volume historical and the second volume ethnographical.[21] Parts of it had been considered politically subversive by the Imperial police, and he was unable to get it published in France. In it he claimed that Napoleon Bonaparte, while pretending to be the heir to the revolutionary principles of liberty and equality had suppressed them. Napoleon had consolidated his power with a bogus neo-aristocracy, dependent on him and on the bribes he dispensed. In other words, he was a corrupt despot; in Bodichon's words, 'an Oriental'.[22] But the book's criticism of Napoleon I was enough to condemn it. Books could be suppressed; laws of *sureté générale* allowed the internment, exile or deportation of any suspect without trial. Public education was carefully scrutinised, the teaching of philosophy in the lycées was forbidden. It was the death of Romanticism in France.

Apart from his suppressed book, Eugène wrote articles on Algeria for the *Bulletin de la Société de Géographie de Paris* and for the *Revue de l'Orient* and had published a book called *Considérations sur l'Algérie* in 1845.[23] To Barbara, Dr Bodichon's Positivism, with its commitment to meritocracy and public health so similar to the Unitarian social stance, must have inclined her to feel that Eugène was a twin soul.

Although seventeen years older than Barbara, he was extremely striking – very tall, and what the Bretons call a 'black Celt', with fine dark eyes and an olive complexion, quite as dark as the Arab complexions around him. Inevitably *The Arabian Nights*, which Barbara so loved, cast a kind of reflected glamour on to Bodichon himself. There are certainly early hints that one of the 'queer liberals' held a special interest for her. Some cartoons accompanying Barbara's letter to Marian include 'the head of a French Philosopher here who will not wear a hat because he says the hair if cultivated to grow like fur, is the best defence against the sun'.[23] Her letter also comments that the philosopher has 'his shoes cut from one piece of leather'; clearly Eugène was somewhat eccentric in his dress, but to Barbara, who was used to the PRB, this would hardly have counted against him.

During their many conversations, Eugène explained to Barbara the ethnological model he had expounded in *Considérations sur l'Algérie*, that of a ladder of races, in which the Arabs were lower down the scale than Europeans. This intellectual framework was typical of contemporary ideas on race. The human races were ranked with reference to classical representations of beauty, in a hierarchy from lightness to darkness of skin colour. In his writings Eugène had little good to say about the Arabs. He considered that their lack of cross-breeding with other races meant that they inherited, undiluted, unpleasant traits such as thieving and raping, alongside such 'hereditary' characteristics as over-excitability and unreliability. Eugène approved of 'amalgamation', considering that if the Arab population would interbreed with more 'civilised' racial groups, they would be improved morally and physically. It was a strange sort of social Darwinism which, uncomfortable as it is to read today, was typical of most Europeans, who, with very few exceptions, saw nothing against Europeans emigrating, settling in other countries and 'developing' the natural resources. This project was imagined and justified in terms of its 'civilising' mission.[24]

The notion of regarding beauty as an index of superiority was a Saint-Simonion one; unabashedly racist, it assumed that the more beautiful the race the more advanced the civilisation, and beauty was always defined by European standards. In *Etude sur l'Algérie et l'Afrique* Bodichon had written:

> In the present state of ethnological science these principles are established: – 1st. Between two races which mix, the more beautiful reproduces its type, in preference to the more ugly. 2nd. Two ugly races who mix, produce, nevertheless, a cross finer than their father and mother. This generic law ought not to surprise us, for nature tends without ceasing to perfectionate humanity.[25]

In his chapter on the indigenous population Eugène described two 'pure' races, the Kabyles and the Arabs, a distinction common at the time but now considered nonsense. He characterised the Kabyles as more open to civilising processes because (he said) they were a sedentary tribe, interested in cultivating their land. The Kabyles, he argued, had a code of honour, honesty and integrity unique among African nations. The Arabs, whom he characterised as nomadic, were, he claimed, pillagers, thieves and rapists, with highly volatile temperaments.

One of Eugène's observations as a *colon* and *médecin* was the unusually high mortality rate among Europeans caused by malaria and diseases they had not been accustomed to. In 1851 he had written two pamphlets *Hygiene à suivre en Algérie: acclimatement des Européens* and *Hygiene à suivre en Algérie: hygiène moral* which were medically nuanced ethnography.[26] He argued that because climate had an effect on human beings, Europeans were sociable and intellectually curious, Asiatics were anti-social and credulous, Africans were violent and instinctive. Fair races had difficulty in adapting to the climate of Africa, he argued, and if they lived there for any length of time it had a debilitating effect on their intellectual and moral faculties. Nevertheless, the fair races must solve the problems of disease.

Judging by the letter to Marian, a romantic interest had sparked between Barbara and Eugène immediately. Barbara spoke appalling French, by her own admission like that of a four-year-old, and his English was equally limited, so just how much they understood of each other's ideas in their short courtship is unclear. The romance developed largely during long walks in the country. Like Barbara, Eugène's religious beliefs seem to have been informed more by Romanticism than specific dogma. In *De l'Humanité* he had written: 'Moral truth exists in God. The best way of conceiving a notion of the Divinity is to study nature . . . The naturalist will be the theologian of the future . . . The Divine word which comes without any intermediary or interpreter is the admirable wisdom visible in every work of the Creator.'[27] Barbara wrote to a friend that 'He is a man who gathers flowers daily for his own pleasure; who walks twenty miles to hear the hyenas laugh. He has for twenty-one years loved to take the same walk to see the sunset from the same place'.[28] He was also a man with an aura of 'hyper-masculinity', a superb fencer who had a cool head in dangerous moments.[29] He was physically powerful, capable of lifting up Barbara and carrying her over a river in flood, and she, after all, was a statuesque beauty, not a tiny creature by any means. Barbara, who was viewed by all her friends as a bold leader, perhaps enjoyed the unusual feeling of being protected by this strange self-contained man.

As the news started to spread among her friends that she was about to marry a foreign stranger, there was a ripple of alarm. Barbara described him to Elizabeth Whitehead as 'a native of Brittany, in fact an ancient Briton. He is forty-six, and very young for his age; has black hair and eyes, the brownest skin you ever saw, and a magnificent head. I think him the handsomest man ever created'. To another friend, she wrote that 'He is tall, grave, almost sombre in aspect, and very eccentric in dress. He never wears a hat, and has black hair as thick as a Newfoundland dog's coat. Some people think the docteur ugly and terrific.' To Jessie White she described him as 'by temperament sensitive, irritable, passionate, violent and reserved' and said that he was capable 'of entire devotion and love to one person' but that he was 'the reverse of me in all natural gifts'.[30] All this suggests that Barbara was drawn on this occasion, not to a man with the promiscuous charm of John Chapman, but to one whose attraction lay chiefly in her conviction that he would be single-minded in his devotion to her.

Anna Mary wrote to Bessie that the news 'came to me like a thunderclap . . . loving Barbara so very much as one does one cannot but feel *very* anxious . . . Where are they going to live – surely in England!'[31] Jessie was clearly alarmed by Barbara's description and asked Bessie about him; her response to Bessie's description indicates that Bessie viewed him with a colder eye than Barbara:

> Yours is the only portrait of Eugène I have had. Bar only raved about his beauty & her reverence for him & to tell the truth his being French and 46 appalled me. Yes I see from her letters that he looks down on art, but she is too intrinsically artistic to be led away. You have described him famously. I see his brain, exactly – all the little packets stowed away so tidily that if one discusses with him in the dark out he brings the right one & puffs his powder conclusions in the face of all your theories, very politely of course. Well, if he lets dear old Bar get her share of good out of life & does not hinder her being & doing all she was meant to be & to do for artists, God bless them both say I . . .[32]

It sounds as if Dr Bodichon's habit of answering any social question by reeling out lists of numerical data was wearying once the novelty had worn off.

At the end of March Bessie left Algiers to meet Anna Jameson in Rome. It was during this stay in Rome that her friendship with 'Matthew' (Matilda Hays) developed, and she no doubt spoke to her of Barbara's and Bessie's plans to run a feminist journal. Almost immediately after Bessie left, Barbara announced to her astonished family that she intended to marry Eugène. For the second time in two years, the Pater was faced with a suitor for his eldest daughter who could not have afforded him the highest satisfaction. He had made Barbara financially independent so that she would not have to marry for money, but, once again, he must have wondered whether he had not simply set her up as prey for unscrupulous and penurious men. Apart from any other consideration, he knew he would miss her acutely if she settled in Algiers. Nannie, who had envisaged an 'art sisters' life with Barbara, possibly in Rome with Hatty Hosmer's group, was utterly devastated. She stirred up Ben and Uncle Jo Gratton, who had joined the party, to make enquiries about Eugène. A letter from Barbara to Bessie in April 1857 expressed her outrage at their interference:

Dearest Bessie,
Ben and Mr Gratton, without telling me, went off and found a Frenchman who gave such an account of Dr Bodichon as to do no end of mischief. I have found out that this man has a bad moral character, and is very ill thought of in the town of Algiers.

Can you think of anything more undignified than that Ben should go to a stranger, and a person who is held in no respect, to ask questions about a man everyone respects? I told my father I know an Englishman, a respected friend of the Mohls, who has known Dr Bodichon ten years, and speaks of him most warmly.

Do tell anyone it may concern that Dr. Bodichon has a very high position in Algiers, not from a worldly point of view, but from every other. He would now be in a high worldly position, had he taken that which was offered to him many times. I am more than satisfied myself, and trouble little about the irrational conduct of those about me here.

Barbara felt that although she had always supported her brother in accomplishing his desires, the men in her family were once again ganging up against her. She was also bitter that although from her babyhood she had always tried to protect her motherless little sister, Nannie had also taken sides against her. Bella, at least, was 'being kinder and more rational about the matter'. Referring once more to the friend of the Mohls she said:

He speaks in the most decided terms of the honour, goodness, unusual morality of Dr. Bodichon, and declares him to be universally respected. Also Dr. Guepin, the chief physician at Nantes, and a well-known author, has known Dr. Bodichon twenty-seven years and spoke of him as an eminent physician and a man of incorruptible integrity.

Barbara concludes by asking Bessie to explain to Mrs Parkes that she is engaged to be married: 'Tell her everything. I don't like writing myself. I feel shy about it.'[33] Barbara's usual self-confidence seems to have taken a hammering, and there is a covert appeal for some kind of 'motherly' intervention from Mrs Parkes.

In response to this appeal, Bessie, who always rushed to Barbara's rescue, persuaded her mother to write to Dr Guepin, giving some account of the kind of person Barbara was, and requesting an honest character reference of Dr Bodichon. As Dr Bodichon's parents were dead, Dr Guepin, who had the same liberal and reforming tendencies as the Pater, was a good choice of referee. Dr Guepin's reply was as follows:

Dear Madame,

In answer to your question I will begin by saying what I consider is to Dr Bodichon's discredit. Dr Bodichon is too eccentric and too indifferent to what people think of him to be liked by those who do not know and appreciate his fine qualities. I speak of men and women in Nantes and La Vendée as well as in Algiers.

And now for his good qualities. There is in his character something knightly and something in him both of Diogenes and of Don Quixote. This admixture irritates his adversaries, and causes them to forget his fine and noble qualities.

As for his family, he belongs by birth to the small Legitimist nobility. Yet as soon as he was grown up he sought the Truth and is, I believe, a Republican. But he is a Republican according to his own manner, and is independent of the false and mean-minded Republicans who put universal safety in front of everything, and especially in front of that education which should be the indispensable right of every Frenchman. At one time he was the best fencer in Nantes, but he never used this gift in a brutal way. He would have despised doing such a thing.

Miss Barbara would, I think, find in him a suitable husband, especially in view of the fine work to which she is devoting her life. A commonplace woman would be very unhappy with the doctor, and would not know how to guide his curious nature. Bodichon is poor, but during the twenty-seven years I have known him he has always acted in an independent way, and has never attached any importance to money. I would willingly give him the advice that I often give myself, that is, to be more prudent with his tongue, his acts can look after themselves.

He has done a great educational work in Algiers, and also in La Vendée, where he worked for a while in collaboration with my father-in-law, Emile Leconte.[34]

Bessie paid highly for her support of Barbara. Ben, previously great friends with Bessie, thought that he would have been successful in preventing the marriage had not Bessie 'interfered'. Ben never really forgave Bessie, although he must have known (as Bessie knew) that 'it would be as reasonable to try and stop Niagara, when Barbara was set on a thing, and set on this she certainly was'.[35] Aunt Dolly, a great peacemaker, did her best to soothe savage breasts and renew friendships although she was not successful in this attempt and was much saddened by it. Ben would not speak to Bessie, which caused her great distress, as after the death of her own brother Priestley, she had looked on Ben as friend *and* brother. Only at Aunt Dolly's insistence did Ben send Bessie a wedding present in 1866, and after Aunt Dolly's death in 1868 Ben became even more intransigent.[36] This family drama was to be re-enacted to everyone's distress many years later, when Ben opposed a penniless suitor of his favourite niece, Amy, whilst Barbara and Bessie allied themselves on the side of love.

When it became clear to him that nothing would dissuade Barbara from giving up what she considered a binding engagement, the Pater insisted that Eugène should return to England with them at the end of May. Possibly he hoped that the romance might cool in the less exotic climate of smoky London. Eugène was not invited to stay at Blandford Square, or at Jo Gratton's house, but placed in lodgings in Paddington. Eugène found England cold in more senses than one. On 2 July 1857, the Pater, Ben and John Thornely witnessed Barbara's marriage according to the rites of English Presbyterianism at the Unitarian Chapel in Little Portland Street. Aunt Ju gave her a little rabbit (for luck) and Aunt Dolly gave her green ribbons, but the wedding seems to have been rather a subdued affair.

On her marriage certificate, under the column for profession Barbara entered 'artist', which makes clear her primary identification. She had been exhibiting paintings at the Royal Academy, the Royal Society of British Artists, the British Institution and at the Crystal Place exhibitions since 1850, to a modicum of critical acclaim. However, her paintings sold neither to a wide range of people nor for vast sums of money (at the time of her marriage the highest figure she had achieved for a single painting was thirty-five guineas). Her main source of income was still from the stocks and shares given to her by her father when she was twenty-one. In this new situation the Pater did exactly what most conventional well-to-do Victorian fathers did to protect their daughters' property on marriage: he had all her assets tied up in a trust, with Julia Smith and John Thornely appointed as trustees. The settlement specifically stated that the annual produce of her shares was for Barbara 'during her life for her separate use independently and exclusively of the said Eugène Bodichon and of his debts, control, interference and engagements'. After her death the trust would administer the annual produce for the benefit of her children, and if she had no children, her assets would go to her sisters, or if they be dead, to her sisters' children. This meant that Eugène could not hope to control his wife's money in her lifetime, nor after it, should she predecease him.[37] This was a sensible move in the light of property laws as they affected married women at the time, but the appointment of trustees meant that Barbara had less financial autonomy than she had had as a single woman of twenty-one years old. As a wedding present Ben made over Blandford Square to Barbara, so that she had a home in England.

Eugène was taken to meet various friends and relatives. On 4 August they dined with Marian and George Lewes at their house in Richmond and went on a boat trip to Twickenham. Marian wrote to give Sara Hennell their first impressions of the bridegroom a couple of weeks later:

> Dr and Mrs Bodichon came a few days after you left us. We think the *essential* is there – that he is a genuine, right-feeling man. They are wisely going to America for a year, and I hope that in time he will learn to speak English, so as to be an 'organ' better fitted to this 'medium' of English life than he is at present.[38]

Some of the Smith relatives felt able to acknowledge Barbara now that she was married; although as an illegitimate daughter she was 'nobody's child', she had gained legitimacy by becoming somebody's wife. Jo Gratton, having satisfied himself that Dr Bodichon was no fortune hunter, reverted to his usual jolly genial self and Aunt Dolly was ever kind. Certainly Eugène felt more warmly towards them than he did towards some of the more arrogant Smith relations, although perhaps this was on Barbara's account rather than his own. Writing to 'dearest Aunty and Mr Gratton' from her honeymoon, she told them:

> When we were in London [Eugène] said he would rather go to see you and Mr Gratton than any of the relations who only knew us lately . . . He says he feels the relations who were good to us as children are the only relations to be treated as relations.[39]

Eugène liked Blanche Shore Smith and her husband, the poet Arthur Hugh Clough, who had married in 1854. Arthur was an idealist, who, in the course of a long courtship had striven to convince Blanche that service must come before love. Eugène's Saint Simonian views and his habit of giving free medical treatment to the poor in Algeria would undoubtedly have impressed Clough. When he heard that the Bodichons were to make a tour of America, he gave them letters of introduction to his friends there. A letter to Charles Norton shows that Clough judged Eugène to be an estimable character from his conversation; he had not read any of his books:

> Have you seen my cousin-in-law and her husband – Dr. Bodichon? . . .
> I think he is really a superior man and he is, so far as I experienced, the least vaniteux of Frenchmen. He was a good deal distinguished in Algeria; he wrote a book about the natives but I don't know what it is . . . [40]

It is useful to note that, although Eugène undoubtedly grew more eccentric as the years passed, he was accepted by at least some of Barbara's family when they were first married.

On their honeymoon Eugène made it clear to Barbara that he could not face living in England, although it was agreed that they would spend the summer months there. Barbara then had to negotiate an existence split between two continents. In a letter to Marian she commented:

> I had such a detestable time in crossing that I said in depths of my heart not an artist's life in Algiers the gardens of Hesperides or the loving and beloved Doctor are worth this dreadful passage *no* but in two days I forgot all about that disgusting experience . . . I was very sorry to leave England when it came to the time because I felt certain I was doing some good to some people and did not feel any certainty that I should do good enough at my painting work to be worth my food and earn the intense pleasure these old mountains give me but I begin to hope and feel so well and so uncommonly jolly that I don't think I have made any profound mistake. [41]

Barbara's comment, 'I don't think I have made any profound mistake' is telling. She needed to believe that this new landscape would inspire her to achieve significant improvements in her stature as an artist. If she had made a mistake in this, she had uprooted herself and quarrelled with Ben for no good reason.

Fortunately, the new landscape was inspirational for at least ten years, although at first she experienced some difficulties in discovering and developing techniques to deal with the exchange of the bluish European light she was used to working in, for the much harsher direct sunlight of Algeria. Initially she experienced a great many technical problems with tonal values. The *Athenaeum* of 3 April 1858, for example, complained that her earliest North African pictures sometimes had a glassy or greyish look, 'the effect not of heat but cold'. She improved with practice, judging by a review the following year in the *Illustrated London News:*

> The series is a highly interesting one, the subjects being taken from the fertile, but hitherto inadequately explored, soil of Algeria. Some of the views are of considerable size, and include features of sea, mountain, and forest in admirable combination . . . Many of the works – and not in themselves the least interesting of the collection – are studies of the peculiar vegetation, flower, shrub, and tree of the place, some of which are extremely beautiful.[42]

Her solo exhibitions at Gambart's French Gallery drew generally good notices, and there she enjoyed a *succès d'estime*, if not great financial success. The *Athenaeum* of 13 April 1861, for example, commented:

> Mrs Bodichon, in Pall Mall, exhibits forty-three drawings of mark. The subjects are mainly found in Algeria, and for powerful rendering of peculiar atmospheric effect, the transcripts from them are eminently successful; they present to us a climatic character always to be found faithfully rendered in this lady's drawings. Singular as these appear, they have a truthfulness and consistency of expression which indicate their complete fidelity . . .

During her career she exhibited about 150 Algerian pictures; her 'Oriental' pictures therefore made up more than half of the work she exhibited publicly.

The exhibitions of her Algerian pictures in England meant that her home in Algeria became an obvious port of call for visiting artists. A friend of her early years, Tottie Fox, made a prolonged visit to Algiers after the death of her husband in 1863. She stayed with Barbara and spent most of her time painting out of doors with her or 'finishing' in Barbara's studio. Like Barbara herself, Tottie had exhibitions in Gambart's French Gallery and her paintings of Algiers made her reputation. While in Algiers she painted a portrait of Madame MacMahon, the wife of the French Governor of Algeria and also a portrait of Barbara in 1868.[43] A later friend, Sophia, Lady Dunbar, an accomplished watercolourist, spent a happy winter in 1866–67 in Algiers, during which time she made a lasting friendship with Barbara.[44] Sophia's first painting to be shown at the Royal Scottish Academy was a view of the Bay of Algiers. As long as Barbara had visiting artists staying with her or nearby, she was happy, but otherwise she felt artistically isolated. She made friends with François Lauret, a French painter of portraits and genre painting who had trained under Hilaire Belloc. He had come to Algiers as many did, in the hope of curing his consumption, but on his return to Toulouse he died suddenly.[45] Barbara wrote to William Allingham,

> I am so grieved – his dear little wife writes to say all his aspirations, all his love of nature; his toil; his watchings, – have brought him to nothing but quatre planches de sapin (four fir boards). If I had but known they were so down-hearted! As it seems they have been! But after all he was much happier than so many who are called fortunate – only, I am so sorry he is dead![46]

As her marriage went on, Dr Bodichon's lack of aesthetic interest created a gulf in their sympathies. Sometimes Barbara could not help wishing that he would take the same compelling interest in her work that George Lewes did in Marian's. It was not for nothing that every one of Marian's manuscripts was dedicated to her 'husband'. Marian wrote to Barbara on 4 December 1863:

> I am sorry to think of you without any artistic society to help you and to feed your faith. It is hard to believe long together that anything is worth while unless there is some eye to kindle in common with our own, some brief word uttered now and then to imply that what is infinitely precious to us is precious alike to another mind. I fancy to do without that guarantee, one must be rather insane – one must be a bad poet, or a spinner of impossible theories, or an inventor of impossible machinery. However, it is but a brief space either of time or distance that divides you from those who thoroughly share your cares and joys . . .[47]

This sense of artistic isolation was something which arose slowly rather than immediately. On her first visit to Algiers, Barbara had had her family about her, and her long-standing intellectual companion, Bessie, to work with. Bessie wrote an article called 'An Englishwoman's Notion of Algiers' for which Barbara did three illustrations, and it was published in the *Illustrated Times*.[48] Barbara was busy writing an article, which later turned into her pamphlet *Women and Work*, and they were also busy formulating plans to provide new work opportunities for women. Bessie wrote to Mary Merryweather:

> I think we shall certainly put in execution, that of establishing a shop, for books, newspapers, stationery, drawings etc. in London. I think it a

grievous pity that women of all sorts of mind should all be crowding into the arts, and that it only wants a start . . . to make setting up in business respectable & profitable. I can see openings in this way for many poor & idle girls if once they were persuaded it could be done. We should make it the place of sale for all our books & tracts, and advertise it well.[49]

This they went on to do, although by making her home in Algiers, Barbara had to rely even more on others, and this often was a wrench to her. It was also sometimes an overwhelming burden on Bessie Parkes, her faithful Ganymede. The most willing worker on the spot cannot help feeling occasionally irritated by criticisms from a (senior) partner who is on the other side of the world, out of the everyday fray. It is a great compliment to Bessie's capacity for love and loyalty that she did not end up utterly furious with Barbara during her days as editor of the *English Woman's Journal*.[50]

Once Barbara and Eugène were married money issues were serious. As a single man Eugène had lived in modest accommodation and he had treated the local poor population for nothing or next to nothing. Consequently, he was in the habit of making enough money to support himself, but no more than that. They both needed to earn if they were to set up home together in Algiers, in a sufficiently comfortable way that family and friends could stay with them. Their first joint enterprise was a hundred-page guidebook, *Algeria Considered as a Winter Residence for the English*, compiled by Barbara of excerpts from Eugène's works.[51] The first three chapters were pretty much wholly his work: the first gave an historical sketch of Algeria, the second dealt with the geography, animals, botany, agriculture and trade, the third chapter with the climate and its influence on Europeans. The section called 'Hints for Artists' with a note to the effect that while oils and paper could be purchased in Algiers, watercolour materials were best brought from England, was Nannie's. The book was published in 1858 and reviewed by the *English Woman's Journal* in March 1859. As the review commented, it was the only guidebook to the French colony then published in England.

While Barbara was away in America, Nannie went out to Algeria in January 1858 and was instrumental in bringing together her forceful sister and another woman, who was just as strong-minded. This was Emily Davies, the daughter of a Gateshead clergyman, who, having been educated at home, had then put her formidable energies into district visiting and Sunday-school teaching. Her sphere widened when her brother Llewelyn was, in 1856, appointed rector of Christ Church,

Marylebone. Once in London, Llewelyn Davies quickly became attracted to the Christian Socialist doctrines of F.D. Maurice, and consequently became involved in the Working Men's College. Through these connections he became interested in women's education, ultimately becoming principal of Queen's College. Emily had a close friend called Jane Crow, with whom she shared an intellectual friendship similar to that of Barbara and Bessie, in that the two women had formed a reading group to educate themselves, and they had tentatively begun to examine women's roles. In the late 1850s Emily's life was overshadowed by the serious illness of her elder sister and two of her brothers, all of whom died in 1858. In the spring of that year she travelled to Algiers to care for her brother Henry, who, in the last stages of consumption, was living in its warm dry climate. Before bringing Henry home to die, she met Nannie and recorded the outcome of this critical encounter in her 'Family Chronicle':

> On my return to Gateshead I went back to parish work, but tried to combine it with some effort in another direction. After making acquaintance at Algiers with Annie Leigh Smith (Madame Bodichon's sister) – the first person I had ever met who sympathised with my feeling of resentment at the subjection of women – I corresponded with her and she introduced me to others of the same circle and kept me up to what was going on. In 1858 the first organised movement on behalf of women was set on foot. The first number of the *Englishwoman's Journal* appeared in March.[52]

Emily Davies's account is interesting in more ways than one. Most noticeable is that fact that she regards the *English Woman's Journal* as the first organised movement because she, Emily Davies, was involved in it. She completely overlooks the important function of Barbara's earlier publication of *A Brief Summary of . . . Laws concerning Women* and the petitioning of Parliament which followed it, which was the real start of an organised movement on behalf of women. Emily Davies's tendency to cast herself at the centre of all feminist action ultimately had the result of underplaying Barbara's significance at key moments. The meeting with Nannie in Algiers led to meetings in London, helped by the happy coincidence that her brother Llewelyn lived near to Blandford Square. Following the death of her father in October 1861, Emily and her mother moved to London in January 1862, taking up residence in a small house at 17 Cunningham Place in St John's Wood. From then on, Emily Davies was right at the centre of the Langham Place group.

In 1859 Barbara paid £800 for a large, straggling, Moorish-looking house in twelve acres of land: at that time it stood almost alone on the eastern heights of Algiers known as Mustapha Supérieure with views of the snow-tipped peaks of the Atlas mountains on the one side and the bay on the other. Barbara wrote:

> The bay of Algiers comes into the flat land like a lip of water kissing the shore; nearer, the wavy hills, one crowned by the new Catholic Cathedral of Kuba, and others clothed with pine-woods . . . and some tracts of brown, uncultivated, rough land, beautifully rounded and modelled, with every now and then a little landslip, newly made by the rains, showing the rich red colour of the earth, and bits of bright yellow sandstone. Over this rough ground, which in three months will be a vast field of asphodel, now browse herds of long-haired goats, and brown sheep with long ears, who look like cousins of the goats, guarded by stately figures all in white, or a little boy in a goat-skin, who amuses himself with playing on a reed pipe as he sits under the great aloe, or with giving his dogs lessons in guarding the flock.[53]

The Bodichons called the house Campagne du Pavillon, the name of the house in which Eugène had grown up in Brittany. This was tactful of Barbara, because its name established it as Dr Bodichon's home in some sense, although paid for with her money. Barbara, writing to Aunt Ju, said of it: 'I doubt if you would think the house 'nice'. It is rough *very* and one has no luxuries. I am afraid of having a well appointed house. I believe I could not work if I had and I want my money for other things.'[54] The rooms had very little furniture, and to heat the house she followed the Algerian habit of burning cork scattered with a handful of wild rosemary to scent it. She did however have an English-style kitchen built and English dinners served at the early English time rather than the late French or Algerian time. Eugène built her atelier himself. The nearest building to them was a European orphanage run by Protestant nuns, which Barbara visited often, taking presents for the children.[55]

Mustapha Supérieure was the most exclusive area of Algiers, where, for instance, the Governor had his country house. Horse-drawn omnibuses went into Algiers every hour and were shared by Arabs, Moors and Europeans quite amiably. The same omnibuses brought meat, vegetables and groceries from the bazaars of Algiers out to the country houses. The arrival of post from England twice a week was eagerly awaited. Barbara wrote to William Allingham in 1862: 'I am always rejoiced when I see the *facteur* plodding up the asphodel field, and I rush down to seize the fat packet of papers, books, and letters with great delight.'[56]

Once settled in Algiers, Barbara experienced difficulties in finding enough of the intellectual companionship that she was used to in Britain, a difficulty she never fully resolved. She established a Saturday *salon* at her home which made it the centre for the overwintering English colony in Algiers, including the Briggs, the Eggs and the Cobdens. More permanent English residents included Mr and Mrs Hermann Bicknell (who lived in a nearby villa and were engaged in translating the works of Hafiz, the Persian poet), Mabel Strawford and Benjamin Woodward, architect of the Oxford Museum. Barbara had many French friends as well, although she never entirely grasped the intricacies of French grammar. Nevertheless, the liveliness of her conversation inclined them to forgive the atrocities she committed with their language. One of her French friends is reported to have said, 'How I love to hear Madame Bodichon talk! Her short-comings as to accent, grammar and idiom are all forgotten, so fresh and interesting always is what she has to say.'[57]

Although she shared historical, intellectual and political interests with Eugène, he did not share her literary and aesthetic interests. A letter to Anna Jameson on 21 April 1859, describing a trip to Sidi Ferruch, points this up:

As usual my Doctor was sent for to visit the sick; we never go out into the country but he is asked to see some one ill of fever or bad eyes. Here there are some hundreds of men, Arabs and soldiers, at work building a fort & he went off to inspect them at the commandant's request . . . Do you remember that Sycorax was born here? . . . Prospero's island may have been near here. As [Nannie and I] searched in the little caves for shell, Venus' ear and others, we thought of Ariel and many passages applicative to the sea shore & yellow sands. I think the Dr. and [the Commandant] were rather out of patience with our groping so long in the caves & could not understand that a certain Tempest gave a beauty to everything which the bright sun himself could not impart & they hurried us away . . .

Our life here is very quiet and hard working & one would have thought perfectly inoffensive to any one on earth, but it is not so! The little foolish circles of French & English talk in the most absurd manner about us & find us very offensive. Have you read Mill 'On Liberty'? It delights us. I wish all these people could read it. To a certain extent we live on his principles! . . .

Next winter I hope we shall have a better supply of English; this year they are not very refined or well instructed & I have not made a single valuable acquaintance . . . Our neighbours are curious – Nuns, Arabs, Jews, & farmers from Italy, Spain & Malta. I know everybody & receive a very mixed society every Saturday afternoon. The most interesting man to me in Algiers is a priest who was in the Crimea. I think we shall be friends; he is a German, very learned & refined & with him I have some sympathy in my art.[58]

Barbara's persistent problem was Nannie's continued dislike of her husband, of whom Nannie complained continually to Isabella Blythe, an old friend from Bedford College days. Isabella replied to one of her complaints that he was 'Godless & hopeless':

> I trust this is outward only, he is good, & has not been like the other people in Algiers. Well, there is no saying what he really is, he is a mystery. I feel him to be a man of very deep feeling Nannie, I think his is a fine Nature soured & changed to a great degree. I should have been very afraid to marry him, I don't know why, but it wd have been awful. You see Nannie how fond his wife is of him and she *must* know him if anyone does. He must have something grand about him to have gained the love of so fine a creature.[59]

Eugène liked Isabella, asking Barbara to add a postscript to a letter she was writing to Nannie to say that if Barbara were to die, he would be happy to marry Isabella instead.[60] Isabella, however, chose to spend her life with Nannie, after the death of her mother, in what was accepted by all who knew them as a romantic friendship. In 1866 Nannie bought a house for Isabella and herself next to the Bodichons', calling it Campagne Montfeld as an echo of Mountfield in Sussex.

One reason why, despite the near residence of her sister and Isabella, and the friends of the 'English colony', Barbara felt intellectually bereft on occasions was her failure to establish any friends who were not European. If her French was unreliable, her Arabic was non-existent. This ruled out any possibility of learning about the lives of Arabic women, or having any close relationships with them. Her feminist framework caused her to regard the position of women in a given society as a useful yardstick for judging its 'maturity'. By this yardstick, she regarded any Mohammedan society as more 'barbarous' than any Christian one, because in Christian theology 'Women are God's children equal with men: in Mohammedan countries this is denied'.[61] On her first visit in 1856 she had written to Marian about her horror at the system of arranged marriages:

> we went to see the women of an Arab prince . . . Fatima (or Fatma as they call it here) has a little daughter so pretty, so graceful with such power of undeveloped thought in her beautiful straight forehead, that

when I thought of her just eleven (the marriageable age) going probably to be tossed out of her home (however dreary still a home) into the power of some strange man whom she will *never* see before she becomes his property, the tears came hot into my eyes and I seized her suddenly with rather a rough grasp, and I kissed her, dear little creature! With feelings mountains above her comprehension, I renewed every vow I ever made over wretched women to do all in my short life with all my strength to help them. Believing that as water finds its level and the smallest stream from the High Reservoir mounts everywhere as high as that high water, so that freedom and justice we English women struggle for will surely run some day into their low places.[62]

Algeria Considered as a Winter Residence quoted a Lady A, who, in visiting a distinguished Moorish lady, had taken a Mrs T with her to translate.[63] Lady A said:

'Mrs T was of little use, for the Moorish ladies have very little to converse about; all the Moorish families are very much alike, the ladies always ask if you are married, how many children you have, and what your clothes cost; and when you have asked them the same questions, there is little more to be said.'

There is no question of Lady A's wondering just how sophisticated Mrs T's Arabic was. The questions and answers could, after all, have been more a function of limited linguistic expertise than anything else.

Barbara was more politically alert than most women of her class at that time; for example, she said repeatedly that the American system of slavery was far worse than anything that occurred in a Mohammedan country. But all of Barbara's impressions of Algeria (apart from aesthetic ones) were filtered through Eugène's particular lens. His (and her) vision was limited and time-bound.[64] Her feminist thinking at least prevented her from falling into an aesthetic which rendered harems 'picturesque', as many nineteenth-century European 'Orientalist' painters and writers did. Perhaps her landscapes, celebrating the beauty of Algeria, could be seen as complicit in the production of an Orientalist Other for the consumption of Western purchasers, but this was certainly not her intention.[65] Her own view of her role in Algeria was more curatorial, capturing a landscape, sometimes peopled, sometimes not, *before* it was overly Europeanised. Like William Morris she agonised about the way cheap factory-made European imports destroyed local crafts and skills, although ironically it was her father's great friend Richard Cobden and his championing of the free trade principle which had, to some extent, resulted in the destruction of indigenous crafts.

One of the women she most admired in Algiers was Madame Luce, who in 1845 had founded a school for Moorish girls, 'the first Christian woman who has made a breach in the prison life of the Eastern women'. Unlike Barbara, Mme Luce had learned 'the native language' in order 'to persuade the fathers and mothers to intrust their little girls to her care for a few hours every day, that they might be taught to read and write in French, and also to sew neatly'. The French government had established schools in Algiers for instructing boys, but they had not bothered to think about girls. By the time Mme Luce was teaching forty little girls she asked for French Algerine government backing, on the grounds that 'it was in vain to hope to rear a better, more rational and civilised race of Musselmans, so long as their wives and the mothers of the next generation were left in worse than the ignorance of the brutes'. The government of a military colony had little interest in the education of Arab girls, so Mme Luce had pawned her few valuables, and relied on private philanthropists. In this way she staggered on for two years. Mme Luce had pledged to the parents that she would not try to instil her own religion into the children. She employed an Arab schoolmistress as her assistant and it was she, not Mme Luce, who gave the girls religious instruction. In 1847 her school had been adopted by the government, and it continued its work of the advancement of female education.[66] Barbara approved uncritically of Mme Luce's efforts, but was herself primarily concerned with reforms in Britain; in Algiers she largely attended to her artistic career. For a time this pattern served her well; in England social work might well have swallowed her up altogether.

Although Barbara praised the French *colons* for opening schools, giving medical advice, including vaccinations, and helping to improve agriculture, she deeply regretted the fact that traditional skills were being lost, because of French imports. She was interested in 'the singular beauty of colour and arrangement in the old Arab work, and within the last two years so great has been the demand, that it is difficult now to pick up good specimens in any of the bazaars'.[67] Afraid lest this old craft should die out, she bought examples and copied them herself. She also liked the Kabyle water jars, which were becoming increasingly hard to find as they started to be replaced by 'hideous and cheap French earthenware'.[68] She made it her mission to send back traditional Kabyle designs to the museum at South Kensington (now the Victoria and Albert Museum), which tried to preserve the finest examples of decorative art. William Morris collected widely on behalf of the museum and he communicated with Barbara about Algerine products on more than one occasion. But, finally, Barbara viewed Algeria as *French*, and her investment in the colony as an Englishwoman was cultural rather than political. This semi-detached relationship with Algeria in the long run proved not deep-rooted enough to sustain her.

CHAPTER 9

The Honey Years

One of the earliest questions Barbara had asked herself was why, when work in the twin senses of 'industry' and 'diligence' was held in such high esteem for men, middle-class women were corralled into lives of enforced idleness? In 1848 as 'Esculapius' she had commented that:

> Women in the ordinary cant of the day, are supposed to have a *mission*. They are not the human creature itself, but attendants sent in some way to refine and elevate man. They are supposed to be a sort of abstract of the moral and abstract principle of the world, and the prominent appearance of intellect is thought to mar the impression. It is said that, to be perfect, women have no need of intellect in its ordinary sense. They may (if possible) possess an intuitive knowledge of many things, but the labour of acquirement is not necessary or ought never to be shewn. That is to say, they are supposed to be somewhat angelic in their capacities or duties.[1]

During her first visit to Algiers Barbara wrote an article called 'Women and Work' in which she developed the same question:[2]

> To think a woman is more feminine because she is frivolous, ignorant, weak, and sickly, is absurd; the larger-natured a woman is, the more decidedly feminine she will be; the stronger she is, the more strongly feminine. You do not call a lioness unfeminine, though she is different in size and strength from the domestic cat, or mouse.[3]

In essence Barbara is attempting to unlock the notion of 'femininity' from the notion of 'silliness', and create a wider, more flexible definition of all the qualities which could be incorporated within the term.

Her opening section, 'Women Want Professions', is a typically Unitarian commitment to action rather than prayer: 'By working for the salvation of this world, we may chance to achieve our own in another, but never by any other means.' Middle-class boys, she argued, were generally educated as well as possible because they were expected to go out in the world and run a business, or enter a profession or public affairs. Middle-class girls, on the other hand, were destined for marriage, and therefore generally equipped only with 'accomplishments':

> Among the rich, music, languages, drawing – 'accomplishments', in fact fill up much of life, and stop the questionings and discontents of heart. In so far as they do this they are pernicious. In so far as they are amusements only, they are killing to the soul. It is better far to hear the voice of the hungry soul loud and crying. It is better to have the bare fact of idleness, than to be busy always doing nothing. Accomplishments, which are amusements only, do more harm than good. Do not misunderstand: all 'accomplishments' may be works, serious studies; and may, by helping others to bear life better, and giving pleasure to those who have none, be made worthy work for women; but for this end they must be studied faithfully and with self-devotion.

This insistence that a young woman needed to stake a claim for 'self-devotion', that is that the young woman had to insist to her family that her studies were *significant*, was more radical than it sounds. In conventional domestic life, daughters were required always to drop their own work in order to be at the beck and call of social 'duties'. Barbara, in her unconventional home, had largely escaped this, but she knew that it was the model for most middle-class homes.

Women and Work went on to tackle the issue of how marriage and a profession could be combined for women. She quoted from Elizabeth Barrett Browning's newly published verse novel *Aurora Leigh*:

> Whoever says
> To a loyal woman, 'love and work with me',
> Will get fair answer, if the work and Love,
> Being good themselves, are good for her, the best
> She was born for.[4]

Elizabeth Barrett Browning wrote of 'love and work' and 'work and love'; implying that for women as well as men it must be recognised that work is as important as love. Barbara wrote: 'We do not mean to say work will take the place of love in life, that is impossible; does it with men? But we ardently desire that women should not make *love their profession*. Love is not the end of life. It is nothing to be sought for; it should come. If we work, love may meet us in life; if not, we have something still beyond all price.' This comment was a quotation from that eminent philosopher, Bessie Parkes, who had written trying to cheer up Barbara after the débâcle with John Chapman.[5] Barbara argued that 'Women must have work if they are to form equal unions . . . The happiest married life we can recall ever to have seen is the life of two workers, a man and a woman equal in intellectual gifts and loving hearts; the union between them being founded in their mutual work.' Here she was possibly thinking of William and Mary Howitt, but it is even more likely that she was referring to George and Marian Lewes, whom she could hardly name, as theirs was an irregular relationship.

Querying the practice of maintaining retinues of unmarried daughters in enforced idleness, Barbara pointed out that if these daughters failed to find husbands, they were doomed to be long-term financial burdens on their families. Barbara stressed the value of work for every human being regardless of gender or class, regardless also of whether a woman was married or single. A central tenet of *Women and Work* was that:

> Every human being should work; no one should owe bread to any but his or her parents . . . rational beings ask nothing from their parents save the means of gaining their own livelihood. Fathers have no right to cast the burden of the support of their daughters on other men. It lowers the dignity of women; and tends to prostitution, whether legal or in the streets. As long as fathers regard the sex of a child as a reason why it should not be taught to gain its own bread, so long must women be degraded. Adult women must not be supported by men, if they are to stand as dignified rational beings before God . . .

She recognised that wives were not necessarily leisured ladies, but were often required to have several managerial skills. Barbara insisted (as had Mary Wollstonecraft) that being a mother should be regarded as a job of work: 'Women who act as housekeepers, nurses, and instructors of their children, often do as much for the support of the household as their husbands; and it is very unfair for men to speak of supporting a wife and children when such is the case.'

The third section of the pamphlet is entitled 'Two Fallacies'. Barbara's friend and mentor, Anna Jameson, in two lectures delivered privately in 1855 and 1856, had argued that traditional feminine qualities such as caring for the young, the sick and the unfortunate should not be confined to family, dependants and friends, but should be expanded into a wider social arena.[6] They could be transferred, she suggested, from amateur visiting of the poor, towards taking part in the administration of workhouses, schools and hospitals. Barbara acknowledged her debt to Anna Jameson's thinking but took issue with the distinction she made between work done for love and work done for money:

To make all work done for money honourable, is what we strive for. To insist on work for the love of Christ only, to cry up gratuitous work, is a profound and mischievous mistake. It tends to lessen the dignity of necessary labour; as if work done for bread could not be for love of Christ too! Mrs Jameson, in her beautiful and wise Essay on the 'Communion of Labour', has we think made a great mistake in this respect, of work for love and work for money. Well-done work is what we want. All work, whether for love or money, should be well done; this is what we should insist on.

The question of payment for work was a central issue for middle-class feminists. Middle-class women occupied their time and energy in activities which came under the broad heading of 'philanthropy'. Much social work now the province of the welfare state in Britain was in the nineteenth century principally undertaken by a vast unpaid labour force of women. It was this volunteer status which maintained gentility; a middle-class woman earning a salary risked losing caste. Barbara quoted Marian Lewes's view that all work is honourable as long as it is done well; this, she wrote, was Marian's comment:

'Ill-done work seems to me the plague of human society. People are grasping after some grandiose task, something "worthy" of their powers, when the only proof of capacity they give is to do small things badly. Conscience goes to the hammering in of nails properly, and how many evils, from trying one's temper to tearing one's garment, have come from imperfect hammering.'

The second 'fallacy' which Barbara attacked was:

that ladies should not take the bread of the poor working-man or woman by selling in their market. The riches and material well-being of the country consist in the quality of stuff in the country to eat and to wear, houses to live in, books to read, rational objects of recreation and elevation, as music and pictures &c. &c. Any one who puts more of any of these things into the country, adds to its riches and happiness. The more of these things, the easier is it for all to get. Do not think of money until you see this fact. This is why we bless steam-engines; this is why we would bless women. Steam-engines did at first take the bread out of a few mouths, but how many thousands have they fed for one they have starved?

Barbara, using the rhetoric of political economy, employs a rather unfortunate Utilitarian Gradgrind tone here. Marian's friend, Charles

Bray, the Coventry ribbon manufacturer, wrote to argue the point with her.[7] Marian wrote to her other old Coventry friend, Charles Bray's sister-in-law, Sara Hennell: 'Mr Bray, I suppose is going to take the field against the "Working Woman" if I am right in my inference from the letter he wrote to Mrs Bodichon. Something will come out of the battle, whoever is right.'[8]

In her 'Concluding Remarks' Barbara praises the 'ladies of the aristocracy' (a rare case) for their sensible attitude to clothing. When they lead an active life in the country, she says, they wear 'short petticoats, thick-ribbed, brown, blue, or barred stockings, and solid Balmoral boots'.[9] She advises women who want to be actively involved in learning and working not to be prevented from useful activities by wearing ludicrous clothes which leave them open to the risk of frequent colds:

> No woman ought to be without a waterproof cloak with a hood. The best can be procured for £2, common ones for £1. Winter boots should always be made with a layer of cork between the two soles; this keeps the feet perfectly dry, and, by adding thickness to the soles, lifts the boot from the mud without adding to the weight.

She also reiterates her central argument that 'women must work both for the health of their minds and bodies. They want it often because they must eat and because they have children and others dependent on them – *for all the reasons that men want work.*'

In the second section of her pamphlet, 'Professions want Women', Barbara had named, like a roll of honour, women whose achievements and expertise had been recognised as equivalent to those of any male professional: Florence Nightingale (nursing reformer), Mary Carpenter (active in the reformatory movement), Dorothea Dix (American prison reformer), Madame Luce of Algiers (educationist), Marie Carpentier Pape (a French educational pioneer), Elizabeth Blackwell (first woman to qualify as a doctor in America) and Anna Jameson (art historian and critic). Barbara comments that she can see no reason why women should not enter the professions; she had, after all, given examples of women doing thoroughly professional work, whom (almost) all were forced to admire. She had also referred to the obstacles placed in the way of women, referring for example to Jessie White's unfulfilled desire to obtain medical training in England. Jessie had made formal application for admission to all fourteen London hospitals; eight of the letters of refusal were exhibited as evidence in the appendix to *Women and Work*. As Jessie White said herself in her letter to Barbara: 'in no single case did

I receive either a sensible or logical reply to my question, "Why may not a woman study Medicine?" . . . a little alteration of Dr Johnson's lines gives you the only reason why I was denied admission:

> "We shan't admit you, Mistress Fell –
> The reason why we cannot tell;
> But this we all know very well,
> We shan't admit you, Mistress Fell!" '

In 1859 *Women and Work* was reprinted in New York with a preface by Catherine M. Sedgwick, in which Sedgwick commented that the women in England faced more difficulties in changing society's attitude than their American sisters, because of inexorable prejudices in the older country. Her judgement seems correct. The *Saturday Review* dismissed Barbara's pamphlet in an article called 'Bloomeriana' on 19 July 1857.[10] Clearly the critic knew that the author of *Women and Work* was also the author of *A Brief Summary*, because the article refers to 'Miss Barbara – we cannot bear to speak of so poetical a philosopher as Miss Smith' with dismissive contempt. The *Review* goes on to say: 'If this is a fair example of what a lady who boasts to have made the subject her own is likely to publish, we are afraid that the sex is really not so far developed as we had hoped. As a piece of "pretty Fanny's" talk it would be charming; but we should be sorry to trust "pretty Fanny" with any business more important and intricate than the payment of a milk-bill.'

Women and Work was not so tightly organised as *A Brief Summary*, but it was dealing with a wider set of interlocking issues. Why, if women worked, should they no longer be considered ladies? Why were women allowed 'missions' but not professions? These were complicated issues. There was not, as in the case of *A Brief Summary*, an established model (such as Wharton,) on which she could build. *Women and Work* represents Barbara's grappling with an idea that we now all take for granted, that the personal *is* the political; she was creating theory on the hoof, so to speak. Her theory was not elegantly refined, certainly, and it moved rather jerkily from sociological critique to reportage of women's experience in their direct challenges to the status quo. Its advice to readers to eschew high fashion in favour of attire suitable for work, whilst eminently sensible, adds an unintended comic dimension, rather vulnerable to *Saturday Review* satire.

In terms of her own chosen profession, Barbara's major feminist campaign of 1857 was to help set up an arena where women painters could exhibit and sell their work. Major exhibiting bodies like the Royal

Academy and the Old Water Colour Society discriminated against women, either by specifically limiting their numbers, or by keeping them in marginal positions as non-members. It is fair to say that women were made more welcome in provincial art societies, but in London itself women artists encountered great difficulties. The title of Royal Academician, by the rules of the Academy, could not be conferred on those who painted *only* in watercolour. The Old Water Colour Society, established in 1804, was therefore anxious to establish its own bone fides and rigorously excluded anything which might smack of the amateur and dilettante. Presumably the society felt women were, by definition, amateur, as they were allowed very limited access to the society, either as members or exhibitors. The New Watercolour Society, founded in 1832, was equally disdainful of women artists. In 1857 Barbara joined forces with Harriet Grote, the wife of the historian and founding member of University College, London, George Grote, and her friend, Mrs Robertson Blaine, to found the Society of Female Artists (SFA) specifically to help women artists get their work exhibited.[11] The sudden increase in the number of women's paintings exhibited meant that they were inevitably of a variable standard, and some male critics took the opportunity to lament the allegedly low ability of painters. The *English Woman's Journal*, however, in an article in May 1858, praised the SFA for 'offering a new industrial opening for women', commenting that 'everything which in the present needs of society at large helps to rouse the energy, concentrate the ambition and support the social relations and professional status of working women, is a great step in advance'.

The SFA gained mixed support from women artists themselves; some who were already successfully exhibiting at the Royal Academy ignored it, and some sent their large historical works to the Royal Academy and smaller works to the SFA.[12] Sympathetic male critics understood the strategy of women exhibiting by themselves, as otherwise 'they would too likely be crowded out of other exhibitions, or so inconspicuously placed that the important fact of the effort that a certain number of women are making to establish in art would sink out of public observation'; nevertheless, the danger of this strategy was that women 'can paint very indifferently indeed, and yet still keep head above water according to the level of the separate Female Exhibition'.[13] An impression was formed in the minds of the public that the SFA might be a good place to pick up cheap pictures, as it was assumed that any woman who had achieved celebrity would of course exhibit at a more prestigious site – a site which would command more money for works sold there. This was probably true; pictures from the SFA in 1868, for example, sold for between two and fifty guineas (whereas at the top of the market in the same year, an oil by Landseer sold for £4,200). Nevertheless, with so many things working against them, an encouraging environment where women could exhibit, and, with luck, sell their paintings was important.

A few weeks after her marriage in July 1857 Barbara and Eugène set out on a trip to America, which, as in all her travels, included a hectic programme of looking at fresh landscapes and painting them, as well as surveying the social/political scene and writing about it. Aunt Julia gave her a black bag with a metal frame in which to carry watercolour paints and brushes. She wrote many letters home to her father, her sisters and to Aunt Dolly and Mr Gratton; some of the letters were private, but some were written in the form of a journal with a view to publication. She did not succeed in this, although many of her observations appeared subsequently in the form of journal articles.

Barbara and her new husband travelled from south to north, often by boat on the great American rivers, learning about the country and its people but also learning to live together. The extant letters start in December 1857 from a southern steamboat travelling along the Mississippi River. Eugène, at forty-six, was sometimes taken for her father. Barbara aged thirty was, if not such a beauty as her sister Bella, nevertheless very striking and attracted a lot of attention from both men and women: 'I happened to have on my green silk shirt, green net on my hair Ellen A[llen] gave me, and to be writing with a green feather pen. This accidental picturesqueness was commented on in the drollest manner!'[14] A letter to Pater dated 7–11 December 1857, describing the company on board ship, included an account of a General Haskell whose unwelcome attentions to her led Eugène to threaten him with physical violence if he pestered her further.[15]

As well as receiving unwelcome attentions from Southern men, Barbara found herself in political contention with the pro-slavery Southerners on board ship. Barbara was well-informed and able to hold her own in any discussions. Her diary entry for Friday, 11 December reads:

Last night I sat finishing up my sketches at the public table. Company: the pretty little Mrs H. and her fair Scotch-looking husband, Mr C. the intellectual-looking Californian gentleman and Mrs B. who has a very beautiful expression and is the most refined woman on the boat. Mr C. is reading a paper and read out loud the announcement of the marriage of a mulatto and a white girl; it excites from all expressions of the utmost disgust and horror. I say, 'It is very uncommon?' Mr C. 'Yes! thank God. Only permitted in Massachusetts and a few states.' 'There seems to be nothing disgusting in it. My brothers went to school with a mulatto and I with a mulatto girl, and I have seen mulattoes in England who were not unlikely to marry with white.' *All*: 'At school! At school with niggers! 'Yes.' *All*: 'Horrid idea, how could you?' *BLS*: 'Why, your little children all feel it possible to come in close contact with negroes, and they seem to like it; there is no natural antipathy.' *Some*: 'Yes, there is an inborn disgust *which prevents amalgamation*.' (Mark this: only one-half the negroes in the United States are full-blooded Africans – the rest [the] produce of white men and black women.) *Some:* 'No it is only the effect of education.' *Mr C*: 'There is no school or college in the U.S. where negroes could be educated with whites.' *BLS:* 'You are wrong, Sir. At Oberlin men women and negroes are educated together.' *Mrs B*: 'Yes, I know that, because Lucy Stone was educated there with people of colour.' *Mr C*: 'Lucy Stone – she is a Woman's Rights woman, and an atheist.'[16]

Barbara was well-informed on this point because Elizabeth Blackwell's brother Henry had, in 1855, married Lucy Stone, after he had promised to support her campaign for women's rights. Oberlin had been the first college in the US to admit African-Americans, in 1835, and the first to award degrees to women, in 1844. It produced many influential female teachers, including many talented African-American ones.[17] The connection between anti-slavery campaigns and women's rights campaigns had been established at least as far back as the 1830s, but the accusation of 'atheism' was perverse, as many of the campaigners were Quakers and Unitarians. However, the slave owners in the South regarded themselves as very religious people, using Bible texts selectively to justify slave owning, such as the claim that slavery began with Abraham or that God's curse on Noah's son Ham, who was ugly and dark skinned, implied that 'blackness' was a punishment for sin. Barbara's eloquent arguments failed to move her Southern listeners; even Mrs B, whom she had believed to be the most sympathetic, had shocked Barbara by expressing her violent hatred of Harrriet Beecher Stowe, whose novel *Uncle Tom's Cabin* (1852) had revealed only too clearly that the skeleton in the South's closet was precisely that the black family and the white family were so often the *same* family. Barbara went on to say:

> I do not know how other people feel, but I cannot come amongst these people without the perception that every standard of right and wrong is lost, – that they are perverted and degraded by this one falsehood. To live in the belief of a vital falsehood poisons all the springs of life. I feel in England how incapable men and women are of judging rightly on any point when they hold false opinions concerning the rights of one half of the human race . . . To hold false ideas on these great questions

which are woven in with every-day life perverts, embitters, poisons the soul more than to hold the most monstrously absurd doctrines of religious faith . . . To believe in transubstantiation or the divinity of the Virgin is not so perverting to the mind as to believe that women have no rights to full development of all their faculties and exercise of all their powers, to believe that men have rights over women, and as fathers to exercise those pretended rights over daughters, as husbands exercising those rights over wives. Every day men acting on this false belief destroy their own moral nature, so injure their consciences that they lose the power to perceive the highest and purest attributes of God. Slavery is a greater injustice, but it is allied to the injustice to women so closely that I cannot see one without thinking of the other and feeling how soon slavery would be destroyed if right opinions were entertained upon the other question.[18]

Throughout the trip Barbara sketched what she could see from the boat in order to 'finish' the best ones in a studio later. Whenever the steamer stopped to take on board wood for burning, Barbara and Eugène went walking. In December she noted a walk

in a wood where all the trees were covered with the grey Spanish moss (not a moss, by the bye, but a parasite, with flower and a pod like a vetch). The effect was strange and beautiful. I enjoyed it more than anything I have seen in America. There are subjects for thousands of pictures. Why should artists born here paint everlasting campagnas, domes and towers? Why, – their forests are a new revelation of nature's beauty. God must have been in an Edgar Poe frame of mind when he thought of throwing this weird grey drapery over their forests. I am bewitched with this new phase of beauty. I never imagined anything like it. Old trees leaning on young trees, the dead prostrate; haughty trees springing straight up to heaven and then spreading out into a fir-like tower – boughs all of them, covered with this grey garment hanging down straight. Some look like Dante Rossetti's figures – clothes and souls and – nothing more. Sometimes the trees look covered with grey icicles – always beautiful and fantastic, sometimes sublime. How grateful we should be if American artists would send us over some of this curious swamp.[19]

This last comment is reminiscent of Barbara's remarks that the artists who flocked to Rome seemed to her to have their vision damaged by the experience; they lost their ability to see what was in front of them and became infected by 'classical' landscapes. In this she is echoing, in her own terms, Ruskin's views in volume three of *Modern Painters*.[20] In the

South Barbara felt that 'there is very little knowledge of art in America, very little love of any art, but scarcely any for landscape art or small treasures like old Hunts. Some people like my drawings because they see they are like their woods but only one person has *enjoyed* them . . . and that was a poor Italian image boy who came two or three times and looked at me painting for a long time through the window and enjoyed the colours, he said.'[21]

Arriving at New Orleans towards the end of December, they decided to take two rooms in a boarding house and stay for a month so that Barbara could settle down to her painting. This could be regarded as their first 'home'. One room is referred to as Barbara's bedroom, and the other as the Doctor's where 'we keep wood and all sorts of things'. The rooms were large, with 'five windows and a door into the veranda – so that we do everything in them with windows open (cooking etc.). Doctor cooks little things beautifully. This is a better way of life than hotel life for us and does not cost quite half as much'.[22] It is clear from these details that the Bodichons were breaking the conventional division of labour. Eugène respected the fact that Barbara's painting is 'hard head work and hard hand work too, and I can be at it all day long except when I take walks for exercise'. Eugène largely took charge of the housekeeping and shopping, and at least some of the cooking. In a letter to Joseph Gratton she said, 'if you were here I would give you a very curious birthday dinner: queer fish, gumbo soup, roast grey squirrel, boiled wild cat, omelette of alligators eggs, & fried bananas &c. &c.' Barbara clearly finds her husband entirely satisfactory; a note to Aunt Dolly assures her that she 'need not be afraid of the Doctor not taking care of me – he takes the same care of me as Miss Hays used to do at Roughwood & you said I should not find a husband who would do so. He is something like her in his ways [though] not so elegant'.[23] The reference to their two rooms as 'Barbara's' and 'the Doctor's' might well imply that the Doctor shared her bed by invitation, but not as a right, which would undoubtedly fit in with the kind of conversations she had with Elizabeth Blackwell where Elizabeth suggested that sexual relations should be organised according to women's wishes, rather than according to men's demands. Barbara's words of assurance to Aunt Dolly might be a coded message referring to the fact that he puts his wife's comfort first, in *all* things.

Barbara painted happily outdoors in the 'forests of oaks draped with the grey moss (a specimen I enclose in this letter) haunted with alligators – these are my subjects. Quite strange – wild, original enough to suit the devil in me'.[24] At her request Eugène brought a young alligator into their rooms for her to draw:

That awful young fiend of an alligator made me so nervous that I fear I shall not bring you the fearful picture I intended. He was tied down for me to draw and I sat studying him – he looking down at me with the vilest demon eyes – and I was thinking [of] the Doctor's ideas that the spirits of animals rose gradually into higher and higher forms until they made the spirit stuff of men. I was thinking what a bad man this devil would make, when suddenly the Doctor went near and the Demon darted up to bite him, tumbled over on his back and bit his own tail and screamed like a child.[25]

Presumably, that particular day Eugène stayed at home to make sure that Barbara was safe with the alligator, but usually, when she was painting, he went off on prodigious walks: 'You never saw anyone walk as the Doctor does 20 or 30 miles all over the country. I am a good walker and think nothing of 8, 9, 10 miles but I can't go the long excursions he does – he walks 6 hours without resting.'[26] Often he would bring Barbara things he thought she might want to draw, such as a branch of the cotton plant.

On 26 December the Bodichons went together to a slave auction room where twenty slaves had just been sold and quizzed the auctioneer, who told them a pack of lies about husbands and wives not being separated, or children not being taken from their parents. Their 'Yankee landlady', however, made no such pretences:

She is no humbug. She says slavery is a good institution, marriage of slaves absurd, and wrong to teach them to read and write. She says as soon as they know how to read they will rise and kill their masters. She says, 'What's to prevent them when they get intelligent!' She has owned slaves – is very sorry she sold one (a woman) because she had children very fast. 'I can't think how I could be so stupid as to sell her – I should have made a great deal – but my husband had died and I wanted money directly, so I sold them all.'[27]

The white Americans in their part of New Orleans (not a fashionable area) were in the main originally from England, Ireland, France, Germany and Spain. Barbara was particularly struck by the fact that this was a society where class did not determine the outcome of one's life, and that the government exemplified the kind of social contract Locke had envisaged. In 1858 in the Union there was universal white male suffrage, with no property qualifications (albeit some literacy tests):

it is exceedingly difficult to compare classes. This is really a free country in the respect of having no privileged class – excepting the class of white over black. White men are free in America and no mistake! My wonder is great at the marvellous manner in which the country governs itself. I find myself saying continually, 'This is a free country.' One is so little used to freedom, real freedom, even in England that it takes time to understand freedom, to realise it. Nothing sent from upper powers to be worshipped or humbly listened to, no parsons sent by a class of born rulers to preach and lecture to another class born to submit and pay. No race of men with honours they have not earned and power over others which the others have not consented them. Heavens what a difference! Here all who hold power are heaved up by the people, of the people. Until I came to America I hardly felt the strange want of rational liberty in England. How came Franklin and Washington to dare to try this huge experiment? Why, because they saw it was *right* and because they saw New England governing herself so gallantly.

I believe one reason why Americans look so careworn is because they all feel so intensely the responsibility of governing the country. What an incredible amount of humbug there is in England never struck me before. They talk Christianity – all men equal before God – but it is only in the Free States of America that the idea of Christ's about equality is beginning to be understood.

I find Germans are very proud to be Americans and when you say, 'You are German?' they answer in broken English, 'I am an American.' So with the French people. This comes of their right to vote. It makes them feel at home, gives them an importance which they probably never had before, makes them respect themselves, gives them a standing which creates a new motive for self-improvement. The effect of right to vote on the people makes me think much of the effect of the right to vote on women – it will do them immense good; just the good it does these poor Germans, used to paternal governments and feudal institutions. American women will not be worth much until they get this right.[28]

This may seem a bit hard on the American women, but at this stage of the tour she had only met a limited range of women. Barbara found the extremely flirtatious behaviour of the women at the lodging house, and their obsession with fashionable dresses and pretty parasols, ridiculous. On their side, the Southern belles found Barbara's outdoor painting attire of a large drawing hat (instead of parasol, in order to leave her hands free), blue spectacles and Balmoral boots, 'monstrous'. 'I never saw such utter astonishment as is depicted on the faces of the populace when I return from a sketching excursion. I do not like to come back alone so the Dr. always comes for me.' Even her more respectable outfits were found sadly wanting by the women in the lodging house, who tried to lend her 'flower garden bonnets if I would but go out in them . . . My little plain bonnet and plaid ribbon is despised, all my wardrobe considered shabby and triste'.[29]

Eugène seemed to fare rather better with the men he met, but they were fellow professionals. The *Picayune* newspaper carried a daily summary of 'Arrivals at the Principal Hotels Yesterday' and he was delighted to see that some friends of his from Algiers had arrived, two brothers, both of whom were doctors, and also some apothecary friends. They advised him to stay in America for a year, because he could earn a great deal of money in New Orleans and then take it back to Algiers. Barbara was not interested in this proposal however; the pull of 'that lovely country' (Algeria) was too strong. Eugène also met Dr Nott, an old acquaintance now lecturing at the University of Louisiana, who called out to him in the street, 'I was speaking of you in a lecture the other day and here you are!' Dr Nott, 'having read [Eugène's papers] on races and the necessity of mixture of races!', had sent copies of his own books to Algiers.[30] The Bodichons went to the City Hall one evening to hear him lecture 'On the Immutability of Human Types':

> Dr Nott proved that races were distinct by referring to Egyptian tombs and showing the drawings of negro, arab, jew, asiatic, mongol, etc. and went on to say that climate and education could not alter races, and ended by saying he hoped that certain plans of certain philanthropists to alter certain races were absurd: that as long as negro was negro they would be inferior to white ('Hear! Hear!') and must hold their present position ('Hear! Hear!) . . . How I did burn to ask a few questions. Is it not true races have been mixing ever since Pharoah's time? How many pure negroes have you here like that type you show us? Do you apply this argument of slavery you build up from the African pure to all – even those who are more white than black?[31]

Clearly, the Bodichons regarded discretion as the better part of valour in this public space, but Eugène had already had a private interview with Dr Nott in which he had tried, but utterly failed to convince him to look at things in a different way. Barbara commented in her journal on 12 January that she thought it unlikely that the two men would agree:

> The Doctor's ideas of Universal Fusion and Universal Brotherhood to spring from it are not popular here at all, though they can't deny the mulatto race here beats the white in health, strength and beauty, and all the men admire the women with some African blood in them more

than they do the whites. And I do not wonder, – the whites here are wretched looking objects, yellow and pale, the quadroons magnificent women, the mulattoes very often beautifully formed and faces of a sort of Memnon cast, very pleasing, the children of mixed unions exquisite little creatures, the white children little miseries.[32]

By 13 February, having finished her paintings and packed up her easel, Barbara visited a slave auction in a dirty hall 'big enough to hold a thousand people':

There were three sales going on at the same time, and the room was crowded with rough-looking men, smoking and spitting, bad-looking set – a melee of all nations. I pitied the slaves, for these were the slave buyers . . . A girl with two little children was on the block: 'Likely girl, Amy and her two children, good cook, healthy girl, Amy – what! only seven hundred dollars for the three? that is giving 'em away! 720! 730! 735! – 740! why, gentlemen, they are worth a thousand dollars – healthy family, good washer, house servant etc. $750!' . . . Then a girl with a little baby got up and the same sort of harangue went on until eight hundred dollars, I think was bid and a blackguard-looking gentleman came up, opened her mouth, examined her teeth, felt her all over and said she was a dear or something to that effect . . . I came away very sick from the noise and the sickening moral and physical atmosphere.[33]

Barbara's sense of repulsion was reflected in one of her published pieces from the American trip in which she described how (to her eye) the Mississippi landscape seemed to mirror the moral landscape:

Here, in this swampy, slimy Louisiana, there is ugly dreariness, ugly wildness, ugly quaintness, and the country often struck me as absolutely ugly, and with its alligators basking in the rivers, as almost revolting, somewhat as if it were a country in a geological period not prepared for man's appearance . . . The state of society was not more pleasant to contemplate than the natural scenery; the moral atmosphere was as offensive as the swamp miasma. [34]

They left New Orleans in the middle of February and set sail on a 'good iron steamer', the *Virginia*. Disembarking at Montgomery they travelled by train, where Dr Bodichon was mistaken for General Commonfort, the ex-President of Mexico. The rumour followed them to Columbus where, despite Barbara's constant denials, the story persisted. Barbara was travelling in a 'little brown waterproof jacket and pockets, black silk shirt, very short leather boots'. To avoid this nonsense Dr Bodichon 'rolled himself up in a white burnous so that nothing was visible but an Arab-like hump . . . All day long this shadow of greatness haunted us, and even at night it was not laid though the Doctor wrote his name in full in the book'.[35]

At Savannah Barbara painted out of doors although 'rather afraid of snakes in these woods but my doctor goes first and beats the woods with his stick'. Writing to the Pater on 3 March she said: 'I will write you very particular accounts of all those places you have seen so that you may see them again.'[36] She assured the Pater that things were going well for them:

> We have had here such delightful walks (the Doctor and I) and have seen such beautiful creatures – birds of all sorts: creepers, perchers, waders, divers. Nothing so lovely as the bluebird. One day we saw fifty of them with their azure backs and wings flying, glancing in the sunlight or picking up seeds. The Doctor is perfectly happy watching birds. I never saw any one with such a love of animals. He is just the creature to ramble with and never minds any trials of temper the incidents of travel or BLSB expose him to.[37]

They arrived in Washington in March; Barbara was there with her husband, just as her mother had been with her father. Bar wrote to Aunt Dolly and Mr Gratton, 'I think of myself & my father & mother here two years – it is a curious life.'[38] She wrote to 'dearest Pater' on 18 April saying:

> Yesterday as we rattled along in the rail, about two o'clock we came to a ploughed field, nothing particular to look at, and in it was standing a stick and (nothing particular to look at) on this stick was a white flag. That was Mason and Dixon's line that was the boundary between the Slave States and the Free between Delaware and Pennsylvania – and though the air did not change or the land look happier as we passed and came on this side, I can tell you my feelings changed so much that it seemed to me that everything was better, brighter, truer, at once.[39]

They next went to visit Lucretia and Thomas Mott at their small farm eight miles out of Philadelphia. They were greeted in Quaker fashion as 'Friend Barbara' and 'Friend Bodichon' and affectionate enquiries were made about Elizabeth Reid, Aunt Ju and Lady Byron, all of whom Lucretia remembered from her visit to London in 1840. Barbara described Lucretia's response to her account of the British women's movement:

She seemed absolutely to chuckle with glee to hear that we hold all that she and 'the Friends' advocated and only wait to claim the suffrage because it would be useless to try for it now ... Lucretia Mott showed me a mass of Women's Right literature and I made my pick for the benefit of B.R.P. and M.H. And she showed me her books of notes for lectures with extracts and little quotations so nicely put together, and as we looked them over she gave me little accounts of the occasions on which they had been used. She says all the Women's Rights conventions had been quiet, orderly and dignified and that the rumours of their vulgarity are absolutely unfounded.[40]

The Bodichons liked all the people they met at the Raritan Bay Union.[41] Each family had a private suite but there was a sharing of work and sharing of communal services – washing, baking, storage, agriculture and education – 'where the advantages of co-operation may be secured and the evils of competition avoided'.[42] Theodore D. Weld, his wife Angelina Grimké Weld, and her sister Sarah Grimké ran Eaglewood School there, which was committed to progressive co-education. Barbara wrote to 'Pater and all' reporting on their positive impressions of the school:

We are both quite convinced that the system is answering perfectly well both for boys and for girls, little and grown (for some of them are eighteen and nineteen years old). I never saw such a satisfactory group of young people in my life. Mr. Weld is working out every day his principles of equal advantages for black and white or male and female ... The children are quite different from all other American children I have seen. They are full of fun and spirits, strong and healthy. I wish you could see Annie Tallmann, a beautiful girl of eighteen. She has short curls, rose cheeks, bright hazel eyes, and the expression of a young Hebe. She is tall and slight and a real young athlete. She jumps three feet four inches like a deer and walks along a ladder hung only by her hands like an acrobat! All the girls practice gymnastics ... A granddaughter of Lucretia Mott is also a fine production of the school. She is a student and one of the most sensible girls I ever met in my life. Some of these girls will be heard of in the world, I am convinced.[43]

They stayed a week in the community, where Eugène (true to the ethos of the place) earned their keep by giving French lessons and fencing lessons.

On 20 May the Bodichons met Elizabeth Blackwell and her adopted daughter, Kitty Barry, for a trip to Niagara. Barbara once more pressed Elizabeth to come over to England to help open up the medical profession to women there. Describing the effect of the Falls, Barbara wrote to Bella:

My dearest Belos . . . Over on the Canada side we dressed up in oilskin and went down behind the fall 'within the veil' only there does one at all feel the awful power of this fall of water. It is very grand, but the noise is so deafening that a few minutes is as much as we could stand . . . We saw two beautiful wolves yesterday taken near here. My Doctor looked at them with profound affection.[44]

They went up to Montreal, which the Pater had told her was the most beautiful part of America. Barbara found she could not understand the French that Canadians spoke, but 'Doctor says it is old French and he can understand them very well'.[45] They found that the Negroes were 'doing well in the money sense, but as yet they have not taken an equal place with the whites and are not equally respected'.[46] Barbara told Pater that Eugène considered that the 'moral level' was higher in Canada than in the United States.[47] In Quebec:

the Doctor finds friends everywhere . . . He made friends with all sorts, from the Governor down to the cooks (newly imported immigrants). Until you travel in America you can have no idea of the extent of the tyranny in Europe. There are hundreds of Frenchmen, thousands I may say, who have left France, though not transported, because they could not bear the suspicions and petty vexations their opinions against Louis Napoleon expose them to. To live in constant fear of being arrested is too terrible to be endured, and we have many who have come here to breathe freely. My heart is ready to burst with indignation when I see how many good, clever men in mid-life have had their whole prospect blighted by this tyrant. The Frenchman does not easily transplant himself and suffers always from homesickness *pour la belle France* . . .[48]

Barbara here is implying that her Doctor is just such a good, clever man, whose status in the world might have been quite different, but for 'political' misfortune. She continually took care in letters home to show that his work on race was recognised and appreciated by liberal intellectuals.

On 1 June the Bodichons arrived in Boston where Barbara had a letter of introduction to Sara Ann Clarke, active in anti-slavery and women's right's campaigns, who was also a landscape painter. Barbara found her 'in pretty rooms in the French style in a large hotel and her studio on the highest floor, five stories up'.[49] She found lodgings for them and offered Barbara the use of her studio while in Boston. On 2 June Barbara went to the American Exhibition of British Painting which had arrived in Boston, having already toured Philadelphia and New York in 1857–8. It contained eight of her Welsh landscapes, including *Thunder Storm near Festiniog, N. Wales* and *Mountains in N. Wales*, as well as *Thunder Shower* and several Sussex paintings, such as *Sunset over Corn and Willow Land* and *The Cornfield*. She was delighted to see 'sold' stickers on two of her pictures. Marcus Spring had bought *The Cornfield* and Margaret Foley had bought *Thunder Storm near Festiniog, N. Wales*. On arrival in Boston Barbara had been invited to a soirée organised by the lady artists of Boston in her honour. There she had met Margaret Foley, a woman the same age as herself, who made a living as a cameo cutter. This encounter had a significant impact on Margaret's life. Barbara advised her to go to Rome if she possibly could to join the group of neo-classical sculptors in the Hatty Hosmer 'group'. It took Margaret until 1860 to save up the money to settle in Rome, but there she met William, Mary and Meggie Howitt. Margaret and Meggie became devoted companions, similar to Isabella Blythe and Nannie Leigh Smith. When Margaret Foley died in 1877, she left Barbara's *Festiniog* to Meggie Howitt. This painting seemed to circulate like an emblem of female ambition and female friendship.[50]

Sara Clarke introduced Barbara to William James Stillman (1828–1901), a friend of Ruskin's, who had founded *The Crayon: an American Journal of Art* in 1855. William Rossetti contributed a column called 'Art News fom England' and in August 1856 the *Crayon* had published Rossetti's report about the exhibition of paintings at Crystal Palace in May, in which he singled out for praise a coast scene by 'Miss Barbara Smith being full of real Pre-Raphaelitism, that is to say, full of character and naturalism in the detail, as well as multiplicity of it'.[51] William Rossetti had sent Stillman some notes in advance on the British artists whose paintings would be shown in the travelling exhibition. In the 'Watercolours' section Rossetti had put 'Mrs Bodichon late Miss Barbara Smith and amateur (I think) of great power'.[52] His comment indicates an uncertainty about Barbara's professional status. She had not, like Anna Mary for example, trained at Sass's, and then worked in a great master's atelier. Her status as a professional artist was probably not securely established until Gambart offered her a solo exhibition in the French Gallery in 1859.

One of the highlights of the Boston stay was going to hear Theodore Parker preach at the Music Hall. He was a militant abolitionist, having once advocated the rescue of a fugitive slave by an attack on a courthouse, and was equally strong on women's rights:

He has a beautiful voice and when he began a noble thanksgiving for the beauties of this wonderful world he spoke like a poet and like a painter, describing the opening summer more like Ruskin than anyone else. He had a glass of wild flowers which he clutched and used as an illustration. He prayed to the Creator, the Infinite Mother of us all (always using Mother instead of Father in this prayer). It was the prayer of all I ever heard in my life which was the truest to my individual soul.[53]

The Bodichons also went to Concorde to see Emerson, who talked to 'Dr. about French political writers, natural history, Africa, Paris, America'. Barbara was slightly disappointed that he did not say anything characteristically Emersonian, but she agreed with Sara Clarke that he looked 'tender and just'.

Their trip came to an end in June. It had been extremely successful in many ways. Firstly the Bodichons had established a way of living together which had respected Barbara's career as a painter. Barbara, as usual, had met many people, looked at many different schools, and thought about political systems. As well as painting, her diary was a distillation of her experiences in America. Although she had hoped to publish her 'American Letters' as a book, she did not succeed in this, but the letters were subsequently transformed into articles for the *English Woman's Journal*. Apart from an article about the Cincinnati school system, in which she observed that co-education and mixed social classes offered the best possibility of upward mobility, most of her articles were about slavery.[54] The October 1858 edition of the *English Woman's Journal* published Barbara's article entitled 'Slavery in America', in which she contrasted the dignity of the people of the free states with the slave states, where she looked in vain for the virtues of republicanism.[55] She pointed out that in the free states 'all is in a state of change, every one hopes to advance, to obtain more power, more scope, more dollars. In the slave states, on the other hand, there is an appearance of poverty; all tells of neglect, and men look listless, and satisfied to let things be'.[56] In the slave states of the Union are, she wrote, '3,700,000 human beings who have no legal rights, no legal right to their labour, and who can be sold from hand to hand like horses or dogs'.[57] Further, she considered that Mrs Stowe had made no exaggeration in *Uncle Tom* in terms of atrocities committed by masters on slaves. In another article, 'Slavery in the South', Barbara denounced the hypocrisy of the cotton planters who, in drawing-room conversations, spoke of their slaves 'as the patriarchs might have spoken of their families, but it is not so; they do not consider their feelings except in rare instances'.[58] 'Slaves married to one another were split up; children of slaves sold to other farms; in cases where masters had used female slaves sexually, the masters sold their own half-caste children.' That there was no absolute standard of 'whiteness' and 'blackness' had been obvious to Barbara; she had noted that many of the 'black' woman in New Orleans were actually paler skinned than her erstwhile governess, Catherine Spooner, and Dr Bodichon himself was often taken for a man of colour in America.

The connection between the condition of slaves and the condition of women was further developed in Barbara's article 'Of those who are the property of others, and of the great power that holds them' in the *English Woman's Journal* of February 1863. Barbara pointed out that there could only be one logical excuse for slavery, and that was if it could be proved that the Negro race were not human beings

> but a kind of monkey race made to wait on men. But facts are too strong, and the Southern upholders of slavery have never attempted to prove that; what they do say is, that the negroes are inferior and cannot govern themselves ... As regards the alleged inferiority, I am convinced that the negro is superior in some qualities, and how far inferior in others cannot be asserted until he and the white man are placed in exactly the same position.[59]

Racist theories and practices were often grounded in part on observable and 'inescapable' physical differences.[60] Barbara had been so much in the habit of refuting arguments about women's 'natural' inferiority that she had no difficulty in rejecting similar arguments deployed as justification for the treatment of people of colour.

Barbara noted that it was illegal to educate slaves above a certain (low) level, which accounted for any so-called inferiority. As there was a 'literacy test' rather than a property test applied to potential voters, the laws were quite deliberately discriminatory. Anyone who attempted to educate slaves faced the rigours of those laws. Barbara made the link between the lack of commitment to girls' education in England, as part of a system of social control, and the concern not to 'over-educate' black slaves in America. She reported the case of 'a poor old Englishman who had sixty slave scholars [who] was sent to prison for eleven months and died from the effects of imprisonment'.[61] Barbara reproduced a conversation she had with some white Southern women, who were discussing whether or not it was a good idea to teach slave children to read the Bible. A Mrs B thought it was self-evident that slaves should not be taught to read as 'you will find that all negroes who run away are those who have learnt how to read'.[62] Even the Bible held potential dangers as a subversive text. Barbara noted that a black preacher used the story of the Woman of Samaria for his text, which included 'a good description of the difference between Jews and Samaritans . . . and I remarked, as I often have before, that the congregation always identify themselves with that chosen people in bondage'.[63]

Barbara also rejected the anti-abolitionist argument that slavery was a ' "divine institution" for civilising and Christianising the savage African races.'[64] Having been in Algiers, she was able to make some comparisons. In the American Union, she pointed out, the law demanded that the status of the children of slaves follow the condition of the mother, and therefore they were owned by the master of the female slave, who was free to sell them. However, in Mohammedan countries, she noted, 'the children of slave women do not follow the condition of the mother, and thus some of the worst and most cruel consequences of slavery are avoided.'[65] She pointed out also that 'In Mahometan [sic] countries a man is allowed by his religion to have many wives, and he brings up his children by different mothers, alike to share his goods and to inherit his position.'[66] The attempted destruction of family feeling brought about by the American slave system she regarded as an unmitigated evil.

One tangible result of her trip was her American paintings, exhibited by Gambert at his Pall Mall gallery in 1861. A review in the *Athenaeum* on 13 April 1861, was full of praise for them, drawing particular attention to 'no. 40', *Swamp near New Orleans*: 'we have palms that droop their many-leaved arms in the sluggish and purple river; the mosses that hang about like flags torn in battle; and the gaunt cypresses looking gloomily on. The whole scene is desolate, aguish and still.' Mrs Gaskell saw either the original or the engraving made from it, because she vividly described the painting as 'a gorge full of rich rank tropical vegetation – her husband keeping watch over her with loaded pistols because of the alligators infesting the stream'.[67] In many ways this picture serves as the best reminder of the tour, and the pattern for the Bodichons' relationship laid down during it. Barbara was committed to taking her career as an artist as seriously after her marriage as before it. The style of her marriage was very much along the lines which Anna Mary had fantasised in her story of 'The Art Sisters'. Eugène respected Barbara's career, did not crowd her, but equally, was there to offer his protection when needed. It seemed a marriage of true minds.

CHAPTER 10

Love and Loss

Barbara asked Ruskin for his opinion of her generally admired *Louisiana Swamp*. As the author of *Modern Painters*, he was probably the most powerful critic of his day, so his views could make or break an artist's reputation. His reply to Barbara was hostile: 'Do you really think that a drawing of an American swamp is a precious thing to bequeath to the world. I don't like your ladies' reading room either, at all . . .'[1] The odd juxtaposition of Barbara's painting and his objection to the reading room which Barbara and Bessie had set up at the headquarters of the *English Woman's Journal*, implies that Ruskin was more interested in keeping female ambition under control than in offering aesthetic criticism. Ruskin's attitude towards women artists was ambivalent, to say the least. He supported women attending schools of design because he deemed *craft* within their capabilities. He was therefore quite happy to train Octavia Hill as a copyist, or to encourage Georgie Burne Jones as an engraver, but at bottom he did not seem to believe that women were capable of fine art.

When Anna Mary Howitt had exhibited a large-scale historical oil painting of *Boadicea* at the Crystal Palace exhibition of 1856 it received mixed reviews. The *Athenaeum* said it was 'Botany not Art'.[2] Barbara had modelled as the warrior queen, with her golden-red hair flying. William Rossetti had praised the picture, albeit slightly tongue-in-cheek: 'Miss Howitt's Boadicea Meditating Vengeance in The Forest, is among the most remarkable of the new oil pictures. History says that the British Queen was exceedingly 'burly' in form; and Miss Howitt, with a conscientiousness which must be respected, although it derogates from the effect of her picture, makes her so undeniably.'[3] Ruskin's response to Anna Mary's painting was unequivocally hostile. He wrote to her privately, rather than making a public criticism, but what he said devastated her nonetheless: 'What do you know about Boadicea? Leave such subjects alone and paint a pheasant's wing.'[4] Ruskin's attack was received as an attack on Anna Mary's right to enter the prestigious field of history painting, and a challenge to her whole imaginative conception.

Both Barbara and Anna Mary Howitt aspired to be professional painters, to have their work taken as seriously as the men of the PRB, whose work Ruskin had famously championed. Yet women artists in Britain in the nineteenth century faced many gendered obstacles.[5] Firstly, they could not obtain the same professional training as men. Having enjoyed the camaraderie of training at Sass's with the PRB men, Anna Mary was barred from the possibility of going on to the Royal Academy schools. Writing to Barbara after attending a public lecture at the RA, Anna Mary said:

> Oh! How terribly did I long to be a man so as to paint there . . . it seemed after all the Royal Academy *were* greater and more to be desired than the Academy of Nature. I felt quite *angry* at being a woman, it seemed to me *such a mistake.*[6]

Anna Mary's chagrin at the exclusion is apparent, and the reference to the 'Academy of Nature' implies that she was taking issue with the message of Barbara's parable 'Filia', although Barbara had argued for nature *and* culture.

The Royal Academy was a gentlemen's club from which women were barred.[7] In the spring of 1859 Barbara mounted a campaign to oblige the Royal Academy to admit female students to its schools. The two-stage battle plan had all the hallmarks of a seasoned political campaign; thirty-nine women artists petitioned the RA for access to the schools. The signatures included several of the usual suspects: Barbara Bodichon, Ellen Clayton, Eliza Fox, Margaret Gillies, Laura Herford, Anna Jameson, the Mutrie sisters, Emily Osborn and Henrietta Ward. The petition was rejected on the ground that it would have required setting up separate life classes, because the Academicians would not allow male and female students to paint nude models in the same room. The second stage was more of a guerrilla strike, when Laura Herford, a Unitarian who had been a fellow student of Barbara's at Bedford College, applied to the Royal Academy School, submitting her work under the signature 'A. L. Herford'. Once a place had been offered to A.L. Herford Esq. the onus was on the Academy to prove that its constitution *specifically* excluded women, and it reluctantly gave in.[8]

In her own artistic career, Barbara had a stroke of luck. The art dealer Ernest Gambart, who had successfully promoted some of the Pre-Raphaelites' paintings, was showing an exhibition of David Cox's later freer paintings. They had initially attracted some criticism, although Cox responded by saying the critics 'forget they are the work of the mind, which I consider very far before portraits of places'.[9] They were, however, popular with the public. Barbara once wrote that her ambition was to 'paint as well as David Cox!'[10] In Cox's works, the landscapes are sometimes peopled by small figures who seem part of the natural order. The figures do not master the landscape but are simply *of* it. Barbara followed Cox in this disposition of figures in a landscape; a relationship suggesting everlasting nature and the limits and fragility of humanity. Cox died in June 1859 and Gambart offered Barbara a solo exhibition at his French Gallery. Writing to Marian on 1 July 1859, Barbara said: 'Everybody is astonished at my good fortune in getting my things shown altogether; for me I feel it a shame to go in after dear old David whom I loved much.'[11] Marian wrote back to say that they were going to see the pictures and that George had already seen Barbara's name 'in large letters on a walking "sandwich" and we were not without sensations at your having that honourable publicity. It is really a step to have your pictures hung together in a regular gallery where you have an illustrious predecessor'.[12] Clearly, Marian felt that a solo exhibition in Pall Mall was more prestigious than work shown at the Society of Female Artists, and honestly said so. She may also have meant that, like Gambart, she recognised that Cox was Barbara's 'illustrious predecessor' in an aesthetic tradition.

To be exhibited by Gambart was a little like crossing the Rubicon: it gave the aspiring artist an opportunity both to make some money and to receive serious critical attention.[13] Gabriel Rossetti rather rudely referred to him as 'Gamble-Art', implying that he was more a speculative businessman than an art-lover, but at least he actively promoted contemporary paintings and stimulated a market for them among the new aristocracy: the captains of industry from Birmingham, Manchester and Liverpool. Marian wrote to Barbara: 'An artist-friend of ours – Mr F.W. Burton – a nice creature, expressed high admiration of your pictures – didn't care about the want of finish in some of them – they had finer qualities than that of finish – he felt they were done on the spot under true inspiration.'[14] The artist's comment which Marian quoted was apt; watercolour as a medium offered the qualities of spontaneity and expressiveness rather than the high degree of finish that could be achieved with oils.

By contrast to Barbara's new success in the professional arena, Anna Mary's career was in a decline. Ruskin's rebuff of her painting at the end of 1856 had a profound effect on her. One reason for this may be that Anna Mary saw herself as a Pre-Raphaelite painter; she had trained at the same school as the PRB and shared their ideals. Barbara, although

interested in Pre-Raphaelitism, painted in a different tradition, in which
Varley, William Hunt, David Cox, or even Turner, were her masters. If
Ruskin, the champion of the PRB, could find nothing to admire in Anna
Mary's painting, then inevitably it struck a deeper blow to her than his
criticism did to Barbara.

The other reason why Ruskin's criticism so demolished Anna Mary
was that her ideas for paintings came to her in the form of visions. Her
vision of 'Boadicea' embodied as Barbara was not therefore simply a
question of a criticism of her style or her technique, which probably she
could have coped with, but was received as a denial of the vision itself.
Barbara had become in some sense Anna Mary's guardian angel. This
was not entirely fanciful in its origins. When the Howitts had first met
the Leigh Smiths they had been stricken by the death of little Claude,
and at the height of their money troubles. Ben Smith had thought up
many tactful ways to help and cheer them, and his offers were always
made on his behalf by Barbara. In truth, Anna Mary knew that Ben
Smith was their major benefactor, but it seemed as if Barbara had
magically appeared in their darkest hour embodying succour and light.
When it turned out that Barbara had an artistic soul, and loved nothing
better than to paint with and learn from Anna Mary, she had assumed
enormous psychological importance in Anna Mary's life. After Barbara
had modelled for Boadicea, Anna Mary had asked her to model for her
picture of Beatrice. As Barbara's golden good looks could hardly have
suggested a medieval Italian heroine, it seems as though she *represented*
Beatrice, 'she who makes blessed', in the symbolic rather than the
physical sense – muse rather than model.

Ruskin's criticism struck right at the roots of Anna Mary's overlapping
identifications – as a professional woman artist, as a seer, as a worshipper.
Anna Jameson, who was also an art critic, had a surer feel for Anna
Mary's intentions and, writing to Bessie, she said that she was 'struck by
the originality and power of the conception. It is very grand and Barbarie
– it shows good progress in all respects – I have written to her'.[15] This
sounds as though Anna Jameson had heard along the grapevine that Anna
Mary's confidence needed building up. The shock of Ruskin's disapproval, followed by Barbara's marriage and removal to Algiers, had filled
Anna Mary with alarm; her 'angel' had deserted her. In 1858 Anna Mary
went to Rouen in Normandy where, long before, another female
visionary, Joan of Arc, had been burnt at the stake. In the museum at
Rouen is a picture of the Virgin and Child enthroned in the midst of
female saints, with St Barbara on the Virgin's left-hand side leaning
over a book. St Barbara is renowned for being studious but she also

stands for fortitude and courage.[16] 'St Barbara' was one of Marian's nicknames for Barbara, and possibly one Anna Mary knew. Anna Mary appears to have made some kind of psychotic identification with these female martyrs, and suffered a nervous breakdown.

Barbara was distressed when the news reached her, and tried to think of a way to rebuild Anna Mary's shattered artistic confidence. Remembering the pleasure the two of them had once enjoyed as members of Gabriel Rossetti's Folio Club, when she arrived in England in the spring of 1859, she started a new club, calling it 'The Portfolio'. It began quite modestly with Barbara, Bella, Nannie, Bessie and Adelaide Procter – three artists and two poets – but also welcomed corresponding members, including Christina Rossetti, who was too shy to be present in person.[17] Over the years, the members of the club expanded to include Willie's wife, Georgina, and her new brother-in-law, General Ludlow, and also some of the women involved with the *English Woman's Journal* – Jane Crow, Isabella Blythe and Emily Faithfull. The Portfolio operated simultaneously in Algiers, drawing in the offerings of any visiting artists or writers who cared to join. But if Barbara's primary objective was that the private space of the Portfolio Club would help rebuild Anna Mary's confidence to exhibit publicly, then she was disappointed, because increasingly Anna Mary shrank away from her old set.

Anna Mary and Barbara met again after a longish interval when Barbara sent her tickets for her 1859 exhibition. Anna Mary wrote to her in September:

> My most beloved Barbara, If you will have faith in me, and kiss my artistic body as it were with tender kisses, and hold me lovingly in your motherly and sisterly arms, and breathe upon me, your *art faith* in me, and be as it were my artistic *mesmeriser* I shall revive, I shall come forth, I shall be newborn! Don't laugh at me! Oh my most dear Barbara, if you ever could comprehend how, for three years or more, I have hung bleeding upon a cross of artistic martyrdom, you would comprehend what it was to lie as I am now lying in a sepulchre buried to the world, but alive to God, and life stirring within me to come forth, but unable to come forth closed in flesh, unless it be held lovingly to a human artistic breast, and be breathed upon by artistic breath.[18]

It seems clear that if Anna Mary's relationship with Barbara was constrained (physically or psychically), then she lost the nerve and desire to create. Without passion, although her work (through long training) would be competent, it could not be an expression of her deepest self, and therefore not be a work of art. Anna Mary's Swedenborgian concept required her 'angel', Barbara, to breathe creative daring into her. Sadly (partly because Barbara was so often away in Algiers) Anna Mary increasingly retreated into spiritualism, calling herself an art medium, producing geometric 'scribble-scrabbles', which she said were dictated to her by the spirits.[19] This move obviated the necessity for taking responsibility for her own creations, for daring to be vulnerable when offering up her essence for criticism. Anna Mary retreated from ambition in the public domain (she did not exhibit after 1857) into an entirely private 'sepulchre'. It was a defeat which caused all who recognised her talent much sorrow.

In November 1859 Anna Mary married a childhood friend Alfred Watts, who looked after her 'with a Mother's thoughtfulness and love'.[20] Barbara gave the Watts two of her watercolours as a wedding present; one of them was *Beanfield in Sussex at Sunset* which Anna Mary delightedly 'read' as Barbara's special message to her:

> I shall so love those drawings which you have given us! They are such a dear love-token to me; the shadow side, with its weird fantastic forms, and the glorious sunshine falling upon the ripened and reaped harvest. Mine is the wild shadow picture half fantastic, half insane, a harvest of shadow tinted shocks which have once been odorous but are now withered; with weird black winged birds fluttering amongst them, and even spreading their mystery athwart a pure sunset sky, a wild flight of shadows as it were flecking intensest purity; and yet my shadow picture must have its symbolic truth of purity, borne out in flowers as well as birds, by God's creatures of the earth as well as of the sky; you have painted therefore bright pure tenderest rose-tinted blossoms (Love's own colour) blossoms brilliant and tender even as sunset cloudlets, and thanked God evanescent! Springing up in shadow, in the gloom, amidst autumn leaves and dry beans and stones. And the whole is a hill side, a steep ascent of earth up to heaven beyond and above! My own darling, that shadow picture is a wonderful picture poem of part of my life, my shadow side – it was painted for me alone, given you from God to me as a lesson, a teaching, a commentary, a page of hieroglyphic – as is all true art, and as is every line, and particle of nature, because *being* nature it is instinct with God's soul.[21]

Barbara also believed that nature was 'instinct with God's soul' but for her, communing with nature restored her to peace and calm; whereas Anna Mary seemed always in danger of frenzied response.[22]

Marriages were taking place thick and fast. While Barbara had been in America, Willie had married Georgina Mary Halliday (a relation of the

Noels) in August 1858 and they had moved into Mountfield Park Farm, to be near to the Pater, although the wedding present itself was Crowham Manor (then tenanted). A year later, Bella was engaged to be married.[23] Her fiancé was Major General John Ludlow, generally referred to by the Leigh Smiths as 'the General', whom they had known since 1853 when he had visited Hastings to get over the death of his brother William.[24] He came from a long and distinguished line of military people, with an ancestor who had served in Cromwell's army. After his retirement, the General's father, Edmund Ludlow, lived at a boarding house in Weymouth Street, Portland Place, as both his sons were abroad in the Indian army and his only daughter lived in Australia. As a shareholder of University College, Gower Street, and a member of the Reform Club, Edmund Ludlow mixed in the same reforming circles as the Smiths.[25] He was proud of his son John, who had obtained his commission in the Indian army in 1819 and had been awarded the Ava medal in 1826 for his services in the Burmese war. The General had then joined the Indian Political Department, where as chargé d'affaires at Jeypore he had successfully campaigned for the abolition of suttee (widow burning).[26] Bella's beloved was a socially reforming pioneer, with 'feminist' credentials which would have appealed to all the Leigh Smiths.[27]

The General was very close to his cousin John Malcolm Forbes Ludlow, whom the Leigh Smiths knew through Gabriel Rossetti and Working Men's College connections.[28] After the death of his brother, Lt.-Col. John Ludlow, in 1821, Edmund Ludlow had become a trustee (and virtually a second father) to this nephew. The General often referred to this beloved cousin as his 'brother John', which indicates the closeness of their relationship. General Ludlow helped his cousin financially quite as generously as though he were his brother.[29] Having lived in France, J.M.F. Ludlow's sympathy with the ideas of Fourier drew him in London to the group of Christian Socialists centred on Maurice and Kingsley. He became editor in 1851 of the *Christian Socialist* and was the promoter of working men's associations, speaking as a 'friend of labour' at Social Science Association congresses.[30] These high-principled cousins were very much to the taste of the Leigh Smiths and their friends, and there was an unmixed sense of delight as the news of Bella's engagement spread through family and friends. Anna Mary wrote that 'This is no surprise at all to either of us as we have always expected it . . . How proud the General must be of his lovely, graceful dear wife elect!'[31]

This universal approval of Bella's marriage must have seemed in stark contrast to the doubt and concern which had been expressed on all sides at Barbara's sudden marriage to a stranger two years previously, although

Barbara, with her usual generosity of spirit, seemed to hold no resentment. She had arrived at Glottenham in September 1859 to find her father in rather poor health, suffering from a carbuncle which, although his doctor said that he would suffer from gangrene if he did not have it cut away, he refused to have touched. Barbara herself 'turned surgeon' (perhaps she had learned from her husband) and within three days it started to get better, although, sadly, he was not well enough to go to Bella's wedding. On 29 September the Pater made a marriage settlement of £5,000 on her. He seems at the same time to have given Nannie property in Bath Street in the city of London.[32] Nannie had shown no sign of interest in any young men of their acquaintance; it may be that Ben surmised that she was not likely to marry, although it is more likely that he simply wanted his affairs in order before his death.

Nannie was also happy at this time in her life, enjoying visiting Algiers in the winters, and in England finding her greatest pleasure in the company of Adelaide Procter. Nannie and Barbara threw themselves into the meticulous preparations for Bella's country wedding. Three carriages set out from Mountfield Park Farm to Brightling Church. The bride and her two sisters were in the first carriage, Aunt Ju and Aunt Dolly were in the second, and the Mountfield servants in the third. Converging on the church from Glottenham were three more carriages: the first held the bridegroom, his cousin John and an old army friend, Colonel Bygrave, the second contained Ben Leigh Smith, Willie and his wife Georgina and Uncle Jo Gratton, and in the third the Glottenham servants, plus Mr Willetts.[33] When the carriages pulled up at the rear of the church most of the parish was waiting for a glimpse of the bride, who walked up the church path with Ben, as the Pater was not well enough to attend. The church had been festooned with flowers by the clergyman's wife, and as they came out the waiting schoolchildren gave them bunches of flowers to take home. Back at Glottenham, they all rushed up to the Pater's bedroom where he, aged seventy-six, and now of 'bearded . . . patriarchal appearance', received the congratulations of the clergyman and his family in his nightgown.[34] Both Aunt Ju and Barbara took the trouble to report the details of the happy day's events to Aunt Patty; Aunt Ju referred to Barbara in her letter as a 'happy married [daughter] of two years sound experience', which was perhaps intended to reassure Aunt Patty that two out of three Leigh Smith daughters were now suitably settled.

Barbara was concerned about the Pater's health when she left to return to her husband in Algiers. She wrote to Marian:

Do you know I am very anxious about Pater he is so very feeble and dependent. I wish I could stay with him very much but I don't think I ought – there are 3 of us & if each is 4 months with him it is taking good care of him & putting myself out of the question I think as I have taken the responsibility of my husband's life & happiness on myself I ought to go back to him. If Pater is ill this winter I shall come over to help Nanny and to nurse him.[35]

It is interesting to note that Barbara regarded the responsibility of looking after the Pater as the responsibility of the three *daughters* and not the sons. However, he seemed to be recovering well, and as Georgie was willing to look after him, Nannie went out to join Barbara for the spring. He died suddenly on 12 April 1860. Nannie wrote to Hannah Walker, their old nurse at Hastings, to let her know. Hannah's idiosyncratically spelled letter gives a powerful sense of her love for all of the Leigh Smith family:

My dearest Miss Anny, i was so glad to hear from you & that you want to come back to Blandford Sq at wonce for you must feel it if you had stayed longer it is a sad blow to you all I know it was to me my poor dear old Master I feel very much for you all I new it would be sad wen it did come. The lord has herd my prayers that you are all grow up to do for yourselves wat a blessing to have him so long and for him not to suffer a long time and Mr Ben to be there and poor willy to.[36]

Barbara and Nannie set out for England immediately; Dr Bodichon followed in May.

Barbara wrote to Marian:

This will await your return for I believe you are on your way home & not really come. Just a word of greeting to you dear friend for your sake coming home, for mine because I have lost so much I feel the want of all I have. Probably you know how my father died on April 12th – died before Nanny and I heard he was ill. It has been a fearful loss to us all, to me more than that of kith and kin. I cannot now write of it, for I can only bear it by turning my mind to other things . . . I think so much of your Mill that I do not like to put it in one sentence. I find it more interesting than AB even. We 3 all do – probably because it touches our private experience that brother & sister are admirable.[37]

Barbara's expression 'to me more than . . . kith and kin' is plain enough. The Pater had been Barbara's role model of how to engage with the world socially and politically. Although Ben, Bella, Nannie and Willie all adored their father, Barbara most closely identified with his politics, and she, rather than any of the other siblings, accepted the role of heir to *this* inheritance. She might easily have said, like Viola: 'I am all the daughters of my father's house, and all the brothers too'.

But Barbara's reference in her letter to Marian to *The Mill on the Floss* indicates some other, and perhaps troubling issues. Anne Longden was, like Maggie Tulliver, a miller's daughter who had run off with a gentleman, had failed to get married to him, and borne the social disgrace. Only in death, had Anne/Maggie's reputation(s) been redeemed. The Leigh Smith children buried their father in the same grave where Ben had buried Anne Longden in St Edmund's Church, Wootton, on the Isle of Wight. Barbara went to great trouble formulating the memorial inscription for her father's grave. She sent a draft to Marian and George Lewes for their comments.[38] This is fortunate as time and the elements have conspired to erode many of the words on the memorial but by interweaving them with Marian's detailed suggestions to Barbara it is possible to refigure what the memorial says:

> He was an ardent advocate of civil and religious liberty and of every measure which could promote the well-being of mankind. He supported for 20 years the first Infant School in England. He gave hearty and generous assistance to migration. He loved the arts and sciences and was an active friend to their Diffusion among the people.

This reuniting of father and mother in the grave was as much a public statement as the memorial itself.

Barbara and Nannie immediately went to stay with Bella in Sussex, where their sorrow was lightened a little by the news that their sister was pregnant with her first child. Barbara then took both Bessie and Nannie to Algiers to spend part of the winter with her. Bessie had been deeply troubled because her fiancé, Sam Blackwell, was facing bankruptcy after some horrendous financial muddle in which he borrowed money from a Mr Shaw, who had loaned it under the impression that Sam was going to marry his daughter. Bessie told Barbara that she hardly knew what she wanted at this point.[39] Perhaps, at some level, Bessie's long-running engagement to Sam suited her, because it kept her free from the pressure of other romantic entanglements. Barbara wrote to Marian on 22 December 1860:

> It is a real pleasure to me and Dr. Bodichon to see Bessie and Nanny getting better & more cheerful. Bessie is like another being here in the country & takes to gardening with great delight – the very best thing in the world for her. Nanny is better but not well, so irritable with

everything and everybody. I am so sorry. She says herself she is better, but that life is nothing to her at all, nothing in it worth living for and nobody in it she cares to live with – lively for a young woman of 29 with nearly £1000 a year! . . . Nanny wants religion with forms and ceremonies, something present, something of routine . . .[40]

Marian's response to this letter, although kindly meant, jarred Barbara's sensitivities. Marian's earlier work in 'Higher Criticism' had entirely ruled out for her the sense of an individual soul surviving death, and she had mistaken Barbara's rather idiosyncratic religious faith for atheism. Barbara's Romanticism meant that her idea of God was as a Great Mother immanent in nature. But she had by no means ruled out an afterlife. Marian wrote: 'As for the "forms and ceremonies", I feel no regret that any should turn to them for comfort . . . But . . . the highest "calling and election" is to do *without opium* and live through our pain with conscious clear-eyed endurance.'[41] Barbara found it impossible to accommodate Marian's stoical atheism and shrank away from her for a time. Marian realised that there had been some kind of misunderstanding, judging by a letter dated 26 November 1862 in which she admonished Barbara: 'Pray don't ever ask me again not to rob a man of his religious belief, as if you thought my mind tended towards such robbery.'[42]

The same year that Barbara lost her father also marked the loss of Anna Jameson, who was precious to her, like all the friends of her early years. As a long-standing friend of Mrs Procter, Anna Jameson had come to view Adelaide, Barbara, Bella, Nannie and Bessie all as quasi-nieces. Her *salon* had offered an opportunity for the aspiring young women to meet older women who could help them or inspire them, such as Elizabeth Barrett Browning and Lady Byron. In Barbara's handwriting inside her copy of Anna Jameson's *Legends of the Madonna* is a note which says, 'A memorial of a motherly friend who can never be replaced – who was to me & to many other young women a guide & companion, ever ready with her sympathy & her experience – the one woman to whom one looked for help and encouragement.'[43]

At the end of December 1860 Bella's baby, Amabel, was born safely in Blandford Square, greatly to Barbara's relief, as she regarded childbirth as the battlefield of women. Marian, who happened to be living at 16 Blandford Square at that time, wrote to tell Barbara that she knew the birth was imminent because she had seen 'straw before the door of No. 5', placed there to muffle the noise of cabs.[44] Hannah Walker came up from Hastings to help Bella through the birth and to help look after the baby, even though she was seventy-five at the time and not herself physically strong. It was just as well the familiar old friend was there; Bella suffered from severe post-natal depression, which included a hysterical rejection of the baby. The General hardly knew what to do for the best. Bella expressed a wish to go to Hastings, but the General was afraid to leave her while he went down to arrange everything, unless Ben could come and stay in the house with Bella while he was away. Hannah wrote to Nannie in Algiers at the beginning of February to assure her that the worst crisis was over:

> My dear dear Miss I was so glad to hear from your self as i ave not rite to you on account of our dear Mrs Ludlow but ham trying to tell you she is sertainly better and will soon be quite well and love her dear litle baby she takes a grate deal more notes of it than she did that will come to her when she gets well for she is a dear good baby and very pretty fair blue eyes you wil love her i know when you see her clearly poor dear I have shed many tears over her and her poor mama to it was very shockin but thank god she had one of the kindes of husbands the ever lived in evry way that could be witch must make you and madame Bodeshon feel very happy please god to restore her to him quite well it is many years since i felt so fritened as wen she was taken first and I had the care of the baby for 10 day and nights to my self it made me feel as if i 20 years younger for sake of the poor baby thank god . . . i ham going down to get us forward as i can before they [arrive?] there will be a great deal to do I wish poor dear she was quite well to help him baby was crisend and Mrs Ludlow churcht on the first of the month and I went to Mr Benn little Miss smith [Julia] and Miss longden was godmother.[45]

The General managed to take a lease on number 9 Pelham Crescent with the hope that it would help Bella to convalesce if she could be in the emotional security of her old home. Nevertheless, when the General dispatched Hannah Walker, with the baby, down to Hastings, his instructions to her included having a partition removed in the dining room and ensuring that Bella could not lock herself in anywhere, which indicates his continued anxiety about Bella's state of mind.

Bella was well enough for the General to bring her to Hastings to join nurse and baby for Easter, and Ben, Mr Gratton and Aunt Dolly all went down to visit them. Isabella Blythe wrote to Nannie on Good Friday: 'Yesterday I met Miss Longden . . . too, and sat with her a long time watching the sea . . . she was lamenting that Mrs. Bodichon does not live in England adding that she always felt safe when she was at home. Poor old lady, how proud of you all she is.'[46] Clearly to Aunt Dolly, although Ben was the 'head' of the Leigh Smith family, Barbara was the one who made everyone feel better.

Barbara spent May in Hastings, reassuring herself that everyone was all right, and then accompanied her husband to Brittany to meet his mother's side of the family. Although Dr Bodichon himself was republican and anti-clerical, and his mother's family was royalist and Catholic, he accepted their convictions as unshakeable but despised the Bodichons' Bonapartist sympathies.[47] By the time of Barbara's visit in 1861, the political situation in France had changed significantly even since the time of her marriage. Napoleon III's (limited) support of the Risorgimento, and the 1860 commercial treaty with Great Britain, ratifying the free trade policy of Richard Cobden and Michael Chevalier, marked the start of an evolution of an absolutist empire towards a more liberal one. Eugène felt more hopeful about the political direction of his native land than he had for several years previously.

The most interesting visit from Barbara's point of view was to Eugène's old home, Campagne du Pavillon at Mauves. From the station they walked up a quiet country road where the only vehicle they saw was a wagon drawn by cream-coloured cattle. Barbara wrote that they

> walked for an hour always up hill, through a beautiful country like Sussex, and the roads just as bad, until we came to an old house in a most solitary place on top of the hill. It made the Doctor cry to see it all so bare, for all the fine avenue of pines and elms planted by his great grandfather have been cut down, nothing left but some plantations he made twenty or thirty years ago, and one beautiful avenue of fine oaks, three rows deep on either side. Le Grand, who lives there alone, one daughter being married, and one at the convent at Nantes, was very affectionate and pleasant . . .[48]

The house itself struck Barbara as quite beautiful, rather like a French version of Brown's where she had spent her earliest years. Sadly, Eugène's mother had found Pavillon too expensive to keep up; the cutting down and selling of the pines and elms was an indication of increasingly desperate attempts to raise money. She had moved to Nantes in 1841 after Eugène's cousin, Amadée Le Grand, had offered to buy it from her. Barbara wrote: 'On the whole it was a pleasure to see the old place in the hands of this cousin, rather than to have it. I should not like to live there, neither would Eugène, and you see his cousin bought it out of love for the family, and it is all very satisfactory, and the peasants are very happy under him.' She was right, of course: the cousin lived 'on the spot' and shared the ardent Catholicism of his community. A natural nostalgia for the scenes of his youth aside, Dr Bodichon no longer fitted into this social environment.

On their visit to Pavillon, Amadée Le Grand's married daughter and her husband rode eighteen miles from their own house in order to meet them for lunch. The conversation inevitably turned to the Revolution, for Campagne du Pavillon had been taken by the Blues (republicans) and held against the Whites (royalists). Barbara wrote that the old well had 'twenty skeletons or more mouldering in its depths . . . every stone, every tree of this country, is a text for a discourse on the French Revolution'. Naturally enough, these aristocratic Whites spoke almost exclusively about the cruelty of the Blues.

In Nantes, they visited Eugène's friend (and referee), Dr Guepin. Unsurprisingly, Barbara felt more comfortable with these friends than with Eugène's family, despite their kindness to her. From the Guepins, Barbara wrote:

> I hear the other side, and see a life of active good works, and immense scientific and literary activity, such a change from all [the Catholic family stories]. Very instructive to hear the history of this strange and wonderful part of France from two such different societies. I have spent a great deal of time with the Guepins, and never been there without hearing of something doing for the good of somebody or other. With Madame Guepin I visited the Protestant school, and some of the places where the horrors of the French Revolution were committed. Dr. Guepin is the author of many works, and well known in France for his devotion to Liberal politics. One of his ancestors was burned slowly, *roasted* alive by the Catholics, because he was a Dissenter, and Dr. Guepin believes that the best blood in France was Huguenot, and that it was a woeful day for France, that St. Bartholomews fete!

Dr Guepin told her a story about an old blind man called 'Jambe de Bois', a fighter for the royalists in La Vendée, who had consulted the doctor although, as a White, he did not trust any Blues. Dr Guepin had casually asked the old fighter what he thought he had gained from his bravery and

> Jambe de Bois scratched his head & said in a slow husky voice 'Why we poor people got *nothing* at all, some of the gentlemen got money & some titles but we poor devils nothing at all!' Dr. Guepin examined his eyes & gave the old hero some hope of sight, whereafter he began to respect the docteur tho' a blue & a republican & Dr. Guepin, who was

very anxious to know the truth of a certain fact in history, at last put the question – if on a certain occasion when his officers had taken about 400 prisoners – young men all the very flower of Nantes – he had not assassinated them all, he & his fellows in the most cold blooded & horrible manner. The old Chaoun hesitated – but at last said it was true. He said he & his men had gone into the prison & hacked & cut up these poor defenceless creatures with their knives & swords in a manner too horrible to relate. He said 'blood makes a man drunk like wine'.

Barbara felt that the Guepins' stories were an important political counterbalance to the stories she was told by Eugène's maternal family: 'I am getting quite tired of hearing these old aristocrats complain, believing firmly as I do that the whites were quite as cruel as the blues in the Revolution whenever they had the opportunity.'

They visited Château de la Pommeraye, at Vallet, the family house built on a fortune made in St Domingo. Madame des Nouhes, the sister of Eugène's mother, and his own godmother, still lived there. At the time of their visit she was seventy-five and in poor health, but was delighted to see her nearest relative and his bride. Barbara wrote to Aunt Dolly that when

> Eugène's mother was a child [she] hid in a wood when her father was obliged to fly, and the republicans took possession of the house. She and her nurse lived in the trees for many days on leaves and wild fruits. Certainly if any house has a right to be haunted, this has, and it made me shudder to go into the big rooms, open to the sky, with the gaping window spaces and cold wide hearth stones.

La Pommeraye was certainly widely considered to be haunted; candles blew out at a certain point on the stairs, horses in the stables would never settle. It was formally exorcised as late as 1914. Vallet was an area made rich by the growing of grapes for Muscadet wine, and the Pommeraye estate had been rich before the depredations of the French Revolution. Following the Revolution, most of the peasants now owned their own land, and Madame des Nouhes told Barbara that there were twenty peasants locally whose income amounted to £800 a year. Now that everybody had property, she said, it acted as a guarantee of order; Madame des Nouhes believed that there was no likelihood of another revolution.

Barbara summed up the whole experience of meeting her husband's family by telling Aunt Dolly:

It has been very pleasant to me to be so cordially and affectionately treated by every one of them, and though I should not like to live among them (indeed it would be impossible for me to live with thorough-going Roman Catholics), I like to see them, and I hope in two or three years we shall pay them all another visit, – they interest me, and I shall want to know how all the young people get on in life. Life in Algeria, with all its drawbacks, pleases me much better than life in La Petite Bretagne.

After the visit Barbara had a clearer picture of Eugène's early life, and could understand why, despite loving Brittany, he had not felt called to commit his life to keeping up an impoverished estate after his father's death.

Drawing on her visits to Eugène's ancestral homes, Barbara wrote a short story (rather like one of George Sand's *bergeries*) which involved real historical incidents entwined with elements of the ghost stories which her husband and his relatives had told her. The persona of the writer is the companion of a Frenchman returning from America with a fortune to rescue his impoverished estate, a fictive healing of Dr Bodichon's self-imposed exile. It appeared in the *English Woman's Journal* as 'Six Weeks in La Chère Petite Bretagne' in May 1863, dedicated to Anna Mary, which was a way for Barbara to tell her that she was still in sympathy with Anna Mary's sense of there being only a thin veil between everyday reality and the world of the spirits. The supposed writer says: 'I cannot say I felt certain that the ghosts of the castle were other than bats, owls, frogs, strange noises of wind in empty chambers, miasmas from the moat, and *the ever present memories of bloody deeds and evil times*, accursed spirits more or less tangible according to the sensibility of the human creature.' Anna Mary responded to Barbara's compliment by writing to her:

My very dear Bar, Was I not very, very much pleased last evening, opening the English Woman's Journal to find your very charming picturesque Brittany article – and that BLSB had dedicated it to AMHW, thank you very lovingly my dear old friend, I felt no little touched by your thought of me – and I think the paper very charming indeed – so fresh and quaint and beautiful! I remember your saying that you had kept a kind of Diary of your visit to Brittany for me, but I did not understand quite in what way – and this took me quite by surprise and brought loving tears to my eyes. I thought I would at once thank you from a very loving heart. I like the manner in which you have wrought the events up into a little history – when we meet you must tell me how much is 'truth' and how much 'poetry' – I expect, however, that all the description is truth, simply the little plot, poetry![49]

179

On Barbara's return to Algiers, she received news that her cousin Blanche was facing tragedy. Blanche Shore Smith had married the poet Arthur Hugh Clough in 1854. During the Crimean War Florence had had Aunt Mai with her and Uncle Sam had acted as London 'banker' for the Crimean nurses who wished to remit money home, and had been patient with his wife's absence, but eventually he was inclined to complain that it would be quite nice to have his wife back. In 1855 when the Nightingale Fund was set up to mark the nation's gratitude for Florence's work in the Crimea, Florence co-opted her cousin-in-law, Arthur Clough, to take on the unpaid work of secretary to this fund. In 1857 Florence had established herself as a quasi-invalid staying in the annexe of the Burlington Hotel, with Aunt Mai and Hilary Bonham Carter (and others) dancing attendance. In June 1858, Florence's sister Parthe had married a widower, Sir Harry Verney, MP for Buckinghamshire and the heir to Claydon House in Buckinghamshire, and he too was co-opted as one of 'Florence's men'. Arthur Clough's health deteriorated until it was damaged beyond repair. He had suffered a bad bout of scarlatina in 1860, resumed work before properly getting over it and also suffered some kind of accident to his foot. By the summer of 1861 he had been forced to relinquish his paid work in order to go on a convalescent tour. Blanche was insistent that he should stay out of England; she assured him that Sir Harry Verney would be able to look after Florence's affairs, and the Education Department where he was an examiner could survive without him. Blanche was terrified that his strong ideal of service would cause him to be sucked back into Florence's web if he were to return. In response to Blanche's rather frantic letters to Arthur, assuring him that Florence said that she did not need him and that he should recover his health abroad, he sent rather woeful letters saying:

> I think it is very funny of you people at home – Flo and all of you – to suppose that it can be so very pleasant or easily endurable to stay poking about abroad for more than two or three months at a time, all by oneself or something no better – or perhaps worse. Coming home did me more good than harm.[50]

Blanche was staying at Combe Hurst with her parents because she was expecting her third child, Blanche Athena, who was born safely at the beginning of August. As soon as she had recovered from the birth Blanche joined Arthur in Paris and they travelled slowly towards Florence, where he died on 13 November 1861. One cannot help wondering whether Blanche in her heart of hearts felt that Florence had killed her husband with overwork. There is certainly something bizarrely fitting, although horrible, about poor Arthur crawling towards Florence to die. Florence promptly appointed her cousin, Henry Bonham Carter, in Clough's place.

Fortunately, Arthur's sister, Anne, managed to get out to Florence three days before her brother died. During those last days the sisters-in-law drew very close, and subsequently Anne was invited to stay at Combe Hurst whenever she wished. There she met Barbara and in conversations about the higher education of women the two women grew to have great respect for each other. Whether they made any private comments about Florence's behaviour is impossible to say. Barbara had noted in America that the rumour that she was a cousin of Florence Nightingale 'added a brilliancy to my reputation'. She had been encouraged to make this claim in order 'to insure a warm reception, but I refused positively'.[51] Barbara had some reason for proud resentment, owing to the long history of the Nightingales' ostracism of the Leigh Smith children. However, it is also possible to suppose that she might have had some additional antagonism on behalf of her gentle cousin, Blanche.

After the frightening time following the birth of Amabel, Barbara was concerned when Bella became pregnant again almost immediately. However, this time all was well and Harry was born without undue difficulty on 22 January 1862. Barbara asked Emily Blackwell to 'Tell Elizabeth Bell has a little boy & is *quite well*'.[52] Bella was never so ill again as she had been after the first birth. Whether it was the confidence that came from knowing that the General would look after her whatever happened is hard to say. Possibly, of course, everyone around her was more alert in helping her get through the early stages. After Harry, she had two more children, Edmund in 1863 and Milicent in 1868. Barbara, who had worried about Bella ever since her breakdown in 1856, at last felt that she could resign the welfare of this particular sister to the General's tender care. She got on tremendously well with her brother-in-law, having in many ways an easier relationship with him than she did with her own brothers following her marriage to Eugène.

After the visit to Brittany, Barbara thought long and hard about replacing in some real way (not only fictively) Eugène's lost home. She had noted that the countryside around Campagne du Pavillon was very similar to Sussex, which was no doubt why he loved it as much as she did. In 1863 she decided to lease from Ben three acres of land on the Glottenham estate in order to build a cottage. She chose to build in Harding's Wood, near to Scalands Farm but closer to the road, so she called the house Scalands Gate. In conversation she usually referred to it as 'Dr Bodichon's cottage', presumably to accord him the dignity that her rich brothers were inclined to deny him.[53] It was designed after the model of an old Sussex manor, so the latched front door opened straight into the living room, with a large bricked fireplace, which her friends used to initial when they came to visit. Over the fireplace was a frieze of the Bayeux Tapestry. As with her house in Algiers, Barbara furnished Scalands Gate simply. The floors were covered with matting, and there were plain white bookshelves running round the lower part of the walls, leaving the upper part free for pictures, and for her collection of Kabyle and Spanish pottery. Cushions were made from Arab embroidery. One of the upstairs rooms, with the best views and strong light, was turned into a studio.

The Bodichons were able to move into Scalands Gate in July 1863 and their Sussex home was a great joy to both of them, perhaps especially to Eugène, whose idea of perfect happiness was a long walk, accompanied either by Barbara or some friendly dogs. Once Scalands Gate was established, whenever Barbara needed to attend to her many-faceted social work in London, Eugène could stay in Sussex. That first summer Barbara planted pale creamy yellow Branksia climbing roses to adorn the sides of the house, chosen because they were fast growing and bloomed in May, to welcome them when they returned to England. Eugène felt at peace at Scalands Gate in a way that he never did in London, and to Barbara too there was a feeling of coming home. Brown's, the house where she had lived with her mother, was only a ten-minute walk through the woods and her Aunt Dolly spent the spring and summer there. As Marian Lewes wrote in *Daniel Deronda*, everyone's life needs to be 'well rooted in some spot of native land'.

In the spring of 1864 Barbara offered Scalands Gate to the Howitts, whose son, Charlton, had tragically drowned in New Zealand.[54] Bessie, recovering from a severe bout of scarlet fever, went to convalesce at Brown's with Aunt Dolly to look after her. She wrote to Barbara in Algiers: 'What an odd turn of fate that instead of being with you on the mountains, I should be landed here with Aunty at Browns. Sitting looking out into the very garden where you had that famous adventure with the muddy points. I have just been looking at your cottage, with its tall chimney which looks just like a hand put up to say "Here I am" to the neighbours.'[55] With her earliest friends all at Robertsbridge, there is a striking sense of the connectedness to the past that Scalands Gate represented to Barbara. Willie and his family were not far away at Crowham Manor. In the summertime, the General and Bella often rented

Glottenham Manor from Ben when they wanted to come down to visit their Sussex relatives. Barbara was resident in Algeria only because her husband lived there. Sussex was the home of her heart.

CHAPTER 11

The Reform Firm

All through their apprenticeship years, Barbara and Bessie had talked about 'reform' in precisely the sense in which Mary Wollstonecraft had talked about a reform in female manners. Wollstonecraft had argued that, as long as middle-class women were held back by social custom from committing themselves to some worthwhile enterprise, they were trapped in a sort of perpetual infantilism. Both Bessie and Barbara had long interested themselves in situations where women had carved out a useful role for themselves, and had between them visited many such women engaged in philanthropic schemes. Bessie had visited Mary Carpenter's reformatory for delinquent children in Bristol and in 1856 she went to see the schools set up by the Unitarians, Samuel and Ellen Courtauld at their silk mills at Halstead. There she had met Mary Merryweather, a Quaker, who had been involved with the Courtaulds since 1847 in providing schools for the children of working women. Bessie was strongly drawn towards Mary Merryweather, almost as though Mary were the mother she would have chosen for herself, were such a thing possible. Many women who, like Mary, forged this kind of philanthropic role for themselves either chose not to marry, or, after a separation or widowhood, formed a close, albeit usually undefined relationship, with another woman. Mary had assumed that Bessie and Barbara had this kind of relationship and would set up home together. Although Barbara's marriage to Eugène had ruled out this option, it had not ruled out putting into practice the plans the two women had made in Algeria, although, because she spent half of every year in Algiers, Barbara perforce had to take a more back-seat role.

In October 1856 on a visit to Edinburgh, Bessie had met Isa Craig, the orphaned daughter of a hosier and glover; like Bessie, she wrote both poetry and articles for journals.[1] Bessie and Isa both sent work that October to a fortnightly paper called the *Waverley Journal*, advertised as being 'published by ladies for the cultivation of the memorable, the progressive and the beautiful'. After her visit to Barbara, Bessie had sent in articles on 'French Algiers' and the 'Physical Training of Females' and in February 1857 Barbara had contributed the article which had subsequently been published as her pamphlet, *Women and Work*. But both of them thought that the standard of the *Waverley* could be improved were it brought under their control, so Bessie had begun negotiations to become its editor. Writing to Barbara on 14 May 1857 she said:

> As to Waverley, I am accepted Editor, & it is ours for all practical purposes . . . I wish you would make due enquiries and invest, say, a couple of hundred pounds in it . . . I think Mrs Jameson & the Brownings will both help. Assuredly nothing would please me better than to see dear Max [Hays] working on it . . . when I have thoroughly got the paper up, I would willingly resign the editorship to her.[2]

Bessie saw in the journal the opportunity to focus on women's need of employment, and appropriate education and training. She said the journal would serve 'working women', an inclusive term which she defined as:

> all women who are actively engaged in any labours of brain or hand, whether they be the wives and daughter of landed proprietors, devoted to the well-being of their tenantry, or are to be classed among the many other labourers in the broad field of philanthropy; – whether they belong to the army of teachers, public or private, or to the realms of professional artist; or are engaged in any of those manual occupations by which multitudes of British women, at home and in the colonies, gain their daily bread.[3]

This letter serves as Bessie's manifesto for the journal she was to edit and which she hoped Barbara would be willing to bankroll. On 19 May Bessie pressed the point again, saying: 'If the Waverley can be got chiefly into friendly hands, & brought to London as [the present owner] wisely suggests, we can have our own book shop, & the beginning of a Club, room for exhibiting pictures etc. etc . . .'[4] These were things the two women had discussed in Algiers: the importance of establishing the kind of meeting place for women that men of their class took for granted (such as the Reform Club, the Athenaeum, or the Oxford and Cambridge Club) as well as running the journal itself. During that first summer, a small reading room for ladies was established at the London office of the *Waverley*: the journal had attracted over seventy subscriptions by 1858.

The first *Waverley* issue under Bessie's editorship came out in July 1857. From September Bessie and Max worked together in the small

London office at 14A Princes Street. Max contributed poetry and Mary Merryweather contributed a series of articles on factory life in Halstead. Bessie sent the first few copies to Marian in September for her comments, as she had edited the prestigious *Westminster Review* and George Lewes had edited the *Leader*. Marian acknowledged receipt of 'the Journals' and commented:

> It is a doctrine of Mr. Lewes's, which I think recommends itself to one's reason, that every new or renovated periodical should have a specialité – do something not yet done, fill up a gap, and so give people a motive for taking it. But I do not at all like the specialité that consists in the inscription 'conducted by Women', and I am very glad you are going to do away with it. For my own taste, I should say, the more business you can get into the journal – the more statements of philanthropic movements and social facts, and the less *literature*, the better. Not because I like philanthropy and hate literature, but because I want to *know* about philanthropy and don't care for second-rate literature.[5]

Marian clearly thinks that a 'woman-only' tag is less important than high-quality journalism and, subtly, indicates that the 'literature' contributions are not up to scratch. Bessie certainly took the hint on the issue of not excluding male writers but, arguably, did not pay sufficient attention to Marian's other two points.[6]

Getting control of a journal was seen by Barbara as a key means of influencing public opinion, just as Barbara's uncle, Octavius Smith, had backed the *Westminster* in order to promulgate liberal opinion. Bessie too believed that the 'growth of the press' offered an opportunity for the 'direct influence of educated women on the world's affairs. Mute in the senate and the church, their opinions have found a voice' in periodicals.[7] Barbara felt that the *Waverley* was not radical enough and complained about it. Bessie replied:

> My darling Barbara
> . . . all goes like clockwork at the office under Max, who is the most methodical of workers . . . Subscriptions come in steadily. We have now close upon 400, & our sales are about 250 a month. This is current, the back numbers keep constantly selling too . . . Max thinks I am far too timid in my expression of opinion, & Mr Fox thinks so too; but I don't believe there is any abstract public for divorce and the Suffrage, and I am far better placed to gain the approbation of our elders and betters, & trust to the gradual working of public opinion

towards further extensions of principle than to smash my head and
your money against a brick wall.[8]

The negotiations for the purchase of the *Waverley Journal* had been put
in the hands of the barrister and reformer, George Hastings (son of Sir
Charles Hastings, the founder of the British Medical Association), but he
ended up advising them to start a new journal. This was named the
English Woman's Journal, and was set up as a joint stock company.[9] They
were able to take advantage of this relatively new legislation to set up a
limited liability company on 13 February 1858. According to law they
needed seven shareholders. Barbara was the major shareholder with sixty
shares (in Nannie's name, as married women could not hold property in
their own right), Bessie had five shares, Matilda had five and Maria Rye
had one. Of the three male shareholders, Samuel Courtauld and James
Vaughan (a barrister and son-in-law of Jacob Bright) held four shares
each, and William Strickland Cookson, a Unitarian lawyer held five.
These seven shareholders were the directors of the new company, with
Cookson assuming the role of chairman.[10]

In February 1858 Bessie wrote to tell Marian Lewes: 'We are
beginning with a £1,000 and a great social interest.' This was clearly true.
By November 1858 the share capital had been doubled to £2,000 and
William Johnson Fox was appointed auditor. By February 1859, 212 of
the available 400 shares had been purchased. The Comtesse de Nouailles,
who had supported Elizabeth Blackwell's medical career, purchased sixty
shares. The Unitarian connection – with Peter Taylor, two related
Taylors and Elizabeth Sturch – was maintained. Bella Leigh Smith, Dr
Bodichon and Mary Merryweather held under five shares each. The
artist, Laura Herford, held one.

In December 1859, Theodosia, Dowager Lady Monson, an old
friend of Anna Jameson, who had given sterling assistance at the cramped
Princes Street office, found new rooms for them at 19 Langham Place.[11]
In March 1860 she too joined the board of directors. Here there was
sufficient space to organise a Ladies' Institute, comprising a reading
room with luncheon room attached, plus offices.[12]

When the first issue of the *English Woman's Journal* was published in
March 1858, it included an article by Anna Mary Howitt, 'A House of
Mercy', on the London diocesan penitentiary for fallen women in
Highgate. Ever since Barbara had written her letters to the *Leader* on the
subject of the 'domestic Moloch' in 1854, Barbara, Bessie and Anna Mary
had made it an article of faith amongst them that they would speak out on
the institution of prostitution. Both Joseph Parkes and Anna Jameson

thought this unwise.[13] After the October issue of the *Journal* appeared, Joseph Parkes was moved to remonstrate with Bessie about Max's article praising George Sand. He wrote to her: 'The French authoress has been a profligate writer; a mischievous one; and in her own early life a bad woman. No reflecting person of commonsense, of experience, or of common virtue, can exhume her in a different light.'[14]

Marian declined Bessie's invitation to write for the *Journal*, mainly because she was secretly writing *Adam Bede* but also because she was not impressed with its standards. She wrote to Sara Hennell after perusing the first issue:

> Did you know that Miss Parkes is the editress of the Englishwoman's Journal, which you see advertised? Co-editress, at least, with Miss Hayes. She gave me the first number the other day when I called on her at the office. It is just middling. Her own first paper on the Profession of the Teacher, has some *good* stuff in it: I can't help crying over the stories of the superannuated governesses. If you haven't seen the Magazine I will send it to you. Bessie has talent and real ardour for goodness, but I fear Miss Hayes has been chosen on the charitable ground that she had nothing else to do in the world. There is something more piteous almost than soapless poverty in this application of feminine incapacity to Literature.[15]

This sounds hard, but Marian Lewes thought from the beginning that Max would turn out to be a liability, not because of any question mark in her mind about her morality, but simply because she thought her writing execrable. Back in February 1856, John Chapman had asked for Marian's comments on an article Max had written on George Sand which he was considering for inclusion in the *Westminster Review*. Marian strongly advised him against using it:

> The *whole* of the introduction, and every passage where Miss H. launches into more than a connecting sentence or two is feminine rant of the worst kind, which it will be simply *fatal* to the Review to admit . . .[16]

This letter indicates that if articles by Max Hays were considered too poor to admit into the *Westminster*'s pages, and she had an editorial position at the *Journal*, then the standard of literature might be variable at best.[17]

When Barbara was away in Algiers, Bessie sent her encouraging reports of the *English Woman's Journal*, and Bessie herself was especially pleased with the articles which gave examples of women achieving in the world. Max was undoubtedly working hard, writing an article on 'Florence Nightingale and the English Soldier' for the April 1858 edition and an article on Harriet Hosmer in June. Anna Blackwell also contributed an article, about her sister's struggle to enter the medical profession. But the new *Journal* was still not sufficiently politically engaged to suit Barbara, and this produced tension between the editor-in-chief (Bessie) and the major shareholder on the board of directors (Barbara), because all along Barbara had envisaged the journal as a progressive *political* organ, and Bessie was more interested in *moral* influence.[18]

Barbara remained irritated with what she saw as the shortcomings of the *Journal*, writing to Marian from Algiers on 26 April 1859:

> I have so much to say to you about the Journal. Bessie writes in such a wild way of its success that I hardly know what to make of her. She has not a big enough head to see the small size of her work! I wish she could. I am sometimes so disgusted with her exaggeration – (the letter I sent you a specimen) that I think she will waste all her pure enthusiasm and do no good in the end.[19]

Marian responded on 5 May 1859:

> I was really glad to read the last passage in your letter about the E.W.J., because I had felt very strongly what you express and had wished your affection for her might not make you too tender to her mistakes. She needs only the sort of correction your mind could give her if you were near her . . . I have been so much vexed by several things in her writing lately that I feel quite guilty for having praised it so much when I saw her.[20]

Barbara did not have unlimited funds at this season. Having purchased the house in Algiers and having helped to finance the *English Woman's Journal*, money matters were somewhat pressing. Marian and George Lewes were both trying (unsuccessfully) to place Barbara's American letters and an article described by Barbara as 'Dr. Bodichon's animal article' for publication.[21] Barbara began to have regrets about investing in the venture. Perhaps sensing her disappointment, Marian sent a word of praise about an article in the September 1859 edition, which cheered Barbara somewhat before her return to Algiers. The article in question was one by Isa Craig describing a group of young girls making shirts for twopence-halfpenny a shirt, one of whom was repeatedly pricking her finger out of sheer exhaustion. Marian wrote:

> I have just been reading, with deep interest and heart-stirring, the article on the Infant Seamstresses in the Englishwoman's Journal. If, as I imagine, Bessie is the writer, just say to her when you happen to be writing to her or seeing her, that I am one of the grateful readers of that moving description – moving because the writer's own soul was moved by love and pity in the writing of it. These are the papers that will make the Journal a true organ, with a *function*.[22]

When Barbara returned to Algiers for the winter, she wrote to Marian to say:

> We (Dr. and I) have had some walks which ought to [be] written or sung or painted – so beautiful! I enjoy myself very much more than I can tell or than I deserve. If my pictures don't tell some of the pleasure I have they are liars. I am anxious that they succeed because if nothing the doctor writes succeeds & nothing I paint it won't do to stay here.[23]

This letter is the first indication that Barbara experienced some strain in trying to attend to all her duties: to her husband, to her family in England, to social reform and to her artistic career. Dr Bodichon's dislike of England, and of London in particular, was a serious problem. Marian sought to reassure Barbara that her social efforts were not in vain: replying to her letter on 5 December Marian said:

> The Englishwoman's Journal *must* be doing good substantially – stimulating women to useful work, and rousing people to knowledge of women's needs. A few mistakes, and rather a feeble presentation of useful matter, will not neutralize the good that lies in a great aim and an honest effort; and I heartily wish all connected with the Journal 'God speed' – except the ignorant and unconscientious writer who sometimes figures as the reviewer of books. I wish Bessie felt more keenly about the immorality of such slack writing as is sometimes admitted into that department of the Journal.[24]

Marian had clearly not revised her opinion of Max's abilities, and her opinion influenced Barbara. Barbara herself regularly contributed articles to the *Journal*, and, although finally she became disenchanted with the quality and focus of the *Journal* itself, she remained an enthusiastic supporter of its outreach activities – both finding jobs for women within Britain and helping to organise female emigration.

As well as publishing feminist articles by established writers, the *Journal* followed George Lewes's idea in the *Leader* by offering an 'Open Council' column in which readers could express their opinions. This helped to establish a communication network between the London feminists and women from the provinces. The offices of the *Journal*, first in Cavendish Square and, from the end of 1859, at 19 Langham Place, acted as a focus and magnet for several interrelated women's issues. At the time of setting up the *Journal* there were ever increasing numbers of middle-class women vying for a very small range of jobs. Unemployed governesses and needlewomen, widows and orphans appeared at the *Journal*'s offices desperate for help. Bessie and Barbara had started to keep an employment register themselves the first summer, but quickly realised that it was a huge job and that part of the difficulty of placing women was that they fell into two distinct groups: women who regarded themselves as 'ladies', who wanted professional jobs for women; and women who were willing to do semi-mechanical work, such as printing, law copying or telegraphy.

The varied activities of the Langham Place office attracted more pioneers. Jessie Boucherett was the daughter of a country squire who was High Sheriff of Lincolnshire. Very much a county woman, enthusiastically riding to hounds, she was also actively involved in philanthropic work. Her elder sister, Louisa, was a pioneer in the movement for boarding out pauper children and Jessie herself supported a dispensary and cottage hospital in Market Rasen. However, Jessie had always felt that a more organised approach to opportunities for work for women was needed. In 1858, when she was thirty-three, she

> caught sight, on a railway bookstall, of a number of the *Englishwoman's Journal*. She bought it, attracted by the title, but expecting nothing better than the inanities commonly considered fit for women. To her surprise and joy she found her own unspoken aspirations reflected in its pages. She lost no time in repairing to the office of the journal, where she expected to find some rather dowdy old lady. But instead a handsome young woman, dressed in admirable taste, was seated at the table. It was Miss Parkes; in a few minutes another young lady, also beautifully dressed, came in, of radiant beauty, with masses of golden hair. Such is the description given by Jessie Boucherett, long years after, of her first meeting with Barbara Leigh Smith and Bessie Parkes. She began forthwith the desire of her life, a Society for Promoting the Employment of Women.[25]

Jessie took charge of the employment register, establishing the Society for

Promoting the Employment of Women (SPEW) in June 1859, with Jane Crow (a school friend of Lizzie Garrett) helping as secretary. SPEW promoted training and looked for job opportunities for women as cashiers and clerks, for jobs in telegraph offices, in printing offices, in lithography and in hairdressing.

Another of the early callers at the Langham Place office was Emily Faithfull, the youngest daughter of a Surrey clergyman.[26] From 1854 to 1857 she stayed with her friend, Helen, the wife of Admiral Henry Codrington. When the Codringtons moved to Malta in 1858 Emily, aged twenty-three, appeared in the offices of the *Journal* in November. Bessie was delighted with the 'hearty young worker', writing to Barbara in January 1859, 'Emily is the nearest approach to my ideal of a canvasser I have yet got hold of . . . rather strong-minded; carried her own huge carpet bag, &c'.[27] Adelaide Procter also liked Emily enormously and immediately invited her to join the Portfolio Club, where she often read Christina Rossetti's offerings. After consultations with Emily, Bessie felt convinced that printing was a business women could be trained to enter, so she undertook to buy a small press and some type and hired a printer to instruct the women. This was undertaken in the spirit of a feasibility study. Emily Faithfull and George Hastings then agreed jointly to finance a press for the employment of women, under Emily's control. They refurbished a house in Great Coram Street (Russell Square) and called it the Victoria Printing Press in honour of the Queen.

The business opened on 25 March 1860 with five women apprentices; by October the number had increased to sixteen. This was the first time in England that female compositors had been trained and employed, and on the production of the Victoria Press's first tracts Bessie wrote to Barbara: 'here are women in the trade at last! One dream of my life!'[28] The Press aroused much public interest, generally favourable, although the women faced a good deal of hostility and even attempts at intimidation from male printers. Despite teething problems, the Victoria Press's contract to print the *Journal* and the *Transactions* of the Social Science Association kept the business solvent in its early stages, and in September 1860 the *Journal* was able to proudly reprint a paragraph from *The Times*: 'The Queen has graciously signified to Miss Emily Faithfull her approval of the establishment of the Victoria Press . . . for the employment of female compositors', adding, 'that all such useful and practical steps for the opening of new branches of industry to educated women must meet with her Majesty's entire approbation.' In 1862 Emily was appointed, by Royal Warrant, 'Printer and Publisher in Ordinary to

Her Majesty'. The Reform Firm was finding its work approved of in the highest quarters.[29]

In 1857 Lord Brougham had established the Social Science Association as an open forum for progressive middle-class ideas.[30] The Association formed pressure groups interested in reforming five areas of government: law, the penal system, education, public health and social economy (industrial, financial and commercial affairs).[31] As Lord Brougham was an old friend of the Pater, Barbara did not miss the opportunity of persuading him to make it open to women. Bessie wrote in her memoir, *A Passing World*, 'In connection with the Social Science Association one name ought to be gratefully recorded, and all the more so because absence from England usually prevented the personal presence of Barbara Leigh Smith at most of the actual meetings. But it was mainly owing to previous efforts and influence of hers that women were freely admitted to all its advantages.'[32] It opened the way for women to contribute in their own areas of expertise. The *Saturday Review* commented:

> There are decided advantages in this Universal Palaver Association . . . It must be remembered to Lord Brougham's credit that he is the first person who has dealt upon this plan with the problem of female loquacity . . . It is a great idea to tire out the hitherto unflagging vigour of their tongues by encouraging a taste for stump-oratory among them . . . Lord Brougham's little *corps* of lady orators, preaching strong-mindedness, gives a new aspect to the Association's presence . . . We heartily wish the strong-minded ladies happiness and success in their new alliance; and do not doubt that they will remember to practice the precept of one of their debaters 'not to mind being thought unladylike'. It is always better not to mind that which is inevitable.[33]

At the first session in 1857 at Birmingham the general secretary appointed for the first five years was George Hastings, one of the shareholders of the *Journal*, and he appointed Isa Craig as his assistant secretary. The 1858 congress had papers by Louisa Twining on workhouses, by Mary Carpenter on ragged schools and reformatories, by Florence Nightingale on health and construction of hospitals and by Isa Craig herself on emigration. The Association offered a unique opportunity for women, still excluded from the political process, to participate in public policy making. Papers presented at congress were often reprinted in the *Journal*. Barbara sent a paper on 'Middle Class Schools for Girls' for Bessie to read on her behalf at the 1860 Glasgow conference, in which she bemoaned the abysmally low standards of girls' schools, and this was reproduced in the November 1860 edition of the *Journal*. The Reform Firm therefore took every advantage of making sure that women's contributions at the Association meetings were fully reported. Although their papers were printed in the official organ of the Social Science Association, the *Transactions*, Barbara regarded this as tantamount to interring them in a 'costly sepulchre', and thought it important to get the women's papers published in the *Journal* as well.

At the Association meeting in 1859 at Bradford, Jessie Boucherett had read a paper about the work undertaken by SPEW and the congress proposed that as there were only two practical societies connected with the Association (the Workhouse Visiting Society and SPEW), they might as well be amalgamated. A committee of twelve women and twelve men was formed. The women included Jessie Boucherett, Isa Craig, Adelaide Procter, Max Hays and Jane Crow (as Secretary). On 1 October 1860 Bessie reported to the Glasgow congress on 'Reform Firm' activities. She dealt with three major areas: Jessie Boucherett's work in training young women to take situations as cashiers and clerks, Isa Craig's work in training women as telegraph clerks, and Maria Rye's law copying office where women earned a living by making accurate copies of legal documents. SPEW had managed to find permanent jobs for up to seventy-five women a year and temporary jobs for up to a hundred. In summer of 1859 Emily Davies visited London and then went off to found the Northumberland and Durham Branch. London SPEW therefore served as an example which could be replicated all round the land.

Maria Rye, a solicitor's daughter born in 1829, had joined the Reform Firm. In 1856 she had summarised the Law Amendment Society's draft for a proposed new Married Women's Property Act and included the text of Barbara's petition to Parliament in the *Englishwoman's Domestic Magazine*. Early in 1860 Barbara took a house in Portugal Street, Lincoln's Inn Fields, handy for all the lawyers' offices. She appointed Maria to run it as a law copying office. It seemed to offer an ideal occupation for distressed gentlewomen, because the only skill required was a fair hand, accuracy and legibility, and the women could work sitting down in a relatively private space. Maria Rye was inundated with applications for jobs there; on one occasion 810 women applied for a single position paying only £15 a year. By June 1860 Maria was able to report to a soirée at Langham Place that the law copying office was employing ten women to copy legal documents. Barbara supplied money for Maria's salary by her usual system of putting some money down herself *pour encourager les autres*, and then writing to the usual round of sympathetic philanthropists.

Given the overwhelming number of women applying for positions at the law copying office Maria often advised them to emigrate in search of work. In 1861, she helped twenty-two educated women reach various colonies by providing loans and arranging contacts. Barbara strongly supported Maria Rye's initiative. At the 1861 Social Science Congress Maria described her work and appealed for help in establishing a formal society to promote the emigration of educated women, because the colonial service only interested itself in the emigration to Australia, New Zealand and Natal of working-class women destined to be domestic servants. With Barbara's help Maria set up the Female Middle Class Emigration Society. Barbara wrote to Emily Blackwell at the beginning of February 1862: 'Miss Rye you know I set up independent of the Society [SPEW] & there have been stupid complaints which I never listen to, as I am sure Miss Rye is a good woman tho' tough & I could not find a better. She without printing or row got £200 for lady Emigrants & sent them off in the most business like manner which Jane C[row] could not do.'[34] This setting up of the Emigration Society separate from its origins as a development of SPEW is perhaps significant. Barbara was committed to emigration schemes largely because her father had believed in it as a solution; the other members of the Reform Firm were not convinced. Barbara used her customary networking techniques to raise money for the emigration society; by the end of July 1862 she had raised £200 and she wanted to raise £200 more. When writing to wealthy people, such as Lord Shaftesbury, she asked directly for a financial contribution, but in the case of poorer well-wishers, Barbara asked them to contact wealthy philanthropists of their acquaintance.

Maria Rye did not fit in with the other women of the Reform Firm. She did not approve of women entering the world of politics or 'male' professions such as medicine. She was an evangelical Christian with a traditional sense of women's special mission. William Rathbone Greg's article 'Why Are Women Redundant?', published in the *National Review* in 1862, had suggested that as the only 'natural' role for women was that of wife and mother, 'surplus' women in England could be conveniently siphoned off to the colonies. Some of the Reform Firm objected to emigration schemes for women as 'amounting to a sentence of transportation or starvation for old maids'.[35] Maria visited British Columbia and, finding that servants, rather than governesses were required, chose to concentrate on working-class emigration. After a visit to Australia and New Zealand in 1865 she left the Female Middle Class Emigration Society in which Barbara had set her up. This was just as well because she was opposed to the campaign for women's suffrage which all

the other Reform Firm members supported.[36] Her work as honorary
secretary of the society was taken over by her co-worker, Jane Lewin.
Jane Lewin returned to the original brief of the society to help middle-
class women, and generally demanded teaching qualifications from the
women to whom the society offered loans. Under Jane Lewin the society
was then run more along the lines of a professional resettlement agency
than a charity, which was the direction in which Maria had taken it. Jane
continued this work until her retirement in 1881, which effectively ended
the connection between feminism and middle-class emigration. Middle-
class emigration subsequently drifted back into the domain of philanthropy, from which it had emerged.

But troubles were coming, not in single spies, but in battalions.
Barbara, in Algiers, started to receive increasingly critical reports about
Max Hays. It is not clear exactly what the letters were about, but it seems
likely that Max, following the collapse of her 'female marriage' with
Charlotte Cushman, had become involved in a passionate friendship with
Adelaide Procter. In May 1858 Adelaide had dedicated her volume of
poetry, *Legends and Lyrics*, to 'Matilda M. Hays' with a quote taken from
Emerson:

> Our tokens of love are for the most part barbarous. Cold and lifeless,
> because they do not represent our life. The only gift is a portion of
> thyself. Therefore let the farmer give his corn; the miner, a gem; the
> sailor, coral and shells; the painter, his picture; and the poet, his poem.

There must have been something about Max's behaviour which was
causing alarm, because Barbara, who had every reason to be grateful for
her stalwart help during the crisis of Bella's 'madness' in 1856, by 1860
was indicating to Bessie that she was extremely concerned about her. It
could also be that the romantic friendships many of these young women
enjoyed, which for the most part were not sexual ones, had blinded them
to the fact that Max *did* desire sexual relationships with women. The
Journal wanted to present itself as the product of high-minded women,
acting from the best of motives, to serve other high-minded women. It
certainly could not afford to be vulnerable to a scandalous attack. Marian,
when writing to Barbara, had referred to the staff of the *Journal* as 'a
coterie of women', implying that there were dangers of being too much
part of an exclusive clique, in that it was easy to lose sight altogether of
the views of outsiders – outsiders otherwise known as the rest of the
world.[37]

The first external attack which drew blood was on Bessie's pride and joy, the reading room. She had described it to Barbara as 'a very Queen of Clubs!' a punning reference to the exclusive Whig King of Clubs which William Smith had attended.[38] At a time when little public space was available to ladies, to have a club which provided similar facilities to gentlemen's clubs was extremely satisfactory. Its prospectus of 1860 advertised the Ladies' Institute at 19 Langham Place as offering:

> A LADIES' READING ROOM. – (1) The Ladies Reading Room is open from 11 a.m. to 10 p.m. Leading Daily and Weekly Papers, Magazines and Reviews. Terms, one guinea per annum. A two guinea subscription enables the subscriber to bring any lady not a subscriber. N.B. Professional ladies half price.
>
> Ladies visiting the West End on shopping or other business, will find it a great convenience, as attached to the Reading Room is a Luncheon Room, and a room also for the reception of parcels, for the use of the subscribers only.[39]

The subscription price established the reading room as a middle-class affair, where ladies could go to read, talk and meet their friends and see the work of women artists (including Barbara's) on the walls. On 7 January 1860 the *Saturday Review* ran a 'most beastly article' attacking the Ladies' Institute which Bessie described to Barbara as 'dirty and indecent to a horrible degree. I expect it will set all the husbands & fathers of our 80 ladies wild with anger'.[40] The writer of this article disingenuously commented that 'we should not like to refer the committee-women of the ladies reading room to the study of Ecclesiazusae and the Lysistrata, for it is very naughty reading, though it does describe what came of the ladies imitating a masculine institution, and combining against the other sex'. The references to two plays by Aristophanes are telling. In the first play the women outwitted the men so that they could rule in their stead, by insisting that the men had to sexually satisfy every old crone before they would be allowed a young wife; the men were thus sexually exhausted and failed to arrive at the senate to cast their votes. The second reference is to a play in which the women went on a sex strike in order to persuade their husbands to give up war. The *Saturday Review* article implies, firstly, that when women get together without men, it always means trouble for the men and, secondly, that women employ their sexuality (either giving or withholding) to control and outwit men. It might seem fairly commonplace misogynist sneering to us now, but, at the time it was written, it was an attack on 'ladies' which would have been considered 'ungentlemanly' at the least.

None of this had anything directly to do with Max, unless the figuring of women going on a sex strike raises the possibility (subliminally) that women who are giving each other sexual pleasure are the most likely to find men redundant. It is possible that Barbara feared the *Saturday Review* might cast more direct aspersions about lesbianism on the Ladies' Institute, given the slightest opportunity. For example, judging by a response from Bessie in a letter of 8 January 1860 it seems clear that Barbara had asked a fairly blunt question about the nature of Max's attachment to Adelaide:

> It has been a long, & at first it was a very hard struggle to reorganise a life so shattered by her own & other's violence; & I must expect relapses from such a temperament so long as she is this side of the grave – but she is *saved* and one must know my dear child to know the full meaning of that word. And the more successful she is the better she will be . . . Remember the difficulties & disgraces of one's work have to be endured with the rest. It is very hard for women in England just now; men fail them & there is a terrible tacit division between the sexes. It is *no wonder* that the warm tender feelings cling too much to each other in *default* of natural ties . . .[41]

Bessie reasonably defends Max, and may not have comprehended, or may have chosen to disregard, the point that Barbara was trying to make. Barbara's brother, Ben, had long been suspicious of Max, and perhaps he had spelled out to Barbara what men of the world would assume from Max's dress, style and, in particular, her behaviour towards other women.

Barbara, apart from having put up the largest share of money for the *Journal*, also contributed articles on schools for girls, on slavery in America and on Algerian women.[42] In April 1861 Bessie found herself embroiled in a difficulty with Barbara when she rejected an article sent by Eugène attacking 'Emperors and Catholics'. Bessie had wanted him to give a brief survey of 'woman articles from the French newspapers', and she wrote explaining her rejection of the article:

> Now, dear Barbara, you know I can't go out of my natural path to touch on political topics which will bar the Journal from entering France, when I am taking such infinite pains to secure a philanthropic connexion; and as to the religious question, I have *numerous* Catholic & High Church subscribers, & (without any reference to my own opinions) how can I throw an apple of discord into the middle of them. I mean to try to get the paper with some liberal journal during the next day or two. I shall copy it and take it myself. I can't bear him to take

the trouble for nothing & yet you must see how impossible it is for me to use such material.[43]

This rejection, and perhaps the privileging of 'philanthropy' over 'politics', irritated Barbara. In June 1861, when Barbara was visiting Brittany, she was annoyed by the consequences of an extract in the 'Passing Events' section of the *Journal* of May 1861 to 'beautiful church windows . . . made by women in Nantes'. She had searched for the atelier in Nantes, and found no sign of it, only to be told by her husband's relatives that the atelier was at Le Mans.[44] Writing to Aunt Dolly, Barbara referred caustically to the typically 'Journal-like incorrectness'.[45] Barbara (the major shareholder of the *Journal*) was exasperated by professional sloppiness. On her instructions Nannie supplied another £200 of Barbara's money, with the proviso that it was to be used to secure a higher standard of writers.

Joseph Parkes had warned Bessie to be extremely cautious about the moral outlook of her fellow workers, but Bessie, rightly, had followed her own judgement. In April 1861 Barbara complained to Bessie of receiving yet another 'exasperating' letter about quarrels among the women workers at the *Journal*. Bessie replied, saying, 'with all our faults & quarrels there is a real spirit of love at bottom'.[46] The letter to Barbara on this occasion appears to have been sent by Adelaide herself; although Nannie and Adelaide had enjoyed a romantic friendship in their youth, Nannie had been ousted from Adelaide's affections by Max. But now there seems to have been a new jealous crisis, when Max transferred her affections to Lady Monson. The upshot was that Barbara insisted that Max should be removed from the *Journal*. Whether her main motive was to protect the women workers from some kind of 'female rake', or to save the *Journal* from sloppy work, or simply to save it from scandal cannot be certain.

Max finally resigned at the end of 1862 and she seems to have been driven out of the Langham Place group. Bessie, who had herself been deeply attracted to Max when she first met her, by January 1864 was writing to Barbara of Max's 'selfish unstable nature'.[47] After Adelaide's death in the same year, Bessie urged Barbara 'never to question to yourself & others the effect of that friendship [on Adelaide]. It lies in the past inscrutable'.[48] Many years later, Bessie's daughter, Marie Belloc Lowndes, was to describe Max to George Eliot's biographer, Gordon Haight, as 'a tall, handsome woman with a strongly featured face, very clever, and with a great deal of charm, particularly for other women. She formed an ardent friendship with Theodosia, Lady Monson, and spent many years as her companion'.[49] Marie must have had these impressions from her mother, who, in her own memoirs, was reticent about Max, saying she liked 'to observe rigorously the old fashioned rule, *de mortuis nil nisi bonum'*.[50]

To replace Max, Barbara obtained the services of someone she regarded as a great deal more thorough, competent and emotionally stable: Emily Davies. Barbara had formed a high estimate of Emily's potential, considering that although her manner was not pleasing, she had enormous capacity for learning and wells of deep-seated determination. In October 1861, when Emily's father died rather suddenly, Emily and her mother left the Gateshead Rectory and in January 1862 moved into a small house, 17 Cunningham Place, St John's Wood. Emily was now exactly where she wanted to be, at the epicentre of the Reform Firm. With Barbara's approbation she quickly established herself as a central player in the Langham Place group, offering to take over the work of editor if Max finally resigned. Emily took over the editorship of the *Journal* for September and October 1862, and then remained editor for seven months.

In promoting Emily Davies's entry into the Reform Firm, Barbara, although entirely correct in her estimation of Emily's abilities, had created a different form of tension. Bessie disliked working with Emily, claiming that she steamrollered over anyone who had a different opinion. On one occasion Barbara objected to Emily countermanding one of her own instructions and experienced at first hand Emily's wrath at contradiction. Bessie wrote to Barbara: 'as to Emily Davies, I am glad you saw her as a sick porpoise crossed in love because, if she could be so to you, whom she admires, what can she be like to those for whom she has a deep-seated contempt which crops up in many ways, of which I really believe she is half unconscious'.[51] Emily was contemptuous of Catholics, and she felt sure that Bessie was heading fast towards Rome. Bessie increasingly saw the *Journal* in terms of a mission, the very thing that Barbara had dismissed as cant in her earliest essays as a journalist. As Adelaide wrote, to Bessie the *Journal* was a 'moral engine', which would not only 'rescue' gentlewomen desperate for work, but also rescue some of the women working at Langham Place itself.[52] Both Bessie and Adelaide had regarded themselves as in the business of 'saving' Max – from herself and for God presumably – whereas Barbara was primarily concerned with whether Max was competent at her job, and had concluded that she was not.

To judge by the market, rather than by any moral claims, when Emily took over the editorship of the *Journal* its readership was declining. In

September 1862 subscriptions were at 697; by January 1863 they had declined to 624. In that month Emily wrote to Barbara saying: 'I am in the last degree of perplexity about the Journal. Ever since I came into it, Miss Lewin has been constantly in distress & difficulty about money, & yesterday she told me she had not enough to pay the rent.'[53] Sarah Lewin, the treasurer, sent Barbara figures which showed falling subscriptions; Barbara promptly sent a cheque for the rent. The shortfall in income meant that the editors could no longer commission articles from good professional writers. Emily Davies was also increasingly critical of the *Journal*'s political value. She wrote to Barbara on 14 January 1863:

> To create an atmosphere we must be *read*, and the EWJ is not. I think it is of very little use as a rallying point . . . The journal has been of no use in the Medical movement. It was of no use in the London University matter, & is of none now, that I can see, in the Local Examns question . . . I wonder how men could be taught to respect women. *Not* by keeping up feeble journals, that I am convinced of.[54]

This gets to the heart of the matter. By this stage Barbara and Emily were campaigning together on various fronts. In April 1863 Emily edited her last edition of the *Journal* and then joined Emily Faithfull at the *Victoria Magazine*, first defining their relationship in a formal written agreement, as she felt the friendship network of the *Journal* had not proved to be sufficiently businesslike.

The divisions within the Langham Place circle began to manifest themselves around religious differences. The original group of shareholders were mainly Unitarians. Adelaide was a Catholic and Bessie, although formally neutral, was, as Emily suspected, increasingly drawn to the Catholic Church. Emily Davies, Jane Crow, Emily Faithfull and Isa Craig were Anglicans.

Emily Davies wrote to Barbara:

> In everything Bessie says I am struck with her amazing ignorance of what other people think & feel about things in general. If she had been brought up among either Church people or orthodox Dissenters, who between them constitute the great mass of English society she would know there is nothing at all new in women's working together. All over the country, there are Ladies' Associations, Ladies' Committees, Schools managed by ladies, magazines conducted by ladies &c. &c., which get on well enough. The new & difficult thing is for men & women to work together on equal terms, & the existence of the EWJ is not testimony with regard to that.[55]

Bessie also complained to Barbara that she was finding increasing difficulty in getting all the women to pull in the same direction:

> I can work with Unitarians, because tho' I am not dogmatically a *Unitarian* I have been trained in and still retain in a great measure their view of life and its duties. And I could work with Catholics because of my intellectual sympathy with their doctrines, and the definiteness of their plans. But I confess that when I get hold of minds which have been trained (or not trained) in the Church of England, I don't know how to deal with them.[56]

Barbara was by this stage thoroughly disenchanted with the *Journal*, feeling that if it was not serving her political interests she was unwilling to fund it indefinitely. Fortunately for Bessie, when Emily Davies left the *Journal* to join Emily Faithfull, and Bessie resumed the editorship in May 1863, she had just received a legacy and was able to become the major shareholder, holding 123 out of the 351 shares taken up.

Bessie had often found Barbara's criticism of the *Journal* and her co-workers hard to bear. During the period of Barbara's increasing pressure on her to get rid of Max, she wrote with some exasperation that 'Emily [Faithfull], who is a splendid worker, full of energy and ability, is even more unsettled morally than Max. You have always held the purse & been able to hire labour, whereas I have had to trust right and left to the independent actions of those I live with'.[57] This seems a just reproach; Barbara was in Algiers six months of the year, sending home critical letters while Bessie was struggling in the thick of things. Unfortunately, events conspired against Bessie which allowed exactly the kind of coarse laughter and innuendo that she had most feared. In September 1862 she had told Barbara that, although Emily Faithfull was '*very* clever and *very* kind in many ways . . . she has that particular screw loose which might in my opinion some day bring her to Millbank [the penitentiary on the banks of the Thames]. This opinion has slowly formed itself in my mind during the last year and a half, owing to numerous occurrences, great and small . . .'[58]

The first intimation of trouble was in the summer of 1862, when Adelaide informed Bessie that she had broken off her friendship with Emily Faithfull. Adelaide would not say exactly why she had broken with Emily, although Mrs Procter told Robert Browning that Emily had told some tale to Adelaide which she had come to know contained lies.[59] Bessie's consequent anxiety was expressed to Barbara in a letter of 18 May 1863: 'The Portfolio is asked to meet tomorrow night at Emily Faithfull's, a sore vexation, for I don't like to go; & yet just now it is doubly ungracious to stay away.'[60] In November Bessie wrote to tell Barbara that Emily was embroiled in a divorce case that was sure to erupt as a scandal in the public domain: 'I do not think you will do harm by visiting her, but I am publicly involved; & must keep clear of the blow-up which I think must by all the laws of chance, come some day.'[61] And so it did. On 14 November 1863 Admiral Codrington filed for divorce from his wife, accusing her of adultery with two co-respondents, one of whom was a Colonel Anderson. He alleged that Emily Faithfull had allowed his wife and Colonel Anderson to use her home for assignations. In December Bessie cancelled the Victoria Press's contract to print the *English Woman's Journal*. Emily Davies also withdrew from the *Victoria Magazine* and ceased to associate with Emily Faithfull.

On 29 July 1864, when the divorce trial began, it became clear that Mrs Codrington had made a countersuit, a situation newly made possible by the Marriage and Divorce Act of 1857. Mrs Codrington, denying adultery, made a countercharge against her husband, which damaged Emily's reputation irrevocably. She accused her husband of the attempted rape of Emily, while Emily was sharing Mrs Codrington's bed. This enticing picture was covered in avid detail, not only by the gutter press, but in great detail by the respectable *Times*. The high social position of the petitioner and the respondent guaranteed the interest of *The Times*, but it was particularly interested in the novelty of a wife being legally able to countersue. Mrs Codrington alleged that:

> She and the Petitioner were by mutual consent temporarily occupying separate rooms at the Petitioner's then residence in Ecclestone Square and that a Miss Faithfull was then and had for some-time past been occupying the same room and sleeping in the same Bed with her; the Petitioner then occupying an adjoining Room. That in the said month of October one thousand eight hundred and fifty six the Petitioner came in his Night dress from the Room which he then occupied into that occupied by the Respondent and the said Miss Faithfull, got into the Bed in which the Respondent and the said Miss Faithfull were then sleeping and then attempted to have connexion with the said Miss Faithfull while asleep. And the Petitioner was only prevented effecting his purpose by the resistance of the said Miss Faithfull.[62]

Emily, taking the advice of her own solicitor, had already fled the country to avoid being subpoenaed by Mrs Codrington's lawyer, and so was not available for cross-examination. An adjournment was granted on 1 August and, after reading *The Times* of 2 August, Joseph Parkes immediately wrote a series of letters to his daughter, warning her that

'Everybody compromises herself, of your sex, who keeps company with any who have publicly violated the great rules of morality.'[63] This was the same advice that he had given her when Marian had 'eloped' with George Lewes, and on the previous occasion Bessie had clung to her own judgement and sense of honour in not deserting Marian. On this occasion, however, she had already started to distance herself from the soon to be notorious Emily.

When the trial started again on 17 November, Emily was subpoenaed by Mrs Codrington's lawyer, Mr Few. By this stage Emily was a hostile witness, apparently afraid of some evidence which Admiral Codrington had against her, with reference to why he had removed her from his house. In court it emerged that, although she had given evidence to Mr Few in an affidavit of 1858 that the Admiral had taken liberties with her, in fact she had been asleep and was only repeating what Mrs Codrington had told her. As Emily had been just nineteen when first living with the Codringtons there is every likelihood that a worldly woman may have used her as a smokescreen for her affairs, and even persuaded her to tell lies for her to a lawyer. *The Times* of 18 November summarised the troubles between husband and wife in a way that was especially damaging to Emily's reputation:

> In April 185[4], the Admiral went to the Crimea, leaving his wife in London, and was absent until August, 1856. After his return differences took place between them, partly arising, as was suggested, by the presence in the same house of Miss Emily Faithfull, a friend of Mrs. Codrington. In the early part of 1857 Miss Faithfull went, or was sent away at the instance of the Admiral, and a sealed packet was placed in the hands of his brother, the General, containing an explanation of the cause of her dismissal, which remains in his custody with the seals unbroken.

As the contents of the packet never came to light, it gave rise to endless gossip, which could never be convincingly denied. Many readers assumed that Admiral Codrington had surprised his wife and Emily in a lesbian relationship, and that this was the evidence that Admiral Codrington held as his ace card and that had caused Emily to change sides in the divorce case. It was the most sensational divorce trial of the 1860s and Emily Faithfull could not escape unscathed; she must have been either a fool, a liar, a lesbian or a pander. It was, as Joseph Parkes said, a 'dirty case [which] will take all the enamel off of Emily's reputation and ruin her business'.[64] Everyone assumed that the Queen would cancel the royal printership, although in fact she did not. The Social Science Association continued to have their *Transactions* printed by the Victoria Press for several years longer. But, like Max Hays, Emily was exiled from the Reform Firm, although she continued to work in the interests of women all her life. After her death in May 1895, an obituary in the *Illustrated London News* by a woman journalist commented: 'she did cause some mischief by appearing always as *manly* as possible. Her torso portrait looks like that of a stout, serious gentleman – such a mistake!'[65] Clearly the 'lesbian' scandal of the 1864 divorce case had never been forgotten. As with Max Hays, her 'punishment' was to be largely written out of the history of the women's movement.[66]

By 1863 many of the 'liberals' (including Barbara) felt that it was time to put an end to the *Journal*. Bessie, in her new position as major shareholder, increased the share capital of the company from £2,000 to £6,000. A shareholders' meeting of August 1864 transferred the entire management of the *Journal* to Bessie. She attempted a rescue bid by restarting it as the *Alexandra Magazine and Englishwoman's Journal*, selling it at sixpence (half the price of the original) and hoping to gain a wider audience. It did not succeed under Bessie's editorship, and Jessie Boucherett inherited the paper in 1865, a move of which Barbara approved as Jessie had the same kind of political agenda as Barbara. She wrote to Helen Taylor in 1866 encouraging her to take out a subscription, 'I think (and Miss Boucherett too) it will do good . . .'[66] Jessie renamed it the *Englishwoman's Review*, and it kept going until 1903.

After her conversion to Catholicism in 1864, Bessie's viewpoint shifted somewhat from the ideals she had shared with Barbara in her youth. Increasingly Bessie condemned married women working outside the home, and seemed more interested in philanthropic efforts by French Catholic women than in the more politically engaged stance of Barbara, Jessie, Isa and Emily Davies. Her love for Barbara never wavered but her increasing focus on (Catholic) religious matters caused pain to both of them. Barbara no longer looked automatically to Bessie to act as her agent in projects of feminist reform. Increasingly it was Emily Davies she saw as the woman most likely to carry through difficult projects. Emily Davies, however, was nobody's Ganymede, and Barbara was to find that in working with Emily she would not be allowed the pleasant role of 'principal' with willing and grateful workers enacting her ideas. This was in itself no bad thing; but it occasionally came as something of a shock to her.

All in all, Barbara found the constant letters about the quarrels and difficulties among the women of the Reform Firm dispiriting. As early as July 1862 she had confessed as much to her old friend, the Irish poet

William Allingham. An unusually long letter from Barbara, in reply to one from Allingham dated 4 and 5 July gives a sense of how, despite her long commitment to social reform, it was her work as an artist which gave her the most satisfaction and a consistent sense of identity:

> Bessie Parkes gave me your letter in the carriage on Monday night as we were rolling off to the 'Portfolio' party, she with her poem, very sentimental, on 'Separation' (the given subject), and I with my drawing, two bulls fighting and a man separating them on the top of a hill with a pale yellow sunset behind. The party was very pleasant to me because it is always pleasant to see old friends after six months absence, and the 'Portfolio' was originated at 5 Blandford Square tho' now it goes on at Eaton Square, and I and my sister Nannie always look on it as our child. Later we went to another party, very grand Michael Chevalier, Cobden and so on, there.[68]
>
> . . . I love my art more than ever – in fact more in proportion to other loves than ever for I confess the enthusiasm with which I used to leave my easel and go teach at the school or help Bessie in her affairs is wearing off, and if it were not that at thirty-five one has acquired habits which happily cannot be broken I should not go on as I do; I could not begin as I used ten years ago at any of these dusty dirty attempts to help one's fellow creatures, and it is quite natural that my life abroad and out of doors should make me more enterprising for boar-hunts or painting excursions, than for long sojourns in stifling rooms with miserable people. I think of the 'Palace of art' and know it is my temptation – but that is enough of that . . .[69]

But Barbara never did give up on reforming activities; she just changed focus. On 23 October 1862 she had attended a meeting with Isa and Emily in which they formed a 'Committee for Obtaining Admission of Women to University Examinations in Art & Medicine'. This was in the first instance in support of Lizzie Garrett's attempt to apply for matriculation at London University. Although Lizzie's father had begun by thinking that the very idea of a woman doctor was disgusting, he became her staunch supporter, offering to pay all expenses for a campaign to gain the admission of women. Feeling that it was not fair for Mr Garrett to fund the whole cost of a campaign which would eventually benefit all aspiring women, Emily asked Lady Goldsmid to act as treasurer of any donations they received for the 'Admissions to University Examination Fund', and appointed herself as honorary secretary.[70] This modest beginning was to lead to the Reform Firm's campaign to open up higher education for women.

CHAPTER 12

Practising the Art of the Possible

For Barbara, from about the summer of 1863, the strain of juggling all aspects of her life seems to have become more intense. Ellen Allen, the head of Portman Hall School, was to get married and to give up her job. As there was no one else whom she trusted to be the chief mistress, this marriage brought an end to the much-loved project. Bessie, the one always to be relied on, was in Ireland visiting Agnes Procter, now Sister Mary Francis of the Irish Sisters of Mercy, and Barbara felt sure that she was going to 'lose' her friend to Rome. Writing to Bessie, she said:

> I am much distressed at your present bias towards Catholicism. Oh dear you must not take the good in humanity from the good in that old structure. I cannot tell you how wrong your views seem to me to be, and what a bar to anything you ought to wish for, & which we both love to do. God forbid you should go over, & God forbid that the Catholic Church should ever take you in. It is no place for women & no religion is more sensual in its views of women . . .[1]

As well as these two 'desertions' Barbara herself had shrunk away from Marian a little following the Pater's death. Marian's stoical acceptance that death was the end of the individual personality threatened the fragility of Barbara's faith. Writing to Bessie from Algiers on 27 December 1861 Barbara had said:

> tho' I instinctly am an immortal being and never feel weariness of the soul or any unit in my own consciousness of the possibility of any end of life, my faith is not so strong for meeting [Marian] again and I want it to be stronger. I told Marian that if I felt *convinced* as she professed to be of *utter annihilation,* I should not have the power to live for this little scrap of life. Do you see Marian? I have not written to her once.[2]

It was because Barbara so respected Marian's intellect that she was afraid of entering into a theological discussion with her. Barbara's faith was

undogmatic and eccentric; nevertheless, she found her faith in immortal-
ity frequently floundering.

However, this interlude of misunderstanding was swept away when
Romola was published in 1863. Initially, Barbara had felt no great desire
to read an historical novel (a genre she did not much care for), but when
she settled down to read it, she experienced it as a revelation of Marian's
view on the complexities of each individual's search for a satisfying
spiritual life. She wrote to her in July 1863: 'My dear Marian, Romola
interested me more than any of your books . . . I can't tell you how your
picture of Romola's love for her father went to my heart – in fact I felt
more emotions in living in Romola for a week than I have felt in a long
time & I am not one who lives like a polyp.'[3] Bessie later wrote that 'it was
an open secret' that it was Barbara herself who had 'suggested the
conception of *Romola* to George Eliot'.[4] In the novel, the heroine, the
golden-haired Romola, loves her father deeply, and respects him,
although finding his absolute dependence on reason not sufficient to
sustain her own spiritual life. As Bessie seems convinced that Marian had
Barbara in mind, it also raises the possibility that Marian's savage
exposure of the moral bankruptcy of the philandering Tito (and his
horrific death) is a fictional revenge on Chapman.

That summer of 1863, Barbara was worried about the state of health of
her husband and that of her two sisters. Her letter to Marian continues:

> We have both been as happy down here [at Scalands Gate] as it is
> possible to be when those very near are in trouble & both Bell & Nanny
> have been ill all the time. Nanny has an internal complaint which is
> very grave & has kept her lying down ever since I told you she was ill
> nearly 3 months ago; I think she is a little better & her two doctors say
> she will get quite well in a year . . . Bell is in the same state so you see
> dear Marian I have had cause for anxiety. I can bear it well here
> because I feel so well in the country and I paint a great deal every day.

Although Bella had been well after her son Harry's birth in 1862, after
Edmund's birth in 1863 she once again suffered from depression and
emotional instability. On this occasion the General was swift to recognise
the symptoms and arrange for Bella to convalesce in Hastings, where she
always felt happiest. A comment by Marian shows her awareness that
Barbara herself was somewhat exhausted from the diverse claims on her:
'your letter brought me needful comfort. I seldom feel any emanation of
sadness from you, but I had a little consciousness of that sort when you
came to say goodbye, looking so weary . . .'[5]

By the time Bessie returned from her stay in Ireland, Adelaide Procter, aged only thirty-five, was in the last stages of consumption. Adelaide by this time was as popular a woman poet as Elizabeth Barrett Browning and Christina Rossetti, her poems having appeared regularly in Dickens's widely read *Household Words*, as well as in the *English Woman's Journal*.[6] Nannie, who had been the closest friend of Adelaide's youth, had gone to Rome for the winter. The Procters thought it best if Max did not visit her, as she had caused such heartbreak, although she wrote daily letters from Lady Monson's house.[7] In her last days, therefore, Bessie was almost her only visitor outside her immediate family.

Adelaide used what remained of her energy to write *A Chaplet of Verses* which was sold for the benefit of Dr Gilbert's night refuge at Providence Row. When she died on 2 February 1864, Bessie wrote to Barbara:

> How exquisitely lovely she looked all the week, shrouded in white & sprinkled with flowers, nor how bright and peaceful the day of the funeral was, at the Catholic cemetery at Kensal Green, I cannot describe to you now adequately. It was both a calm and a happy death bed dear Barbara. The suffering was so gallantly even gaily borne; her resignation so perfect. Anything of melancholy had long disappeared . . . Her own idea of life and death was thoroughly supernatural. I have tried hard to make everybody about us, about Langham Place see & feel this, and not treat it as a dreadful gloomy misfortune. I believe with my whole force of my soul that she is with Jesus, & being with Him is still closely linked up with His interests here. If I had looked at it in the natural way, simply *death*, removed into an unknown sphere, removed from us, the Church on Earth, the loss would have killed me. But I never could look at it except in the light of her own faith. And I thank God it is so.[8]

Adelaide's death seemed to emblematise the end of youth and all youth's highest hopes. In March that same year William Hunt, Barbara's earliest painting master, died and Bessie wrote to Barbara: 'Henceforth dear, we shall be constantly losing! Presently most of our love will be garnered up in the other world. I feel no doubt of an individuality do you? When I think of my Adelaide's *single* mind & soul, perfect in power to the very last, I am sure she is truly *herself*, there as here, loving & remembering, tender, witty, teasing the Angels! Quite herself!'[9] It is clear that Bessie's growing faith in Catholicism sustained her; Barbara, however, was not comforted. She wrote to Bessie:

> Adelaide's death has come to me like an earthquake. The news of it, even though I knew it would come, shook me from head to foot . . .

Death to me is so very dreadful, and hoping and believing in a future would not make it less so. They who are gone from us here and are deaf and dumb for us all the years we live – it is very dreadful to me . . . I feel Adelaide's death is as a light gone from among us, and that though she did not mean as much to my life as she did to yours.[10]

In March 1864 Bessie's own life was in danger when she caught scarlet fever visiting her friend Mary Merryweather in Liverpool. After training at the Nightingale School at St Thomas's Hospital Mary had become the superintendent of the Training School for Nurses at Liverpool Infirmary, established in 1862 by William Rathbone, Unitarian and Liberal MP. Bessie was critically ill and had to spend a convalescent month with Mary in Liverpool, rather to Barbara's disappointment, because she had hoped that Aunt Ju could bring Bessie out to convalesce in Algiers. Bessie, herself, wanted to join Nannie in Rome, having got into a panic that Nannie was herself at death's door. (Nannie's letters, all her life, made much of her own sufferings.) Nannie, however, made it quite clear that she did not want Bessie with her, having a prejudice that anyone tempted by the Catholic faith should be kept well away from Rome. Bessie respected her wishes, simply commenting to Barbara that 'Nannie seems to have none of the mental & bodily spring which you & I possess – a certain aptitude at seizing the sources of health, oxygen both in the air & in the world of thought. I feel as if I longed to put some of my own life into her'.[11] Nannie spent all winter in Rome where no physician was able to diagnose a physical reason for her ailments; she was still 'delicate' by March 1864 and, having exhausted conventional doctors, was consulting a homoeopath.[12] Barbara increasingly suspected that Nannie was suffering from an hysterical paralysis. Her problems at this point may well have been related to the death of Adelaide.

In April 1864 Barbara arranged for Bessie to have a convalescent holiday at Brown's Farm with Aunt Dolly, in close proximity to Mary Howitt, who was staying at Scalands Gate. Bessie wrote to Barbara saying 'I have just been looking at your cottage [Scalands Gate], with its tall chimney which looks just like a hand put up to say "Here I am" to the neighbours . . . I feel with my dear Adelaide a great chapter of my life were dead & past. It has made me feel strangely as if I were beginning quite another part of my life'.[13] Bessie was indeed drawing closer and closer to the Catholic Church: a letter to her mother again emphasises the failure of Unitarianism from her point of view: 'With regard to Unitarianism, I have the greatest respect and affection for them as they have existed in the last three generations. But I do not believe they have any standpoint from which they can work upon sinners. It seems to me a sort of religion for good people but not for naughty ones; of whom there are an awful number.'[14] Bessie grew ever closer to Monsignor Gilbert, the Irish priest who had opened a night refuge in Providence Row, Finsbury Park, in 1860. As Bessie had never been baptised, her reception into the Catholic Church was simply a matter of being privately baptised by Monsignor Gilbert at St Mary's, Moorfields, in 1864.[15] The event Barbara and Nannie had so long feared, finally took place. Barbara had lost, not her friend certainly, but her Ganymede.

If Barbara experienced some sadness because of Bessie's 'defection' to Rome, that same year she achieved a long-held desire. In November 1864 Barbara went to Paris to work under the tutelage of Camille Corot.[16] It is not surprising that Barbara admired his work. Often described as the poet of French landscape, Corot exploited tonal contrasts rather than strict drawing in his compositions and specialised in the rendering of skies, and particular effects of light on landscape and buildings.[17] Through working with Corot Barbara made a new friend, Charles François Daubigny, a member of the 'Barbizon School', who took their name from a small village on the outskirts of the forest of Fontainebleau where they had settled during the latter half of the 1840s.[18] The forest of Fontainebleau had long provided neo-classical artists with an alternative to the Italian landscape for the backgrounds of their historical or biblical paintings. The forest services maintained strict control over the use of land: it was forbidden to graze cattle, cut wood, or light fires so it retained the density and mystery of a primeval forest. Barbara had certainly been to Fontainebleau before her formal studies with Corot because she had compared the 'tall oaks' of Louisiana with those of Fontainebleau on her American tour of 1857–58.[19] Corot himself went almost every year to Chailly and Barbizon, and increasingly, influenced by the naturalism of the seventeenth-century Dutch landscape painters, the Barbizon School painters moved away from the idealised neo-classical landscapes. Daubigny was probably the highest paid artist of the *paysagistes* of the Barbizon School after Corot. From 1860 onwards Daubigny concentrated his efforts on trying to record transient effects of cloud and sky, working quickly to catch effects before the weather changed. This resulted in an increasing 'simplicity' in his work which has often led to him being called a precursor of Impressionism. This catching of the moment was exactly what Barbara prized: as she wrote to Allingham, 'I do not think a perpetual blue sky is a joyous thing. I like clouds and chasing shadows better.'[20] Barbara and Daubigny enjoyed a long-standing artistic friendship.[21]

Barbara's artistic Romanticism was closely tied up with her own religious feelings; although a free-thinker intellectually, she was not an atheist. As a Unitarian with a strong reliance on knowledge, particularly the power of scientific knowledge to advance humanity, she regarded Catholicism as a backward step (in the ladder of civilisation) in the direction of outdated superstition. Having grown up in Sussex, where anti-Catholicism was particularly virulent, it is hardly surprising that she should feel this. Her marriage to Dr Bodichon, who was violently anti-clerical, further intensified her hostility to its doctrines. Nevertheless, despite the common joke that Unitarianism was just a net to catch a falling Christian on his way to full-blown atheism, this was not the case with Barbara. James Buchanan's Swedenborgianism had laid the ground for an almost mystical spirituality in her, a feeling recognised and shared by Anna Mary Howitt. This sense of God immanent in nature is a feature of all her landscape paintings. On her tour through America she had heard a prayer to God the Mother, and she translated this into her view of nature itself as a kind of maternal God. In short, she thought the duty of man was to improve society, and she accepted the dogma of no specific church, but for all that, she struggled to maintain a spiritual perspective.

Some of her most revealing remarks on her own idiosyncratic religious position were made to her cousin, Hilary Bonham Carter, the eldest daughter of Joanna. Hilary, like Barbara, had had the potential to become a fine painter. However, when in 1838 her father died she had become her mother's main support. In 1850 Mary Clarke Mohl ('Clarkey'), a family friend of all the Smiths, had persuaded Joanna to let Hilary stay with her in Paris and work in a studio there. This, coincidentally, was the year in which Barbara visited Anna Mary and Jane Benham in their Munich studio, a visit which had confirmed Barbara in her ambition to become a professional artist. But although Hilary's talents were considered remarkable, and Clarkey pleaded with her mother to let Hilary work seriously at her painting, Joanna considered that she could not be spared from family duties, and so she was allowed painting lessons only when social engagements permitted. In about 1860, she had gone to serve as helpmate to her adored cousin, Florence Nightingale, who had made use of her rather in the same way that she had previously made use of Aunt Mai. In 1862 Hilary became ill and Florence had sent her away. Again Clarkey tried to protect her favourite from grief. Writing to Florence on 5 February 1862 she said, 'if she is as useful to you as a limb, why should you amputate her? . . . the thing she likes best in the world is being with you and being useful to you.'[22] Florence Nightingale, although like Barbara in having the ability to lead great enterprises, was in this way quite different. Despite her claim to follow a call from God, all her dealings with people seem to have been on the basis of how they could serve her; nothing in her character appears to match Barbara's constant attempts to empower other people. Hilary, once useful to Florence, now felt utterly discarded.

She wrote to Barbara in January 1865, feeling that her life had been a waste of her talents and speaking of her sorrow in experiencing a loss of religious faith. Barbara's answer from Algiers, sensitive to Hilary's crisis, reveals her own religious position, and also her view of the complexity in maintaining the delicate balancing act between duty to one's talent and duties to other people:

> My dearest Hilary, I was going to write you another letter when your very long and sad letter came. I wish I knew better how to answer it. *I wish that* with all my heart. As I do not know how best to answer with the *great consolation* which I believe in as existing somewhere, you must take the second best, on which I live myself, always feeling that there is some way of solving the riddle of the suffering of the world which I cannot see. I have faith, but I am ignorant, and do not live religiously. If I bear troubles and get on in life at all, it is on very second-best expedients which I do not much respect myself – a sort of rough wooden scaffold bridge of life where some day I hope to see a perfect arch. I do not understand God's ways at all in this world. I have not harmonised or made a theory of the facts, I know. I live from hand to mouth. *I try never to think of myself;* when I do I am very unhappy. I say 'Cosmos' when little things annoy me. When I am exaggerating things that happen I say like old Corot, 'il faut chercher les valeurs'.
>
> Then every day of my life I remember what the Pater used to say – 'Direct your thoughts and you will save yourself much suffering' – and I make myself think of what is good and noble, or what is to be done at once. In the morning I plan my day, and I keep my plan unless something more worthy opens, 'mais il faut chercher les valeurs' – and so on . . .
>
> I think you have been very happy in having so many good friends; every good friend one has is a fortification against evil, an extra arm for good. So good habits are all helps, and a routine life if one is dissatisfied or in a weak state of mind. But you know all this. I don't despise any small means of keeping myself in good cheerful working order. Dress helps me. If I am going down, I put on a better and brighter gown, and confessing myself a creature of many wants and many weaknesses, I take anything which can help me. I hope you will be so well and strong when you get this letter that you will laugh at it.
>
> After all, the feeling that others rely on me has given me most

strength of all things. If one leans on one side and one on another it gives strength to what is weaker than either . . .[23]

This tactful letter assuring Hilary that a life spent largely serving other people was not a wasted life but a good one, gives a clear sense that Barbara feels her duty is to support both her husband and Nannie, and that her awareness of their reliance on her helps to keep Barbara herself upright. Barbara, in quoting Corot's views on finding *valeur* (which he had used in the sense of integrity in artistic practice) uses the word also to mean integrity in the sense of moral principles. She implies in her letter that whereas she feels Hilary has succeeded in 'harmonising' her world, she, Barbara, tries, but does not always succeed in harmonising both senses of *valeur*. In April 1865 Hilary was diagnosed as having cancer and she died in September. Florence Nightingale told everyone who would listen how Hilary had allowed her family to destroy her, implying, by contrast, that she, Florence, had been too strong-minded to allow such a thing to happen to her. Florence does not appear ever to have seriously examined her own behaviour towards Hilary. Again, what Barbara thought about all that remains unknown.

When Barbara had invested money and effort in the *English Woman's Journal* she had assumed that, just as the *Leader* and the *Westminster Review* had been committed to the extension of the suffrage, so the *Journal* would become a powerful advocate for women's suffrage. In fact, Barbara had regarded the *Journal* from the first as overly cautious on the political front. Barbara's and Bessie's forebears had pushed for manufacturers, merchants, professional men and farmers to have direct representation. However, although the 1832 Reform Act had enfranchised the heads of middle-class households (the wealth generators), it had also specifically limited the franchise to 'male persons'. James Mill, one of the leading Philosophic Radicals, considering the reform of Parliament had argued in his *Essay on Government* (1824):

> One thing is pretty clear, that all those individuals whose interests are indisputably included in those of other individuals, may be struck off without inconvenience . . . In this light . . . women may be regarded, the interest of almost all of whom is involved either in that of their fathers or in that of their husbands.

Women were assumed to have their interests represented by their fathers, or, after marriage, by their husbands. The whole thrust of Barbara's feminist politics was to establish an individuated legal and political identity for women, and to show that they could contribute to the wealth of the state directly, if given the appropriate education and opportunities to work. Like Mary Wollstonecraft, she also argued that a mother bringing up future citizens should be considered as doing an important job which indirectly, if not directly, contributed to the wealth of the state.

The Social Science Association, as we have seen, had proved an opportunity for women to participate in public policy. At its annual conferences various members of the Reform Firm had offered papers, served on committees, made useful connections and honed their campaigning skills in a neo-political sphere. In June 1862 the Association was allowed to hold a soirée for 8,000 people in the Palace of Westminster itself. There was no historical precedent for such a privilege. The *Spectator* of 14 June said: 'for the first time the volunteer legislators of Great Britain assembled in the halls consecrated to regular legislative business and boldly took possession of the House of Commons', commenting that the Treasury Bench was 'entirely occupied by a group of very determined-looking Social Science ladies'.[24] The sight of the women made the correspondent of the *Daily Telegraph* remark on 9 June that he could 'almost imagine that "women's rights" had been ceded'.[25] The Social Science ladies, having gained a political education, only awaited the emergence of a committed feminist champion in Parliament itself.

1865 was an auspicious year. After a long campaign Elizabeth Garrett became the first woman in England to be submitted to the Society of Apothecaries. Although she could not call herself a doctor until she had completed her studies in Paris, it was, nevertheless, another small triumph for the Reform Firm. In May 1865, a women's discussion and campaign group was set up at the Kensington home of Charlotte Manning. Called the Kensington Society, its founder members were pretty much the same group who had been involved in the married women's property agitation, plus the women who had struggled to open local education examinations to girls. It had about fifty members, including Barbara, Emily Davies, Jessie Boucherett, Dorothea Beale (principal of Cheltenham Ladies' College), Frances Buss (headmistress of North London Collegiate School), Elizabeth Garrett and Helen Taylor.

Helen Taylor's presence in the group was crucial. She was the daughter of Harriet Taylor, who had married John Taylor, eleven years her senior, when she was eighteen. John Taylor was a Unitarian of William Fox's circle and he had met John Stuart Mill there around 1830 when he was recovering from a nervous breakdown. Harriet Taylor and Mill became strongly attracted to each other, and Harriet became estranged from her husband, although not formally separated from him.

Mill and Harriet's relationship was conducted discreetly, and they finally married in 1851, two years after the death of her husband. Harriet subsequently died from tuberculosis while the Mills were travelling in France in 1858 and her daughter, Helen Taylor, born in 1831, took over the role of John Stuart Mill's housekeeper, secretary, and intellectual companion. Helen regarded Mill as her father, and John Stuart Mill regarded it as a sacred trust to his dead wife to assist the feminist cause. In 1861 in an article called 'Considerations on Representative Government', Mill made plain that he disagreed absolutely with his father's position that women's interests could be adequately served by anyone else but women themselves:

> In the preceding argument for universal, but graduated suffrage I have taken no account of difference of sex. I consider it to be as entirely irrelevant to political rights, as difference in height, or in the colour of the hair. All human beings have the same interest in good government; the welfare of all is alike affected by it, and they have equal need of a voice in it to secure their share of its benefits. If there be any difference women require it more than men, since being physically weaker, they are more dependent on law and society for protection.[26]

Mill's stress on 'graduated' suffrage is significant because it implied that the right to vote should be related to an educational benchmark, rather than one of class or gender.

In May 1865 Mill was invited by his fellow Liberals to stand for Parliament for the City of Westminster and made an election promise that he would bring women's suffrage to the attention of Parliament. Barbara campaigned for him by driving her carriage covered with campaign posters through the borough, accompanied by Bessie, Isa Craig and Emily Davies. Emily Davies, ever cautious, wondered whether this flamboyant activity would do Mill more harm than good, 'as one of our friends told us he had heard him described as "the man who wants to have girls in parliament".[27] Whether their election campaign was a help or hindrance, Mill was duly elected on 12 July 1865 and used his election address to reiterate his intention of persuading Parliament to extend the franchise to women.

At the second meeting of the Kensington Society on 21 November 1865, Barbara and Helen Taylor mailed in papers from Algiers and Avignon respectively, advocating the extension of the franchise to women. A resolution in favour of women's suffrage was carried. Barbara spent the winter planning, and when she returned from Algiers in May 1866 she was ready for action. She wrote to Helen Taylor on paper headed 'Society for Promoting the Employment of Women in connexion with the NAPSS, 19 Langham Place, London'. The headed notepaper clearly identified Barbara's Reform Firm position to Helen Taylor, whom I assume she had not previously met, judging by the formal opening of the letter:

Dear Madam,

I am very anxious to have some conversation with you about the possibility of doing something immediately towards getting women voters. I should not like to start a petition or make any movement without knowing what you and Mr J.S. Mill thought expedient at this time. I have only just arrived in London from Algiers but I have already seen many ladies who are willing to take some steps for this cause. Miss Boucherett who is here puts down £25 at once for expenses. I shall be every day this week at this office at 3 p.m. Could you write a petition – which you could bring with you. I myself should propose to try simply for what we were most likely to get immediately . . .[28]

Helen Taylor replied the same day:

Dear Madam,

It seems to me that while a Reform Bill is under discussion and petitions are being presented to Parliament from different classes – asking for representation or protesting against disenfranchisement, it is very desirable that women who wish for political enfranchisement should say so, and that women not saying so now will be used against them in the future and delay the time of their enfranchisement . . . I think the most important thing is to make a demand and commence the first humble beginnings of an agitation for which reasons can be given that are in harmony with the political ideas of English people in general. No idea is so universally accepted and acceptable in England as that taxation and representation ought to go together, and people in general will be much more willing to listen to the assertion that single women and widows of property have been overlooked and left out from the privileges to which their property entitles them, than to the much more startling general proposition that sex is not a proper ground for distinction in political rights . . . We should only be petitioning for the omission of the words male and men from the present act . . . If a tolerably numerously signed petition can be got up my father will gladly undertake to present it and will consider whether it might be made the occasion for anything further. He could at least move for a return of the number of householders disqualified on account of sex, which could be useful to us in many ways if it could be got. I shall be very glad to subscribe £20 towards expenses.[29]

Mill's strategy was to limit his appeal to single women and widows of property who were being taxed without being represented. Mill also thought that Russell Gurney, from a Quaker banking family, who had been elected with Mill in 1865 after a distinguished career as a judge and Recorder of the City of London, might be persuaded to make the motion that a report of 'return' be made to the House giving the actual number of disenfranchised female house owners. Gurney was a Conservative (albeit a 'wet' one) and his support might have helped to establish women's suffrage as a cross-party issue.

Much encouraged, Barbara replied on 11 May 1866 saying that 'Miss Davies Miss Parkes Miss Boucherett Miss Garrett Miss Jane Crow and myself will begin at once to get signatures. I believe Miss Isa Craig would be our secretary – but she could not be asked at present as she is otherwise engaged.'[30] On receiving Helen Taylor's draft petition, Barbara, as the experienced 'old hand' at petitioning, thought it much too long, commenting: 'it would be better to make it as short as possible and to state as few reasons as possible for what we want, everyone has something to say against the reasons . . . none of the five ladies I have named would consent to be secretary and they insisted on my accepting the post pro tem. On my return to France this autumn I believe Miss Craig will be willing to be permanent secretary. I am not a good secretary I am well aware, being legally a Frenchwoman and having a French name, but I could not refuse under present circumstances. Last evening I called on Mrs Peter Taylor ['Mentia', wife of the radical MP Peter Taylor] who is willing to do all in her power. Miss Garrett has lent us the drawing room of this house for any meetings and will allow all letters to be addressed here . . .'[31]

Lizzie Garrett's home at 20 Upper Berkeley Street, which she shared with Jane Crow, was the ideal base for the committee, because she was an independent woman householder, exactly the category of woman who could say, without fear of contradiction, that she was being taxed without being represented. Having co-opted Mentia Taylor on to the committee, the women set to work using the chain-letter system which Barbara had used before in 1855 to petition for changes in the Married Women's Property Laws. Barbara was once again in her political element. On hearing from Barbara less than a month later that the committee had collected nearly 1,500 signatures, Helen replied on 6 June: 'My father will present the petition tomorrow (if that is still the wish of the ladies) and it should be sent to the House of Commons to arrive there before two p.m. tomorrow, Thursday June 7th directed to Mr Mill, and petition written on it. It is indeed a wonderful success. It does honour to the energy of those who have worked for it and promises well for the prospects of any future plan for furthering the same objects.'[32]

There was a small setback on the morning of the 7th when Barbara received a letter from Helen saying that 'My father saw Mr Russell Gurney last night and found that he shrinks from identifying himself with our movement just at the beginning of his parliamentary life – agrees, sympathises, looks forward to helping in the future, but would prefer to do nothing in it at present.'[33] Although timid on this occasion Joseph Gurney was a genuine advocate of women's rights, and helped them later. On the day itself Barbara was ill, so Emily Davies and Lizzie Garrett took the petition to Westminster. There is a (possibly apocryphal) tale that feeling rather encumbered by the huge petition they hid it under the stall of an apple woman, while they went into the lobby to find someone to hand it over to. If it *is* true, it is a wonderful moment; the apple of knowledge and power proscribed to Eve serves as a wonderful metaphor for the ambitions of the Reform Firm. Mill presented the petition of 'Barbara L.S. Bodichon and others', containing the signatures of 1,499 women, in Parliament on 7 June 1866.[34] The names then reel off in alphabetical order; there is no attempt this time to emphasise a leading group of 'respectables' as Barbara had done with the petition to amend the Married Women's Property Laws. The familiar names of the Reform Firm are dotted among the rest: Isabella Blythe, Jessie and Louisa Boucherett, Mrs Lee Bridell (Tottie Fox's married name), Emily Davies, Elizabeth Garrett, Matilda Hays, Jane Lewin, Sarah Lewin, Elizabeth Malleson, Mary Merryweather, Rebecca Moore, Bessie Parkes, Elizabeth Reid, Anne Leigh Smith and Helen Taylor.

Barbara suggested that an association should be formed, with an executive committee of five members, to keep political momentum and pressure on Parliament after the presentation of the petition. On 10 June Helen wrote to say that first she must make clear to Barbara her idea of 'the part men should take'. She wrote:

In the petition it seemed to me desirable that we should not even consult them, in order that Mr Mill might be able to say that it was entirely women's doing. Now although I know that no man suggested *one word* of the petition . . . yet you see the Spectator today insinuates that it was written by a man . . . In our new plan I do not see the same reason not to consult men. We may do as men always have done, consult our relations and friends, as we do not want to say, and therefore require to be able to say with the strictest verbal accuracy, that no men are concerned. But to admit men into the governing body is merely to give over the whole credit into their hands – all the women concerned will merely be considered to take their usual and proper subordinate position. The greatest thing to my mind, that this society can do for us for many years to come is to present the example of women quietly and steadily occupied with purely political work.[35]

During the month of August most of the women were out of town. Mill and Helen were in Avignon where, ever since Harriet's death there in 1858, they had spent half of each year.

Barbara reworked the article she had sent to the Kensington Society on 'Reasons for the Enfranchisement of Women' with the hope of getting it published in the *Fortnightly* or the *Macmillan*. Given Barbara's always forthright, but sometimes wandering arguments, this document was well put together and may have benefited from Helen's editing. A letter from Barbara in August 1866 thanks her for her 'kindness in correcting my MS. I have been all over it again and shall adopt most of the alterations'.[36] The paper made three central arguments. The first concerned the anomaly of taxation without representation, for which she presented the particular example of her friend Matilda Betham-Edwards, a woman farmer who did not have the vote, whereas, as she pointed out, any male keeper of a low beer-house did have the vote. She went on to say, however, that the case 'is scarcely less strong as regards all women, who, as heads of a business or a household, fulfil the duties of a man in the same position'. The second argument was that any class which is not represented is likely to be neglected. She quoted the truism that out of sight is out of mind, and offered as an example the fact that girls had a very small share in educational endowments. Her third argument was centred on the issue of citizenship itself; Barbara considered that a sense of citizenship promoted 'a healthy lively, intelligent interest' in the nation and 'an unselfish devotedness to public service'. 'Public spirit,' she went on to say, 'is like fire: a feeble spark of it may be fanned into a flame, or it may very easily be put out.' Underpinning this central notion of citizenship is a question of dignity: 'Citizenship is an honour, and not to have the full rights of a citizen is a want of honour.'

In September 1866 Barbara had been dismayed by an article in *Blackwood's Magazine* in which Margaret Oliphant dismissed the signatories of the petition as a mere twenty 'unnatural' women, malcontents who, unlike the rest of their sex, refused to content themselves with their divinely ordained domestic sphere.[37] Barbara first considered sending a letter of correction to the magazine, pointing out that nearly 1,500 women had signed the petition, but decided instead to respond to the kinds of argument Oliphant deployed, adding letters she received at the time of the petition. Her pamphlet was published as *Objections to the Enfranchisement Considered* in 1866. In it Barbara countered the assertion that women did not want votes by pointing out that, at the very least, the 1,499 women who had signed the petition demonstrably wanted the vote. She then dismissed the argument that women should not be citizens because of their domestic duties, by pointing out that men had other duties too:

> however important home duties may be we must bear in mind that a woman's duties do not end there. She is a daughter, a sister, the mistress of a household; she ought to be in the broadest sense of the word, a neighbour, both to her equals and to the poor. These are her obvious and undeniable duties, and within the limits of her admitted functions, I should think it is desirable to add to them – duties to her parish and to the State. A woman who is valuable in all the relations of life, a woman of a large nature, will be more perfect in her domestic capacity, and not less.[38]

At the Social Science Association in Manchester, in October 1866, Barbara's paper on *Reasons for the Enfranchisement of Women* was heard by Lydia Becker, a Manchester woman who ran a Ladies' Literary Society but who had no prior connection with feminist circles. She became converted to its ideas and joined the Manchester Women's Suffrage Committee as secretary when it was formed early in 1867.[39] This committee wrote to Barbara asking for '3 thousand copies of my paper on thin paper to send round to 3000 female householders in Manchester' in support of a new suffrage petition.[40] This was an encouraging sign of feminist activism growing all over the country, despite discouraging signs in other quarters. Lydia Becker went on to found and edit the *Women's Suffrage Journal* in 1870, which served the purpose Barbara had desired for the *English Woman's Journal*.

On 20 October 1866, before Helen had returned from Avignon, the other women met and formed a general committee, intended to be a *permanent* suffrage committee. This general committee included five men – George Hastings, the Dean of Canterbury, Russell Gurney, Professor Cairnes and John Westlake. At the same time they formed a smaller provisional committee formed 'for obtaining the abolition of the legal disabilities which at present unqualified women as such from voting for Members of Parliament'. This group was essentially the working group and consisted of Jessie Boucherett, Frances Cobbe, Isa Craig (now Mrs Knox) Miss Lloyd, Lizzie Garrett, Emily Davies and Bessie Parkes. Barbara did not join either committee, because, as she explained to Helen Taylor, she was only in London for a few months a year. She promised always to work as an 'outside scirmisher', which she insisted was her forte.[41] On receiving Barbara's letter, Helen promptly objected to there being men on the general committee. Mentia Taylor (the treasurer) and Emily Davies wrote to Helen urging her to reconsider her position.[42] Barbara also attempted to convince Helen that her concerns about the men's presence were unfounded:

> I have thought much of your reasons for wishing to have women exclusively on the Committee and I do not think they are good. I believe it will be the better to have men and women. I do not think men will get the credit of the movement and I do not think the educational utility of an exclusively woman's movement would be of much value. Women do manage things now and after all what we aim at is getting the suffrage and I think we shall get it 10 years quicker by working the association with a small committee composed of men and women . . . I think a woman as sec. and a woman as treasurer will give a decidedly female character to the association.[43]

Helen does not seem to have fallen out with Barbara directly – it is more likely that she had expected to be the acknowledged leader of the group, and that when she found that Emily Davies was far more centre stage than she could ever be, then she did not want to play at all.

While Barbara was in Algiers during the winter of 1866–67, the Reform Firm kept up the pressure. The suffrage committee collected signatures for two kinds of petition – one with the names of female householders seeking the franchise (the Women Householders' Petition) and the other including the names of all sympathetic men and women (the General Petition). Barbara's pamphlets (*Reasons* and *Objections to the Enfranchisement of Women Considered*) were circulated in order to present the arguments for signing the petition. In January 1867 Jessie Boucherett published a modified version of 'Reasons for the Enfranchisement of Women' in the first edition of the *Englishwoman's Review of Social and Industrial Questions*, under the title 'Authorities and Precedents for Giving the Suffrage to Qualified Women'.

Emily Davies thought it prudent to keep her own name 'out of sight, to avoid the risk of damaging my work in the education field by its being associated with the agitation for the franchise'.[44] Consequently, Lizzie Garrett's older sister, Louisa (Mrs J.W. Smith), took on the role of secretary and figurehead, but tragically, died of appendicitis on 6 February 1867.[45] As the time for presenting the petitions was so near, Barbara's name was entered as Secretary of the suffrage committee, to honour her important work of propaganda.

A General Petition of 3,559 signatures was presented in Parliament on 28 March by the Hon. H.A. Bruce and another, with over 3,000 signatures, was presented by Mill on 5 April. Russell Gurney presented the signatures of 1,605 women householders on 8 April.[46] The *Saturday Review* of 30 March, commented that although Mill himself usually commanded respect he 'can hardly be surprised at finding that his proposal for giving votes to women is generally treated as a joke'. Undaunted, on 20 May, Mill moved an amendment to the Representation of the People Bill (clause 4) 'to leave out the word "men" in order to insert the word "person" instead'. Although the amendment was defeated by a majority of 123, Mill gained 79 favourable votes. Emily wrote to Barbara saying, 'I am glad you thought the Division good. It was pretty much what I expected, and certainly on the whole, encouraging.'[47]

After this there was a move to dissolve the original suffrage group because there were divisions within it. Mentia Taylor and Helen Taylor insisted on a women-only suffrage group. Emily Davies wrote to Barbara on 3 June 1867, wondering what they should do next:

> We *might* have two Committees, one moderate, and the other under Mrs. [Mentia] and Miss Helen Taylor's leadership. But that would expose our divisions to the world, and it would be said that 'women can never work together', etc. which would be very damaging. So on the whole I think with Lady Goldsmid that 'We had better quietly withdraw and stick to our middle-class' [to girls' education]. The best course will perhaps be for you to write to me resigning the Secretaryship. If you could at the same time suggest that the Committee might be dissolved, we could call a meeting for the purpose of receiving your resignation, and discussing whether to dissolve or not.[48]

At a meeting on 14 June, which Barbara attended, she tried to persuade Helen Taylor one last time, but Helen remained adamant that men should be excluded. The original committee was then formally dissolved and a new women-only committee was set up with Mentia Taylor, Frances Power Cobbe and Millicent Garrett (now Mrs Fawcett) of the London National Society for Woman Suffrage. The new committee found themselves in the unenviable position of being subject to the absentee control of Helen Taylor, which turned out to be unworkable.

Frances Power Cobbe resigned in December 1867. Mentia stayed on for a few years, struggling to do Helen's bidding, and as a consequence was herself unable to give strong leadership. Helen continued to cause trouble within the women's movement, having a bitter quarrel with Lydia Becker of Manchester in 1868 and also with Mill's parliamentary successor as champion of the woman's suffrage societies, Jacob Bright, in 1871. Helen Taylor's obduracy may well have set the cause back by driving away many of its most experienced and capable campaigners. Millicent Fawcett later managed to re-form and reunite the suffrage campaign, and the rest, as they say, is history.

Emily Davies refocused her energies immediately on the improvement of girls' education. Barbara had been so debilitated by typhoid fever in January 1867 that she spent most of that year simply trying to recover from it. Barbara was a political pragmatist; she had had no illusions that the struggle for female suffrage would be anything but a long haul. She reputedly said to Emily Davies: 'You will go up and vote upon crutches and I shall come out of my grave and vote in my winding-sheet.'[49] If true, this was an accurate assessment; Emily was eighty-eight when she walked to the poll in 1919. Barbara had been dead for nearly thirty years.

CHAPTER 13

Losing the Honey

Barbara continued to move between England and Algiers. In 1865 Matilda Betham-Edwards, visiting Algiers for the first time, was taken to Campagne du Pavillon by the artist Sophia, Lady Dunbar, who assured her that 'at Mme Bodichon's you will meet all the best people, French and English, in the place'.[1] Milly was a novelist, poet and journalist from a farming family in which many of the women had a literary bent.[2] She was a great Francophile, contributing to the *Daily News* for many years on French topics and writing a guidebook on central France for John Murray. Arriving at Campagne du Pavillon, Milly was struck by Barbara's appearance:

> my hostess entered, looking as English as it was possible to do, and strikingly contrasted to her exotic surroundings, her long sumptuous golden hair ... simply dressed, her Titianesque colouring matching such superb goldenness; looks, words, gesture expressing that love of life, that intense interest in the life of humanity – alike collective and individual – rendering her own so full to overflowing and so serviceable to her generation. This was my first meeting with one who was to become my close friend so long as she lived ... [Dr Bodichon was] bronzed to the hue of a Bedouin and hardly European in his dress. A striking point about the former army surgeon was his hair, an iron-grey poll, so thick, frizzed and fine that during one of his bivouacs in the desert a mouse curled itself up in the mass and lay there till dawn. A passionate lover of birds and beasts, not for worlds would the doctor have dislodged his little intruder until absolutely necessary ... I had here, indeed, the open Sesame for all that Algeria had to show and to teach.[3]

Barbara always enjoyed the company of intellectual women, and Milly's fluent French meant that she was able to converse with Eugène. She suggested that Milly should move out of her hotel and stay with them at Campagne du Pavillon during April. Milly enormously enjoyed the experience of being part of their household:

One day Mme Bodichon's young Arab servant brought in a little wild boar offered for sale. My friend was always ready to buy anything which pleased her, and the few francs demanded were immediately paid down. Hamet used to bring in the baby boar at times to divert us with his infantine antics. It was carried home by the proud purchaser and presented to her husband. Long, I believe, it flourished under the doctor's care. Dr. Bodichon adored animals, and had a pet pig in their Sussex home; the maids used to play at hunting him in the adjoining wood, greatly to the animal's delight.

'Voila', said the doctor, 'une bête qui a énormément d'ésprit!'[4]

Milly described this first visit to Algiers in her book, *A Winter with the Swallows*, which was dedicated with a poem to 'Madame Bodichon of Algiers'.[5]

> Fain would I link your dear and honoured name
> To some bright page of story or of song;
> That so my praises might not do you wrong,
> And I might take your thanks and feel no shame.

Milly used as a frontispiece an engraving of Barbara's picture of the Bay of Algiers plus a drawing of Arabs at prayer by Tottie Bridell Fox. The book is a nice example of the coming together of three talented women's work.

Shortly after Milly's return to England she received a letter from Barbara, dated 26 April, reporting on a plague of locusts which had broken into her paradise:

Last Thursday morning one of our maids – little Katherine [the daughter of a French colonist with a small farm] . . . came running into my room, looking white and ghastly, and crying, 'Les sauterelles! Les sauterelles!' I rushed to the window and saw what looked to be some small glittering birds flying over my lower field. It was the beginning of a great storm. They came in millions and trillions of billions! I can give you no idea of their numbers. The air was full of them. It was like a black hailstorm of the largest hailstones you ever saw. If you could only have seen the wondrous sight!

In a moment, as it were, the whole population were in a state of frightful excitement, and many were weeping aloud. Poor little Katherine's heart was all but breaking for the expected desolation of her father's and brother's little farms. The people turned out shouting, screaming, beating kettles and frying-pans with sticks and stones, firing guns, and waving handkerchiefs, to prevent the destroyers from settling on their field. This has been going on around Algiers during the last few days till the poor people are quite worn out . . .

Just now the air is so thick with them that it is quite unpleasant to be out. You have to keep waving your parasol to keep them off your face, and they alight on your skirt, and stick there by means of their hooked feet. In look they are like immense grasshoppers, with yellow and green bodies, as long and thick as your middle finger. Dr. B tells us that each female lays ninety eggs. The weather is close and warm, with sirocco blowing. We can only hope for a strong wind to come and blow them into the sea.[6]

The following winter, Barbara suggested to Milly that she accompany her to Algiers, travelling slowly through France and Spain, taking a different route to her usual one. They visited a *colonie pénitentiaire agricole* which had been founded in 1839 at Mettray in the Loire valley, in which Matthew Davenport Hill had taken an interest.[7] Barbara described her meeting with its founder Frédéric-Auguste Demetz in a letter home to Marian:

M. Demetz is left now an old man 71. In the village are 10 houses & in each a family of boys 600 in all. Nearly all of them have been condemned to some sentence. 3000 have passed thro' M. Demetz' hands & nearly all have been changed from criminals into useful citizens. It is by far the most remarkable establishment I ever saw in any country & well worth everyone's while to see it . . . He struck me as a man of immense judgement of character & power of organisation – everything in fact in this establishment as in all others depends on the choice of teachers employed. M. Demetz educates his own teachers – he has a college on the estate & tries to get young men to go into it, who, having thought of the church & still wishing for a religious life yet also desire the 'joys of the family'. If we could judge by the teacher who went over the institution with us he has admirably succeeded . . . There are omissions at Mettray but what a difficulty even to make anything so perfect as it is! So I hardly like to mention them – tho' it is that there are no women in his families – and is it not absurd to call anything a family with no woman in it. I felt the want of some good motherly woman for each of the homes. These poor low natured children with bad brains & poor health wanted tender comfortable women; I saw one boy cry because he was scolded for having said some bad word & I felt a woman would have known best how to take advantage of that soft mood. The teacher was kind but it was a military sort of kindness & the boy was too little to be treated as if he had been only a number & not a child.[8]

They also visited another experimental community at La Force in the Dordogne, where Pasteur John Bost had founded 'la famille évangélique' in 1848 for abandoned girls. In 1855 he had added 'Bethesda' for physically and mentally handicapped people. As Barbara described it to Marian:

> he has collected the waifs and strays from the roadsides of life & put them into as good order as human limitations admit of. I learnt a great deal from his orphan girls school . . . but what is the strangest sight is his institution for incurables . . . Here again are small houses & the family arrangements preserved as much as possible. The admirable way in which he makes the deaf lead the blind & the cripple use his head for the idiot & the sound faculty of one help out the imperfection of another is marvellous – the whole spirit of the place was hopefulness and peace.

Barbara eagerly lapped up the landscape between Burgos and Madrid, viewing it in terms of the pictures she would like to paint:

> There were 3 great divisions of pictures which I saw – the horizontal deserts with towers in the faint distance or towns near – the wavy rock deserts – & the pine wood sandy deserts . . . I saw more things I should like to paint in one day than I see in 6 months in Algiers . . .

She had by this time spent ten years painting in Algiers and its attraction to her as a painter was starting to pall. Increasingly she need to refresh herself with new landscapes. In Madrid, Barbara went immediately to the Prado Museum where she had been advised to go by her friend, the painter Brabazon, in order to study the Velázquez paintings. Barbara wrote to Marian:

> Do you care about painting which is quite perfect, as art? Don Diego Rodriguez de Silva y Velasquez is the greatest painter the world has produced. He is not the greatest colourist, he is not the greatest poet, he is not the greatest master of expression. *But he is the greatest painter.* I do not think many people can or ought to care for painting pure without thought of what it says therefore I say it is not worth many people's while to see Velasquez. But I do care for painting and this collection is therefore one of the greatest intellectual pleasures I ever enjoyed in my life. I mean most people like a touching story told badly by painting better than the inside of a dead ox painted miraculously by Rembrandt or an onion & a herring by Chardin who is in fact the only artist I can think of like Velasquez in manner of painting.

Milly went to a bullfight, which Barbara refused to do as the Pater had warned her that he had nearly fainted at one. Typically, she went instead to look at something very few tourists ever did:

> I took a man servant & went to the stables at the back of the Playa de Toros & saw the picadores dress & mount after they had prayed to the Virgin in the dirty little chapel yard. Dreary, dirty and dull it all looked; the horses were horrid scrags from a knackers yard & yet poor brutes they would suffer as much at being disembowelled as the finest arab [horse] in all Algeria & I could not bear to look at them with this anticipation. You know they are blinded to face the bull. They had their eye bands ready – only slipped up a little – dirty bits of rag; the horses were dirty, not cleaned and their harness all rubbish not picturesque . . . The dresses of the picadores were dirty, torn & tinselly & there was not a bit of eager conversation, not even in the crowd round them. I went into every corner & saw the places where the men are taken when wounded etc. You know they had confessed & received absolution & in fact they looked as if they had just come from a stupid sermon & not like men going to join in a national sport . . . I was not allowed to see the bull; he was in the dark to make him savage on coming to the light.

When Milly got back to the hotel she was physically sick from her experience, and rather cross that Barbara had not dissuaded her from going. Barbara's grandfather, William Smith, had himself campaigned against bull-baiting in England, at a time when it was considered a perfectly legitimate rural pastime, rather as some people regard fox-hunting today.

Barbara's package of letters caught up with Marian at Bordeaux, who wrote on 4 January 1867 to say that she was 'so delighted with the letters' that she thought they should be published in a 'good organ'.[9] As a consequence of her efforts an edited and abridged version of the letters eventually appeared as the article 'An Easy Railway Journey in Spain' in *Temple Bar* in January 1869. Inspired by Barbara's letters, Marian and George Lewes did 'go and see' Spain on a ten-week visit. On reaching home on 16 March 1867 Marian plunged into her new work while her impressions were fresh in her mind. During the winter of 1864–65 she had been writing an epic poem called *The Spanish Gypsy*; after her visit to Spain in 1867 she rewrote and amplified it. The role of Fedalma in *The Spanish Gypsy*, as the political leader of her people, suggests something of the *spirit* of Barbara, and it was written at the precise moment when

Barbara was leading her people (women) in the struggle to establish their political identity.

In the mid-1860s Barbara lost two more links with her past. After retiring from actively running his corn dealing business, Uncle Jo Gratton had moved out of High Street, Shoreditch, and into a new house in Gower Street.[10] On 3 November 1865 he died, and was buried according to his wishes in his mother's grave in the north transept of the Abbey of St Albans. He left his house and the residue of his £50,000 estate to Dolly.[11] On different census forms Dolly is variously described as 'housekeeper' or 'wife' to the head of the household, Joseph Gratton.[12] In his will, however, she is simply described as 'my cousin'. Whatever the formal or informal status of their relationship may have been, Dolly had lost her protector and chief companion of many years. Ben Leigh Smith, as one of the will's executors and trustees, managed her affairs for her. Ben was able to use the Gower Street house as his London base, and in spring and summer Aunt Dolly stayed at Brown's (at this time known as Fir Bank in honour of the five fir trees) where her sister Anne had lived so long ago with her five young children. It meant that she was only ten minutes' walk from Scalands Gate, when her beloved Barbara returned every May.

The next loss was 'old Nurse', who was buried in the churchyard of All Saints, Hastings, with a memorial inscription, 'In Memory of Hannah Walker who died November 3 1866 aged 80 for many years the faithful and beloved nurse in the family of the late Benjamin Smith Esq. MP for Norwich.' The inscription was undoubtedly organised by Ben on behalf of all five.

Increasingly, Barbara was lonely within her marriage. As Eugène had made no attempt to learn English, he was dependent on her company and that of her French-speaking friends. When they arrived in England Barbara tended to expect Bessie, whose French was better than Barbara's, to come to Scalands Gate to keep Dr Bodichon company. Bessie started to resent this, writing to her mother that Barbara 'likes to force me to go to Scalands when it suits her, and I feel that more and more I am becoming a sort of cushion between her and Eugène Bodichon'.[13] Barbara had to seek congenial company for her husband, partly because she was busy with her social duties, but also because neither of her brothers ever showed any wish to get involved with him.

In 1864 when Bessie had been taken dangerously ill with scarlet fever Barbara had written to her: 'take care of your precious self, and do not go and die! I do want us all to have some children, including yourself. It would be such a pity if none of us have any. If I can create one in the next three years, I will.' That same year she had written to Nannie, 'Did you hear about the storks building on my studio top in Algiers? I hope it is a good omen.'[14] But by 1867, aged forty, she was beginning to despair of ever having children. Her picture entitled *Solitude* with its blue tones and one lonely wheeling stork perhaps represents the depth of her disappointment. In the mid-nineteenth century women's periods usually ceased at about forty-five years of age, so Barbara would probably have already been suffering the typical pre-menopausal symptoms of broken sleep and hot flushes which accompany decline in fertility.[15] She had always suffered from irregular periods so, as she approached menopause, she was possibly suffering hormonal swoops and dives. She appears to have described some of her symptoms to Marian, judging from her response:

> My dear Barbara . . . George and I have both been more suffering than usual, but we are always grumblers, so there is no use in dwelling on what is so far from exceptional. *Your* illness is much more of a case to inquire about. Why did you not tell me what was the matter with you? – Palpitations – or what else? And are you well again? I am terribly afraid that you are worrying yourself about the unchangeable – looking for fowl's milk or some other impossibility – when half the great lesson in life is to adapt one's soul to the irremediable.
>
> Confess and be healed by adopting the prescriptions you have had over and over again. There are no other. Certain human natures, have limits as immovable as the Jura. You may say you can't help feeling anguish, and that is true enough. But the anguish is fed by false hope, as fire is fed by fuel . . .
>
> When you write again, remember to tell me particularly about the progress of Nannie's health. I want to hear that she is thoroughly restored to all the enjoyments of life – that she can walk, ride, paint, and be active in the many valuable ways her nature prompts.[16]

It seems likely that Barbara had once again asked her husband whether he would live with her in England, and he had once again refused. The question of Nannie's health is a more vexing mystery, for despite her well-established persona of semi-invalidism Nannie lived well into the twentieth century, long after both her sisters were dead.

What is certain is that Barbara continued to regard her 'baby' sister as her own special responsibility, even though Nannie had chosen Isabella Blythe as her life partner. She had first met Isabella at Bedford College. Isabella was training to make her living as a governess, and, through Nannie, had also become involved with the Reform Firm and the Portfolio Club. Faced with the near certainty of permanent exile in

Algeria, and with the decreasing likelihood of having children, Barbara persuaded Nannie to buy a house next door to her on Mustapha Supérieure.[17] Meanwhile Nannie and Isabella moved into Campagne Montfeld. This was to prove less than an ideal solution. Between Eugène and Nannie there existed, almost from their first meeting, feelings of mutual antipathy. In her efforts to manage the problem Barbara was simply denying uncomfortable facts by trying to mould them into a more tolerable shape.[18] Instead of analysing the real roots of her feelings of isolation, she had created a situation in Algiers which could only make for unhappiness.

As a couple of people determined to quarrel with one another, almost any pretext would have served, but an opportunity was already to hand. Eugène had long been interested in the health-giving properties of plants, and the possibilities of exploiting them in different landscapes and climates. He wrote:

> The introduction of an unknown plant is often the only benefit accruing to humanity from wars and wholesale migrations . . . What were the results of the gigantic struggles between Europe and Asia in the Middle Ages? Four or five millions of men perished. Their ashes have been scattered to the winds; but meantime, the mulberry tree, the sugar-cane, and buckwheat were introduced into Europe. Such is the real result to humanity.[19]

In France in 1804 seeds of the *Eucalyptus globulus*, commonly called the blue gum, had been imported from Australia and planted on the Riviera.[20] These blue gums had then been introduced into Algeria in 1854, where a M. Trottier had successfully grown them from seed. In 1864 Eugène had visited these plantations, and transplanted many young trees on to the Bodichons' twelve acres on Mustapha Supérieure.[21] The trees were faintly aromatic, the crushed leaves giving off a cooling camphor-like scent even on the hottest day, and the eucalyptus oil obtained from the dried leaves could be used as an antiseptic in the treatment of nose and throat disorders, and as a prophylactic against malaria and other fevers.[22] As Barbara wrote in an article for the *Pall Mall Gazette*:

> Dr. Bodichon insists that Africa has a deteriorating effect on men, principally owing to the irritating effects of the dry air and of the sirocco . . . There is in Australia a wonderful tree, the Eucalyptus or Gum-tree, which will probably be of enormous benefit to Algeria in this particular. It grows there as well as in Australia, and has this

valuable quality, that, though it is a tree growing with extraordinary rapidity, its wood is of extreme hardness, and much esteemed for building and for the construction of vessels. It overturns all our ideas of the supposed relation between slowness of growth and hardness of wood. The Eucalyptus globulus at fifteen years of age is as valuable as an oak tree of one hundred years.[23]

However, the gums were already three feet in circumference, at only four years old, and extremely fast-growing, likely to reach a height of anywhere between 200 to 300 feet. Nannie strenuously objected that Dr Bodichon's 'forest' would soon block out her views down to the bay, which was the chief charm of living on Mustapha Supérieure. Nannie expected Barbara to take her side; but Barbara backed her husband's project. These little trees were his 'children', his hobby, and they might even eventually provide him with an independent income. So, ironically the 'healing' eucalyptus was to be both source and emblem of a bitter and long-running battle between Nannie and Eugène in which Barbara was the unhappy pig-in-the-middle.

Despite the supposedly prophylactic qualities of the eucalyptus trees, in the early spring of 1867 Barbara contracted typhoid, was briefly extremely ill, and returned to Europe earlier than usual. One cannot help wondering whether she was glad to have an excuse to get away from Algiers early that year. Marian wrote to her, deeply concerned, on 18 March 1867: 'Dearest Barbara, We got home only the day before yesterday (Saturday the 16th) and there I found Bessie's letter enclosing your own few words in pencil written from Marseilles. That was the first news I had had of your illness, and it was a painful shock to me – all the more because the information I got left me still ignorant as to the nature of your illness, and the reasons why you are moving northward into a horrible climate. Pray let me hear somehow what has been the matter with you, and where you are going.'[24] From Marseilles Barbara and Bessie stayed in Avignon briefly, each accompanied by a maid. As soon as they arrived in Paris, however, they sent their maids back to England and Algiers respectively, so that they could enjoy an uninterrupted tête-à-tête.

In Paris they asked Clarkey (Madame Mohl), who knew everybody and everything, if she could recommend a peaceful spot for Barbara to take a convalescent holiday. She suggested that they rent a chalet at La Celle St Cloud, a beautiful village between Versailles and St Germain, only twelve miles from Paris, owned by her friend Mme Belloc. This suggestion strongly appealed to Barbara because the owner was the widow of the painter, Jean-Hilaire Belloc, and her friend Lauret had trained under him. In addition, Louise Swanton Belloc was a woman who earned her living as a writer. She was the editor of two periodicals and the author of over forty books, including a life of Byron, and had translated into French books by Maria Edgeworth, Dickens, Mrs Gaskell and Harriet Beecher Stowe.[25]

They took the chalet for six weeks and while Barbara slowly recovered by throwing herself into her painting Bessie became exceedingly attached to Mme Belloc. Louise Swanton Belloc was of Irish and French ancestry and at seventy-one still showed signs of the extraordinary beauty she had possessed as a young woman.[26] She was a compelling character, who in the 1820s in Paris had attracted the love of several women.[27] In particular, Adelaide Montgolfier's love for Louise was a possessive and jealous one, and she had succeeded in breaking up Louise's friendship with Clarkey (for a period of twenty years) for both women were determined to be the 'first friend'. After Louise's marriage to Jean-Hilaire Belloc in 1821 Adelaide spent every summer with them, collaborating in Louise's writing, and she was her 'most intimate friend for close on sixty years'.[28]

Bessie's intense attachment to Louise Belloc was perhaps a deep-seated need for someone to love, and her new friend seemed a sort of ideal woman. Her beloved friend Adelaide Procter was dead. The *English Woman's Journal*, with all the excitement of working for a great moral cause, as she had seen it, was also gone. Her father, Joseph Parkes had died on 11 August 1865 and was buried next to her brother in All Saints churchyard, Hastings. She was finally free of Sam Blackwell. Bessie's loyal nature meant that she would not have abandoned Sam because he had money troubles, but she was finally persuaded that he had behaved dishonourably both in business and in an affair of the heart. Consequently she felt free to break off her engagement at the beginning of 1866. Marian wrote to Barbara that she was 'delighted to know of Bessie's final decision against the marriage. She seems bright and happy, and courageous in the hope of working with her pen so as to eke out her income'.[29] For two years Bessie had also been pressed by Henry Fawcett, Professor of Political Economy at Cambridge University and a Liberal MP, to marry him. He had been blinded in a shooting accident but had bravely carried on almost as before. Although Bessie regarded him as a noble man, she was not romantically inclined towards him. This was possibly just as well, as he seems to have proposed to quite a surprising number of women. He had already asked and been refused by Lizzie Garrett and in October 1866 had been accepted by Lizzie's young sister, Millicent.[30] Lizzie did not like to tell her sister that a man who kept proposing to one woman after another was hardly a good bet, but had suggested that Millicent might ask Barbara for advice. Millicent rejected this idea rather forcibly, saying that 'judging from Dr Bodichon's appearance, I should say that it was improbable that we should agree in the choice of husbands'.[31] Bessie, although she believed Fawcett to be a noble soul, did not feel that 'we should ever have done together' and so she was both pleased and rather relieved when he married Millicent Garrett on 23 April 1867.[32] Barbara promptly offered Scalands Gate to them for their honeymoon.

Barbara had been deeply disturbed by the quarrel between her husband and Nannie, and was relieved to be away from them both. She was happy to be with dear Bessie, who loved her, and made no claims on her. As soon as she felt better, she reverted to her usual habit of spending many hours a day painting outdoors. While she was busy, to her utter astonishment, Bessie fell suddenly and completely in love with the son of the house, Louis Belloc, a man who had been an invalid for thirteen years, following some kind of brain fever and breakdown. Before Barbara had the slightest inkling of what was going on, Louis, aged thirty-seven, had proposed marriage to Bessie, also aged thirty-seven, and she had accepted.

When Bessie told Barbara that she was going to marry Louis, Barbara was thunderstruck.[33] Even Louis's mother was astonished that Bessie should accept, and felt that she must be marrying him out of pity. In a letter in which she described the inflammation of the brain which had reduced her son to an invalid, Louise wrote to Bessie:

> Your letter has not only much surprised me, it has also profoundly moved and troubled me . . . You do not really know Louis, and so you cannot realise, as I do, that while he possesses exceptional kindness of heart, delicacy of nature, and certain important high principles, he now lacks all initiative. Any woman who married him would have to lavish on him the affection of a mother, as well as that of a wife. Is not this too much to ask of human nature?[34]

It may be that Louis's 'feminine' nature was exactly what allowed Bessie to contemplate the marriage. The most significant relationships she had had till this moment had been with women, and she disliked any kind of 'coarseness' in men.

The other person deeply shocked by this strange and sudden turn of events was Bessie's mother, Elizabeth Parkes. Her marriage had not been entirely happy, but nevertheless, she missed her husband after his death in 1865, and she had clung to Bessie more and more. She was now faced with losing her only remaining child. She was devastated that Bessie was about to marry someone she hardly knew and (presumably) live abroad. It was perhaps the sense that either her mother or Barbara would simply lay claim to her life that incited Bessie to make her escape. After spending another two weeks with the Bellocs (and without Barbara), Bessie wrote to her mother:

> I cannot allow, my dear mother, that 'marriage is a lottery'. I believe too firmly in the special leading of Providence not to believe that, in certain cases at any rate, marriages are directed. I even believe that the marriage of Barbara and Dr Bodichon was made in Heaven, and I have never regarded her marriage to that singular man with any regret. Difficulties and dangers would have come with anybody the dear woman had married. The dangers to be feared in any marriage seem to me to lie in character. And as we ourselves are always half of any tie we form, the first thing we have to consider is whether we are ready to do our share. I am certain that if one half thoroughly does its duty, the other half in the end will do its duty too.[35]

Leaving France and arriving in England, Bessie went to stay with Barbara at Scalands Gate, where she endured the utter misery of Barbara's impassioned attempts to talk her out of the marriage. Barbara's intense concern that Bessie should not marry a foreigner was perhaps a reflection of her own sense of the sacrifice she had made by living mainly away from her native land.

Barbara remained depressed by the whole business, although she was somewhat cheered by a visit from Emily Blackwell, Elizabeth's sister. At St Cloud, Barbara had received a letter from Marian, urging her 'not to come to England till there is no risk of your being overdone by affectionate friends. So many are interested in you that I feel a sympathetic fatigue at the idea of the kindness that would be poured out upon you; Bessie would be crushed in attempting to defend you from it.'[36] Marian's letter also brought news of the death of their mutual friend Joseph Neuberg, who, long ago, had wanted Barbara to marry him. At that time, she had been too wrapped up in the 'affair' with John Chapman to respond, but perhaps, in this mid-life crisis, Barbara indulged just a little in contemplating some of those alternative scenarios. She continued to brood over Bessie's impending marriage, which had originally been planned for the following spring, when to her horror Bessie told her that she had decided to marry on 19 September. Perhaps Bessie felt that in the face of opposition from her mother,

Barbara and even her beloved Mary Merryweather, it was better simply to get on with it.

Still feeling sure that the marriage would prove a catastrophe, at the end of August Barbara wrote to Louis's mother, sending a copy to Bessie:

> Dear Madame Belloc, – Although you are not aware of it, for after all you do not really know her, Bessie is far too nervous and too delicate to undertake married life under what would be, as I am sure you must agree, unusual difficulties. She is unaware of it, but *I* know that in time she will feel intensely the abandonment of all she has gained by her noble life of work for others in England. She has built up, though she may not be conscious of it, a position of great distinction. All this she now proposes to give up, apparently without a thought. And I fear she has not consulted any man who would give her honest and impartial advice.
>
> As for me, her oldest, closest, and most devoted friend, I feel compelled to tell you that I entirely disapprove of this hasty marriage, and I beg you earnestly to ask her to pause, and to think, even now, well over what she is about to do. I was amazed when I heard the news. Indeed it was a fearful shock. I also feel the terrible responsibility of being the only person who knows both Bessie and Monsieur Belloc. Should the marriage take place, I implore you, Madame, to try and feel – not as a mother-in-law feels, but as a real mother feels.
>
> Still as Bessie knows, I feel that I am her sister, and, as I am constant in my relations, if she marries Monsieur Belloc, then I shall consider him exactly as I should do were he in truth my brother-in-law. And I am not going to tell anyone but Bessie and you what I think.
>
> I hope you will not think it strange of me to say that I shall feel free, if you all wish it, after having told you my opinion, to continue my lifelong relation to Bessie. But I was bound to write this letter, on no other terms could I have done so.[37]

This letter suggests more explicitly than any other statement Barbara ever made in her life, that ten years after her marriage she had huge regrets about its consequences, primarily that of having to live out of England, estranged from the pulse of social affairs. Had children resulted from the marriage, the regrets she experienced would probably have been less acute. Madame Belloc, not surprisingly, having been doubtful about the marriage in the first place, now agonised over 'the disapprobation of the woman who loves you so deeply'.[38]

Bessie was hurt and angry at Barbara's intervention, especially when she herself had supported Barbara in her desire to marry Eugène, and in so doing had forfeited Ben's friendship. Louise Belloc wrote to Barbara, assuring her that she had encouraged Bessie to take her time, and that Bessie had quite made up her mind. Once Barbara realised that the wedding would go forward, she sent invitations to Louis and his mother to stay with her in Blandford Square at the time of the wedding. She had behaved honourably, and as Louise wrote to Bessie, she would have been 'ashamed not to recognise your friend's fine nature, and I am glad she will never know the agonising hours she caused me to endure'.[39] Bessie and Louis married at the Catholic church in Old Spanish Place, London on 19 September. For a wedding gift, Mrs Parkes gave her daughter's bridegroom her most treasured possession, Priestley's dressing-case, given to him by his parents as a twenty-first birthday present. Bessie and Louis moved into the chalet at St Cloud, which had so recently been occupied by herself and Barbara. Bessie wrote to her mother in November:

> How strange that Barbara should think I ever feel lonely! There have been times in my life when I have felt painfully alone, but never since the fortunate day when she and I settled into the chalet last spring. I remember feeling that evening as if I had stepped into a new dimension, and in that dimension I have, thank God, dwelt ever since, with increasing joy and peace. I am naturally glad of letters from England, and I delight in any newspaper sent me. Still, I am becoming in a real sense a Frenchwoman.[40]

Barbara was left behind, forlorn and depressed. She was somewhat comforted by receiving letters from Mary Howitt, now living in Rome during the winters and in Dietenheim in the Austrian Tyrol during the summers. The Howitts and their daughter Margaret had come to know and love the American sculptor, Margaret Foley, whom Barbara had met in America back in 1858 and had recommended to join Hatty Hosmer's group in Rome. Nannie and Isabella Blythe had joined the Howitt group in the late summer in the Tyrol, which again made Barbara feel somehow alone and inconsequential. Mary, as ever, was maternal in her solicitude for Barbara's welfare:

> My dear Barbara,
> It is with deep sorrow that we hear of your great illness. We heard of it from [Anna Mary] first, then from Dr Elizabeth Blackwell, then from Isabella Blythe – all within a few days. Very sorry indeed are we to know that you – the very embodiment of health & strength have been thus suddenly smitten down . . . You have been for years a sort of ideal person a strong glorious powerful woman, gifted by God with your

endowments, my living representation of a northern heroine, a modern Valkyria & though it is years now since I saw you, – you remain large and beautiful in my memory & in my heart as you were in those far off days when we were all younger.[41]

A letter from Barbara to William Allingham of 10 September 1867 serves as the clearest indication of how low she was feeling:

> I have been very ill in Africa with the fever of the country and I have a better perception than I used to have, of the dreary moods of life – for a long time I was so weak that hope and life seemed to have gone out. But no more of that – courage and health seem to be coming back together and perhaps being ill has given me a wider sympathy. No! I shall not be in London at all this year. I mean to stay here until the woods are too damp and wet to allow me to live out of doors, – at present I am out on horseback at 8 a.m. and the rest of the day very nearly all the hours of it are spent in my little wood; I have got an old wood-cutter to cut out paths and glimpses of views, and now we are cutting a clearing to build some cottages on to let for two shillings a week each (when built), and perhaps I may build a little school if the good clergyman's family don't worry me too much (every one wanted to convert me when I looked so ill). I want to have an infant school here very much.[42]

In this letter Barbara shows signs of a deep desire to bed down in Sussex; setting up an infant school there would have given her an 'excuse' to remain, rather than going back to Algiers.

Fortunately, perhaps, the campaign to establish a women's university college was just beginning and aroused Barbara's long-held interest and ambition. Emily Davies had been to spend the month of August with her in the Sussex woods, where she was shocked to see how ill Barbara appeared. Writing from Scalands Gate, Emily observed that 'Mrs. Bodichon is, I am sorry to say, sadly broken down by her fever. It was a very bad attack and she has never had a fair chance of recovery, for people *won't* let her alone. It is quite a caution against forming the habit of benevolence, it is so difficult to break it off'.[43] Emily clearly did not regard herself as belonging to the category of people who would not let Barbara alone, although she herself had gone down to see whether Barbara would make a firm financial commitment to the establishment of a university college for women.

Barbara continued to feel unwell, and was irritated with any attempts to persuade her to go back to Algiers that winter. A letter from Scalands

Gate to Emily Blackwell begun on 28 September and bearing the instruction 'Burn this' reveals a fury at Nannie's attempts to make her come and at Bessie's complicity (as she sees it) in her predicament:

> Nanny is cross with me because I cannot go back to Algiers & Bessie has persuaded her (*I think*) that there is nothing much the matter. In fact Bessie is a sort of special pleader who turns me & Nanny & any one round her fingers. She *always misrepresents facts*. I am grieved for poor Nanny. But *she should not write unkind letters to me*. As for Bessie I have done all she asked me about her affairs, & I am grieved at her persistent wrongheadedness about mine.
>
> Nanny will see you & you will judge for yourself but I am sure (I feel it) tho' I do not know it! that Nanny was not pleased with your letter & that Bessie's wiles have perverted her clear eyesight. I have been getting better but when Nanny & Isabella & all the Ludlows came at once it upset me & I have got back that confused head & railway rattle again *so bad sometimes,* for 2 weeks before that I was without it.
>
> Bessie hopes I shall 'cross the channel soon'!! If she had any idea how I suffered in France! Good heavens! she would not hope any such thing! I am shocked at Bessie's marriage but you can see & judge for yourself – & I think you will not expect me to go to La Celle St. C. even if every stone there were not a reminder of hours & weeks of *agony of fatigue without sleep* . . .
>
> 29th. My dear you must come and spend as much time as you can with me before you go. I do so want to see you & I do so want to get back my *good working brain* which I don't think I should have lost if I had not gone to Algiers. I can bear anything in England. My not going back to Algiers is a terrible disappointment to Nanny. I cry when I think of it; but she is so much better now! That is a comfort. I am better too so perhaps I may get well.[44]

Much of what Barbara was suffering were the after-effects of typhoid, which lowers the immune system, so that convalescence is a long-drawn-out affair. Added to her physical state, Bessie's unexpected marriage, and the death of Bella's third child, Edmund Villeneufe (at only four years old), that same troubled year combined to make the usually buoyant Barbara feel fragile, both physically and emotionally.

After three months of marriage, Bessie wrote saying that she was pregnant, and Barbara replied in a doom-laden letter. Bessie wrote back, amused rather than offended by Barbara's 'croaking':

> My dearest Bar, – I could not help smiling as I read your dreadful letter. I am remarkably well – in fact much better than I was before my

marriage. Do believe me when I say that it is very wrong of you to anticipate any special trouble. I hope to have at least two – perhaps three – children. I don't feel I could go in for more at my time of life.[45]

Bessie returned to London to have her baby, because, as she wrote to her mother, 'our only doctor for miles around is very old-fashioned ... I naturally intend to have my monthly nurse chosen by Mary Merryweather. She has one in her mind who has already brought forty-eight babies into the world without a doctor'.[46]

At the beginning of January 1868 Barbara went to stay with Willie and his wife Georgina at their house, Crowham Manor, still feeling curiously redundant. She missed Bessie terribly, but could not face seeing her. Perhaps the fact that Bessie was about to have a child was impossibly painful, when her own chances of maternity now seemed hopeless. Writing to Emily Blackwell, still wishing that Emily and Elizabeth could come and stay with her, she said:

> I am pretty well but as for plans I have none. I have no one to stay with me particularly, I dont know exactly what to do. It is snowing hard or I should have gone to the cottage [Scalands Gate] & I suppose I shall go to London tho' Bessie Belloc is there for a month. You see the very few people I am fond of are all at work for others & I really have no one. I can get on very well in London & I think I shall have a French girl to stay with me there but in the country or at the sea I cant read or draw long enough to be all alone. It is very cold but I do not mind it much. I think I had best go to London & just keep out of Bessie's way as much as I can.[47]

Her chief enjoyment at this period when everyone except herself seemed full of work and plans was the time spent with Willie's '3 little chicks whom I love very much and 2 more at Bell's not far off'. The eldest of Willie's children, Amy, was her favourite; perhaps she served as a substitute for the child she longed for but did not have.

Bessie, despite Barbara's forebodings, at thirty-eight safely gave birth to a little girl, Marie.[48] Bessie was at first rather nonplussed by the experience and wrote to Barbara: 'I feel like a traveller on the banks of the Amazon who is suddenly approached by a small unknown animal, and is, if charmed and interested, yet not sure how the little animal will turn out.'[49] Bessie felt surprisingly well, and three weeks after the birth felt ready to go back to her French home. Barbara invited her to come and stay with her baby at Scalands Gate. Bessie refused, saying, 'you are the only one of my friends who knows my beautiful home. Surely you can understand how I long to be back there?' For Barbara, 1868 produced only another death. Aunt Dolly died at on 25 October at Brown's, and was buried in Brightling churchyard. The link with her mother disintegrated with the death of Aunt Dolly. Barbara was nobody's daughter and nobody's mother.

CHAPTER 14

The Hitchin Years

Despite the after-effects of typhoid fever, Barbara was not idle in terms of her 'social' efforts, for she had mentally returned to her early dream of a university college for women, the dream of Ida in *The Princess*. In 1858 a Royal Commission on Popular Education had been set up to investigate education provided for working-class children. This commission broke new ground, because 'for the first time, women were invited to give expert advice in a written circular . . . The twelve female witnesses were questioned because of their activities in running elementary ragged or charity schools'.[1] The fact that Barbara was one of the twelve women invited shows that her contribution to popular education had been officially recognised. In August 1859, when she gave her testimony, she deplored the lack of properly trained women teachers for girls' schools, and blamed fathers for not investing money in the education of their girls. Her analysis made it clear that the education problem was symptomatic of a wider social malaise: 'I believe', she wrote:

> the laws and social arrangements affecting the condition of wives in England, to be one of the causes why good teachers cannot be found for girls' schools, and why girls' schools deserve the bad character the Rev. J.P. Norris so truly gives them. I believe that, until the law gives a married woman a right to her own wages, and an independent legal existence, some control over her children, and social arrangements admit a woman's right to more liberty of action, that the education of girls will be miserably neglected.[2]

Barbara had also contributed a paper on 'Middle-class Schools for Girls' to the fourth annual meeting of the Social Science Association held in Glasgow in September 1860, which was read in her absence by Bessie, and later published in the November 1860 issue of the *English Woman's Journal*. Here, Barbara had pointed out the difficulty in establishing any reliable data:

It is exceedingly difficult to visit such establishments; they are *private* and I have found the mistresses exceedingly jealous of inspection, most unwilling to show a stranger (and quite naturally) anything of the school books, or to answer any questions.

She had referred to the inequity of endowments for boys and girls of the middle class, and had expressed her desire that the rich should be persuaded to give money to provide for girls an equivalent to the boys' grammar schools. Her argument was that 'giving education, the very means of self-help, is the safest way of being charitable'.[3] She further argued that the gulf between the education of middle-class girls and boys of the same class was wider than the gulf between the education of working-class girls and boys. The gulf widened between the genders when middle-class boys went first to public schools, and then to Oxford and Cambridge.

Adelaide Procter's desolate poem 'Philip and Mildred' published in *Legends and Lyrics* in 1858 represented just such a gulf. It describes a young village couple, sweethearts in their youth, who engage to marry before he goes away to university. He returns and marries her, but the long-awaited happiness has become hollow:

Darker grew the clouds above her, and the slow conviction clearer,
That he gave her home and pity, but that heart, and soul, and mind
Were beyond her now; he loved her, and in youth he had been near her
But he now had gone far onward, and had left her there behind.

Inevitably there are varying accounts of the beginning of the movement towards the founding of the first university-level college for women in Britain, but in 1857 and 1858 Oxford and Cambridge established a 'local' or 'middle-class' examination designed to provide boys' secondary schools with standards for their graduates (serving roughly the same function as our own day's A-level examinations). In the summer of 1862 Emily Davies had made informal enquiries to both universities about the possibility of extending these examinations to girls. From Oxford she had received a polite but unmistakable rebuff but Dr Liveing of the Cambridge Local Examination Syndicate could see no objection *in principle* to the examination of girls. This chink in the armour was the signal for the formation of a committee in October 1862 consisting of Social Science Association members who were committed to the higher education of women. The committee included Barbara, Emily, Eliza Bostock (a friend of Mrs Reid on the committee of Bedford College), Isa Craig, Russell Gurney, George Hastings, James Heywood,[4] and Lady Goldsmid.[5]

The committee organised a petition to the university for the formal opening of the local examinations to girls. Following Barbara's strategy when she petitioned for change in the Married Women's Property Laws, they put the names of supporters who seemed likely to impress the senate on the top sheet. The 'high status names' on this occasion included seventeen teachers and officials connected with Queen's College and thirty-four from Bedford College. Two particular friends of Barbara's were on the list. One was Anne Jemima Clough, the sister of the poet Hugh Arthur Clough who had married Barbara's cousin, Blanche Shore Smith.[6] Another was that veteran of Portman Hall School and the Married Women's Property Campaign, Octavia Hill. Altogether 1,200 signatures were presented to the university and the council of the senate appointed a syndicate to investigate the request. In February 1865, Cambridge officially opened local examinations to girls.[7]

After the campaign to admit women to the franchise Barbara and Emily returned their energies to education. On 9 March 1866 Emily wrote to Barbara to say 'We are about to organise a Schoolmistresses' meeting, a thing analogous to a clerical meeting, which I expect will be useful, partly as a propagandist institution, the more intelligent gradually enlightening the dark and ignorant, and partly as a body (if it ever grows strong enough) which can speak and act with some authority.'[8] Octavia Hill, Frances Buss and Elizabeth Whitehead Malleson were among the number who met at Emily's home and started the London Schoolmistresses' Association, for which Emily Davies acted as secretary for more than twenty years. These meetings in autumn 1866 (from which Barbara was absent) were regarded by Emily as the founding moment of the plan for a university college for women.

Barbara wanted to discuss the material reality of the college, as Emily wrote to a friend:

> Mrs. Bodichon is quite fired by the vision of it . . . It is to be as beautiful as the Assize Courts at Manchester and with gardens and grounds and everything that is good for body, soul, and spirit. I don't think I told you how intensely we enjoyed the beauty of the Assize Courts. I have seen no modern building to be compared with it, and the delight we felt in it made one realize how much one's happiness may be influenced by external objects.[9]

On 29 January 1867 Emily wrote to Barbara in Algiers to say:

> I have drawn up the Programme of which I enclose a proof . . . The next question will be how to set about raising the money . . . Will you

consider what you can do, and will you also talk to Nannie about it. The money need not of course be paid at present. What we want is a few promises of large sums, to lead other people on . . . As soon as I hear from you, I shall go to Lady Goldsmid, Mr Russell Gurney, Mr James Heywood, the Westlakes, and two or three other people who are likely to be interested, and we may then I hope make a beginning at looking out for a site, etc.[10]

Emily took the view that if they were to be successful in founding a university college for women, a new committee (separate from the London Schoolmistresses' Association) was needed, firstly to collect money and subsequently to administer a building fund. She wrote down the names of various people she considered to be suitable. In her 'Family Chronicle' she noted: 'it may be observed that the list includes no one specially known as advocating the Rights of women. It was felt to be important to put forward only such names as would be likely to win the confidence of ordinary people.'[11] She therefore left Barbara's name off the list, feeling that her advocacy of political rights for women might scare off some potential friends of a women's college.[12] As Barbara was still suffering the after-effects of typhoid during the spring and summer of 1867, she remained at Scalands Gate and some early resolutions were passed by the executive committee which Barbara would not have approved of, had she been consulted.[13] The fact that her name was not on this first committee list has meant that some historians of education have tended to give Emily Davies *all* the credit as the initiator of Girton College.[14]

Most of the historical accounts of the 1850s and 1860s have regarded Barbara as the 'political' leader of the Langham Place group and Emily as the 'educational' leader. Yet both women were interested in education, opening up the professions to women, women's status as citizens – in fact the whole range of feminist movements. Both women had leadership qualities, although they had very different leadership styles, and different roles. Emily was an excellent committee woman, having the patience and tenacity to attend to the minutest nuts and bolts of business, essential in any long and difficult campaign. She was not, however, a leader who inspired people by the force of her personality; rather she overpowered people by sheer force of purpose and wore them down until they acceded. Bessie, we may remember, regarded her as a steamroller. Barbara, on the other hand, was what the French call an *enthusiaste*, and her presence inspired almost everyone with whom she came in contact. Unless (and it is very unusual) all of these attributes are found in one person, both kinds of leader are necessary for long campaigns. The founding of a university

Barbara in 1861, the year that she went to
Brittany to meet her husband's family

Campagne du Pavillon, the
house where Eugène Bodichon
grew up, at Mauves in Brittany

Scalands Gate, the house Barbara
built for herself and her husband on
the Glottenham Estate in 1863

In her dining room at
Scalands Gate Barbara's
visitors used to sign their
names round the big fireplace

Barbara was saddened not to have children. Her picture *Solitude*, with its blue tones and one lonely, wheeling stork, suggests the depth of her disappointment.

Barbara's picture of the bay of Algiers was engraved as a frontispiece to
A Winter with the Swallows (1867) written by her friend Milly Betham Edwards
following her stay with the Bodichons in Algiers

The first permanent College building at Girton in 1873 was in bare wind-swept fields, far from Barbara's vision of a dignified building surrounded by beautiful gardens

The Girton College Fire Brigade 1880, which was proposed by Hertha Marks, Barbara's protégée and beloved 'daughter'. Hertha is the student second on the left, holding a bucket.

This portrait of Barbara, by Samuel Laurence, hangs in the dining hall of Girton College

This portrait of Emily Davies, painted by Rudolph Lehmann in 1880, hangs in the dining hall of Girton College

Barbara painted Chateau Gaillard on the Seine on her painting trip to
France in 1870 with her friends Henry Moore and Reginald Thompson

Barbara's pencil
and ink sketch of
Segovia shows
her skill in
draughtsmanship

Near the Land's End was painted in 1875, the year
she bought The Poor House in Cornwall

Gertrude Jekyll was a close artistic
companion of Barbara's later years.
Barbara left her Cornish house and
her Spanish pottery to her

Mary Ewart, a major
benefactor of Newnham
College, Cambridge,
was another close
friend of the latter
part of Barbara's life

Marianne North, painter,
traveller and naturalist,
whom Barbara knew both
as a child in Hastings
and in her later years

Milly Betham-Edwards,
whom Barbara met in
Algiers in 1866, was
one of the few friends
who enjoyed Eugène
Bodichon's company

Barbara's friend 'Brabbie',
the painter Hercules Brabazon
Brabazon

Barbara's protégé, Norman Moore, had an illustrious career as Warden of St. Bartholomew's Hospital and the representative of the college of Physicians on the General Medical Council

Amy, Barbara's favourite niece, was considered the beauty of the family

Benjamin Leigh Smith, on board the *Hope* in 1882, after being rescued from the Arctic following the sinking of his own ship, the *Eire*

Emily Osborn's portrait of Barbara, given by her friends to
Girton College in 1885, now missing

This portrait of Barbara by Emily Osborn,
is now at Girton College

Barbara bought The Poor House at Zennor as a haven for herself and other artist friends. She suffered her first stroke there in 1877

After suffering another stroke in October 1884 Barbara engaged Mrs. Hornsby, a nurse from St. Bartholomew's Hospital, to look after her at Scalands Gate

college for women, like most feminist campaigns, needed a group of people to make it happen, and within that group Emily and Barbara were *both* key players.

In August 1867 Emily went down to Scalands Gate to spend a month with Barbara doing some detailed planning of the projected college, both its buildings and its curriculum. There were two areas where they did not see eye to eye – the religious allegiance of the college and the issue of the young women's physical well-being. The Smith family had always put their money into secular educational institutions, such as the Pater with Westminster Infant School, Octavius Smith with University College, London, and Barbara herself with Portman Hall. Emily, however, was an Anglican, and she wanted to persuade Barbara that they would have a better chance of being accepted by the Cambridge establishment if they were nominally Anglican, although no student, in practice, would be obliged to attend Anglican services and instruction. Barbara was unhappy about it; every fibre of her own political instinct, and the agenda of her family over three generations, had been to remove religious disabilities from public institutions.

Barbara was also concerned about the possible toll on women's health if Emily persisted in her insistence that *no* concessions were to be given to women students that were not given to men, despite the fact that they knew that young women would be handicapped by inadequate secondary education. On her American tour in 1857–58 Barbara had been impressed by the sense of physical well-being she had perceived in the young women studying at Eagleswood School, New Jersey. She considered that if parents were to allow their daughters to leave home to study, the college must regard itself as to some degree in *loco parentis* and assume responsibility for the health of the young women in its care. Consequently, although Barbara pledged £1,000 to the projected college, she wanted to make it a condition of her donation that Elizabeth Blackwell should hold a professorship of hygiene. She made her position crystal clear in a letter to Emily dated 31 October:

> A danger of working too hard exists always for young women if they have to do things in a given time I think. I give you permission to express my intentions where you can do it fully. I desire to see some one in power who has made the physical constitution of women a study and if I give my £1,000, as I am not rich, I must be sure it is used in accordance with my best judgement of what will really promote the great object we have in view, the ennobling, morally, intellectually and physically one half of humanity . . . We must do this well if we do it at all. My whole heart is in the idea.[15]

Emily nevertheless persuaded her to promise her £1,000, writing that 'this is the only way, as you will not be on the Committee, that you can be counted among the founders of the College . . . you know how much pleasure it would give me to feel to be doing it *with* you, who have believed in this idea from the very first'.[16] In other words, with Barbara still too unwell to attend committee meetings, only her money would qualify her as a 'founder'.

Barbara, always mindful of her father's maxim, *bis dat qui cito dat*, despite her misgivings promised Emily, on 22 November, to donate her money without formal written obligations. Barbara wrote: 'I do still think something special must be done about hygiene, but I have decided to leave it to your influence and mine over you! So now you can say you have my £1,000 promised.'[17] To rely on her influence over Emily was an error of judgement. Emily relied solely on her own judgement, and that of *no one* else. She was an indefatigable worker, and therefore invaluable, but the price of her work was her insistence on doing everything her own way. Emily was very similar in temperament to Barbara's cousin, Florence Nightingale, an unstoppable force, achieving high goals, but willingly sacrificing individuals to her cause.

Emily continued to push Barbara to accept the Anglican foundation of the prospective college. When Emily convened the first meeting of the College Committee on 5 December only four people attended and Emily had no trouble in persuading Mrs Manning, Mr Sedley Taylor and Mr Tomkinson to accept her resolution: 'That the religious services and instruction shall be in accordance with the principles of the Church of England, but that where conscientious objections are entertained, attendance at such services and instruction shall not be obligatory.'[18] The immediate result of Emily's Anglican stance was, as Barbara had feared, the loss of some radical support, but it was a *fait accompli*.

Not surprisingly, as many of her friends were Unitarians, Barbara had trouble persuading them to fund the project; after a year's campaigning only £2,000 had been pledged, half of which was Barbara's original £1,000. Emily began to think of a small beginning in a rented building, much to Barbara's dismay. After hearing from Barbara, Marian wrote to Emily on behalf of George Lewes and herself, saying: 'We strongly object to the proposal that there should be a beginning made on a small scale. To spend forces and funds in this way would be a hindrance rather than a furtherance of the great scheme which is pre-eminently worth trying for. Everyone concerned should be roused to understand that a great campaign has to be victualled for.'[19] She offered her own financial contribution: 'My dear Miss Davies, Whenever it will not be a bad example to set down subscriptions of £50 for the Ladies' College, Mr Lewes begs that you will enter that sum on the list as coming from "the author of 'Adam Bede' or of 'Romola' " – whichever title you may prefer.'[20] The gift was entered as from 'the author of Romola'.

As well as money, they needed champions within the university itself. Emily's brother Llewelyn sought to help them by introducing them to Professor Seeley, a Cambridge don, who had previously expressed interest in the women's college. But when Emily and Barbara met him in March 1868 he seemed in a very negative mood, more inclined to talk about all the difficulties than to try to help them find a way through the obstacle course. Barbara, whose cheerful spirits could usually be relied upon to stir up other women's flagging energies, felt disheartened by this meeting and wrote to Emily:

> There is a frightful coolness about the college. I felt it at your house that Mr Seeley was bored by it and if I had followed my instinct I should not have mentioned it to him that night at all. Perhaps another time he might not have been slightly oppressed and apposite (if there is such a word). I don't know him, but I felt he was not inclined to discuss. Did not you?[21]

This letter points up the difference in style between their approach; Emily ignored Seeley's negativity, putting it down to the usual 'cool Cambridge manner' and determinedly pressed on with her enquiries. She replied to Barbara's note: 'I thought you were more discouraged than need be by other people's coldness, because you expected more from them than I did. You go about bravely talking to people and expecting sympathy from them, when I should not open my mouth, and so you get the cold water showered upon you . . .'[22] In turn, Barbara reassured her that she had not lost faith, saying, 'I know you thought I was damped but that is not true, but I should have shut my eyes and closed my reason to all evidence if I had not seen up and down the world this last two months that there is a frightful coolness about the College.'[23] The empirical evidence suggests that she was right. The subscription list inserted into the programmes showed Barbara's £1,000 and £100 each offered by Emily, Lady Goldsmid, Mr Heywood, Mrs Manning and Mr Tomkinson. But apart from this the only other firm offers were Marian Lewes's £50 and Lizzie Garrett's promise to give £100 over a period of five years. By virtue of the first money as well as a further contribution of £5,000 in 1884 and the £10,000 left to Girton in her will, Barbara was without a shadow of doubt the college's principal financial benefactor.[24]

Having given £50 Marian felt entitled to press Emily on the points she felt to be important. In a letter of 8 August 1868 Marian strove to make her own position a little clearer. She was not so concerned as Barbara about 'hygiene'; her concern was that 'there lies just that kernel of truth in the vulgar alarm of men lest women should be "unsexed" . . .'[25] Marian accepted innate differences between the sexes, but she did not accept the interpretations of the significance of these differences as theorised by Herbert Spencer and Charles Darwin, that women were doomed to lag permanently behind men. Consistent with her concerns about women's writing, she had a deep concern that women should not lose their 'precious speciality', by which she meant their nurturing qualities.[26] In short, she wanted Emily to beware lest her dogged insistence that the college women should be just the *same* as the men might result in a loss, rather than a gain.

Initially, plans to open university education to women received support from several university men who were anxious to change what they saw as excessive commitment to classical languages, instead of to modern languages, science and social science. However, Emily's absolute and unshakeable conviction that the women must jump the same hurdles as the men, and that no concessions must be made to women, meant that the supporters of higher education for women effectively split into two camps. Henry Sidgwick, a philosopher and fellow of Trinity College, felt that it would be mad for a new women's college to copy slavishly the old colleges' curricula.[27] Neither could he agree with Emily that there should be formal subscription to the tenets of the Church of England and eventually parted company with Emily to join forces with another group, the North of England Council for Promoting the Further Education of Women, to press for 'special' examinations for women. Consequently Sidgwick worked with Anne Jemima Clough, Blanche Shore Smith's sister-in-law. It is ironic not only that someone with Barbara's progressive views about education found herself in the educationally conservative camp, but also that there were family connections in the progressive camp. Nevertheless, once Barbara gave a good worker her backing, she stuck with them, and she accepted Emily's insistence on proving the intellectual equality of the sexes by following the existing University of Cambridge syllabus.

Unlike Emily, however, Barbara simply felt that all roads led to Rome, and she did not regard folk in the other (Newnham Hall) camp as enemies. She formed a close friendship around this time with a woman of exactly similar principles, who happened to be in the Sidgwick camp. This was Mary Ewart, whose father, William Ewart, had been a friend of the Pater. After her father's death in 1869 Mary came to live in London and supported several initiatives for the better education of girls and women.[28] For Newnham College, she put £1,000 down for a building fund, plus a series of small sums over a period of time, finally bequeathing £30,000 in her will. As well as sharing Barbara's commitment to women's education she was also an enthusiastic traveller, who, like Barbara, enjoyed studying the art, history, flora and fauna of all the places she visited. She became one of Barbara's closest friends and a highly valued travelling companion during the latter years of her life.

The only thing which distressed Barbara was that Sidgwick's group were establishing themselves right in the centre of Cambridge, exactly where Barbara had wanted 'her' college to be. Emily, however, was still not certain whether London University or Cambridge University would be the more likely to forward her schemes, and was unwilling to set up a women's college in close proximity to men's colleges, for fear that middle-class fathers would not send their daughters to live close to swarms of hot-blooded male undergraduates. Emily favoured setting up in Hitchin, approximately equidistant from Cambridge and from London, which Emily thought a politic strategy, especially after she discovered that 'in the adjoining parish of St Ippolyts there were two Trinity livings whose incumbents were Cambridge scholars'.[29] At her first Executive Committee meeting Barbara objected to establishing a college out of the reach of museums and libraries, where not even clean tap water, gas lighting, decent roads or railway station were to be relied on.[30] She wrote to Emily commenting that she could surely see that 'a hired house is not good husbandry'.[31] A letter from Emily to Adelaide Manning, of 26 February 1869, said:

> I am glad you do not want us to start at Cambridge. Mrs Bodichon has gone off upon that tack, and has been talking to Lady Goldsmid about it. She (Mrs B.) seems to have made up her mind that we shall have no more students than we have promised now, and that we ought not to provide for, or look forward to, any more ... I fancy it is partly that Mrs Bodichon has taken a dislike to Hitchin, and that being of a physical turn of mind, she cannot separate the essential idea of the College from the accident of the place in which it is located ... I was obliged to tell Lady Goldsmid that Mrs Bodichon has had an attack of timidity, and she said she thought I had got an attack of audacity, but she seemed rather to admire it than otherwise.[32]

Barbara was not being timid so much as realistic in guessing that they would be starting with only five students, not the twenty-five which

Emily had confidently assumed would appear. She also thought it was simply wrong-headed not to begin in Cambridge if that is where they ultimately wanted to be, and she did not like the idea of wasting scarce resources on temporary accommodation. Nevertheless she caved in to Emily's wishes.

The Executive Committee met on 16 April 1869, when Emily proposed the appointment of Mrs Charlotte Manning as Mistress at Hitchin. She was the widow of Sir William Spear and in 1857 had become the second wife of the distinguished lawyer, Serjeant Manning. She was rather delicate and only agreed to stay for one term, but she suggested that her stepdaughter, Adelaide Manning, could come with her as unpaid secretary, and together they seemed to offer the best start the new college could have; the offer was gratefully accepted by the Executive Committee. Emily reported to Mrs Manning:

> Our number was small today, only Mrs. Gurney, Mr. Roby, Miss Metcalfe, Mrs. Bodichon and Mr. Tomkinson. We were sure however that the absentees would agree with us . . . Mrs. Bodichon was very cordial.[33]

There was also a debate about choosing an 'euphonious feminine' name for the resident female head of the College. Rector, Warden, Provost were all used for heads of Oxford colleges. The term 'Dean' had a feminine form, which was briefly considered, but 'Duenna', they felt, struck the wrong note. As Master was the normal form in Cambridge colleges, and Cambridge was where they felt they were ultimately heading, they finally agreed upon 'Mistress', which presumably they did not regard as unfortunate. These issues were not as trivial as they sound; as there had never been a university college for women before, the Executive Committee were inventing their own traditions.

In October 1869 Emily arranged to rent Benslow House in Hitchin (thirty-five miles from London and twenty-seven from Cambridge), which had the single advantage of not putting all their eggs in one basket. If Cambridge would not adopt the 'little sister', then maybe London would. Everything else was a disadvantage. The Cambridge dons who supported the idea of women's higher education were condemned to prove their allegiance by spending hours on trains to and from Hitchin in order to lecture to the women students. Eighteen young women took the first entrance examination for the college, held at the University of London. After the examination there was a reception to introduce the students to the committee. One of these, Emily Gibson, wrote:

It was then that I first saw Madame Bodichon, and the little talk I had with her went straight to my heart. I felt that the college meant a great deal to her, and that it was a great privilege to have a chance of making it a success. I seem to remember that her face was framed in a cottage bonnet that made a halo for her blue eyes and golden hair.[34]

In October 1869 three more candidates were examined at 5 Blandford Square, including one of the five pioneers, Louisa Lumsden.

The college at Hitchin opened its doors on 16 October to Emily Gibson, Louisa Lumsden, Anna Lloyd, Isabel Townsend and Miss Woodhead. They undertook exactly the same course as Cambridge undergraduates (the Little-go followed by the Tripos) in the same time-scale (ten terms) as the men. The Little-go, also known as the Previous, had been established in 1822 and tested Latin, elementary Greek and mathematics. The Sidgwick progressives argued that the time spent on a second classical language could be more usefully spent on a modern language or a science. Nevertheless, despite Barbara's reservations about Emily's insistence that the young women followed to the letter the old-fashioned, but prestigious, Cambridge syllabus, she had such faith in Emily's determination to see any project she undertook through to its conclusion that she supported her decisions, even though her own instincts were more progressive.

Perhaps slightly smarting under the sense that Emily always had things her own way, Barbara was rather cheered on spotting a letter in the *Spectator*, signed 'Helen T.' which commented that to Madame Bodichon 'not only the college at Hitchin owes its origin, – not less to her energy than to the gift of a thousand pounds, – but the women's suffrage cause two of its best and most widely circulated pamphlets'.[35] Barbara mistakenly assumed that Helen Taylor was the author and wrote to her on 1 August 1869:

I do not think I deserve to be called the originator of the College for though ever since my brother went to Cambridge I have always intended to aim at the establishment of a college where women could have the same education as men if they wished it, I certainly could not have carried out the plan as Miss Davies has done. I am not strong enough, or orthodox enough. Of course you understand that I do not approve of the Cambridge education as much as Miss Davies does but I think we are likely to get something really good in time if we attach ourselves to Cambridge and Cambridge to us and such good workers as Miss Davies ought to be helped and not hindered with criticism . . . When I was reading the other day 'Mozart's Letters' I was struck with the fact in his life that his sister would probably have had as great a musical career as himself if she had been allowed the same advantages . . .[36]

In August 1869 Barbara had attended the first large public gathering on women's suffrage and writing to Helen Taylor she expressed her pleasure that 'the adherents of the suffrage number all sorts and conditions of women . . . you might have found 1000 instances'.[37] Helen Taylor replied very graciously on 7 August, saying that although the letter marked 'Helen T.' was not her own, she was 'sure that all the various movements for improving the condition of women help one another, and all ought to go on simultaneously if we are to hope to see any considerable effect produced in our time. I am glad to see the progress which the College is making – progress which I think is in reality as great as could possibly be expected.'[38]

Barbara spent most of the summer of 1869 at Scalands Gate with Eugène and on 16 June she was delighted to hear from Elizabeth Blackwell that she had at last surrendered to her oft-repeated persuasions: 'I am coming with one strong purpose in my mind of assisting in the establishment or opening of a thorough medical education for women in England.'[39] Barbara offered her Blandford Square and from there she went with Barbara on 15 August to visit Benslow House. In the same month Barbara invited her old friend Florence Davenport Hill, who was no doubt interested in Barbara's latest educational venture, to spend a month at Scalands Gate. Jessie Boucherett was staying in nearby Hastings trying to recover her health, which had at that time rather broken down. Following her work at SPEW, in 1866 she had founded and edited the *Englishwoman's Review and Home Newspaper*. Barbara went to Hastings to see her, commenting to Helen Taylor that 'she is very delicate but full of ardour and life when we talked of [women's rights] but I feel her health is broken for ever, I could not help thinking when I was there how much she herself had gained in happiness by allying herself so bravely with us. She has a vivid interest in life which nothing in "the society" she was born in could have given her'.[40] Happily, Barbara was wrong in her gloomy prognostications of Jessie's health; she continued as editor until 1871 and as late as 1896 (five years after Barbara's death) she published a book, *Condition of Working Women*, before retiring to her estate at Market Rasen, Lincolnshire, where she lived until her death in 1905.

During that same summer, Emily had turned to an old Gateshead friend, Mrs Austin (née Crow), for whom she had been bridesmaid back in 1857. Widowed early, she had been a willing background helper in many of Emily's projects. Mrs Austin went down to Benslow House with her two maids and cleaned it, aired it, received and arranged furniture, and stocked the kitchen. In short she attended to all the domestic arrangements, so that the college would be fit to receive its Mistress and students.[41] Domestic work seems to have been the only area of work Emily was willing to delegate. When the college at Hitchin opened in October 1869 Emily insisted that the Mistress and her friends sat at a separate table from the five students. Given the small number of inhabitants of Benslow House it struck the students as rather ridiculous, but it was an early example of Emily's insistence that they must follow the model of the Cambridge colleges, including 'High Table', right from the outset. Marian wrote to Emily on 19 November 1869: 'I am cheered by hearing that the beginning at Hitchin looks so happy and promising. I care so much about individual happiness that I think it is a great thing to work for, only to make half-a-dozen lives rather better than they might otherwise be.'[42] Emily and Barbara's ultimate aim was to achieve a college community of 200 young women, and, knowing this, Marian wanted to reassure Emily that the venture was worth undertaking, even for the sake of five individuals. She sent some books for the library, which was inevitably rather meagre, and during the Christmas vacation Barbara sent some of her sketches over to brighten the walls.

In January 1870 Barbara went to see her old friend, Gabriel Rossetti, who was suffering both physically and psychologically. He had been inflicted with a persistent eyesight problem and began to fear that he was going blind. Perhaps as a consequence, he felt desperate to bring out a new collection of poetry to establish his reputation as a poet. In one of the more bizarre incidents in literary history, in October 1869 Gabriel had obtained an exhumation order to open Lizzie Siddal's grave and retrieve the manuscript of poems which had been buried with his wife in February 1862. The manuscript had to be disinfected before he could set about transcribing and reworking the poems, and was marked by a worm hole. His aim was to disguise the poems inspired by his new adulterous love for Janey Morris, by intermingling them with the poems dedicated to his dead love. The combination of grinding out new poems, retrospective guilt about Lizzie and guilt circling round the Arthur–Lancelot–Guinevere triangle of his new love affair meant that by the time his new collection was published in spring 1870 Gabriel was close to nervous collapse. Barbara offered him the use of Scalands Gate, which appealed to him because William and Janey Morris were staying at Hastings. In March Gabriel went down to Sussex with his friend William Stillman, the editor of the *Crayon*, who had done much to advertise the

Pre-Raphaelites (including Barbara) in America. Gabriel wrote to Barbara on 15 March thanking her for providing 'a much more independent and promising *pied-à-terre* than I could have found in the tents of the stranger'.[43]

Although he wrote amusingly to Barbara of Stillman as Don Quixote and himself as Sancho, all was not well. Gabriel was in a stew of emotions, strung out by their intensity, and quite unable to get deep refreshing sleep. Stillman, no doubt meaning well, recommended that he should try chloral hydrate, a relaxant then fashionable because of its mildly hypnotic effect. It was the chosen drug of bohemians in the 1870s, considered harmless, rather as cannabis was viewed in the 1960s. Certainly its initial effect was to make Gabriel more cheerful, as a letter to William Allingham of 17 March shows: 'Barbara does not indulge in bell-pulls, hardly in servants to summon thereby – so I have brought my own. What she does affect is any amount of thorough draught, – a library bearing the stern stamp of "Bodichon", and a kettle-holder with the uncompromising initials B.B. She is the best of women, but I fear, from what I last saw of her, that her health is failing like my own.'[44] On 26 March the Morrises came over from Hastings and stayed with Rossetti and Stillman for a few days, and it was arranged that Janey should stay on at Brown's while William returned to London. Stillman went back to London, so Gabriel and Janey had their tryst, with only the ghosts of dead loves to keep them company.

At Hitchin, in the Lent term Emily Shirreff, the daughter of Rear-Admiral W.H. Shirreff, succeeded Mrs Manning as Mistress. The students were keen to have a resident tutor in classics so Julia Wedgwood, of the pottery family, offered to come temporarily to help.[45] She had taught girls in a village school which her father, Hensleigh Wedgwood, had set up, so she had proven teaching skills. Miss Gibson commented: 'We should no doubt have been the better in those early days for a little more advice and teaching. Our lecturers came once or twice a week, and there was no one to appeal to in between. Miss Julia Wedgwood stood in the gap for a time. I do not know that her classical teaching was any great assistance, but she was an interesting and delightful personality, and enriched the life of our little community.'[46] Her presence at least made the students feel less isolated; they were away from home, living in rather uncomfortable conditions. They were engaged in strenuous studies under women 'leaders' who did not know from experience how the Tripos worked. It was often a case of the blind leading the blind. Their lectures were at odd times, fixed more by train timetables than anything else, and the teaching arrangements were frankly inadequate. Two of the lecturers,

Professor Seeley[47] and the Revd Hort, were not committed to preparing the women for examination, and were only interested in broadening their students' general culture. As these young women were facing a desperate race against time and needed to stick rigidly to the rubric there was a sense of despair and outrage when the students discovered that the Revd Hort had given them seminars on Acts when the prescribed book was Luke. In the ensuing argument, Professor Seeley withdrew his support from Hitchin.

Louisa Lumsden said that the first group of students only managed to succeed because 'a sort of mutual help society had existed among us from the first, and thus to some extent we supplied gaps in teaching by coaching one another' for the Little-go.[48] This sense among the pioneers of having taken responsibility for their own learning is important: on the occasions when Emily tried to treat them like schoolgirls, they not unreasonably objected strenuously. Another area where Emily's extreme reluctance to share power proved problematic was that of the role of Mistress. When Miss Shirreff took over from Mrs Manning, she wished her role to be something more than that of a glorified housekeeper and to include the role of 'Director of Studies'. Emily, however, had no wish to delegate any real power to the Mistress and achieved this by keeping the Mistress off the Executive Committee.

The issue which continued to niggle Barbara was the college's 'exile' from Cambridge itself. In January 1870 Mr Sedley Taylor wrote to Barbara commenting that the ladies' lectures Sidgwick was organising in Cambridge were bound to be 'very much more comprehensive and . . . cheaper' than anything Hitchin could offer.[49] Barbara replied that she 'wished to go to Cambridge, but she thought no one else on the Committee did'.[50] She then raised the question of removal to Cambridge at the next committee meeting. The committee had realised by this stage that the original plan of raising £30,000 was entirely unrealistic and that the most they could set their sights on was a sum of £7,000 to buy a building site for a college of about thirty students.

During the summer of 1870 Barbara enjoyed a painting expedition to Normandy with the painter Henry Moore and a new friend, Reginald Thompson, a doctor who was a good amateur painter. Possibly they went to join a community of marine painters based on the coastline between Trouville and Honfleur, an area Corot much favoured. Certainly she went to Richard Coeur de Lion's castle at Les Andelys, because a watercolour of *Château Gaillard on the Seine 1870* was one of a group of paintings she lent to Girton College in 1875, and bequeathed in 1891.

Moore had started out painting landscapes with a marked Pre-Raphaelite influence, but after about 1857 had specialised in marine painting.[51] He was a fine colourist, and extremely sensitive to the shifting details of atmospheric effect. Marine painting is notoriously difficult, as the surface forms of the sea are constantly changing. According to effects of the sky, the sea can appear opaque and sombre or transparent and full of colour. Moore was a faithful student of all the sea's moods. To Barbara, having grown up at Hastings, to paint the sea satisfactorily had been one of her earliest challenges and one which had often defeated her. On 14 January 1856 she had complained to Marian: 'I am wild just now – the waves will not let me catch them.'[52] Moore helped Barbara in this area, and there can be no doubt that she would have valued a painting expedition in the company of such an accomplished artist.[53]

Her other companion on the 1870 painting expedition, Reginald Thompson, although a doctor by profession, was also an accomplished amateur artist and musician, who became one of Barbara's most trusted friends.[54] When Barbara first met him he was assistant physician to the Brompton Hospital where his research field was that of hereditary phthisis. Reginald was a close friend of William de Morgan, the Pre-Raphaelite potter and decorative tile maker. Morgan had developed the use of a film of copper or silver on glazes, to give a rich red, gold or bluish-grey colour to pots and tiles, which he decorated with plant or bird forms in luminous blue, green and yellow enamels, and he and Reginald used to compete to see who could produce the most fantastic creatures.[55] Clearly the 1870 painting expedition was a great success, for in the following summer Barbara went on a painting expedition to Holland in the same company.

It seems hardly surprising that Barbara was eager to go off on expeditions with her artist friends. Uninterrupted sojourns with only her husband for company no longer seemed to satisfy her. Unless she was ill Barbara was an early riser, because she liked to enjoy the morning light for painting, or riding, while Eugène preferred to rise late. Fortunately he was a self-contained man, content to walk by himself with the dogs. If he did not help, neither did he hinder Barbara from making painting expeditions with artist friends; nor did he object to being left to his own devices.

In November 1870 Elizabeth Blackwell and her adopted daughter Kitty were invited to stay at Scalands Gate, and Kitty's letter home to America yields a glimpse of why Dr Bodichon could hardly be 'translated' into polite society:

Dr. B never appears till 11 a.m. when he takes breakfast arrayed in a long garment of white flannel, just like a lady's waterproof sack, with its hood. All day long he wanders about in the wood hatless, umbrella tucked under his arm, & wearing his flannel garment. At 7 we dine – Dr. B then arrays himself in a grey garment made like the white one, puts the hood over his head – also a blanket shawl, & thus sits down to dinner. He always takes eight or nine glasses of wine, & is greatly concerned because I drink nothing but water. After dinner Dr. B has three dogs seated by him and feeds them on crackers and cheese, and as the dogs *always* quarrel, it is very unpleasant.[56]

Elizabeth undoubtedly believed that Barbara's marriage was a great mistake. She found little to like in Dr Bodichon, although at the very least they had common ground in their abhorrence of vivisection. But Elizabeth strongly disapproved of drinking, so Kitty's comment about how much wine Eugène drank may well be prejudiced by her mother's view. On the other hand, Milly Betham-Edwards noticed that Barbara was in the habit of watering the claret, slightly unexpected behaviour in a generous woman. Possibly Barbara found her husband inclined to become more dogmatic and argumentative with each glass of wine and quietly reduced his alcohol intake by judicious watering. But by comparison with Kitty's account, one of the early Girton students, Emily Gibson, who stayed at Scalands Gate over the summer vacation of 1871, held a quite different view:

That visit was a revelation to me. It showed me a new way of life, the charm of simple surroundings. The living-room with open hearth, wood fire and round table spread for a meal beside the open cottage door was entirely different from anything I had seen . . . Her little sitting-room, a frieze of the Bayeux tapestry its only decoration, was delightful by lamplight when William Allingham, the only other guest, read aloud to us Shakespeare's sonnets and now and then a poem of his own.

The whole picture was French rather than English, and the illusion was completed by the wonderful apparition of the master who appeared only at meals clad in his blue peasant's blouse, and by the French talk which one had to take part in when he came in.[57]

Meanwhile, from Hitchin there was excellent news. At the end of Cambridge University's Michaelmas term the first Hitchin students had tackled the Little-go examination. The council of the senate had given no formal permission, but had felt that there could be no objection if a private arrangement was made with the examiners. On 10 December 1870 the five pioneers took and passed their viva voce examinations. *Punch* recorded this unique event in its own inimitable style, under the headline THE CHIGNON AT CAMBRIDGE:

> At the examination lately held at Cambridge, a number of students from the Ladies' College at Hitchin passed their 'Little-go', the first time that such undergraduates ever underwent that ordeal. It is gratifying to be enabled to add, that out of all those flowers of loveliness, not one was plucked. Bachelors of Arts are likely to be made to look to their laurels by these Spinsters . . .[58]

During the winter of 1870 when the Franco-Prussian War was at its height and Paris was enduring its fourth month of siege, Barbara overwintered in England. Eugène was in Algiers heartbroken at France's humiliation and Barbara, herself a French citizen by marriage, was infected with sadness. She was relieved to hear that Bessie and Louis Belloc had arrived safely in England. Daubigny, whose home in France had been destroyed, was staying with his parents in cramped lodgings in Kensington. At the beginning of December Barbara whisked him off on a painting expedition to the Isle of Wight. Even in those sad circumstances the two friends enjoyed each other's company. Barbara wrote to William Allingham:

> A three day visit from the French painter Daubigny did me worlds of good; we went for one afternoon under the cliffs at Niton, don't you remember where those little antique thorns are? he enjoyed it as only people of genius can enjoy things.[59]

She decided to stay on the Isle of Wight over Christmas, and rented a house at Ryde, where Milly Betham-Edwards and the Leweses joined her. George was on top form, playing practical jokes to take their minds off the terrible stories of the conditions in Paris. People who met Marian and George Lewes only briefly tended to regard the pair rather in the light of a Titania who had been unfortunately bewitched into falling in love with Bottom. In fact, George's puckish sense of fun was the perfect antidote to Marian's anxious nature. As Barbara's family had always been partial to high-spirited fun, she enjoyed his company uncritically, without thinking him incapable of seriousness. She knew perfectly well that despite their differences in style, George was Marian's intellectual equal. Barbara was pleased for her friend that she had a partner who shared so closely her literary life. It was an increasing sorrow to her that Eugène, although he loved her dearly, had little empathy with her artistic life. He wished her success with her efforts, but she could not *share* her aesthetic interests with him.

As well as trying to make useful introductions for Daubigny, Barbara was also busy trying to think of ways to keep up the spirits of the poor women students at Hitchin, in the grip of an exacting regime and usually with only a sketchy 'secondary' education to underpin their undergraduate efforts. It proved fortunate that Barbara had remained in England that winter. In March 1871 a few of the Hitchin students, feeling they had deserved a bit of light relief after their struggles to pass the Little-go, decided to act a few Shakespearean scenes for the pleasure of the other students, the dons who had volunteered to teach them, and for Emily Davies and Julia Wedgwood. Emily was outraged that the students had dressed in male attire in front of the visiting dons, and her response almost led to a mutiny. She was concerned lest any scandal should ruin Hitchin's reputation: this was not in itself ridiculous, bearing in mind the troubles at the *English Woman's Journal*. Emily insisted that the students involved in the theatricals should be disciplined by the Executive Committee, and the students threatened to leave the college as a protest against Emily's high-handedness. Barbara, who had dressed up and acted in charades and theatricals in her youth, thought Emily had over-reacted and persuaded her to leave the Executive Committee out of the matter, promising that she herself would come to Hitchin to mediate.

Emily promised to postpone taking the 'student difficulty' before the committee until she saw what Barbara's visit achieved. Writing to Mrs Manning on 17 March 1871 she said:

> Mrs Bodichon has promised a visit to Hitchin next week, and Mrs Austin thinks that will do more good than anything. Mrs Bodichon thinks the students *must* see what a mistake they are making, if we give them time, and they are more likely to listen to her, as an artist and a theatre-going person.[60]

On 23 March Barbara spoke to the students, almost certainly suggesting to them that what they were doing was not wrong *per se* but that in their circumstances discretion must be the better part of valour. Emily was satisfied that Barbara seemed to 'have spoken wisely as well as strongly' and no doubt she took the trouble to explain Emily's fear of bad publicity.

Barbara's diplomatic skills, in the crucial early days of the college, were of vital importance, as necessary in their own way as Emily's determination and persistence. One of the rebels, Emily Gibson, gave an account of the event:

> To me the most important outcome of the imbroglio was an interview with Madame Bodichon who was deputed . . . to pay me a domiciliary visit, and reason with me with reference not only to my role as ringleader in the theatrical revolt, but to the style of dress which I was beginning to affect. With regard to the latter I scored. It happened that I had recently gone into mourning and, as a protest against the hideous and fussy fashions of the time, I had contrived a simple little frock of fine parmetta not unlike the coat-frocks of to-day . . . It was jeered at, at home, as my 'preacher's gown', but when Madame Bodichon found me in it in my room at Hitchin she was charmed with it. It was a case of the prophet coming to curse and remaining to bless, for she asked me for the pattern and said she would have a gown made like it to paint in.[61]

As an artist, Barbara was more insouciant than Emily about dress code, but she also knew the value of offering encouragement and praise, not merely proscriptions against everything which seemed like pleasure. She was able to convince the students that if she asked them to give up their acting, it was a sacrifice which needed to be made in order to achieve their long-term aim. In fact, this was exactly Emily Davies's position too, but she was inclined simply to issue orders to the students, rather than to explain her motives. But Emily never entirely forgave this revolt against her authority, or the particular students who had dared to challenge her. She wrote to Barbara on a later occasion: 'Is it not vexing to see such a spirit shown? I am afraid we shall have no lasting peace while any of the pioneers remain.'[62] She missed the point that only young women of the highest spirit and courage would have chosen such a brave course as to attempt the Cambridge University Tripos in the first place. It was precisely this spirit which Barbara admired in them, even if, on occasion, it proved expedient to urge caution for fear of what a largely hostile world might say.

All in all, Emily found spring 1871 rather a distressing time. Mrs Manning, the first Mistress at Hitchin, died in April. The next blow was the news that Henry Sidgwick had rented a house at 74 Regent Street, Cambridge, where women who came from a distance to attend his 'ladies' lectures' could reside. Emily felt utterly betrayed by this move, regarding Sidgwick as setting up a rival college. She wrote to him on 19 May saying, 'I am sure it is generous inconsistency and not cruel mockery that makes you say you are willing to help us, when your scheme is the serpent which is gnawing at our vitals.'[63] The Sidgwick philosophy was that as women did not receive an adequate secondary education, the sensible way forward was to allow them to work at a variety of levels, and for periods as short as a term. Emily felt that this flexible opportunity would divert women from her college, which insisted on a ten-term commitment, leading to the Cambridge Tripos. In this view, she was to some degree correct. Barbara herself advised her niece Amy to attend lectures at Newnham when she realised that she did not have the application and drive to commit herself to the full-time and demanding regime which Emily insisted on. Once again Barbara pressed for the permanent college to be built in the centre of Cambridge, like the Sidgwick initiative. She did not entirely achieve her object, but a compromise was reached. Emily wanted any new college to be well away from Cambridge itself, but for once the committee stood firm and insisted that it should be no more than three miles out of Cambridge.[64] A sixteen-acre site was found in open fields near Girton village, at the junction of the Girton and Huntingdon roads about two miles from Cambridge, which was accepted as a suitable compromise.

By September 1871 Emily was exhausted and went down to Sussex to stay with Barbara. Despite her initial panic about competition from Sidgwick, the number of students at Hitchin was slowly growing. The main comfort for Emily, however, was Barbara's reassurance that there was no danger of her reneging to the other camp. She would continue to support their original vision of a women's university-level college. Writing to a friend from Scalands Gate, Emily said:

> We had a great deal of talk about the College building and garden, etc. I hope you agree with us in liking an old-fashioned and useful garden with autumn and spring hardy flowers all about. I think we ought to plant a belt of trees as soon as we can round our own domain, as we are sure to want that at any rate. Mrs Bodichon recommends Austrian pines . . .[65]

Emily had already spoken to Alfred Waterhouse, an architect with the reputation for working strictly to budget. Barbara took the role of chair of the Building Sub-Committee, which met in October and approved the proposals to buy the land at Girton and to engage Waterhouse. Raising the £7,000 they would need for bricks and mortar was not easy, as Barbara wrote to Marian following a somewhat depressing building meeting:

I have had some qualms of conscience about our College or rather about my want of vigour when you asked me about the College & if we wanted help and how we were getting on – We had a meeting yesterday and I went up & Emily Davies as usual came from Hitchin to attend & I was more than ever struck with her extraordinary power of doing well all she undertakes. She is really a precious & rare creature & I hope she will not be too much tried but will live to see her work fairly begun & the buildings up & free from debt with 20 pupils installed . . . The fact is we want money very much indeed & I do not think I insisted enough on this point. I hope if you have the power of saying a word for us to rich people [that] you will. To me one of the morals of your work is [to] help the highest education of women – open all the doors & I hope if anyone comes to you & asks you how they can practice your sermons you will tell them to help us. I am very grateful to you dear Marian for that book & I know it will help us, in fact when some of our Council were very down I felt partly hopeful because [of] the last few pages of Middlemarch.[66]

It is not surprising that Barbara occasionally became discouraged about the fund-raising, even though a great deal of effort had gone into it. Beginning on 15 May 1871, at St James Hall, Piccadilly, a series of public meetings had been held to try to convince the public of the importance of higher education for women, and to get promises of money to establish a permanent college. The St James Hall meeting brought in promises of £600. Even the *Saturday Review*, usually patronising at best, and downright hostile at worst, to any kind of female endeavour, had written a favourable report of this meeting and its intentions. Similar meetings followed at Leeds, Birmingham, St Leonards and Nottingham. The experience of speaking in public at the Social Science Association meetings had been invaluable, as both Emily and Barbara were by this stage skilled public speakers. Although the money came in much more slowly than they had hoped, nevertheless it did come in. It probably seemed an unkind twist of fate to Barbara that Smith family money was going into the Sidgwick camp rather than to her own establishment, although there is no evidence that she fell out with her cousins over this.

As well as financial uncertainties, various personnel crises had to be dealt with, some of which arose directly as a result of Emily's uncompromising personality. In the summer term of 1870 Emily Shirreff had resigned as Mistress because Emily would not allow her to assume the role of Director of Studies or to become a member of the Executive Committee. Annie Austin had been willing to fill the breach (strictly under Emily's terms of reference) and had taken over at short notice, but in the spring of 1872 she fell ill with pneumonia and had to leave before the end of Lent term. Her sister, Jane Crow, then offered to live at Cunningham Place and look after Emily's mother so that Emily herself could go down and hold the fort at Hitchin. For the summer term of 1872 Emily, Lady Stanley and Barbara took turns as Acting Mistress at Hitchin. If only very briefly, and as an emergency measure, Barbara entered into the day to day running of Hitchin College. Emily felt that Barbara's influence on the students was a good one: 'She is so clear and firm, and at the same time so winning and bright, and they know how much she does for the College, that I think her influence is about the most useful we can have.'[67] Barbara used her time as Acting Mistress as an opportunity to persuade Cambridge dons to consider the issue of women's higher education favourably. In a letter from Hitchin, Barbara told her niece Amy: 'Miss Jones and Jane here for tonight & we go on to Cambridge tomorrow where there is to be a party about the new college & we are to see Cambridge & a great many people.'[68]

At the end of those fraught Hitchin years, the two prime movers had great respect for each other's talents. Barbara had enormous respect for Emily's ability to navigate her way through tortuous committee work; Emily, on the other hand, recognised and appreciated Barbara's skills with people, the way her presence always seemed to lift the spirits of the students. No one but Emily could have stood the terrible dreary rounds of committees and negotiations with the university, but she lacked Barbara's abundant warmth and charm which impressed everyone she met. Barbara's networking skills and powers of persuasion were also an important asset. She was so very different from the *Saturday Review* stereotype of the dried-up old spinster bluestocking that her glamour held a kind of promise that intellect in a woman did not automatically mean a lack of what the nineteenth century saw as womanliness. This was reassuring both to doubtful supporters and to the students themselves.

CHAPTER 15

The Girton Years

The move from running a small college in a rented building on a short lease, to establishing a permanent college in its own grounds was, of course, a momentous step. On 15 May 1872, seventeen people including Barbara signed the Articles of Association for the new college, and this document marks the first moment of Girton College's legal existence. The Executive Committee named Emily as secretary, which, as there was no permanent chairholder, was the most powerful position. Emily's aim from the beginning was to persuade Cambridge University to incorporate the women's college and she never deviated from her chosen path. Aspiring women students had to pass an entrance examination, so in this way she set out her stall from the very beginning. Once the college's legal existence was established, there was increased urgency in both raising money and in finding sufficiently well-educated young women who could pass the entrance examination and whose parents were willing to spend a hundred guineas a year on a girl's education.

Emily regarded Barbara as a 'perfect treasure' on the Building Committee. She was in her element, interpreting her brief widely and interested in every detail, right down to the route of the coal carts to the basements and the siting of the hot-water furnace, tiles, material for curtains, the planting of trees and obtaining gifts of books for the college. Consultations with the architect continued all through 1872. Waterhouse's plans shows the main principles of the design.[1] The idea was that rooms (apart from service rooms) should be built on only one side of the corridors, which should be wide, light and airy. The Building Committee expressed some concern that the attenuated layout might act as an invitation to intruders. Iron bars to the windows were considered but, as Emily wrote to Barbara on 21 April 1872:

> they would be a great expense (£60 at least) and not an effectual protection after all. It was concluded that we had better have a catch in the windows, & for our principal protection rely upon a little dog running about the corridors.[2]

Building started in 1872 and the first phase, the 'Old Wing', overlooking what is now called Emily Davies Court, was built in order to be ready for Michaelmas term 1873. It was in the currently fashionable Gothic revival style: as Emily said, 'as we cannot have tradition and association, we shall want to get dignity in every other way that is open to us'.[3] The difficulty was in achieving dignity economically. Economy, for example, ruled the choice of long corridors (wings), rather than a staircase system like that of the medieval men's colleges. The college was built solidly with sixteen-inch-thick walls out of 'best red kiln burnt' brick from Haverhill pointed in 'black ash mortar'.[4] The design had an air of enlarged but dignified domesticity, as befitted an institution of learning. Barbara and Emily were agreed in wishing to provide each young woman student with a set of two rooms, a bedroom and a sitting room, with wide double doors between them. Barbara, true to her early concerns about women's health, was insistent on the provision of a gymnasium, although it was not built until about a year after the college was occupied, when money became available.

From the beginning, Old Wing was envisaged as the first stage of a much larger scheme, with extra parts of the college to be built as money arrived. At the beginning of September Barbara and Emily spent some frantic days at Girton trying to make sure that the windows opened properly, arranging curtains and blinds, and ordering blue carpets for the students' sets. However, in October 1873, when the nine Hitchin students and six new ones arrived at Emily's and Barbara's embodied dream, the actuality was a long way from the vision. The building was hardly finished; builders' rubble littered the space between the Huntingdon road and the college, carpenters' tools cluttered the corridors. Emily Gibson, writing home to her parents, described Girton College as 'a red raw building among bare fields with windows and doors still being fitted into their frames'.[5] The lone building standing naked and exposed in flat windswept fields without any trees, lawns or flowerbeds to offset the bleakness can hardly have lifted the spirits of the young women entering it.

Emily had reluctantly taken on the role of Mistress as no one else at the time would do it. Barbara knew that Emily would not give time to making *herself* comfortable, so she sent a bookcase and a carpet specifically earmarked for the Mistress's room and chairs for the students and offered to pay for the decoration of the Mistress's room and the reception rooms.[6] She continued to raise funds and visited Girton frequently, often bringing friends, not merely to show the college off, although she was very proud of it, but always in the hope that the friend would either contribute some money or, if poor, at least speak well of Girton to a wealthier friend. Alternatively she persuaded her friends to offer what they had in different ways. Sometimes, as with Charles Darwin and George and Marian Lewes, they were encouraged to donate their books to Girton's library.

In April 1874 Barbara was troubled by an article by Dr Maudsley in the *Fortnightly Review* called 'Sex in Mind and in Education'. The article implied that sustained mental work made women unfit for their reproductive functions, and that the educational reformers neglected physical training because they only cared about intellectual prowess. Concerned about the possible impact of these views Barbara wrote to Emily on 5 April 1874:

> I have read Dr Maudsley's article with care, and I think it will do us much harm because there is much truth in it, and because what is not true is exactly the most difficult sort of error for us as women to discuss. I wish we could find some man to answer it. I should like to see you and Mrs Anderson . . .[7]

Barbara thought that the best way to deal with the matter publicly was to ask Lizzie Garrett (now Mrs Anderson) to reply, as her medical qualifications gave her the authority to respond to Dr Maudsley. In the May issue of the *Fortnightly* Lizzie sensibly pointed out that 'The schoolmistresses who asked that girls might share in the Oxford and Cambridge Local Examinations were the first also to introduce gymnastics, active games, daily baths, and many other hygienic reforms sorely needed in girls' schools'. On this occasion Barbara pressed Emily on the issue of the health of the young women in her care, as not only she, but several committee members were not entirely satisfied on this point. Emily's view was that a college was not a school, and that it was therefore the responsibility of the young women themselves to take care of their own health and, to some extent, take care of each other.[8]

Emily was suffering from the not unusual irritation of the person doing the work on the spot, receiving criticisms from others. But she was an autocrat; she was determined to run the college her way and if she and the London committee were to be at 'cross-purposes', as she put it, she was not prepared to stay on as Mistress. The students, naturally enough, wished their views to be represented on the committee and they wanted Louisa Lumsden, now classics tutor at Girton, to be their representative. Barbara proposed that Louisa should be elected but Emily was implacably opposed to this, writing to Barbara, 'I think you are in much too great a hurry to get an old student put on. I have the strongest objection to this movement for putting the Mistress under the control of the students, for that is what it comes to.'[9] Emily wrote to Charlotte Manning (Hitchin's first Mistress), on 3 January 1875: 'I think Madame Bodichon goes too much by the temporary opinions and tastes and requirements of the existing generation of students, as e.g. she asked anxiously about the housekeeping – Are they satisfied? When I think the questions should have been, Is it satisfactory? And are they showing a more reasonable contented spirit?'[10] Barbara wrote to her young friend, Norman Moore, from Blandford Square on 3 March:

> We have a committee of Girton today & I am troubled in my mind about it, the students want Miss Lumsden to stay as tutor & she is going. Miss Davies does not like her tho' the students do. It is very difficult to govern this College living here in London. I confess I should like to put 3 Cambridge men on our Committee. Can you think of any one who would be useful to us? And who would come?[12]

Barbara was correct in assuming that Emily would win the day. The committee always bowed before her forceful will. At one point Barbara expressed her opinion that if Emily insisted on everything being done her way, a governing committee was something of a waste of time. Emily replied rather sharply, 'As to your saying the College is mine, you know that is nonsense. It has taken all of us to get so far, and it wants us all still.'[13]

Emily's victory, as Barbara predicted, resulted in the loss of Louisa, the first Girton student to become a college lecturer, who resigned from the college in spring 1875.[14] Although Louisa admired unreservedly what Emily Davies had achieved on behalf of women's education, she regarded her style of leadership as unfortunate: 'the student was a mere cog in the wheel of her great scheme. There was a fine element in this, a total indifference to her popularity but . . . it was plain we counted for little or nothing except as we furthered her plans.'[15]

Emily always missed Barbara when she was away in Algiers. A letter in January 1874 looking forward to Barbara's return in March, said:

> I hope you will give Girton an early place among your necessary visits . . . There are such endless things to talk to you about which can only be done satisfactorily on the spot. You don't know how I miss you. I had got so much in the habit of looking to you for advice and help about all sorts of things that I am always feeling after it still . . .[16]

Barbara's concern was always whether the students were happy and comfortable. She wanted to apply the good work begun with carpets and curtains to internal decoration generally, and with Gertrude Jekyll's help she worked out a colour scheme for papering and painting the inside of the college. Emily wrote to Barbara, explaining that she did not feel that this was the priority for the moment:

> It does not seem as if this work was of urgent necessity. Of course the place looks unfinished, but this is not altogether a disadvantage. It brings home to people that we have not money. When everything looks smooth and nice, it does not occur to people that it is not paid for. And for the students it is not amiss I think to have a reminder that the place did not grow up of itself without any trouble.[17]

Emily's principal feeling was that the students should be grateful for the opportunity to study and that there was no need to coddle them. Barbara had to be content with creating as many opportunities as she could for them, by inviting them to Scalands Gate for country breaks, and to parties at Blandford Square.

To her Girton parties she often invited a young medical student at St Bartholemew's Hospital and any friends he cared to bring. This young man, Norman Moore, twenty years younger than Barbara, was to feature very largely in her life. His father, Robert Ross Rowan Moore, was the Anglo-Irish barrister and anti-Corn Law orator who had contested the borough of Hastings for free trade in 1844 and had become a friend of Ben Smith's. Moore senior had eloped with Rebecca Fisher, a young woman from an Irish Quaker family, but had then deserted her before Norman's birth, to run off with another woman. Rebecca Moore had supported herself and her young son by running a school in Higher Broughton, Manchester, and was, as Anna Mary said on meeting her in 1855, 'a capital woman belonging to the readers of the "Una" and that class of American literature, a woman who has ideas, and very clever ones too upon policies, morals and literature and education and homeopathy – all alive and full of intellect'.[18] Her son Norman was something of an infant prodigy; when Anna Mary met him, aged eight, his conversation struck her as intellectually precocious and he looked 'keen as steel'.[19]

Anna Mary's description of the young Norman proved accurate. He possessed formidable intellect and drive, working as an apprentice in a cotton factory during the day and attending evening classes at a working man's Natural History Society in the evenings. At sixteen he had travelled by foot to Walton Hall, Wakefield, and there formed a firm friendship with the elderly Charles Waterton, the traveller and conservationist, who was clearly more of a father to him than his own father (who had died in 1864) had ever been.[20] When Waterton himself died in 1865, Norman's sense of loss was tremendous; Waterton had been a Catholic, and it may well be that Norman was drawn to this religion by his close involvement with Waterton, as he was ultimately to join the Catholic Church. After graduating in natural sciences in 1869 he went on to Bart's for his clinical studies in medicine and comparative anatomy. At this point Rebecca Moore wrote to Barbara from Manchester asking if she would take an interest in her son. Rebecca had first met Barbara at the Manchester Anti-Corn Law Bazaar which Barbara had attended with Aunt Ju when she was 'quite a girl'. She had followed Barbara's subsequent 'career' with interest, and was full of praise for 'all the good she was doing'.[21]

Barbara immediately invited Norman to Scalands Gate, where his enthusiasm for natural history and great love of animals endeared him to Dr Bodichon. Norman was no more bothered by Dr Bodichon's eccentricities than he had been by Waterton's. They were interested in all flora and fauna and engaged in esoteric activities, such as skinning dead vipers and drying out their skins to create vellum for bookbinding.[22] There is a distinct sense that the young Norman always attached himself to intellectual mentors, especially to one who could double as a father figure. Both the Bodichons enjoyed Norman's company. Barbara had never herself learned to play an instrument very well, but she derived great pleasure from music, especially enjoying traditional songs. One of her fondest memories was of her nurse Hannah Walker singing old Sussex folksongs to help her get to sleep. Norman, perhaps by way of trying to replace his lost Irish father, took a deep and scholarly interest in Irish music, and often arrived with 'new' Irish songs. For an impoverished but brilliant young man, regular invitations to the country cottage must have been a welcome relief from hard study. By a strange coincidence the Waterton family motto was 'Better kinde frende than strange kyne', and for Norman Moore, first Charles Waterton and then the Bodichons became the kind of friends who are as good or better than family. As a childless woman, Barbara enjoyed befriending this brilliant young man. She also regarded his conscientious and rather high-minded character as a good role model for her somewhat worldly nephews and nieces.

She took great interest in the well-being of her various nephews and nieces, although here her interventions were not always welcome. Although she had been great friends with her brother Willie in their youth, she felt that he and his wife, Georgie, had become rather locked into a country gentry mould. She was concerned that the two elder girls, Amy and Georgina (usually known as Roddy), were being inadequately educated. Certainly they seemed to have a series of rather inadequate governesses, whom they easily terrorised and drove away. Her favourite niece was Willie's eldest daughter, Amy, whom she often referred to as 'princess', partly because Amy was extremely beautiful but also, more ironically, because she was afraid that Amy cared more about frocks than the things which Barbara believed to be important. A series of letters from 'Aunt Bar' reveals her sending Amy books, pushing her to study French and music seriously and to come to Barbara herself for drawing lessons. Barbara also made clear her opinion that the governesses Willie employed were more 'finishers' than educators' and offered to pay for lessons by good teachers herself. Having paid for them, Barbara then asked for progress reports: one letter to Amy says 'I am quite satisfied with your report of your lessons. I think you must be learning a little every day & if you go on for 2 years hard at work you will not be "shockingly ignorant" we will hope. Does Roddy like her lessons? Ask her to write and tell me'.[23] Willie regarded himself as a gentleman farmer, and perhaps he thought that his daughters only needed to be 'ladies'. Barbara, true to form, wanted them to be educated women. She came to think that Norman Moore might be a good influence on Amy, rather as Philip Kingsford had long ago exerted a good influence on Barbara herself in establishing systematic, rather than random, habits of study. Writing to Norman in June 1871 she said that Amy 'has driven away a 3rd. Governess and now there is an interregnum of doing nothing & I have not the least idea what her parents will try next! But while she is here I like her to see my friends & get out of her defiant state of mind. I think you can help me because she likes you & I think you can give her an interest in the country things among which she walks rather blindly at present.'[24] Over a period of time, just as Philip Kingsford had fallen in love with Barbara, Norman quietly fell in love with Amy.

On 6 March 1873 Bella, aged forty-three, died at home of the consumption which had so long threatened her.[25] Three of her children survived her: Amabel was thirteen, Harry eleven, and her youngest child, Milicent, was only five years old. Marian wrote to Barbara:

Dearest Barbara,
The word you send me of a life so bound up with your early years being so suddenly brought to a premature close, makes me imagine how your thoughts are saddened and solemnised in these first

succeeding days. For her sake – even for the children's – the passing away seems a good. But every death that comes at all near to one makes one in some sense a mourner. The precious flowers are duly cherished.[26]

Nannie was ill with grief at the news of Bella's death.

Barbara felt a strong sense of responsibility towards Bella's young children. She visited Yotes Court whenever she could and, when busy herself, urged Norman Moore, whom General Ludlow liked, to visit the children and encourage them in good paths. Norman was teetotal, which she felt was important in the General's household. Writing to Norman on 3 September 1875 she said:

> I am very glad you liked Yotes & are going again. I want you to be friends to those children very much. You see their mother was subject to fits of insanity & it is just madness to let a boy like Harry drink wine i.e. poor boy says it affects his head & just before I left my bedroom at Yotes Ct came in & said he would try & refuse it when it was offered to him at dinner & asked if he took the pledge would it help him. I said, your father would not like you to do that but you can refuse & must &c &c &c. You can do a great deal for the boy if you get his love & he is very much inclined to like you so please take the trouble to know him.[27]

After a successful visit to General Ludlow's children, Barbara wrote to Norman's mother, 'My children at Y Ct. are delighted with your boy – I am so glad for I consider him as half mine.'[28] Rebecca Moore felt that the Bodichons' interest and patronage of her son went some way towards making up for what he had lost as a result of his father's desertion.

After Bella's death, Barbara felt more strongly that her place should be in England. Algiers, which had originally seemed an artistic paradise and a place where she could practise her art without the distractions of her 'social' work, was beginning to wane in its appeal. The artistic camaraderie and critical response she had enjoyed in the 1850s with Anna Mary, Jane Benham and the young men of the PRB was something difficult to replicate in Algiers. There, she found it hard to get enough artistic stimulation, except when her English or French artist friends came out to visit. In England, however, she had established a new circle of artistic friends with whom she enjoyed painting, including Henry Moore, Reginald Thompson and Hercules Brabazon Brabazon, usually known as 'Brabbie'.[29] Brabbie and Barbara were similar in temperament – generous, intelligent, full of humour and zest for life. He lived near her at Oaklands in Sedlescombe village in Sussex, and being financially independent was able to devote himself to music and art. As he never had to satisfy a specific patron or market, he was free to paint 'impressions' in watercolour.

Largely self-taught, he had studied the painters he regarded as masters, David Cox, De Wint, Turner and Velázquez, and made hundreds of studies which were not so much copies as *interpretations* of the essence of master paintings. These were remarkable paintings, almost dialogues between one painter and another. His motto as a painter was that 'the best art is to suggest' and most striking in his paintings is his use of colour and light to suggest a landscape, a building or a bowl of flowers as though the viewer is also involved in the creative space. There was an affinity between Barbara's and Brabbie's work which made their painting sessions together very enjoyable to them both. Like Barbara, Brabbie obtained enormous satisfaction from travelling and studying the old masters in museums all round the world, but when he was at his Sussex home he always looked forward to long days of painting with Barbara.[30]

It was through Brabbie that Barbara had met Gertrude Jekyll, now revered mainly for her garden designs although she was a woman of many talents: an artist and a craftswoman as well as a gardener.[31] She had the use of a room at her brother's flat in Morpeth Terrace, a few doors from Brabbie's London flat. Gertrude was frequently invited to the musical evenings held by Jacques and Leonie Blumenthal at 43 Hyde Park Gate where Brabbie often entertained with his virtuoso piano playing. In the autumn of 1873 Gertrude accompanied Barbara when she went to spend her winter in Algiers. They began by staying with the Blumenthals at their mountain chalet, at Les Avants above the Lake of Geneva. They travelled through Turin, Genoa and the Riviera on their way to Marseilles, visiting art galleries *en route*.

When they arrived in Algiers on 3 November, it was too hot for Barbara's taste: '70 degrees in the shade in my north room at 7 am – that is too much when I go out. I get much too hot walking.'[32] Fortunately, it cooled in December; Barbara, writing to Norman, said: 'We have been painting a good deal out of doors & I hope some of my work is good at all events I have enjoyed it – painting is nearly all I do enjoy here & of course the natural things, flowers and insects.'[33] She enjoyed Gertrude's company, fortunately; she was 'quite as perfect a companion as I expected – a great many things have been uncomfortable & without her spirit and cleverness in contrivances I never could have inhabited this bare house with these bad french Algerian people as servants'.[34] Increasingly it seems as if Barbara only liked Algiers when she had English artist friends with her; the company of her husband, and of Nannie and Isabella in the next-door house, clearly did not make her happy. Once they had arrived in Algiers, she and Gertrude spent a lot of time with George Cayley, an authority on Arab decoration. While Barbara was painting Gertrude spent her time copying designs for dresses, embroidery and tiles. Some of the 'oriental' designs, she noted, were of European and especially Dutch origin, brought to Algiers in the vessels captured by Barbary pirates.

Towards the end of January 1874 they enjoyed the company of the painter, Frederick Walker and his friend, J.W. North.[35] There was a quality in Walker's paintings that reminded Barbara of her first master, William Hunt. Walker had come to Algiers in the hope of a cure for consumption, but he felt artistically adrift. He was one of those painters whose talents were finely tuned to his native countryside, but who could not resonate with any other. He told his mother, for instance, that a crocus she had sent him through the post 'licks into fits anything here'. He was rather moody, partly due to poor health. Barbara, having witnessed Bella's long sufferings with consumption, was well aware how ill he was, and helped in various practical ways, including finding him models. His paintings increasingly seemed to express a kind of wistfulness for the earth he was soon to leave. All of Walker's friends were inclined to laugh at the ferocious expressions he pulled when in the throes of production, gritting his teeth and chewing his nails to the quick. Gertrude Jekyll described an occasion that winter, when she and Barbara took Frederick out on a painting expedition:

> One of my pleasantest recollections of him was when standing one bright afternoon on the rocky coast, looking westward at a distant low mountain that bounded the view and showed between sea and sky; a sort of lowering frown that seemed habitual to his face, replaced for the moment by a bright smile; he kept repeating to himself: 'Pure ultramarine – pure ultramarine!'[36]

Frederick's letters home suggest that the times spent with Barbara and Gertrude were the most enjoyable part of his visit to Algiers. He described pleasant evenings at Campagne du Pavillon when he played Mozart on his flute, and the best of the expeditions were the ones Barbara, with her artist's eye and intimate knowledge of the landscape, arranged for him. He wrote to his mother that it was only 'the society of two good clever women' which made Algeria pleasant to him.[37] Frederick rather aptly sums up the company for which Barbara herself always panted, that of 'good clever' people; she simply could not find enough within the expatriate English and French community to satisfy her. That winter, she arranged to go back to Europe with Gertrude on 25 February, not waiting until May, which was Eugène's favoured time for arriving in England. Following the meeting in Algiers, Walker went to visit Barbara at Scalands Gate in February 1875, but in June of that year he died of consumption. Barbara was saddened, for she thought him enormously talented. For Gertrude and Barbara, however, their five and a half month sojourn together had cemented an artistic friendship that was one of the great joys of the latter part of her life.

Yet another artistic friendship established in the 1870s was with Marianne North, whose father had been MP for Hastings.[38] Although they had known each other as children, after Marianne's mother had died in 1855, her father had let the house in Hastings and taken a flat in London. There Marianne, apart from keeping house for her father, spent much of her time painting specimen flowers in Chiswick Gardens and at Kew. With her father she enjoyed travels on the continent and into Egypt and Syria. After his death in 1869 Marianne visited Jamaica, Brazil, Singapore, Borneo, India and Ceylon, always making detailed accurate paintings of plants in parts of the world few people ever visited. The friendship between Barbara and Marianne seems to have rekindled at the beginning of 1875, judging from a series of letters from Marianne to Barbara describing her botanical observations.[39] Marianne gave her paintings to the Royal Botanical Gardens at Kew, building a gallery for them at her own expense, where they may still be seen.[40]

The renewed friendship with Bessie and her new friendships with Brabbie, Gertrude Jekyll and Marianne North were fortunate, because after January 1875 came a period of misunderstandings, upset and disagreement between Barbara and Emily Davies. Barbara had always felt that Emily had been wrong in (effectively) getting rid of Louisa Lumsden. Emily, in turn, accused Barbara of favouring the eccentric students, rather than the ones who quietly got on with their work (suggesting that Emily identified herself as the one who quietly got on with the work, while Barbara was merely eccentric). Barbara continued to be concerned about the lack of pastoral care for the young women who were away from home for the first time.

Emily was exhausted following the task of moving the college from Hitchin to Girton, and she did not want to continue as Mistress, preferring to live with her mother in London. However, she retained the powerful position of secretary of the Executive Committee. When Emily herself had been Mistress, and she did not want to work with Louisa Lumsden, she had insisted that Louisa had to go. In other words, when Emily was Mistress, she had behaved at though *the role itself* conferred power. But now she no longer wished to be Mistress, she made sure that she kept her controlling position by overruling the wishes of some of the committee, who thought any new Mistress should have a seat on the Executive Committee. She effectively downgraded the position of Mistress, by arguing that if the Executive Committee found the Mistress unsatisfactory and wanted to sack her, then it would be very difficult if the Mistress were one of the committee discussing her own deficiencies. As usual, Emily insisted on keeping the reins of power in her own hands.

A Mistress who was willing to be resident at Girton was advertised for, and Miss Frances Bernard (whose uncle, Lord Lawrence, was the Viceroy of India) seemed the most promising candidate. She went down to Scalands Gate to meet Barbara in April 1875, and was duly appointed in June. She took on a college of twenty-three students in Michaelmas term 1875. Having been brought up in diplomatic circles, Frances Bernard was more skilled at exerting authority without exhibiting the iron hand in the velvet glove to students (or tutors) so nakedly as Emily. She also made efforts to cultivate Cambridge society in the way that Barbara had always hoped for. Although Emily's capacity for work was both admirable and prodigious, and she was successful in her enterprises through sheer doggedness and determination and was an outstanding committee woman, her personality was such that she had not been an ideal Mistress. It is only fair to Emily to say that there is nothing more annoying to the worker on the spot than to receive criticism from a major financial backer who does not have to deal with day to day pressures. Bessie had felt this irritation when she was running the *EWJ*, and Emily too sometimes felt an acute sense of annoyance when Barbara criticised her from the safe distance of London, Sussex or Algeria.

One example of Emily's inflexibility concerned Agnes Amy Bulley who, having attended Hitchin, decamped for Sidgwick's college, Newnham Hall, because Emily would not consent to her postponing her Tripos for a fourth year.[41] This must have been a moment when Barbara seriously wondered whether she was backing the right horse in the race. Another 'old girl', Constance Maynard, joined the staff in 1875 and, like Louisa, found Emily rather autocratic. Also like Louisa, she instinctively looked to Barbara for support in achieving more democratic structures in the young college. Inevitably this caused tension between Emily and Barbara; Emily was inclined to regard anything less than a hundred per cent approval of her actions as a betrayal. One issue that caused bitterness between them was Barbara's view that as founder, her nieces (as she had no daughters) should have a semi-automatic right to study at Girton. Emily insisted, quite rightly, that they must pass Girton's entrance examination like any other student. Nevertheless, Barbara continued to chase tirelessly everyone she knew for money to continue the building projects at Girton.

One of the early Girton students must have a special place in this story, because, to all intents and purposes, she came to represent the daughter whom Barbara never had. Sarah Phoebe Marks, born in 1854, was the daughter of Levi Marks, a Jewish refugee from Poland and of Alice Moss, the daughter of a glass merchant in Portsea. Levi Marks had earned his living as an itinerant watchmaker, and when he died in 1861 Alice was left with seven children and pregnant with an eighth, as well as having substantial financial debts. She kept the whole family going by means of her talent for exquisite needlework. Recognising that Sarah was extraordinarily intelligent, she accepted an offer from her sister, Mrs Hartog, to educate her in a school she kept at 300 Camden Road, London. Sarah went there when she was nine years old and was well served by it; her relatives were remarkably talented and, as a conse-quence, it was an unusually good school. From her Uncle Alphonse Sarah learned good French and from her Aunt Belle a love of music. Her eldest cousin, Numa, when he was down from Cambridge, taught her mathematics and Latin. This cousin was the first Jewish student to become a senior wrangler and his death from smallpox when he was only seventeen was a great tragedy. At sixteen Sarah had to go out to work as a resident governess, to help support her family in Portsea.

Sarah was befriended by another Jewish family. Karl Blind was one of the many German émigrés who had washed up in London following the 1848 revolution. His stepson, Ferdinand Cohen, had attempted to assassinate Bismarck in 1866 but was so short-sighted that he missed and ended up committing suicide in prison.[42] Sarah formed a lifelong friendship with Blind's daughter, Ottilie, who nicknamed Sarah 'Hertha' after the eponymous heroine of one of Frederika Bremer's novels. It suited her so well that it stuck, and most people assumed it was her real name. Ottilie encouraged Hertha to study for the Cambridge University local examinations, which she passed in 1874 with honours in English and mathematics. Ottilie introduced her to Eliza Orme, a law student who had been a member of the suffrage committee in 1866, which proved a vital link. Through Eliza, Hertha heard about the existing college at Hitchin, and learned that three scholarships were to be offered to students who wished to attend the new college being built at Girton.

Hertha wrote first to Emily Davies and was interviewed by her. Emily was not impressed, but Barbara, independently, decided to interview her as well. Hertha went to see Barbara at Blandford Square in July 1873, and was struck by the older woman's beautiful hair and also by her dress. Barbara was still a remarkably handsome woman, who continued her early practice of wearing gowns with an unfussy line, often made from tussore, a coarse brown silk imported from India. Hertha was strongly conscious of dressmaking, from the years she had spent helping her mother, so even during this important interview she noticed the cut, fabric and style of Madame's dress. Barbara's first note to Hertha was treasured and marked as 'Madame's first letter' in her papers, alongside a lock of her red–gold hair.[43] William Allingham and his fiancée, the artist Helen Paterson, happened to have called on Barbara at the time, so Barbara asked them to go and look at her pictures while she paid attention to Hertha. Barbara, in her turn was struck by the nineteen-year-old girl's beautiful eyes and great bush of curly black hair and, above all, by the earnest eager expression of her face. After that first meeting, Barbara determined to give all the help she could. Her heart was drawn to Hertha, by the young woman's unselfish assumption that she must put her family's needs before her own ambitions.

In September 1873 Barbara invited Hertha to stay with her at Scalands Gate, advising her to bring strong boots because it was a 'rough place'.[44] This visit was the start of a close friendship between Hertha and the Bodichons. Her excellent French meant that she could converse well with Eugène, and her scientific curiosity also appealed to him. She had a lovely, rather low-pitched, singing voice and learned from Eugène the words and melodies of old French songs, which she sang unaccompanied to the great pleasure of visitors to Scalands Gate. Barbara introduced her to her cousin, Elinor Bonham Carter (now Mrs Dicey), who was also impressed. Writing to Barbara on 11 January 1874, she said, 'Please tell me if you are doing anything about getting that nice little Miss Marks to Girton? We should like to help if you are.'[45] Elinor Dicey was true to her word in collecting money from her part of the family in support of Hertha's early career.

In 1874 Barbara was delighted by the marriage of her friend, William Allingham, to Helen Paterson whom Barbara had known since 1866. Helen had been only eleven when the news of her aunt Laura Herford's victory over the Royal Academy schools in 1860 (a campaign in which Barbara had been involved) had caught her attention and provided her with a role model of a professional woman artist. William had endured a chequered career in the twenty years following his first meeting with Barbara at the Hermitage in the early 1850s. In 1874 his luck changed when he became the editor of *Fraser's Magazine* where he met Helen Paterson in her capacity as a professional illustrator. Although he was twenty-four years older than her, his proposal of marriage was accepted. Helen was a staunch Unitarian so on 24 August they married at the chapel at Little Portland Street just as Barbara had done in 1857. Barbara sent William a letter of congratulations on 28 August, offering some furniture, an Arab brass bowl and three of her pictures as wedding presents.[46] Barbara liked Helen and respected her as a talented professional artist, even though at a later stage in her career, Helen's paintings tended to move towards a prettified pastoral age where the sun always shone, very different to the unquiet landscapes in which Barbara excelled. The Allinghams had a happy marriage, a marriage of equals, and Barbara enjoyed the company of both her old friend and her new friend.

In October 1874 Hertha's younger sister Winnie fell ill, and had to be brought to London. Hertha had to give up her private teaching to look after her and so needed to earn money in a way that would not leave Winnie unattended.[47] Barbara offered to loan her money, but when Hertha refused, Barbara, knowing her sewing skills, sent her an embroidery frame, some examples of traditional Arab embroidery she had collected from Algeria as patterns, plus a commission and an advance payment. Hertha relied: 'My letters to you always say the same thing. They say thank you, thank you, thank you, and yet they never say enough to thank you! I received the Arab work to-day and the silks . . . It is very unbusinesslike of you to pay me for undone work. Suppose you do not like it when it is done?'[48] Hertha's work was excellent and when Barbara showed it to other friends, including Brabbie, she was soon receiving plenty of commissions. Hertha wrote that 'the more I see of other people, the more I feel sure that there is no one else at all like you; no one so good and clever & having so many interests & caring for so many people'.[49]

Part of the joy of the friendship between the younger woman and the older one was that Hertha felt that she could discuss anything she was thinking about, without fear of disapproval. Both women could be described as free-thinking in the intellectual sense, but with a strong spiritual sensibility. Hertha, having lost her religious faith when she was sixteen, although not her sense of identity or pride in her race, sometimes felt the need for a fixed system of ethics, which would save her having to puzzle out the rights and wrongs of the world on each occasion from a purely personal viewpoint. She wrote to Barbara:

Every day now, more and more, I am feeling the want of a guide in the way of principle. Every question of morality presents itself to me, to be traced back to utility. If I had time, I should like to do this for myself, but I haven't, so I want very much to get a book on the subject.

Though I threw off my religion five years ago, yet I have never realized this want so distinctly before. But now, every day it presses on me: why is it right? I am not referring to questions about my own conduct; they rise so seldom that it is not difficult to solve them.[50]

One ethical question that Hertha pondered over was that of abortion which, having grown up in a large and poverty-stricken family, she thought a better option than the dreadful consequences of having too many mouths to feed. Barbara disagreed with her on this, saying 'I think that foeticide is a crime; it is false to say it does not injure the health of the mother; Dr Blackwell and I have talked of this, and I will tell you her opinion.'[51] Barbara spoke (and wrote) to Hertha like a mother, or godmother.

By the summer of 1875 Hertha's own health was beginning to give way under the strain of working and looking after Winnie; Barbara had her to stay in Sussex and also arranged for her to have some mathematics lessons from a M. Merlieux. Hertha's plan was to send Winnie to their aunt's school, where Hertha could part-pay her fees by giving mathematics lessons there. Barbara thought this situation not at all promising for Hertha's ultimate success and once again pressed her to accept a loan so that she could attend Girton. Just at this delicate moment matters were further complicated as Barbara lost £400 of her money in a bank failure towards the end of 1875. For Hertha to attend Girton College, Barbara needed to raise enough money to maintain Winnie during that period; so she looked to her friends and relatives to help out.

Barbara had introduced Hertha to Marian Lewes in 1873 when she was already planning her novel, *Daniel Deronda* (1876), the whole structure of which relies on two entwined themes, the progress of women in society, and the progress of the Jewish people towards a homeland.[52] Hertha must have seemed almost like the embodiment of her two themes in one person. Barbara's Shore-Smith relatives also started to take an interest in Hertha, having been encouraged by Elinor Dicey, who subsequently pledged money from an anonymous donor. Eliza Orme offered to act as the treasurer for Hertha's 'Girton Fund', and she herself wrote to solicit help from Helen Taylor on 13 November 1875:

The girl is about 20. She is the daughter of a Jewess a widow in poor circumstances at Southampton . . . I taught her mathematics for some time and she passed the Cambridge exam for women over 18 with honours in mathematics. Since then she has been earning her own living by teaching and with Madame Bodichon's assistance has had further tuition in Mathematics from a Frenchman. I think she has very decided talent, Mme Bodichon will pay what is necessary at Girton but she wishes to [try?] for the London Univy. Exam 1876 (May) to try for the Gilchrist scholarship which wd. pay half her expenses at Girton. I do not think she can as she is working too hard at teaching to prepare for the exam. What is needed is a loan or gift of £92 a year until Oct 1876 to enable her to live without teaching and devote herself to her work. She pays £50 a year for board and lodging at the house she lives at, £20 (she reckons) for dress, books & such; £22 towards the education of her younger sister who is now at school at Mrs Hartogs.[53]

Helen Taylor promptly sent £25 towards Hertha's expenses. Marian Lewes gave £10, writing to her on 21 September 1875 promising to try to find her a governess's position: 'My dear Miss Marks, I enter with the keenest interest into your needs – so does Mr Lewes – and we are longing to see some avenue of light on the probabilities of your finding what will meet the rather difficult conjunction of requisites, especially as to salary and freedom from dogmatic prejudice . . .'[54] Clearly, not all homes were prepared to take a Jewess, however clever, as a governess to their children. Eliza Orme's letter of 20 December 1875, thanking Helen Taylor for her cheque, and informing her that Lady Goldsmid (the wife of Sir Francis Goldsmid, the first Jew to become a barrister, and a MP) had promised money for Hertha, repeated: 'She is a Jewess by birth but without any stated creed I believe at present and yet the Girton authorities have expressed their wish that she should obtain a scholarship – so I suppose the Church of England is less prominent than it was in their minds. I am told the new lady Principal is more successful in a social way than Miss Davies was, the girls being at ease with her.'[55] There is just a hint in this letter that Emily Davies's Anglicanism may have made her disinclined to find Hertha's intelligence as remarkable as Barbara did.

Having met the great 'George Eliot', Hertha was interested in reading her latest work. On 1 March she wrote to Barbara in Algiers saying:

> The second part of *Daniel Deronda* is out, and Miss Orme says that Mrs Lewes had drawn a young Jewess that is in it from me; but I have read the part, and I must say I cannot see the likeness. One thing she says of her, she did once say of me – that is that her utterance sounds foreign from its distinctness.[56]

Barbara was also reading *Daniel Deronda* with enormous pleasure and had, as usual, written to Marian to say so. Marian replied to Barbara: 'I am well pleased that Deronda touches you. I *wanted* you to prefer that chapter about Mirah's finding, and I hope you will also like her history in Part III which has just been published.'[57] Mirah's attempted suicide, when she dips her cloak in the river in order that the weight will help her drown more quickly, refers obliquely to Mary Wollstonecraft, a shared heroine, who had acted in the same way.

But Barbara was now troubled by Emily's high-handed attitude towards the pioneer students; Hertha had passed on to Barbara what one of the these students, Isabel Townshend, had told her. Writing to Hertha from Algiers on 6 and 7 March 1876, Barbara said:

> I think we all felt the want in Miss Davies of genial wisdom and influence, but where do young people, men or women, find that? We do our best to get it for our students but I fear natural selection from bodies, people, & all sorts of influences alone can teach each of us wisdom . . .
>
> The College cannot do much more than give *quiet liberty* and *opportunity* & Miss Davies never had any other idea. That is a great deal & she who has an immense love of justice for women would die to give young women what she never had herself in early life, ah, die to get it for them, though she might hate every individual – she is intense for an idea, truly disinterested & great. I do not think anyone does her justice.[58]

Barbara was loyal to Emily, even when she did not entirely agree with her behaviour.

Hertha was at this stage studying Greek in preparation for her examination for the Girton scholarship. In April 1876 she sent Barbara a progress report:

> I can translate two pages of Xenophon now, twice a week; and Mr Walker seems to think I am all right about my Greek, but I don't feel as if I were all right about anything. The nearer I get to my exam, the more sure I feel that I shall not get the scholarship. The kind of work wanted for examinations is, I am sure, not the kind I can do . . . Besides, I'm sure I shall lose my head in the exam-room. Altogether I am not in a lovely state of mind about myself . . . Will you lose all your faith in me if I don't get it?[59]

Barbara's reply was a model of good sense: 'I shall be sorry if you don't get £300, but if you don't, I shall try to get the £150 for you, and I shall never think less of you in some ways, though of course I shall think I over-estimate you relatively to the other students. *Have you good food?*[60]

This last question from Barbara was typical, but also insistent because Eliza Orme had warned Barbara that Hertha's health was breaking down from overwork.

During the winter of 1875–76 Barbara was having an unusually good time in Algeria as she had the company of Mary Ewart and Katie Scott. Katie was one of the sisters of Charles Prestwich Scott, the editor of the *Manchester Guardian*.[61] As Barbara had been becoming somewhat aesthetically jaded with the now familiar Algerian landscape, the three women went off on an expedition to a province which Barbara had never visited before. The strangeness of Constantine excited her. Writing to Norman Moore on 21 April 1876 she said:

> We coasted in the steamer to Philipville & then came by a bit of winding railway up 2,000 feet in 60 miles to this strange mountain top which is a city on a mile sqre of flat ground split off from a lime stone mountain. Cliffs a thousand feet like rifts going round it or rather 3 sides of it for it is a rounded triangle . . . Most of the many cliffs here are absolutely inaccessible to man & the river is the receptacle of the dead things & refuse of the city – you can imagine the number of vultures hawks &c. Looking down on their backs from the walls of the French side of the town is one of the most curious sights I ever saw. You see a constant hovering of winged creatures & on the arab side you see storks generally now standing on the houses building their nests or motionless guarding something . . .[62]

During this winter Barbara discussed her desires for a new landscape and a new base for painting with her two friends. At the beginning of June she and Katie borrowed a house called Eagle's Nest in Zennor, near St Ives, Cornwall, from Barbara's friends, the Westlakes. Barbara had first been to the Westlakes' house some time in 1874, and had been enchanted with the wild, bleak landscape. This extreme south-westerly point of England attracted her because of its dramatic coastline, with sheer cliffs and turbulent sea, and also because it was drenched with a light of extraordinary, almost Mediterranean brilliance. At least one of her pictures from that summer, a watercolour with body colour of a stormy seascape entitled *Near the Land's End*, was shown at the Dudley Gallery in 1875.[63]

From Eagle's Nest Barbara saw an older house which had served as the parish poorhouse. On 8 July 1875 she bought it from the Penzance Union Guardians, although, because of the Married Woman's Property Laws it was bought in the name of Catherine Scott, who held it in trust for Barbara, thereby ensuring that her husband had no legal claim on it.[64] It may be that Barbara simply wanted a new painting base, but it is interesting to note how little time she was spending with her husband by this stage in their marriage. In Algeria, she frequently went off with artist friends on expeditions, and had started returning to England in March, two months before her husband arrived. Even when Eugène had arrived at Scalands Gate, increasingly she went off on longish painting expeditions without him.[65] This is not to say that the arrangement did not suit both husband and wife, however; Eugène was a singularly self-contained man and Barbara loved the company of her artist friends.

By May, confirming Eliza Orme's fears, Elizabeth Garrett Anderson ordered Hertha to stop work and rest. The Girton examination took place on 30 June, and, sadly, Hertha was correct in assuming that she would not win a scholarship. She wrote to Barbara on 11 July:

> I will begin my letter with what I know you care most about, the doctor's verdict. He said that I have not entirely spoilt my constitution, and that I shall be a good worker. But I must rest entirely until October, living in the country, being as constantly as possible in the open air . . . I want to thank you for my visit, but I can't. How can one say anything to express thanks for acts of kindness that occur as often as you breathe? You can't tell how happy I was with you, even in spite of my disappointment about the scholarship.[66]

Elinor Dicey wrote to Barbara to say that she was sorry for Hertha's disappointment but that, considering the strains under which Hertha had worked, was not surprised and that the money she had promised on behalf of the 'unknown' would still be forthcoming. Hertha was therefore able to accept a place at Girton, knowing that Barbara (and Barbara's friends) would sponsor her.

Hertha went up to Girton in October 1876; her first letter to Barbara gave her address as 'Girton College, 7th Room, 3rd Corridor'. During Hertha's Girton years Barbara had direct information on how it felt to be a student there to compare and contrast with Emily's. For example, a letter from Hertha of 30 October says:

> The new building is going on very well, but on the top corridor of the new part they have cheated us of our window, and the consequence is a long bit of blank wall outside, which is very ugly. Directly you have finished this wing, you will have to begin on some more, for there are so many girls coming that I am sure there will not be room for them. As it is, one girl lives in the prayer-room, and two others share a room. I am the only heathen of my year, out of eleven students. After that, let

people declare that ours is a secular college! . . . The College is most decidedly divided into the religious set and the non-religious, and I don't know how they are to amalgamate, for they are like oil and water. This matters much less now than it did, and the more the College increases, the less it will matter . . .[67]

There is here once again an implicit comparison with the Sidgwick camp's institution, first called Newnham Hall, and subsequently Newnham College, which because of Henry Sidgwick's resolute agnosticism did not incorporate a college chapel.

In November 1876 Eugène went back to Algiers but Barbara remained behind, probably because Norman had dropped a bombshell by declaring his love for Amy, who was only seventeen. Barbara, who always admired anyone with an original mind, saw nothing dishonourable in his love, other than Amy's youth and silliness. As Barbara had always treated Norman with respect, he was utterly unprepared for the extreme hostility and suspicion with which he was met, first by Willie and subsequently by Ben Leigh Smith.

One might wonder quite what Ben had to do with Amy's romance but it was largely a question of how he saw his role in terms of the Leigh Smith family. After the Pater's death, and then Mr Gratton's, Uncle Octavius had seemed the nearest thing to a father figure to the Leigh Smiths as, of all the Pater's brothers, Octavius was the most similar to him in temperament. He was a competitive businessman, impatient of government restrictions, but he had supported both the *Westminster Review* and the *Leader* in order to spread liberal opinion. When he retired from the distillery, immensely wealthy, he had become the paternalistic landowner of Ardtornish estate in the West Highlands, building model houses while his wife Jan set up an infant school.[68] After Octavius's death, in February 1871, Ben regarded himself as the head of the Leigh Smiths, whose approval should be sought on any important family matter. It probably did not occur to him that Barbara, as the eldest Leigh Smith sibling, might also lay claim to that role.

Barbara tried to get Ben to revise his views of Norman, pointing out that although he had no inherited money (or expectations of it) it was hardly his fault that his father had deserted his mother. On the other hand, he had a Cambridge degree, and an MB from St Bartholomew's where he was a lecturer in comparative anatomy. In 1874 he had been appointed Warden of the College, an enormous honour for a young man of twenty-seven. In a letter to Ben on 3 December, she wrote:

I know Norman well & I think him a very fine character. He is upright persevering & very affectionate. He has brain enough to take a good place in his profession. Thousands of English girls do marry struggling professional men & get on very well & are very happy.

Whether Amy has the stuff in her to undertake this externally hard life I am not sure. Her education has been frightfully neglected but if she is as serious as she thinks she will work to learn something for a year & then come to this point again with Willy Georgina & you.[69]

Again, in this new struggle with Ben, Barbara was able to count on Bessie's support. Despite Barbara's 'croakings' during Bessie's pregnancies, Bessie had safely produced two children, Marie in 1868 and Hilaire in 1870.[70] The slight estrangement between the two friends had ended abruptly in August 1872, when Louis Belloc died and their close friendship strongly reasserted itself. Bessie was not well off because 'owing to her trust in a friend's son, who was part owner of a firm of outside brokers' she had lost most of her money.[71] She lived with her mother at Wimpole Street and came for holidays at Scalands Gate. Although she no longer involved herself in Barbara's feminist campaigns directly, her love for Barbara, undiminished, was a continuing sweetness in Barbara's life, and a much-needed comfort.

Girton business went on regardless of family turmoil. In January 1877 Barbara wrote from London to Amy:

On Friday night I went to Ldy Stanley's to a Girton meeting – we were 4 gentlemen & 4 ladies, we had rather a fierce discussion about admitting outside ladies to our lectures at Girton . . . we were all against it as a rule. I knew that this term there were 30 ladies going to study at Cambridge *not* under Miss Clough so was quite determined.[72]

Clearly, Barbara and the rest of the committee were confident by this stage that Girton College would survive, despite competition from Newnham Hall. Barbara pressed Amy to go to Newnham Hall for a term at least, thinking that, were she to marry Norman, she simply must have a better education than she had received thus far in her life. Barbara recognised (or had been made to recognise by Emily) that Amy had neither the commitment nor had received sufficient 'secondary' education to attend Girton. But believing that she would end up by marrying a man of quite extraordinary intellectual acumen, Barbara remained concerned that Amy was such a 'goose':

As there is no entrance examination you could go if your father & mother like it & it would show you another world worth seeing quite, – shall I propose it? There is no forced line of study there, you could go to History lectures and music & drawing or only one thing. But you would see other girls big girls, some going to be married, all over 17 some 20 or 25. It is you know a very nice house & Miss Clough liked you at first sight. Did I tell you, you spelt *piteous* wrong – all other words right in last 3 letters.[73]

Either Amy did not care to go, or her parents were a good deal more interested in getting her out of the country in the hope that she would forget Norman, but, in any event, Amy went neither to Girton nor to Newnham. Instead she was whisked off by her father to France and Switzerland on an extended continental tour.

On 8 January Barbara sent Norman birthday wishes, some salt cellars, and some encouraging words:

To give salt cellars is more lucky than to spill salt. You will see if it is not a good omen. You put 'sal salvit omnia' on my salt cellars at Scalands. My father used to say to me 'Salt of the earth ye virtuous few' &c as an encouragement to stand up against the crowd of worldlings – the word salt is in consequence very pleasant to me as well as the taste.[74]

The letter implies that she regarded Norman, like her father, as an intellectual leader, whereas she felt that Ben and Willie, in becoming the lords of the manors of Glottenham and Crowham respectively, had become too closely identified with the conservative landed gentry. She continued to rally support in the rest of the family by arranging for Norman and his mother to visit the Bonham Carters at Ravensbourne. This visit achieved Barbara's object of obtaining Bonham Carter approval of the Moores, both mother and son: she thereby gained a potential pressure group on the side of Amy's romantic hopes. She orchestrated the strategy for the acceptance of Norman with the same finesse with which she habitually organised political campaigns. She advised him to join the Reform Club, which she felt would give him the stamp of a (liberal) gentleman. She felt that once Ben saw how well respected Norman was by members of his own club, he would have to revise his views.

As well as worrying about her various nieces and nephews, in September 1875 Barbara had been faced with a sudden new and entirely unexpected responsibility. One of her servants at Blandford Square, Esther Grealy, had given birth to an illegitimate child, whom she had given up to a foundling hospital.[75] Barbara could not bear this; perhaps her own illegitimate birth gave her a special sympathy for the 'outlaws' of the world. She rescued the baby from the foundling hospital, offering to have him looked after for a few months at her own expense to give Esther time to decide what she wanted to do. She arranged to have the baby nursed by a Mrs Haseldew in Robertsbridge, so Henny took him down to Sussex. Writing to tell Amy all about it Barbara said, 'Alfred came last night quite safely & slept quite well last night & is flourishing . . . Your Mama was quite excited about my baby & wants to see it very much indeed.' Barbara hoped to persuade someone well off to adopt him, if Esther would not take him back. By March 1876 Elizabeth Blackwell (who was now living in Hastings) had persuaded Barbara to face the fact that, despite her earlier hopes, Esther would not want her child back: 'she is very poor and very friendless. I do not see what she *could* do if she had a baby to support, and ruin her character'.[76] Barbara wondered whether her sister-in-law, Georgie, who had shown an interest in the baby, could be persuaded to take him on, as she had four children already and therefore, in Barbara's mind, could easily tack Alfred on after Willy, born in 1873. Georgie declined Barbara's suggestion, and went on to have two more children of her own (Bella in 1879 and Dolly in 1881). Again Elizabeth Blackwell advised Barbara to lower her sights somewhat. Elizabeth's letter of 19 July 1876 says: 'It seems so extremely improbable that people of position should take a fancy to poor little Alfred, that it would hardly be worthwhile to take much trouble in the matter, with so very slender a chance of success.'[77]

Barbara then turned, more realistically, to Jessie Boucherett's older sister, Louisa, who was a pioneer in the movement for the boarding out of pauper children. With Louisa's help, Alfred was boarded with Mrs Alice Breach, the wife of a boatman at Eastbourne. Alice Breach was a kindly soul who earned money by fostering to help out the family's income, as her husband's trade was seasonal. In January 1877 Barbara and Hertha visited Eastbourne to make sure that little Alfred was thriving and 'found all very satisfactory'.[78] Elizabeth Blackwell advised Barbara to limit her interest in Alfred to saving him from a criminal life by getting him apprenticed as a carpenter or as a sailor. Barbara established herself as Alfred's legal guardian and set up a trust fund for him, which Elizabeth Blackwell promised to manage in the event of Barbara's predeceasing her. All in all, it is surprising the number of people for whose welfare Barbara felt responsible, despite, or possibly because, herself being a childless woman.

Meanwhile, in January 1877, Barbara's other protégée, Hertha, had suffered a breakdown in her health, mainly from overwork but also from distress at the death of Eric Noel, a little boy to whom she had been governess. In February Barbara paid for Hertha to have a holiday with Alice Breach at Eastbourne, to get some sea air. While Hertha was at Eastbourne Barbara received sad news from Mary Howitt in Meran, in the Austrian Tyrols, that 'Peggy' Foley had died. Following her meeting with Barbara in America, Margaret Foley had joined the circle of women sculptors in Rome centred on Harriet Hosmer. There she had earned her living by making a series of cameo portraits and busts of notable visitors. She had exhibited these to acclaim in Dublin, Paris and London, at both the Royal Academy and the Society of Women Artists. As Foley's reputation grew she was able to make large free-standing sculptures, one of which she had sent to the Philadelphia Centennial in 1876 shortly before her fatal illness. Meeting the Howitts in Rome, she had been virtually adopted by them, and had become Maggie Howitt's beloved companion. Mary wrote:

> Our poor Maggie will long bear the scar of this deep wound – I believe she will never lose it – though time brings us, we know, wondrous healing. But these two Margarets were so much to each other – each supplied what the other lacked. But God who has taken the one will not forsake the other.
>
> Poor Margaret Foley suffered great anxiety regarding her money matters during the last twelve months of her life – all her little capital being sunk in the marble work which she sent to America . . . And no sooner was she gone than money came & orders for copies of her most beautiful work – showing that it was appreciated – so much that would have cheered her up had it come in time . . . I must tell you dearest Barbara that your lovely Welsh drawings which were the ornaments of our poor dear Peggy's rooms in Rome and which had become so dear to her, will now fall to Meggy.[79]

Barbara was planning to go down to Zennor to paint so Bessie and her two children went to Scalands Gate for five weeks. Bessie assured Norman on 16 March that 'I will do my best to see Amy & ascertain her mind – but unless I am very careful not to show any special anxiety I shall not be able to do it, as I am always considered the Double – "Doppel Ganger" – of Madame Bodichon.'[80] Aunt Ju offered to take Hertha up to Lea Hurst in Derbyshire for the summer, which pleased Barbara as she knew that 'At Ju will help Marky all she can'.[81] All in all, Barbara had done the best that she could for all her various protégés.

Her enormous delight in the foundation of Girton College continued unabated. Writing to Amy on printed college paper on 17 April she imagined herself as the eponymous heroine Ida of Tennyson's poem, *The Princess*, describing herself as 'in the College for 3 days resting in my own Palace! Certainly it is very delicious & our 35 students & their 35 little houses very jolly.'[82] She visited students in their rooms, joined them at lunchtimes and watched them working with their microscopes in Girton laboratory. She was full of joy that the long-held vision had been brought down from the clouds and made a material reality.

Barbara was awaiting the arrival in England of her old friend, Jessie White Mario, who had been suffering badly from pains in her writing hand. She described her to Amy:

> You know she nursed sick and wounded & was a very great friend of Aunt Bella's, who I remember said she was never happier than with Jessie White. She is *very* clever and generous & courageous. She used to teach in my school years ago & we had lots of work & lots of play together 25 or 30 years ago, so I feel as if it would be splendid to cure her hand . . . It is bitterly cold here. Mr Brabazon looks shrivelled up & he is going to Paris he says and then to Cornwall.[83]

When Jessie arrived at Blandford Square Barbara took her to visit the Leweses before leaving for Cornwall and George made some suggestions about how Jessie should remedy her condition.

Barbara was in high spirits when they set off for Zennor. She was happy about Girton. She had done what she could to help Norman and Amy. She had put her business affairs in order by asking Reginald Thompson to replace Aunt Ju as one of her two trustees (because of Aunt Ju's age). During her stay with Gertrude Jekyll in Surrey she had finished some of her pictures in Gertrude's studio, and had sold pictures shown at both the Society of Lady Artists (the erstwhile SFA) and at the Dudley Gallery. At the Crystal Palace exhibition in April of that year she won a silver medal for a watercolour called *The Sea*. It was now ten years on since the crisis of 1867, when facing up to the fact that she would probably never have children of her own had caused her deep depression. Her interest in the careers of Norman and Hertha had to a great extent answered that need. She had also faced up to the fact that Dr Bodichon did not have a deep empathy with her artistic ambitions, but at least he did not try to circumscribe what she did or where she went with her wide circle of artistic friends. Perhaps no more nor less than many middle-aged people in a marriage of some years' duration, they had come to a comfortable accommodation of each other's needs and desires.

CHAPTER 16

Reduced Powers

For Barbara, the only cloud in the spring of 1877 was Ben's continuing fury over her steadfast promotion of Norman's courtship of Amy. Bessie, well aware of Barbara's distress at Ben's anger, advised her to make a tactical retreat, while she took over as the standard bearer for love's young dreams. Barbara turned her attention to succouring Jessie White Mario who was still writing a commissioned article, despite the fact that she was supposed to be resting her hand. She ordered a 'writing machine' for her, to be sent down to the 'Poor House'.[1]

Barbara herself was thoroughly enjoying the ambience of her old granite cottage, built on the edge of moorland high above sea level and with spectacular views down to the Atlantic Ocean. As ever she was invigorated by the sound of the sea's rough surge and the extraordinary atmospheric effects, including the famous 'green flash', but a crisp, chill east wind had started to blow, so she retreated indoors and started to experiment with the newfangled machine, which she nicknamed 'Tryphena' (after a Smith ancestor). Writing to Hertha at Lea Hurst, she said:

> I can't tell you how much I like this place, but as for drawing, it has been too cold – colder than it was in March . . . I think the machine is a great success, but like all machinery it wants a head to keep it up to the mark. It would not be worth £20 to any one who had a free right hand. The 'manifold copier' is carbonised paper put on the roller, the inked ribbon being taken out. That ribbon is the devil to manage because it gets ruffled and cross . . .[2]

It remained cold at Zennor. Barbara was busy painting the green granite rocks and looking forward to the arrival of Henry Moore and Brabbie. Norman had just arrived for a holiday towards the end of May, when she was struck down with a stroke. As a medical man, he was competent to treat Barbara himself, but wisely telegrammed immediately for Reginald Thompson who, as doctor, friend and also trustee to Barbara, could take charge of everything. As soon as Reginald arrived

Norman left for London. Reginald wrote to Benjamin Leigh Smith on 27 May:

Dear Sir,
I wish to tell you, more explicitly than can be done by telegraph, that Madame Bodichon was seized on Wednesday last [the 24th] with sudden illness resulting from exposure to East wind & an exhausting walk. I arrived here on Thursday to find her suffering from symptoms due to cerebral injury, paralysis of [?] & motion affecting the right side with loss of power of articulation. She is doing now as well as could be expected but I do not anticipate a rapid recovery.[3]

The degree of Benjamin's displeasure with Barbara after their quarrel is perhaps indicated by the fact that he made no immediate plan to see her. Reginald had to write again on 30 May to prompt him:

Dear Sir, It would I am sure be a great consolation to your sister if you could run down only for a day. There is no need for longer stay as merely the sight of you would do much to relieve her mind. Although her speech is affected by the injury to the brain her intellect is clear.[4]

Following this second letter, Ben set off for Cornwall, arriving at the Poor House on Sunday, 3 June. Barbara had suffered terribly from Ben's fury following their latest quarrel and she was desperate to receive his forgiveness and the assurance of his love. She could not, at the first moment of the stroke, have known for certain that she would live. Her need for a reconciliation with him was paramount.

For Barbara herself, after the first horrendous days of panic and disorientation were over, her most intense concern was whether she would ever again command a paintbrush well enough to paint. By the end of June Bessie went down to Zennor to see how things stood with Barbara and wrote a detailed account to Norman on 5 July:

1. Firstly then, I have satisfied myself that she is absolutely unchanged intellectually – quite lucid, quite vigorous.
2. The paralysis of leg & hand is now very slight. She complains of varying sensations of cold & weakness in the leg; but she can walk slowly. As to her hand I perceive no difference – she seized my sketchbooks & pencil one day, began to draw & said 'I must not; Dr Thompson forbids me to try'. The impression on my mind was that she could have drawn as well as usual, for a few minutes.
3. But she is very weak; yesterday she half fainted, from having wilfully insisted on performing parts of her own toilette. She requires

incessant care in regard to small doses of food, cannot bear to be read to more than half an hour at a time (tho' asking to be read to constantly) and

4thly I do not think the speech improves. When *fresh* she can talk on familiar topics with very few trips; but if she tries to tackle proper names, in history or science, she cannot manage it at all.

5th. She went nearly an hour's drive the day before yesterday with no bad results & *great* enjoyment

6thly She tells me, with great decision that much as she loves Amy she does not want her at Zennor, as she should feel Amy's presence a great responsibility on account of her youth.

And she always speaks of you with great affection but says to me privately that under all the circumstances of your engagement to Amy you cannot help her *now*. I am so loath to write this to you; but I *cannot* help it. It is evident that the quarrels with her brothers gave her frightful anguish, & she cannot bear the slightest recurrence to the subject of it . . .[5]

Hertha was desperate with worry when she heard of Barbara's attack and wrote to Bessie pleading to be allowed to visit her. Hertha took over from Bessie at the end of July and was there when Eugène arrived at Zennor. She reported to Amy: 'The doctor has just come today, & Madame is so glad, & they are both so happy.'[6] The old affection between them had sprung up with renewed vividness; perhaps Barbara's stroke had the effect of wiping her memory banks of difficult times, whilst bringing into sharper focus the feelings at the very start of their romance. Writing on the same day to give Norman a progress report on Madame's recovery, Hertha said: 'Her hand has quite recovered its power, & she walks quite well, when she does walk, which is not often yet, nor for more than about a minute at a time. Only her speech still remains wrong, though it is improving, only more slowly than any of the rest.'[7]

A chain of friends including Mary Ewart, Gertrude Jekyll and Elizabeth Blackwell went down to Zennor to keep Barbara company, to read to her, and to encourage her to believe that she would recover. Barbara stayed in Cornwall until the beginning of October 1877, and then went to Blandford Square, with Hertha accompanying her on the journey. Hertha then went up to Girton while Sarah Scott, Katie's youngest sister, took over for the month of November, finding herself extremely busy dealing with Barbara's extensive correspondence; all through her adult life Barbara wrote an average of fifteen letters a day, including family and 'social' letters. Marian wrote on 16 November 1877 to Sara Hennell:

Do you know that our dear Madame Bodichon, whose life was so full of active benevolence, was some months ago stricken with an attack of aphasia and other signs of nervous weakness? She had gone to a cottage she has in Cornwall for the sake of taking there Madame Mario, whose overtasked frame was much in need of rest and change, and lo Barbara herself was stricken and Madame Mario became her energetic nurse. The attack has long passed its worst, and she is completely like herself in everything except strength.[8]

George Lewes's great affection for Barbara was expressed in the form of regular letters designed to lift her spirits. He had never forgotten the dreadful summer of 1869 when his son Thornie was dying from spinal tuberculosis and Barbara's twice-weekly visits had cheered him more than anybody else's.

Hertha took over from Sarah Scott when the Michaelmas term ended and once again conscientiously kept all of Barbara's friends informed of her progress. A Christmas Day letter from Marian Lewes thanked Hertha for her diligence and hoped that she would find time to visit the Leweses to give a fuller account 'Your good news about our dear Madame Bodichon was the best of Christmas gifts to me this morning . . . I long to have more minute details about Mme Bodichon than a note can give me. But that she has a drive and a walk every day is at least a starting point for pleasant fancies about her.'[9] In January 1878 Barbara's troubles were augmented by a bad bout of toothache, which abated after the removal of the culprit. She enjoyed the hordes of letters, but was especially grateful to George Lewes for taking time to bring the outside world into her convalescence. She was particularly interested by one letter in which he described a visit with Huxley and Paget to 'see a patient from whom a Glasgow surgeon had removed the *whole of the larynx*, and this he had supplied by an artificial larynx with which the man could speak. It was most interesting. He spoke in a monotone but with perfect distinctness. What will science do next?'[10] When Hertha went back to Girton for the Lent term, Sarah Scott took over as Barbara's companion once more, followed by Aunt Ju.

The most distinguished physician of the day, Sir William Jenner, Physician-Extraordinary to Queen Victoria, had been put in charge of Barbara's convalescence as soon as she had returned to Blandford Square. Jenner's advice by the end of April 1878 indicated that arrangements for a succession of 'minders' should continue, to keep away the numerous visitors who would otherwise exhaust her. As a consequence of this advice, when Elizabeth Blackwell came to see Barbara at the end of May she took lodgings near to Blandford Square, rather than staying with her, as she usually did when in town. Elizabeth wrote to give Jessie White Mario the benefit of her professional opinion on 23 May:

> for the first time she conversed with me rapidly – in the strong clear spontaneous way with which she used to pour forth her ideas – not hesitatingly painfully and with apparent confusion at times. I did not notice one hesitation for words, whilst talking with me – although there was such difficulty when she gave the coachman directions – neither did I observe any exhaustion at the end of the drive. This of course was only a temporary flashing back of the old life – but it was an immense comfort to find it could so flash.
>
> The one inevitable care that presses upon her, and from which she cannot possibly be freed until it pleases Providence to withdraw from our world this peculiar being who has so mysteriously been allowed to cross Barbara's life – is her husband. It is quite certain that any attempt to render her indifferent to his welfare, would be worse than unavailing – for that great crisis was past through years ago, and she elected to hold to him with that tremendously womanly power of sex which seems unapproachable by men . . .[11]

As Barbara started to feel better she became increasingly insistent on moving out of London and down to Sussex. With Hertha to look after her, on 8 June she moved into one of the small cottages she had built in 1867 next to Scalands Gate. On the same day the South Kensington Museum purchased from her 'a very fine unfinished picture by Van Dyke' as it would be 'a splendid example' for their students to copy.[12] Barbara wanted the money for a new project. She had asked Gertrude Jekyll to draw up plans for the addition of a large room to the ground floor of Scalands Gate, changing the existing porch so that, in the new arrangement, a right turn would lead into the house, but a left turn would lead into the new 'reading room' which was to serve as a library and as a night school for local working men.[13] This scheme was set in hand with help from her old friend, William Ransom, who had retired from his job as editor of the *Hastings and St Leonards News*. He now served as chairman of the Hastings School Board and he offered to come and teach in the school in the winter months, defined as those of November through to April, when Dr Bodichon was not in residence. Bricks were ordered for the extension but during the course of the work, the builders reported on their concerns about the condition of the well water at Scalands, so Hertha sent some up to Norman to be analysed. As the results were rather shocking she gave instructions for the well to be cleaned out and cemented.

To Barbara's great relief, Willie and Georgina had accepted Norman as a prospective son-in-law and resumed their old friendly ways. In token of this Willie had a nice quiet horse sent over from Crowham so that Barbara could go riding.[14] Eugène arrived for the summer as soon as the building works were complete, and Emily Davies came on her usual summer visit. In September Barbara rented 7 Pelham Crescent to enjoy the health-giving effects of Hastings.

She could not prevent herself from continuing her struggle to persuade Amy to educate herself, offering to pay for her to attend the Slade School.[15] Amy was no more inclined to take up this offer than she had been to respond to Barbara's attempts to get her to attend Newnham.[16] Barbara kept up the pressure, suggesting that perhaps she could attend Bedford College for drawing lessons. By 1879 she was writing to her in frustration:

> I think Gertrude [Jekyll] is right about the drawing. You see this last 2 years you have lost some power of observation & exactness & tried to make up by vulgar dash which is not genius . . . never work except you work with *mind* as well as hand. You seem to have lost the idea of religion in your work.[17]

Barbara was never going to win this battle. Amy was entirely satisfied with drawing as a 'feminine' accomplishment; she subscribed to the very model of education which Barbara had fought against all her life.

Marian missed Barbara's company. Writing to her on 15 October 1878 she commented:

> The days pass by without my finding time to tell you what I want to tell you . . . I miss so much the hope I used to have of seeing you in London and talking over everything just as we used to do – in the way that will never exactly come with any one else. How unspeakably the lengthening of memories in common endears our old friends! The new are comparatively like foreigners, with whom one's talk is hemmed in by mutual ignorance. The one cannot express, the other cannot divine.[18]

Shortly after this letter, Marian began to stare tragedy in the face. George's health rapidly declined. Although he tried to keep from Marian the pain he was intermittently suffering, by November he was bedridden. Sir James Paget was called in and on 25 November she wrote to Barbara to say that she had 'a deep sense of change within, and of a permanently closer relationship with death'.[19] Lewes died of enteritis on 30 November

1878 and after a Unitarian service was buried in the Dissenters' part of Highgate Cemetery. Now it was the turn of the receiver of comfort to send comfort in her turn. Barbara asked Marian to come and live with her and Dr Bodichon, an offer which was refused.[20] She sent many letters and enquiries, offering to take Marian away for a holiday with her, but all offers were declined. A reply of 7 January 1879 says: 'Dearest Barbara, Bless you for all your goodness to me, but I am a bruised creature, and shrink even from the tenderest touch.'[21]

Marian was putting what energy she had into getting ready for publication George's last two volumes of *Problems of Life and Mind* with the help of her stepson, Charles Lewes. In January 1879 she changed her name by deed poll to 'Mary Ann Evans Lewes' as a preliminary to setting up a George Henry Lewes Studentship which 'would be a sort of prolongation of *His* life. That there should always, in consequence of his having lived, be a young man working in the way he would have liked to work, is a memorial of him that comes nearest my feelings . . .'[22] In June 1879, on a visit to Marian, Barbara persuaded her to make the studentship open to women.[23]

The chief pleasures of this recovery period of Barbara's life were going painting with Gertrude Jekyll and the new night school, which from its inception was to be Barbara's principal social work following her stroke. When she had first built Scalands Gate, however, she had made only an informal arrangement with Ben who, as the owner of the Glottenham estate, was her landlord. Presumably in 1863 they had been on sufficiently good terms that no one, not even Barbara's trustees had ever worried about it. After their great falling out over Norman, there seems to have been a move towards greater formality in matters of business; in February 1879 a formal conveyance had been made between Ben and his sister of 9 acres 3 rods and 3 perches of land called Harding's Wood including Scalands Gate and its three cottages, subject to right of way for Ben from his adjacent land to the road. This was a significant moment. The original purpose of 'Dr Bodichon's cottage' was to establish a place where her husband was happy to stay when they came to England, but after her stroke she was thinking of it is as her own principal residence. In May 1879 she let Blandford Square for two years.

On 3 March Barbara had heard that William Howitt had died in Rome, still in harness, working on a life of George Fox. Anna Mary wrote to her: 'My father met death with the same brave heart which he had ever shown throughout his career. He told us not to mourn for him; he sent his love and blessing to all his friends and I send you your share . . .'[24] Mary Howitt wrote to her in September of that year from Dietenheim in the

Austrian Tyrol: 'I was not prepared for dear William's death – I always thought he would outlive me – so bright as he was – his heart as warm & true & his enjoyment of life & his interest in all passing events as keen & active as ever – & this to the very last!'[25] Whether Barbara had a direct hand in it, I cannot tell, but in the year of William's death, Mary Howitt was awarded a Civil List pension. It seems at least possible that Barbara had been sending letters to the various influential politicians she knew.

Emily went to stay with Barbara in the summer of 1879 and she reported to Adelaide Manning:

> She can paint a little most days, and walks about, but is still very much an invalid . . . I have been telling Madame that this is a place to grow handsome in, and that I felt it coming on. She said it was quite true, and I was already 20 per cent better-looking than when I came. Then it struck her that it would be a good place for the Portrait to be taken, and asked if I could come and have it done here. I said Yes, but I scarcely think it can come off, as she will have to go when the leaves begin to fall.[26]

The 'Portrait' of Emily Davies was to be painted by Rudolf Lehmann, a German portrait painter who had settled in London. It was subscribed for by Girtonians and its intention clearly was both to honour the 'originator' of Girton and to augment the sense of Girton having a history and a dignity commensurate with that of older Cambridge colleges.

Barbara's health improved slowly but steadily and she enjoyed visits from Nannie and Isabella and from Bessie and her friend Emily Greatorex.[27] At the end of September she went to see Marian at Witley and found her slowly recovering her spirits, but by October she was absorbed by Hertha's problems. Winnie had suffered a nervous breakdown and Hertha's immediate response was to give up Girton to look after her. Finally Hertha was persuaded to take a loan from Ottilie Blind to continue her studies while Barbara paid for Winnie to be nursed first in lodgings in Hastings and subsequently in Robertsbridge.[28] She and Ottilie were equally determined that Hertha, after all her struggles, deserved the chance to undertake her third year at Girton and complete her Tripos. By contrast, Amy continued to resist renewed efforts by Barbara to persuade her to go to Newnham Hall.[29] On 2 February 1880 Fanny Nightingale died, aged ninety-two. It can hardly be supposed that Barbara mourned deeply for her, but she mentioned it to Marian Lewes, who responded, 'I know how you feel the successive deaths of aged relatives . . . especially as to your remaining associations with your father.'[30]

However, that same month, Barbara had reasons to rejoice. Charlotte Angas Scott was placed equal to the eighth wrangler in the Tripos, the first Girton student to achieve the distinction. Hertha wrote describing the scene to Barbara:

> When the list was read in Cambridge this morning and the man came to 'eighth', before he could say the name all the undergraduates called out 'Scott of Girton,' shouting her name over and over again with tremendous cheers and waving of hats . . . She bore it very composedly, blushed and smiled a little . . . One of her papers – algebra and trigonometry – was better than any of the men's, and at the end of the three days' subjects she was third on the list; she lost the five places afterwards by not having read enough – the result of having read so very little when she came up.[31]

Charlotte Scott's triumph, getting the equivalent of a 'first' today, must have been joy to Barbara's ears. Charlotte had managed this magnificent feat despite her inadequate secondary education, a problem all the pioneer Girton students faced. Marian Lewes wrote to congratulate Barbara, saying, 'I saw all about Miss Scott's success in the Times, and was the more interested in it because Miss Marks had described her to me.'[32] For the pioneer students, to feel that older women like Barbara herself, Marian Lewes, Lady Goldsmid and Ottilie Blind were cheering them on was a significant psychological support. It amounted to a new kind of improvised female mentoring which had to stand in for all of the formal structures which supported male undergraduates in a long-established university.[33]

At the end of April 1880 Barbara received a slightly odd note from Marian saying, 'You must not tell Miss Marks to call on me, for I shall not be in town. I have changed my plans and am going abroad for a little while. But I shall write to you again before long and tell you more.'[34] At the beginning of May Barbara was staying with General Ludlow and his family at Yotes Court when she was astonished to see a notice in *The Times* recording Marian's marriage to John Cross on 6 May. She wrote immediately to Charles Lewes who replied promptly, supporting his stepmother's action. He explained that John Cross, a close friend of George and Marian Lewes, who had been treated by them more or less as a nephew, had recently lost his mother, and, turning to Marian for comfort, had ended up falling in love with her. Despite being twenty years younger, Cross had proposed marriage (three times) and finally Marian had accepted his offer. A letter from Barbara thanking Charles said: 'Your letter is a great comfort to me – *thank you for it*. I know nothing – only the "Times" was a shock to me. I hope when I come you will tell me more.'[35] Barbara left Yotes Court to visit her little foundling, Alfred Clements, at Mrs Breach's house in Eastbourne and then travelled along the coast to Hastings. From there she wrote to Marian:

> My dear I hope and I think you will [be] happy.
>
> Tell Johnny Cross I should have done exactly what he has done if you would have let me and I had been a man.
>
> You see I know all love is so different that I do not see it unnatural to love in new ways – not to be unfaithful to any memory.
>
> If I knew Mr Lewes he would be glad to hear you were going to Italy but I did not guess this. My love to your friend if you will.[36]

Marian was especially delighted to receive Barbara's generous letter because the letter she had addressed to her on the day before her marriage had never been posted, but had been stuck out of sight in a drawer. Marian's letter from Italy says:

> Ever since Charles forwarded to me your dear letter while I was in Paris I have been meaning to write to you. That letter [is] doubly sweet to me because it was written before you received mine, intending to inform you of the marriage before it appeared in the newspaper . . . I had more than once said to Mr Cross that you were one of the friends who required the least explanation on the subject – who would spontaneously understand our marriage.[37]

Marian's brother, Isaac Evans, who had broken off all contact with her when she set up home with George Lewes, on reading of her marriage to John Cross wrote offering his congratulations. Marian answered him without hesitation, saying: 'it was a great joy to me to have your kind words of sympathy, for our long silence has never broken the affection for you which began when we were little ones.'[38] Marian at last had the desire of her heart, the return of her brother's approval, and she accepted it without any complaint that he had been unfair to her in the past. Barbara longed for the same blessing from her own brother.

She had hopes of receiving it once Amy married Norman at the end of March in Westfield Church, Willie and Georgina having come to accept that Norman, despite having no family money behind him, had capital in his own intellect.[39] As Warden of St Bartholomew's Hospital he had a house with his job, so there was no problem about accommodation, even if it was not the country manor that Willie would have liked for his daughter. It seems likely that Barbara eased their way by promising Willie that she would leave Amy something in her will to help her buy a home when it was needed. Barbara gave them four candles and possibly the portrait in oils painted in 1861 by Samuel Laurence for their wedding present, as this painting was in their house in 1880.[40] Ben seems to have stuck rigidly to his view that Norman was a fortune hunter and that the match would inevitably end in disaster. He made it clear that he would visit neither Crowham nor Yotes Court, nor Scalands Gate were the couple to be there.

In the summer of 1880 Barbara's long-serving housekeeper, Henny, retired and in her place Barbara appointed a woman of about thirty, Eliza Sanderson, whom she liked very much. Nannie and Isabella came to stay in August, but Nannie immediately fell ill, and at the beginning of October had still not recovered. Barbara wrote to Amy to say:

> I am sorry to say Nanny is not yet out of bed. I think she is very delicate but will [with] care live longer than Aunt Bella did but not to be old. You see my mother died at 32 – chest disease – & all her sisters but Aunty [Dolly] died young so on that side we have not a good chance.[41]

Nannie's delicacy, a thing always taken on trust by Barbara, seems more like Aunt Patty's hypochondria than anything else. She outlived her two sisters by many years.

At the beginning of November Barbara heard from Marian in Witley that her health, which had never been robust, was particularly poor:

> Three weeks ago I had rather a troublesome attack but I am getting on very well now, though still reduced and comparatively weak . . . Mr Cross has nursed me as if he had been a wife nursing a husband, never leaving me except to get his walk.[42]

The attack referred to was a bout of pain from kidney stones, which she had suffered on and off since 1873. This was her last letter to Barbara. On 3 December Marian and John Cross moved into their new home in Cheyne Walk. She had another severe attack on the 18th and died of heart failure on 22 December. Her husband made some attempts to get her buried in the Poets' Corner of Westminster Abbey, but she was far too heterodox for this plan to have any chance of success. Instead, on 29 December, she was buried in Highgate Cemetery, in a plot touching Lewes's grave at one corner. Isaac Evans attended his sister's funeral. Dr Thomas Sadler, who had conducted George Lewes's funeral, conducted Marian's funeral service 'using most of the Prayer Book' with 'discreet

Unitarian omissions'.[43] Barbara had once told Amy that when she was with 'thoroughly great people', among whom she included Marian Lewes, 'I feel that the intellect is not the quality which strikes me most, it is the power of being truthful & having a soul which is pure & active'.[44] John Cross had inscribed on Marian's coffin lines from Dante: 'quella fonte/che spandi di parlar sì largo fiume'.[45] Barbara's words to Amy serve as her epitaph to her friend.

Barbara was only just getting used to the idea of this sad loss when, at the end of January 1881, she received a forlorn letter from Hertha:

> I am only fifteenth in the Third Class. I am so sorry. I am afraid you will be very disappointed in me . . . I think it is very hard on you, after all you have done for me, that I should do no better. It is not for want of work, however, nor even entirely want of brains, but rather want of memory, and still more of presence of mind in the exam. room. So I have turned out a failure.[46]

Barbara replied by return: 'My dear, you are not a failure! Your life will not be a failure . . . Tell me if you are well and sleep well. Write by return. Always your B.'[47] To help Hertha's finances, Barbara found private pupils for her, including a young cousin, Rosalind Shore Smith.[48] To Barbara's enormous delight, Rosalind, after Hertha's careful tutoring, passed her entrance examination for Girton. She went up in Michaelmas 1880 and by the end of term reported that she liked it 'tremendously'.[49]

Aunt Ju stayed at Scalands Gate during December 1880 and January 1881. Barbara told Amy: 'She is very well and teaches the boys but she is not so quick as she was last year in understanding things & she is deaf – but she is 82 & wonderful for that . . . We have such a school! It is quite a rage to go to school & learn, poor fellows like it so much. One walked 22 miles one night & come to Scalands School after.'[50] At this point Barbara seems happily engrossed by her life at Scalands Gate, although still going up to London on business occasionally. The 1881 census, taken on 21 April, offers a snapshot of her life. She is recorded as the 'head' of Scalands Gate, and her occupation given as 'painter'. Her staff consisted of a housekeeper (Eliza Sanderson), a cook (Mary Morgan), a parlour-maid (Emma Payton) and a housemaid (Matilda Fuller). Two of her cottages were occupied by farm labourers and their families; the third she liked to keep as reserve quarters for guests, when they arrived in what she called 'horrid great lumps'.

In May 1882 Barbara finally decided to sell Blandford Square, her political base for so many years. She sold it to Llewelyn Davies, Emily's brother.[51] In this way she could reduce her expenses to running Scalands Gate and Campagne du Pavillon, sending out sufficient money for Eugène to pay Madame Victor, his housekeeper in Algiers, and all his living costs.

At the beginning of February 1882, Barbara was delighted to hear of the safe delivery of Amy's first child, for it briefly took her mind off her violent anxiety about Ben. After inheriting Glottenham estate, Ben could live off the rents and indulge in his greatest loves, sailing and exploring. The endless publicity which had surrounded Sir John Franklin's lost Arctic voyagers had captured his imagination and served as an enticement to the icy wastes.[52] He took the Board of Trade 'ticket' to command his own ships and invented an instrument for computing time at sea. From 1871 to 1882 he made five exploratory voyages in Arctic waters; for the fourth and fifth voyages he had a 300-ton vessel, the *Eira*, built to his own specifications. This set sail from Peterhead with a crew of twenty-five on 14 June 1881. As they travelled northwards the ice became ever more packed. On 21 August the *Eira* was crushed between pack ice and land floe off Cape Flora, and sank in two hours. Ben, although shy and quiet, had solid leadership qualities, as the ship's company later testified. With the ship's dog, a black retriever called Bob, he turned his hunting skills to good advantage, finding and shooting bears, walrus and birds. The steady supply of meat from the hunting expeditions meant that the men neither starved nor got scurvy.

When the *Eira* had not returned by autumn 1881 Ben's family and friends were exceedingly alarmed. Valentine Smith (Octavius's son) put up £10,000 of his own money, the Royal Geographical added £1,000 and Parliament voted £5,000 towards the sending of a relief vessel. Under Ben's sensible leadership the crew survived the winter and in the spring took to their boats for the homeward passage, safely reaching Novaya Zemlya, where they were picked up by Sir Allen Young in the *Hope*, the vessel sent out to find them. The whole crew disembarked safely at Aberdeen at the end of August 1882; the only casualty was the first mate, who had injured an arm.

Barbara had greatly feared that Ben might be dead in the Arctic wastes, and was delighted at his safe return. This was to be Ben's fifth and final expeditionary trip. He was lauded in the press, received the gold medal of the Royal Geographical Society and was made an honorary fellow of Jesus College.[53] Nannie sent copies of articles in the *Graphic* and the *Illustrated London News* to Mary Howitt at Marienruhe, who replied in October:

We are interested in every incident of your brother Ben's voyage to Franz Joseph land, the loss of his ship, and the return of the explorer and his crew from Nova Zemlya. We were glad to have a peep of them in their hut on Cape Flora. But above all were we thankful to see that the brave man himself was so little changed; that notwithstanding the sufferings and hardships, it was just the same calm, thoughtful face that I remember thirty or more years ago.[54]

On 30 November 1882 Barbara wrote: 'General is dead suddenly.'[55] Her brother-in-law had had the kindest of deaths; although eighty-one years of age, he had been full of vim and vigour until the last moment. Barbara was sad nevertheless, because her brother-in-law's deep and consistent affection for her had been in sharp contrast to the semi-constant aura of disapproval which emanated from Ben.

Barbara was still a member of the Executive Committee of Girton, but around this time her relationship with Emily Davies became troubled. Barbara's aesthetic senses were rather appalled by Emily's procrastination in creating Girton gardens. Although Barbara and Gertrude Jekyll had planned the planting of college gardens, Emily always used any available money to build new rooms for students. Barbara was willing to give trees, but the exposed situation and poor soil meant that a garden could only have any hope of survival if it were to be carefully tended. Barbara considered that Emily's total disregard for how things looked was a tactical error.[56] She had an ally in Frances Metcalfe, who wrote to her:

> I am quite of your opinion that it is useless to give gifts to a garden so utterly uncared for . . . I am certainly not tall, but the weeds are taller than I am . . . I think the Committee are very short-sighted in leaving the garden as the last thing and doling out such scanty supplies, when I believe if it were fairly kept it might be a powerful attraction to students – and I see certain signs of the London University advantages, as well as Newnham, becoming a serious rival.[57] I cannot tell you how my heart sinks whenever I see the dismally uncared-for state of the garden front and back.[58]

To Barbara's enormous relief, Miss Metcalfe set about raising £400 and lawns, trees and shrubs were established under her direction. In 1883 a garden steward, Miss Welch, was appointed who planted Yew Walk, Honeysuckle Walk and Old Orchard.[59]

At the beginning of 1883 something occurred which, despite her insouciance about personal fame, rather upset her. Constance Jones, a student who had gone up to Girton in 1875 when Miss Bernard was Mistress and had herself gone on to become a Mistress, wrote an article which gave Emily Davies *all* the credit for being the 'originator' of the idea of a university college for women. Barbara must have expressed her disappointment at being so cavalierly treated because Emily replied to Barbara, trying to establish a distinction between 'originator' and 'founder', which was a reasonable and possibly useful distinction. On 14 January, Emily wrote:

> As to the early history of the College, I think from something said in a letter from Amy Moore that you must be under a mistake about dates. I understood you to be under the impression that the beginning of the College dates from my visit to you at Scalands in August 1867. This is not the case. The idea of starting a new College suggested itself to me in Oct 6th 1866, after a meeting of schoolmistresses at Manchester. By February 1867 I had arrived at the printed programme ... You see these preliminary steps were being taken while you were in Algiers or somewhere abroad; so that it must be a mistake to speak of conversation at your house 'which led to the issue thence of the first letters on the scheme'.[60]

Hertha, not surprisingly, as Barbara had been her benefactress, was outraged at what she saw as Emily Davies's duplicity. She wrote to Amy on 21 January: 'I don't for a moment believe that Miss Davies had any idea of the college till she talked it over with Madame, but in the face of what she says, I don't see how we are to prove it ... She is a vile reptile, viler than even I thought her.'[61] Nannie, who had always thought that Emily Davies had taken Barbara's money and then ignored her specific wishes for the college, was also offended. She suggested that a portrait of Barbara should be commissioned and hung at Girton, as a clear indication that she had been a founding member of the college, and discussed it with Emily Greatorex and the Cobden sisters. Barbara was with Aunt Ju in Bournemouth at the time, but she wrote to Hertha on the 22nd, saying:

> *Private* When Dr E[lizabeth Blackwell] is in London will you see her and tell her the story, she will be prudent & not say too much, but it will be a great thing to get my portrait in Girton. As E. Davies wishes it too there will be no difficulty ... I did give ED the first idea in conversation but she may have forgotten it. I have talked to other people since 1849 when 1st I brooded the idea, but more to ED than to Bessie, as ED cared for education. Don't let it be a quarrel as Nannie would make it. Unless my portrait is done soon the committee will forget I ever did anything & will not accept it as a gift.[62]

Barbara's other worry at this time was the decline in Eugène's health. During the summer of 1883 he was noticeably frail and beginning to wander in his mind. Norman escorted him back to Algiers in November. Barbara set off on a painting expedition with Mary Ewart and Emily Greatorex to the French Riviera. She visited Cannes, then a simple fishing village, which had been 'discovered' and recommended by her old friend Lord Brougham. Barbara especially enjoyed Hyères, where she went exploring on a donkey, describing it to Amy as 'an island covered with pines which I think is the most beautiful place I ever saw in my life . . . there is a fine old ruined castle standing in the sea & near it on the land a palm tree – in fact it is a place to write a poem about'.[63] On 21 December 1883, while Barbara was still in France, Aunt Ju died; another link to her childhood was gone.[64] Barbara came home in slow stages, visiting Grasse and Valescure. Her paintings from that trip were particularly strong and vivid; looking at them now one is aware of a sense of poignancy, because this was to be the last trip in which she had her full artistic faculties.[65] Hertha had joined them at Cannes, and she too was to look back on that trip wistfully, remembering Barbara's enjoyment, painting in the company of excellent friends.

As an intelligent woman Barbara must have known that another stroke could come at any time and she put her affairs in order. Not having children, she felt free to donate a substantial amount of her money to Girton College. On 15 May her solicitor, Mr Shaen, accordingly sent a letter on Barbara's behalf, offering the college £5,000 in exchange for a deed securing to her an annuity during her life of £250. This offer was gratefully accepted. The Executive Committee put on record their 'sense of the interest taken by Mme Bodichon in the welfare of the College from the beginning'. The amount of £3,000 was sufficient for the immediate building expenses, and the college was able to invest the other £2,000.

Meanwhile, Emily Greatorex, following Nannie's hint, pursued the issue of commissioning a portrait of Barbara for the college. Emily Osborn, whose powerful picture *Nameless and Friendless* (1857) was akin to some of Anna Mary's 'social' pictures, was chosen to undertake the commission.[66] Barbara had known her since 1859 when she had been a signatory of the petition to the Royal Academy to open its schools to women. The list of subscribers for Barbara's portrait included Lady Stanley of Alderley, Frances Metcalfe, Emily Davies, Rose and Florence Davenport Hill, the four Cobden sisters, Catherine and Sarah Scott, Sir Thomas Brassey (of Hastings), Norman Moore, Anne Leigh Smith and Emily Greatorex.[67] Emily's portrait of Barbara destined to hang in Girton College was first exhibited at the Grosvenor Gallery in London in 1884 and was described by Henry Blackburn as 'a life size portrait of Madame Bodichon, the wife of Dr Eugène Bodichon of Algiers. Madame Bodichon, herself a landscape artist of considerable repute, is best known in England by her philanthropic work in connection with the education of women, and as one of the founders of Girton College at Cambridge. Miss Osborn depicts her friend at work in her country house at Hastings, in Sussex'.[68] The portrait showed Barbara seated at an easel, with a palette in her left hand and a brush in her right. She appears to be contemplating the picture she is working on, as though considering her next brushstroke. She is dressed simply, and she appears to be working in oils, as though to establish more firmly the emblems of a professional painter. It seems possible that Emily Osborn may have painted Barbara looking significantly younger than she was at the time of painting; perhaps given Barbara's anxieties about being written out of the Girton story, this was a deliberate attempt to represent Barbara as she looked before her stroke, indeed as she would have looked around 1873 when Girton College first opened its doors. On 16 October 1885 Emily Greatorex wrote to the Executive Committee:

> I have the pleasure of offering for acceptance to Girton College a portrait of Madame Bodichon painted by Miss E. Osborn. I enclose the names of the friends who have subscribed for the portrait, & we hope that it may serve as a remembrance of the great interest that Madame Bodichon has always taken in the College.[69]

In short, having accepted Barbara's £5,000, the Executive Committee now 'gratefully accepted' the portrait of its benefactress to hang alongside that of Emily Davies.

But misfortunes were beginning to crowd in on those she loved. Reginald Thompson's beloved wife Annie had died in January, leaving him with three children to bring up. Bella's eldest boy Harry died returning from India, leaving Mabel and Milicent Ludlow to be looked after primarily by Aunt Louisa Shore. In July 1884 Barbara heard that Anna Mary had died while visiting her mother at Dietenheim in the Austrian Tyrol; it was their first meeting since Mary had been confirmed in the Catholic faith. Mother and daughter had not met for nearly three years, possibly because of the religious difficulty. Mary Howitt wrote of Anna Mary's death: 'In July the weather was intensely hot. On the 19th a violent gale came suddenly up from the north. The icy wind seemed to pierce her. She complained of a sore throat, which rapidly developed into diphtheria; and on the night of July 23rd. she passed away.'[70] What painful thoughts went through Barbara's mind at this time can only be guessed at. Anna Mary was the first kindred spirit she had ever found, but the ambitious young artist had been defeated by a combination of events. Barbara's life, so full of friends who adored her, was also punctuated by strands of loneliness. One of those painful places was the gap left by the loss of her sister in art, Anna Mary, who, despite all her talent, had retired defeated from the fray.

In September she received disturbing news from Algiers about the state of Eugène's mind. Like Anna Mary, he was becoming the prey of the spirit world. Milly Betham-Edwards had once observed Dr Bodichon saying, 'Our life was yesterday, is today, and will be tomorrow. The Jehovah of religious life among the Jews meant the three tenses of the verb to be – the present, the past and the future. There is no disjunction. Death is only a transition from this present life to a superior one.'[71] Milly had been impressed with this sentiment at the time, regarding it as the high-minded response of a rational man of science, who was nevertheless possessed of a calm religious certainty. Unfortunately, Dr Bodichon, always a great raconteur of Breton ghost stories, seems at the end of his life to have slithered over the edge of a mental precipice, hardly able to distinguish between the living and the dead.

In October Barbara went to stay with Norman and Amy in the Warden's House, to see if Norman could go out to Algiers to sort things out for her. Norman tried to explain to her that Dr Bodichon was no longer responsible for his own actions and that some more radical action needed to be taken. Perhaps partly as a result of the shock, Barbara was taken suddenly ill. Sir William Jenner was consulted, confirmed that she had had another small stroke and insisted on absolute quiet for several weeks.[72] As soon as it was possible to move her, Reginald Thompson removed her to his house at 48 Cheyne Walk, Chelsea, where Hertha looked after her convalescence. Unfortunately, this was the start of a quarrel and prolonged estrangement between Barbara and the Moores. Nurses had been put into the Moores' house by Sir William Jenner to look after Barbara, and it seems that there was some kind confusion over money. The Moores' housekeeper, Mrs Dick, wrote to Hertha asking for money to pay for Jenner's services and the nurses. Hertha informed Reginald Thompson (as Barbara's trustee), who sent three cheques to the Moores. The cheque for housekeeping expenses was promptly returned with a stiff note:

I had hoped I had explained quite clearly that we would much rather not receive any money for any part of the expenses incurred by us whilst Aunt Barbara & the nurses stayed in our house. Therefore I have returned the cheque for £25 sent to me. I hope you received the receipt from Dick safely. It was sent last night.[73]

In upper-middle-class families such as Amy's, money was given to servants, or social 'inferiors', not to 'equals'. Amy's reference to her housekeeper as 'Dick', with no courtesy title, indicates an absolute regard to rank which Barbara did not share. Amy, encouraged by Nannie, essentially regarded Hertha as 'Marks' because she was a paid amanuensis to Barbara.

The bad news which Barbara had received from Algiers came from Louis Le Grand, one of Dr Bodichon's relatives who was a physician, aged forty-two. Eugène was still physically strong but his mental health had deteriorated rapidly. After staying in Nannie's house to observe Dr Bodichon's condition, Le Grand had concluded that a curator should be appointed to look after his financial affairs, a local doctor (Dr Gerenti) should be put in charge of the medical aspects of his case, and a male 'nurse' found to take charge of him in his own house. As Nannie wrote to Norman and Amy:

> Dr Louis of course thinks as I do – that Dr Bodichon never has been sane! I really cannot imagine that this aggravation can be any great *shock* to Barbara – she must have known so much for so long – only I think she imagines him to be perfect when she is not with him! I dare say she will be displeased with what is done – & somehow no one ever seems able to tell Barbara the truth about things, but this time she *must* be told – if this plan had not been kindly carried out by Dr Louis – a cruel one wd. have been by the authorities. Twenty seven years of trouble in a family – & this is the end! It almost makes me a convert to 'mariages de convenance' – for no Frenchwoman wd have been allowed to marry the Doctor! He had neither money nor sense! . . . You may imagine Dr B's lost state when I tell you he is letting people cut down his eucalyptus in the upper field – (oh, if only down below what a chance!) and giving them to the man that cuts – he is being horribly exploited.[74]

Things moved swiftly to a crisis. On 3 December the bank refused to pay him his dividends, quite correctly as he had been judged 'interdit' (not competent to deal with his own finances) and this incident seems to have finally tipped him over the edge. He spent the night walking naked round his house and in the morning he went to Nannie's house to ask if it was time to go to Scalands Gate. Barbara continued to send her husband regular and frequent letters in French. There is something especially distressing at the thought of Barbara and Eugène both ill on different continents, unable to help each other.

The worst of everything in this horrible situation was that Nannie continued to have an *idée fixe* that Hertha was plotting against the interests of the family. On 10 January 1885 she wrote to Amy:

> Barbara said before Miss Marks to Isabella that my asking her to beg the Doctor to cut down some Eucalyptus here was the cause of all her discomfort with the doctor!!! As tho' she had not been wretched long before the Eucalyptus was planted . . . but the misery is that poor Barbara always wants to find the cause of her misery in the actions of others – & not in the doctor himself – who has always been mad from the beginning & could only make her miserable.[75]

Barbara seems to have been doomed in her life to being pig-in-the-middle of various quarrels – between the Pater and Ben, between her husband and her sister, between Norman and her brothers. Now, once again, she was mired in the middle of distrust between Norman, Amy and Nannie on the one hand and Hertha and Reginald Thompson on the other. As she loved them all, it could only have been acutely painful.

Barbara's recovery from the stroke was slow. It took until January 1885 before she could walk without help. Even so, one foot dragged and she needed someone to write her letters for her. Reginald Thompson wrote to the Moores on her behalf: 'She sends her love to you – this is an express message which I am to send you.'[76] Finally she managed a note to the Moores in her own shaky hand: 'Dear Norman, I can write now and I want to thank you for your careful & successful medical care. I have engaged a Bartholomew nurse to go with me to Scalands. Her name is Mrs Hornsby.'[77] Typically the letter went on to ask if Rebecca Moore could go and see someone on Barbara's behalf, because *she* was ill. Whenever Barbara was well enough to think at all, she was concerned about other people's welfare.

On 20 January Dr Bodichon had an apoplectic fit. Nannie told Norman that Barbara had better be made to understand that the *docteur* was 'imbecile – & happy – & that he gets everything he can possibly need'.[78] As the Doctor had been adjudged incapable of managing his own affairs the administrator who had been appointed to deal with them went to Campagne du Pavillon and found there 3,500 francs which Barbara had sent out for his care, but which he had hidden away and forgotten about. He died of pneumonia on 28 January 1885.

Back in England an obituary was placed in *The Times* on 31 January. No doubt this was written either by Barbara, or by Barbara with help from Hertha or Reginald Thompson. It stands therefore as Barbara's assessment of her husband's life:

> Dr Eugène Bodichon, one of the last of the little group known as the 'Republicans of 30' and the author of many valuable works on Algeria, died at Algiers on the 28th inst. aged 74. Born of a noble Breton family at Nantes, Dr Bodichon early showed that adherence to Republican principles shared by his intimate friends, Ledru Rollin, Louis Blanc, Guepin of Nantes, and others, and was associated with them in their work of political propaganda. Dissatisfied with the condition of things in France, he settled in Algeria 40 years ago, devoting himself to gratuitous services as a physician among the poor, and amassing materials for his 'Considerations sur l'Algérie', cited by the late eminent historian M. Henri Martin as second only in interest and importance to the writings of the late General Daumas. In 1848, on being appointed Corresponding member of the Chamber of Deputies for Algiers, he immediately advised the liberation of the slaves throughout the province of Algeria, which was done. On the establishment of the Empire his movements were closely watched, and the types of his work 'De l'Humanité' were broken up by the Imperial police. The work, which contains a striking study of the first Napoleon, was afterwards published at Brussels. Dr Bodichon was one of the first to draw attention to the valuable febrifugal qualities of the eucalyptus globulus, and of late years entirely devoted himself to its dissemination throughout the colony.

Just before Dr Bodichon's death, Barbara had sent for her lawyer, Mr Shaen, and made her will. It dealt with English property and made no reference to the Algerian house. Under the terms of her marriage settlement, she was able to make these dispositions as long as she had the agreement of her trustees. The most significant family features of this will were that Scalands Gate and its contents were to go to Nannie for her lifetime and Amy was to have £1,000. The Poor House (her artists' haven) was to go to Gertrude Jekyll. In terms of 'public' money, she intended to leave £10,000 to Girton College and £1,000 to Bedford College. There were various annuities to friends, including one of £40 a year to Hertha. Barbara clearly wanted to get her affairs in order, as she no longer knew exactly how long she would live, nor how long she would be mentally fit enough for her will to be proved.

CHAPTER 17

The Last Years

After Eugène's death, Nannie's hostility to his memory continued to pain Barbara, and also the sense of the growing distance between herself and Norman and Amy. Nannie had done irrevocable mischief in persuading the Moores that Hertha was duplicitous. Writing to Norman on 14 February 1885 Nannie commented: 'I ignore her existence in writing to my sister, & when she serves as an amanuensis – I take no more notice of it – than tho' it were the maid. But it is trying that things sd. pass through her hands.'[1] For the age in which she lived, Barbara had rather close and informal relationships with her own servants, sharing a room with Eliza Sanderson in hotels, for example, if that proved most convenient, but clearly Barbara resented any suggestion that Hertha should be treated as a servant.

In March Elizabeth Blackwell went to see Barbara at Scalands Gate, and reported to her friends that her health was failing. Norman went to see her that spring, hoping to patch things up, but their meeting was a disappointment. Their conversation confirmed to her that a gulf in their sympathies existed and that Norman disliked her radical friends, judging women whom Barbara had loved best in the world, like Jessie White Mario, quite differently from her. Barbara's bleak letter following his visit is indicative of her sorrow:

> March 19th. Here is the beginning of a letter I meant to have written to you long ago. But writing is a great fatigue.
>
> The end of my thought is that I think you do not know I was nearly doing a great many things which would have made you *prevent* Amy from coming to see me. I asked George Eliot to come live with Dr Bodichon & me, when Mr. Lewes died for instance.
>
> You do not think of the truths of things but accept what religion your country has &c &c. I dare say as years do [go?] on you will become more & more catholic & Amy too.
>
> I shall have more sympathy with your mother I think! You see I feel more & more since I have been ill the want of strong minded women.[2]

Barbara seems to feel that Norman has somehow retreated into a stiff conventionality. She had promoted him when all seemed against him, yet they ended up intellectually and emotionally estranged. Her intimacy with Norman and Amy was never re-established.

The 'strong minded' little Hertha was indisputably the daughter of Barbara's heart. She was never disappointed in her, despite Hertha's relatively modest examination results. Barbara knew that Hertha's secondary education had not been adequate, and that her work in supporting her sister Winnie had further undermined her energy. But also – and this was probably the most important thing – she recognised that originality of mind was frequently antagonistic to receptivity. Hertha did not learn by being told things, or even by reading them in books, she learned by experimenting. As early as February 1883 she had invented a useful little device called a 'line-divider'. Barbara and Ottilie had advanced her the money to take out foreign patents on it. The *Academy* discussed her invention in a way that must have thrilled them both:

> The question has often been raised whether the higher education of women in science can conduce to anything more than their own intellectual benefit, and whether they are able to contribute to its advancement by means of original work. We are glad to have to record one more instance showing that this question must be answered in the affirmative. The mechanical division of a line into any number of equal parts is a problem that has often taxed the ingenuity of technical men, and has only just been satisfactorily solved by a former student of Girton College.[3]

This success confirmed Barbara's long-held faith in Hertha's talents and she had offered her financial help to limit the number of pupils she took so that she could continue with her research into electricity, the branch of physics which interested her the most. She had begun her studies in autumn 1884 under W.E. Ayrton, then professor of physics at the Technical College, Finsbury. He was a widower; his first wife had been one of the medical pioneers at the newly established London School of Medicine for Women and the Royal Free Hospital.[4] Hertha married Will Ayrton on 6 May 1885, and was a devoted stepmother to little Edith.[5]

In May, Katie Scott, Gertrude Jekyll and Elizabeth Blackwell all went to visit Barbara at Scalands Gate, being well aware, no doubt, that her spirits needed cheering at the time of year when her husband had usually arrived. William Ransom was her most frequent visitor, her local guardian angel. In his retirement he devoted himself during the winter months to the Scalands night school and to Barbara.[6]

But she was dying by inches. In spring 1886 she had another small stroke. When Elizabeth Blackwell went to visit her at the end of May she was disturbed to find that Barbara had suffered an attack of 'amnesia', having forgotten that Eugène was dead, and expecting his imminent return.[7] She was disorientated, and suffering from the emotional lability which is typical of stroke patients. In November 1887 her health took another turn for the worse. Hertha sent for Dr Frederick Bagshawe, the physician at the Hastings, St Leonards and East Sussex Hospital, to oversee her case.[8] The strokes and the accompanying aphasia made up a dreadful catalogue of loss. The area of the brain which controlled language was by now badly affected, making it increasingly difficult for her to organise and express her needs and feelings. To a woman for whom the stimulus of conversation with intellectual friends had been one of her greatest pleasures, this incapacitated state was truly horrific. The only bright note of 1886 was that Hertha had a little girl, named Barbara Bodichon Ayrton, and Barbara's delight and interest in 'the little professoress' was one of the few cheering thoughts of her last years.

One of Barbara's visitors was a Girton friend of Hertha's called Eugénie Sellers. Like Hertha she was a financially impoverished student.[9] After the death of her father in 1877, Eugénie had taught for a year and then entered Girton. On graduating she had shared rooms with Hertha where they supported themselves by preparing girls for the London University matriculation and the Cambridge Higher Local examinations.[10] Eugénie was a brilliant young woman with a passion for archaeology. Barbara had first invited her to stay for a week in August 1884.[11] Eugénie had a younger sister to look after, Charlotte (usually known as Charlie), who lived with them at their Regent's Park flat, nominally as their housekeeper.

After Dr Bodichon's death Ben regarded himself as responsible for Barbara's welfare, and started to make frequent visits to Scalands Gate. Ben, who had always seemed more interested in conquering the 'the White Ladye of the Pole' than any warmer-blooded maiden, met several of Barbara's young friends, including Charlie, then aged nineteen.[12] Perhaps feeling that his expeditionary days were over, and with his beautiful niece Amy married and already a mother, he was unconsciously replacing her young beauty in his life with that of another young woman. Or maybe he had just come to think that he would like heirs. He was fifty-nine, about the age his father had been when he had taken up with Jane Buss. Nannie caught a whisper of family gossip with incredulity:

'Do not please suggest that yr Uncle Ben is going to be so mad as to marry a beautiful young girl . . . he wd be certain to repent & the girl still more – such marriages always turn out ill.'[13] She was further incensed when she found out that the girl was a Catholic. Writing from Venice on 27 June 1887, she said: 'Men, certainly about Uncle Ben's age, seem to go crazy & I am sure it ought to be illegal for men to marry girls 40 years younger than themselves . . . I feel that she must be doing it for the money.'[14] Presumably Barbara felt no such hostility, as she made a codicil to her will in October 1887, revoking an element of the first will and leaving Scalands Gate (previously left to Nannie for her lifetime) to Ben.

In January 1888 Mary Howitt, after an audience with Pope Leo XIII, died in Rome aged eighty-eight. She was buried in the cemetery at Rome, next to her husband in 'a long garden of roses'.[15] In February 1888 Barbara had yet another small stroke, and was increasingly in a state of confusion about what was present and what was past. In August Charley Leigh Smith gave birth to a son and Ben went over to Scalands Gate to tell Barbara personally.[16] The return of her brother's affection was very sweet to her.

On 18 November 1889 William Allingham died, leaving Helen a widow at forty-one with three children to support. Barbara was by this stage not well enough herself to help anyone very much, but she had introduced the Allinghams to Gertrude Jekyll and after the death of both William and Barbara, Gertrude proved as good a friend to Helen as she had been to Barbara. In December 1889 Gertrude wrote to Brabbie: 'We are very glad to have news of you after rather a long interval . . . It is just that with our dear Madame Bodichon – an enduring joy to have known her. It is always good news to hear of her being in any degree well and able to enjoy anything, as she really does in spite of her crippled state. I hope to be with her again in March and to find her no worse again.'[17]

Towards the end of January 1890 Reginald Thompson noticed that Barbara's 'memory was not so good as usual & she asked after friends long dead'.[18] At the beginning of February he was called back to Scalands Gate by Eliza Sanderson and subsequently reported to Amy:

Last Friday night as your Aunt was getting into bed she was seized with a very slight fit of speechlessness & I went down to see her on Saturday & found a little more difficulty of speech but the attack was a very slight one and she wrote me a letter two days ago to say she was better . . . Of course the serious aspect of the matter is the chance of more haemorrhage and she will have to be kept very quiet . . . Your

Aunt's speech has come back but it is more difficult to hear than it was. I am going down again on Saturday.[19]

After his next visit, on 23 February, Reginald reported to Amy that 'she is certainly not so well & her mental and bodily powers are weaker. She gets up & is in very good spirits but she is more difficult to understand & her memory for recent events is much impaired'.[20] On the 28th Barbara had yet another small stroke. Reginald wrote yet again to Amy saying, 'I have been down to Scalands and had a consultation with Dr. Bagshawe. I find her a good deal more feeble than at the beginning of this month & I see she is losing ground. She is very conscious of her weakness. I need not say that I am very anxious about her.'[21]

While Barbara's own health was slipping away, she was also anxious about Ben, who, at the beginning of the year, had lost the use of both of his arms in a bad cab accident. He was attended by Sir William Jenner and it was not until April that he was pronounced to be out of danger.[22] She continued to be distressed by Nannie's demands for permission to chop down Dr Bodichon's eucalyptus trees in Algiers. In October 1890 Milicent Ludlow acted as intermediary and finally made Barbara understand that the trees were blocking out Nannie's view of the bay. She finally authorised their removal.

In March 1891 Barbara's cousin, Alice Bonham Carter, went over to Scalands Gate to keep Barbara company and to undertake any business that she wanted doing. While there she wrote to tell the Executive Committee at Girton that:

> she definitely makes over all her paintings now on the walls of (or in) Girton College to the College . . . She is certain that she cannot leave the paintings in a better position – or in better hands – always with the hope that they may be a source of pleasure to some of those who will come year after year to reside and work at Girton. Her hope indeed is always to impart to others through her paintings some of the strength and happiness that her intense study of nature has brought into her own life.[23]

Barbara clearly felt that her time was running out and she must get her affairs in order.

The 1891 census, taken on 5 April, no longer records Barbara as a 'painter', but simply as a widow 'living on her own means'. She was, more accurately, dying on her own means, but, as Hertha wrote to her stepdaughter, Edie, when visiting Barbara in May 'her household will not let her die'.[24] Barbara asked her foundling, Alfred Clements, now

317

employed by a grocer in Eastbourne, to come over to visit her in June. She told him that she had put £200 in his trust fund so that after her death he could buy a business. He was still there when she died on 11 June.[25] The news of her death was sent out by Reginald Thompson from Scalands Gate; telegrams to Benjamin, Willie and Nannie and dozens of letters to other family and friends. His letter to Amy says: 'With much sorrow I have to tell you that your Aunt has passed away. She died quite quietly & without pain this morning at half past twelve. She had been much in the same condition as when I last wrote until yesterday morning when she became unconscious.'[26]

Reginald's letter-writing task to Barbara's friends was a painful duty, for Reginald had loved her too. Barbara, as Lady Goldsmid had once remarked to Hertha, had been a kind of 'universal friend' to many.[27] Hertha herself was heart-broken, and Bessie, with her usual exquisite tact wrote to her swiftly: 'What a blessing for you to know how much she loved you.'[28]

On 15 June Barbara was buried in Brightling churchyard in Sussex, once the happy scene of Bella's marriage to General Ludlow. Her body was interred in a simple granite grave next to that of her beloved Aunt Dolly. The style of her grave was identical to Dolly's, which suggests that Benjamin Leigh Smith had taken charge of the arrangements. As well as her immediate family and friends her funeral was attended by Alfred Clements and a long procession of scholars from her night school.

CHAPTER 18

The Legacy

After Barbara's death, her brother placed a formal obituary in *The Times* of 15 June 1891, which made her sound more of a philanthropist than a political activist. Bessie wrote a more personal obituary for the *Englishwoman's Review* which said: 'She had essentially the initiative mind, and it may truly be said of her that she scattered ideas broadcast, and that they took root far and wide.'[1] In one of her notebooks, Barbara had referred to 'Padaretus in ancient story . . . [who] remarked that all the faculties a rational being possessed were capable of a moral use, and that after having spent his life in the service of his country, a man ought if possible to render his death a source of additional benefit'.[2] This is an apt epitaph for Barbara herself, who left money which supported both individuals and institutions after her death. The largest single sum went to Girton College.[3]

She left Scalands Gate to Ben. When he died in 1913, he too was buried in Brightling churchyard near to Barbara and Aunt Dolly.[4] As Marian Lewes had written so poignantly about a brother and sister who had quarrelled then reconciled in *The Mill on the Floss*: 'In death they were not divided'.

The significance of the Scalands Gate night school to local working-class people is hard to quantify. Mr Ransom sent a paper with a sketch of Barbara's life in it to two ex-pupils who had emigrated to Connecticut. One of them wrote back:

> Although I was not surprised to hear of the death of Madame Bodichon, I was nevertheless deeply grieved to hear of it, as was also John. On opening the paper that you sent me, containing the news of that most noble of Nature's noblewomen's death, my first words were 'Scalands Gate is no more!' It was a few evenings ago, about a week, that I received the paper, and I had occasion to go down into a lot, or field, to see if some calves there had enough water. I took the paper along with me. As I walked along, I was startled and pained when I saw the announcement of Madame's death; and there I stood, in the middle of the lot, until I could not see the print very clearly. So I doubled the

paper and went on down to the spring and found water, then returned to the house and finished reading your sketch of the life of my benefactress, for such was Madame Bodichon, for to her nightschool do I owe what education I have received . . . I would have liked to have been able to pay my last respects to Madame Bodichon by attending her funeral, and am sorry that I could not be present.[5]

Recent scholarship has assessed Barbara Bodichon as 'perhaps the most important unstudied figure of mid-century English feminism'.[6] Compared with the reputation of her cousin, Florence Nightingale, for example, who reformed nursing, her name was quickly forgotten. Yet in terms of women's progress as citizens, Barbara's contribution might reasonably be considered to be as great or even greater. Bessie was the first person to point out the reason for the lack of public recognition. In *A Passing World* she wrote:

She was struck down in the very middle of her career, and during years of lingering illness the memory of what she had done faded more rapidly than would have been the case had she died, and her death been recorded in print. But of that she took no heed, and she lived to know that her countrywomen were succeeding in innumerable spheres of worthy endeavour, a success to which she had more largely contributed than any can realise but they who bore the burden and the heat of the day.[7]

Bessie was right to point out that after her stroke in 1877 Barbara had been unable to do the committee work she had done before. At Girton College, which Barbara saw as her crowning achievement, the memory of her vivid presence and her significant founding role began to fade. Her friends had organised the portrait of Barbara by Emily Osborn and in a similar attempt to keep her memory alive Nannie offered Emily's second portrait of Barbara (which had stayed in Emily's studio) to the National Portrait Gallery, but the offer was rejected, 'on the grounds that the ten-year rule required a decade to elapse after the death of the sitter'.[8] In January 1913 Nannie gave this same portrait of Barbara to the Hastings Museum and Art Gallery.[9] The painting which had been commissioned for Girton College was removed by Milicent, Lady Moore, in 1929. She offered in exchange the Samuel Laurence oil painting of Barbara. This is perhaps unfortunate, because Emily Osborn's painting represented Barbara as a professional artist, whereas, although Laurence's shows an unmistakably handsome woman, she could be (merely) a philanthropist.[10]

After Barbara had been obliged to retire as an invalid, Emily Davies continued the extraordinarily long and complicated campaign to get Girton College fully incorporated into Cambridge University. It took until February 1881 for the senate of the University, following campaigns from both the Girton and the Newnham camp, to vote in favour of admitting women to the BA examinations (although they were not awarded degrees). Nevertheless, this gave Girton College the formal relationship with Cambridge University which Emily and Barbara had so long desired. When in 1887 a student of Girton, Agneta Frances Ramsay, was placed in the first class of the Classical Tripos ten memorials were submitted to the council of the senate requesting admission to degrees by women.[11] A majority of MAs gave a negative vote of *non placet* (it does not please).

In 1896, a few years after Barbara's death, 1,234 past students of Newnham and Girton petitioned the senate to have their degrees awarded just like the men, rather than being offered a Tripos 'Certificate'. The vote to admit women to degree titles was arranged for Friday, 21 May 1897. *The Times* took the trouble to point out that special trains of the Great Northern Line would leave King's Cross for Cambridge in time for MAs to register their *non-placet* votes. There seems to have been some rabble-rousing going on among the undergraduates (who could not vote) for there were near-riots in the streets of Cambridge. Undergraduates in one-horse hackney carriages met the MAs at the station and rushed them at breakneck speed along Regent Street, through the market place to the Senate House. There, they had to press through excited throngs, under the gaze of undergraduates leaning out of Caius College with banners and effigies of women students hanging out of the college windows. One of them was the lay figure of a woman with red hair wearing cap and gown suspended with a banner which reads: 'Get you to Girton Beatrice Get you to Newnham Here's No Place For You Maids Much Ado About Nothing'. This figure with its red hair and the connection with Beatrice, the Shakespearean heroine who proved she had an equivalent intellect to Benedick, almost seemed to conjure up Barbara's ghostly presence.

On this occasion the women were defeated. It took until 1921 for the senate to grant titles of degrees to duly qualified member of women's colleges. The women, however, were still not members of the university. In March 1923 ordinances were passed securing women students the right of admission to university lectures and laboratories; before this they had only been able to attend by the invitation (and therefore the whim) of individual lecturers. Emily Davies and Barbara Bodichon were the pioneers who had dared to begin the process; Emily's peculiar talent was in spotting any chinks in the armour of the ancient edifice and then relentlessly thrusting forward, taking no prisoners. Cambridge University proved a most difficult dragon to slay, only admitting women to full membership in 1948.[12]

Marian Lewes had recognised and praised Barbara's singular talent of being 'wonderfully clever at talking to young people'.[13] One of the early Girton students referred to her 'wonderful gift of speaking the right word at the right moment – a gift that came I think from a combination of kindness and candour'.[14] As well as the early Girton students, Marian Lewes's stepsons, all Barbara's nephews and nieces, the young Norman Moore and Hertha had all benefited from her easy informal manner and genuine interest in both their troubles and their successes. Of all these, Hertha had responded most vividly to the love which Barbara had to offer. A writer in the *Girton Review* (Michaelmas term, 1923) said: 'It may be counted as one of Madame Bodichon's many benefactions to the College that she made it possible for Miss Marks to become a student.' Barbara had recognised an original talent in Hertha and had nurtured that talent by nurturing the young woman. Hertha became a renowned physicist; in 1898 she was elected to the Institution of Electrical Engineers, where she was the only woman member. Hertha realised the career which Barbara, a generation before her, could not achieve. Her own political activities and those of her daughter, Barbara Bodichon Ayrton, were a living testimony to Barbara's beliefs.

Barbara's faith in Hertha's abilities had led her to organise what amounted to a personal scholarship to Girton, followed by a postgraduate research fund. A letter from Marian Lewes in 1880 asked Barbara to give her best wishes to 'our little dark eyed friend who is "delightful to you". I dare say she would consider that a good final cause for her existence.'[15] Barbara's will, which left Hertha half the residue of her estate, plus the annuity of £40, provided her with an income independent from that of her husband, which gave her conscience permission to employ a housekeeper and resume her scientific research. In other words, Barbara supplied Hertha once again with a room of her own. In 1893 she began the work on electric arcs which was to make her reputation. Her book, *The Electric Arc* (1902) bears the inscription: 'to Madame Bodichon, whose clear sighted enthusiasm for the freedom and enlightenment of women enabled her to strike away so many barriers from their path; whose great intellect, large tolerance and noble presence were an inspiration to all who knew her; to her whose friendship changed and beautified my whole life, I dedicate this book.' In 1902 Hertha was nominated for fellowship of the Royal Society, although the council found it had no legal power to elect a married woman to this distinction.

During the First World War she invented the 'Ayrton fan' for dispersing poisonous gases from the trenches.[16]

Hertha was undoubtedly Barbara's 'daughter' in the political sense too. Hertha's daughter, Barbara's namesake, went with her on political demonstrations from an early age. Barbara became organiser for the Women's Social and Political Union and in 1910 married Gerald Gould, poet, essayist and literary critic. In March 1912, when the suffragettes demonstrated by smashing shop windows, Barbara was arrested for smashing the display window at Debenham's. Hertha wrote to her stepdaughter, Edie, 'Barbie is in Holloway, having, with all the others, refused bail . . . She is to be tried on Wednesday. I am *very* proud of her.'[17] Barbara became increasingly disillusioned with the way Emmeline and Christabel Pankhurst were running the WSPU, and in 1914 she helped form a new society, the United Suffragists, including both men and women. Hertha gave £100 of the money Barbara Bodichon had left her to this organisation, believing it to have been left to her in trust for the women's movement; she became one of the vice-presidents and her daughter Barbara the honorary secretary. The First World War finally delivered the vote for women. Barbara Gould entered Parliament as a Labour MP in 1945, thus realising Barbara's dream of full political participation by women.

When Hertha died in 1923, her stepdaughter, Edith Zangwill, wrote a fictionalised version of the campaigning years with a woman scientist as the heroine in her novel *The Call*.[18] It was dedicated 'to all who fought for the freedom of women'. Barbara Leigh Smith Bodichon, who had honoured her early pledge to brave 'ridicule for the sake of common justice to half the world', had surely earned her place in that dedication.

ABBREVIATIONS

Manuscript Sources

ALCF	Bodichon Letters in Autograph Letter Collection, Fawcett Library, London Guildhall University.
BCFP	Bonham Carter Family Papers, Hampshire Record Office, Winchester.
Beaky	Letters of Anna Mary Howitt transcribed by Leonore Beaky for PhD dissertation, Columbia University.
BMC	Barbara McCrimmon Papers, Fawcett Library, London Guildhall University.
BPG	Bodichon Papers, Girton College, Cambridge.
BRP	Papers of Bessie Rayner Parkes, Girton College, Cambridge.
BRP/A	Typescript of Margaret Crompton's 'Prelude to Arcadia' (unpublished biography of Bessie Parkes's early life), Girton College, Cambridge.
BRP/B	Typescript by Marie Belloc Lowndes, Girton College, Cambridge.
CSS	Clough/Shore Smith Papers, British Library, London.
EB Columbia	Microfilm of Blackwell–Bodichon Correspondence, Elizabeth Blackwell Collection, Butler Library, Columbia University, New York.
EB Congress	Microfilm reel 142, Blackwell Family Papers, Library of Congress.
EB Radcliffe	Box 3 of Blackwell Family Papers, The Arthur and Elizabeth Schlesinger Library on the History of Women in America, Radcliffe College, Massachusetts.
EDFC	Emily Davies's 'Family Chronicle', Girton College, Cambridge.
GLRO	Greater London Record Office.
Hcox	Papers in private collection; photocopies deposited in Girton College, Cambridge.
MT	Mill–Taylor Collection, London School of Economics.
SPRI	Letters of Benjamin Leigh Smith, Scott Polar Museum, Cambridge.
Verney	Verney Papers, Verney Archive, Claydon House, Buckinghamshire.
WS/CUL	Papers of William Smith and his family, Cambridge University Library (Add. 7621).
Yale	Letters from Barbara Bodichon to George Eliot, George Eliot and George Henry Lewes Collection, Beinecke Rare Book and Manuscript Library, Yale University, New Haven (microfilm, Eliot III, R1 Pos).

Published Letters

AD	*An American Diary, 1857–1858,* ed. Joseph W. Reed Jr. (London, 1972).
Buchanan	*Buchanan Family Records,* ed. Isabella Buchanan (Cape Town, 1923).
Burton	Hester Burton, *Barbara Bodichon* (London, 1949).
Cross	J.W. Cross, *George Eliot's Life as Related in her Letters and Journals,* 3 vols (Edinburgh, 1885).
GEL	*The George Eliot Letters,* ed. Gordon S. Haight, 9 vols. (New Haven, 1954–78).
Letters to WA	*Letters to William Allingham,* ed. H. Allingham and E. Baumer (London, 1911).
Selections	*Selections from George Eliot's Letters,* ed. Gordon S. Haight (New York, 1985).
Sharp	Evelyn Sharp, *Hertha Ayrton, 1854–1923: a Memoir* (London, 1926).
Stephen	Barbara Stephen, *Emily Davies and Girton College* (London, 1927).

Abbreviations of Names

ALS	Anne Leigh Smith
AMH	Anna Mary Howitt
Ben LS	Benjamin Leigh Smith (Barbara's brother)
BLS	Barbara Leigh Smith (before marriage)
BLSB	Barbara Leigh Smith Bodichon
BS	Ben Smith
EB	Elizabeth Blackwell
ED	Emily Davies
GHL	George Henry Lewes
MH	Mary Howitt
ML	Marian Lewes
PK	Philip Kingsford
WLS	William Leigh Smith

NOTES

PREFACE

1 Bessie Rayner Belloc, in *Englishwoman's Review* (July 1891) p. 146.
2 See Candida Ann Lacey's useful introduction to this collection of source materials in *Barbara Leigh Smith Bodichon and the Langham Place Group* (New York and London, 1987).
3 Bessie Rayner Belloc, in *Englishwoman's Review* (July 1891) p. 146.
4 BLS, 'Abstract of Mill', BPG.
5 Mrs Gaskell to Charles Eliot Norton, 5 April [1860] in *The Letters of Mrs Gaskell*, ed. J.A.V. Chapple and J. Arthur Pollard (Manchester, 1966) pp. 606–7.
6 BLSB, *An American Diary 1857–1858*, ed. Joseph W. Reed Jr (London, 1972) p. 30.
7 *Letters of Dante Gabriel Rossetti* ed. O. Doughty and J.R. Wahl, 4 vols (Oxford, 1965–7) I, 163.
8 BLSB to Elizabeth Whitehead Malleson, quoted in Barbara Stephen's *Emily Davies and Girton College* (London, 1927) pp. 38–9.
9 Bessie Rayner Parkes [Belloc], *A Passing World (London, 1897)* p. 21.
10 Ray Strachey, *The Cause: A Short History of the Women's Movement in Great Britain* (London, 1928) p. 71.
11 Olive Banks, *Becoming a Feminist: The Social Origins of 'First Wave' Feminism* (Brighton, 1986) p. 133. See also Jane Rendall, *The Origins of Modern Feminism* (Basingstoke, 1985).
12 Elizabeth K. Helsinger, Robin Lauterbach Sheets and William Veeder, *The Woman Question in Britain and America 1837 to 1883* 3 vols (Manchester, 1983) II, 147.

13 Hester Burton, *Barbara Bodichon 1827–1891* (London, 1949); Sheila R. Herstein, *A Mid-Victorian Feminist – Barbara Leigh Smith Bodichon* (New Haven and London, 1985); Jacquie Matthews, 'Barbara Bodichon: Integrity in Diversity' in *Feminist Theorists*, ed. Dale Spender (London 1983); *Barbara Bodichon 1827–1891*, centenary exhibition catalogue ed. F. Gandy, K. Perry and P. Sparkes (Cambridge, 1991); Pam Hirsch, 'Barbara Leigh Smith Bodichon: artist and activist', in *Women in the Victorian Art World*, ed. Clarissa Campbell Orr (Manchester, 1995).

CHAPTER I: THE SMITHS

1 BLSB, *An American Diary 1857–1858*, ed. Joseph W. Reed Jr. (London, 1972) p. 134.
2 BLS, *A Brief Summary, in Plain Language, of the Most Important Laws Concerning Women* (London, 1854).
3 Samuel Smith (1728–1798) proprietor of The Sugar Loaf, Cannon Street, a wholesale grocer's.
4 See Isaac Kramnick, 'Eighteenth-Century Science and Radical Social Theory: the case of Joseph Priestley's scientific liberalism', *Journal of British Studies*, 25 (1986) pp. 1–30.
5 William benefited from an outcome of the French Revolution, which was that important collections of paintings were sold by ruined aristocratic owners. We know, for example, that William bought *The Mill* by Rembrandt in 1793, when the Duke of Orleans's collection came on to the

market in London. He had a special liking for Dutch masters. He owned two other Rembrandts: *Portrait of a Rabbi* and *Rembrandt's Mother*, several fine Cuyps including *Horseman and Herdsman with Cattle*, Hobbema's *Water Mill* and two Ruysdaels: *Country Scene with Ruined Castle* and *The Castle of Bentheim*. Of the Italian masters he had paintings by Carlo Dolce, Guido Reni and Sassoferrato, and three Rubens and a Van Dyck, representing the Flemish school. In the French school he favoured landscapes by Claude and Poussin. Nor did he neglect English paintings; he had two by Reynolds: *Mrs. Siddons as the Tragic Muse* and *Ariadne*; *Two Keepers going up a Wooded Lane* by Gainsborough; *Horse and Lion* by Stubbs; *Celadon and Amelia* by Wilson; also landscapes by Wright of Derby, George Barrett and Richard Westall. He was involved in the founding of the National Gallery and of the British Institution, a gallery in Pall Mall designed to encourage the exhibition and sale of works by contemporary British artists; he was a patron of the Norwich landscape painter John Sell Cotman and the portrait painter, John Opie. He regularly lent his old masters to the British Institution for students to copy.

6 Evangelical Christians, who gathered round the Reverend John Venn's church. They included William Wilberforce, MP for York, the barrister, James Stephen (Wilberforce's brother-in-law), the banker, Henry Thornton (a second cousin of Wilberforce), Charles Grant (chairman of the East India Company), Zachary Macaulay (editor of the *Christian Observer*) and Granville Sharpe (a seasoned philanthropic campaigner). See James Stephen, *Essays in Ecclesiastical Biography* (London, 1860).

7 He was not the first member of his family to express moral unease. His bachelor uncle, William, who had emigrated to the West Indies and become a prosperous merchant in Antigua, had written a letter to his sister Elizabeth (Mrs Benjamin Travers) in which he described the black slaves on the island as 'the most miserable People on Earth: and that to be a Freeborn Subject is the Greatest Blessing in this Life'. Stephen ts, WS/CUL.

8 Sydney Smith (1771–1845) founded the *Edinburgh Review* in 1802, the 'house journal' of the Whig party, championing political economy, the abolition of slavery and law reform. See Alan Bell, *Sydney Smith: A Biography* (Oxford, 1980).

9 Zerbanoo Gifford, *Thomas Clarkson and the Campaign against Slavery* (Fakenham, 1996) p. 25.

10 WS/CUL.

11 Eventually the Home Secretary sent royal troops to restore order, but in the note George III sent authorising the troops, on 14 July 1791, he commented: 'I cannot but feel pleased that Priestley is the sufferer for the doctrines he and his party have instilled, and that the people see them in their true light.' George III to Henry Dundas, *The Letters of King George III*, ed. B. Dobree (London, 1935). Although Priestley received messages of condolence from the Academy of Sciences at Paris, the Royal Society in England shamefully remained silent and did nothing to help its illustrious fellow.

12 The best account of William Smith's political career is R.W. Davis, *Dissent in Politics* (London, 1971).

13 Stephen ts, WS/CUL.

14 Ibid.

15 At one stage there seems to have been a Smith distillery next door to a Cooke distillery, but at some point the Tate family dropped out of the partnership.

16 Frances Smith to Fanny Nightingale, 2 September 1819, Verney.

17 Ibid.

18 Nightingale was highly eligible, having inherited a fortune at twenty-one

from his uncle, Peter Nightingale, who had made a fortune from lead smelting in Derbyshire, and thereupon changed his name from Shore to Nightingale. Cecil Woodham-Smith, *Florence Nightingale 1820–1910* (Harmondsworth, 1955) p. 11.

19 The committee included James Mill, the Marquis of Lansdowne, Zachary Macaulay, John Smith MP, Henry Hase (cashier of the Bank of England) and Joseph Wilson of Spitalfields.

20 James Buchanan (1784–1857), who was thirty-two years of age and an ex-serviceman of the Scottish Militia.

21 W.A.D. Stewart and W.P. McCann, *The Educational Innovators 1750–1880* (London, 1967) p. 247.

22 Copy of a letter from BLSB to Florence Hill, *Buchanan*, p. 22.

23 Patty Smith to Ben Smith c. 1848, WS/CUL.

24 Buchanan decided to emigrate to New Zealand to start infant schools there, under the auspices of the New Zealand Land Company. However, *en route* to New Zealand, he disembarked at Cape Town in order to see his son, and decided to settle there. Ben once again helped financially so that his wife and his daughter Annie could join him. Mrs Buchanan died soon after landing, however, and James Buchanan went to live in Pietermaritzburg, where he died in 1857.

25 Julia Smith's 'Recollections', WS/CUL.

26 Letter from Julia Smith to Patty Smith, ibid.

27 See R.S. Fitton and A.P. Wadsworth, *The Strutts and the Arkwrights 1758–1830: A Study of the Early Factory System* (Manchester, 1958) for a full account.

28 Ben Smith to W.E. Nightingale, 7 March 1826, Verney.

29 Gordon Haight's not entirely correct version of the story is that 'about 1826, when he was a bachelor over forty, he saw in the street a ravishingly pretty girl of seventeen, followed her home, and discovered that she was a milliner's apprentice named Anne Longden, daughter of a Norfolk miller. Leigh Smith seduced her, "took her under his protection", and though he never married, had five children by her before she died of tuberculosis in 1834.' See Gordon S. Haight, *George Eliot: A Biography* (Oxford, 1968) p. 105.

30 John Longden was the son of Samuel and Sarah Longden of Woodthorpe Mill. Dorothy and John were married by licence in the church at North Wingfield on 4 August 1789, witnessed by her sister Elizabeth Ashmore and John Cupit (Lichfield Joint Record Office).

31 Copies of Alfreton baptisms and burials made by Derbyshire Ancestral Research Group.

32 Anne Longden's grandparents were Joseph and Elizabeth Gratton of Woodthorpe, Derbyshire, who, judging by the gritstone memorials in St Lawrence churchyard, North Wingfield, seem to have been a fairly substantial family.

33 In 1820 Anne's sister Jane had married John Smedley Junior, the son of the Alfreton postmaster, but she died of consumption in 1825. Her father John Longden died in 1838. The Longden women are commemorated on limestone memorials at St Martin's Church, Alfreton, where Anne Longden is clearly named 'Anne Smith'.

34 See Land Tax Records, Derbyshire Record Office. In 1805, Revd Henry Case, the second husband of Helen Morewood, paid land tax on behalf of 'Mr Longden'. The Morewoods money had come from lead and coal.

35 Rachel Walker of Alfreton Heritage Centre who furnished me with detailed local information.

36 'The Miller's Daughter', *Tennyson's Poems* (London, 1866) p. 94.

37 Either Petley Lodge or Leaford Lodge.

38 Unidentified handwritten note stating that Ben had a mistress called 'Mrs Leigh', WS/CUL.

39 See L.G. Mitchell, *Charles James Fox* (Oxford, 1992).

40 Frances Smith to Fanny Nightingale, 6 November 1832, Verney.

41 Patty Smith's 'Reminiscences', WS/CUL.

42 Architectural Report no. 1264, Field Archaeology Unit, Institute of Archaeology, University College, London.

43 Joanna Bonham Carter to Fanny Nightingale, 31 July 1823, Verney.

44 See Land Tax assessments for Westfield, County Records, Lewes.

45 WS/CUL.

46 See Charlotte Erickson, 'Agrarian Myths of English Immigrants', in *In the Trek of the Immigrants*, ed. O.F. Ander (Illinois, 1964).

47 According to Burton, 'Intensely interested in the experiment in emigration, Benjamin had followed some of the former pupils of his ragged school to America to see how the young pioneers were succeeding in their new life. Later, in an attempt to popularise emigration in England, he published many of their letters home.' (p. 119).

48 Patty Smith to Fanny Nightingale, 1 October 1828, Verney.

49 Burton, p. 119.

50 Patty Smith to Fanny Nightingale, 1 October 1833, Verney. Fred, who had a commission in the Indian army, had become involved with a woman they regarded as unsuitable in India, and who was now threatening to turn up in England with her two children. The sisters judge that if Frederick wants to live with his amour, he had better settle in Van Diemen's Land; the colonies were evidently seen by them as the place where irregularities could be discreetly covered up (Patty Smith to Fanny Nightingale, 30 January 1834, Verney).

51 Ibid.

52 Wootton parish burial records, Isle of Wight Record Office.

53 Patty Smith to Fanny Nightingale, undated but likely to be September 1834, Verney.

54 Ben Smith to W.E. Nightingale, 15 September 1834, ibid.

55 Joanna Bonham Carter to Fanny Nightingale, 25 May 1835, ibid.

56 Christie's catalogue, July 1835, reveals what was left of William Smith's estate: a Mieris, two Rubens, a Jacob Cats, a Rembrandt, a Van Dyck and a Guido.

57 It was appropriate in another sense. After Waterloo an Act of Parliament was passed in 1818 to raise a million pounds as a national thanks offering for peace. St James was one of the so-called 'Waterloo' churches built with this money. William Smith as a notable friend of peace, is, very suitably, interred there. There is no memorial to him there, but Richard Davis, whose biography of William Smith was published in 1971, petitioned the GLC to have a blue plaque erected at 16 Queen Anne's Gate (formerly 6 Park Street). It was put in place in 1975 and says: 'William Smith MP 1756–1835 Pioneer of religious liberty lived here.'

CHAPTER 2: THE EARLY YEARS

1 The 1837 street list of registered electors for Hastings identifies Benjamin Smith, MP, as residing in Pelham Crescent.

2 J. Manwaring Baines, *Historic Hastings* (St Leonards on Sea, 1986) p. 314.

3 William Ewart (1798–1869) was successively MP, for Bletchley, Liverpool, Wigan and Dumfries and an active campaigner on behalf of the establishment of schools of design, free public libraries and the College of Preceptors. See W.A. Munford, *William Ewart: Portrait of a Radical* (London, 1960).

4 Burton, p. 14.
5 'In devotion to the great cause of National Improvement – in ardent desire to follow out safe Reforms, I yield to no one; but at the same time I must declare my conviction, that all change, to be secure, must be gradual, and according to the spirit of our ancient Constitution. My wish is, not to debase the high, but to raise the depressed – to ameliorate the condition of all classes, by lightening the taxes, by removing every impediment to national prosperity, and above all, by the system of universal education.' BS election pledge published by Bacon, Kinnebrook, and Bacon, Printers, Mercury Office, Norwich.
6 My comments on Ben Smith arise from consulting Parliamentary Papers and those at Norfolk Record Office (reference MC 79 fo. 41).
7 BLSB to Florence Davenport Hill, ts copy, WS/CUL.
8 Ibid.
9 Unpublished 'Memoirs' of Anne Mary Wood (née Maw), Hastings Museum and Art Gallery.
10 Burton, p. 24.
11 Bill from Rock & Baxter, Hcox 2/029.
12 Burton, p.13.
13 BS to BLS, 25 October 1841, Hcox 2/034.
14 Elizabeth Malleson, *Autobiographical Notes* (printed for private circulation, 1926) p. 36.
15 Beaky, letter 4.
16 Se J.L. Dobson, 'The Hill Family and Educational Change in the Early Nineteenth Century', *Research Review*, September 1960.
17 Hcox 2/002.
18 William Henry Hunt (1790–1864).
19 Thomas Girtin (1775–1802).
20 Hcox 2/049 and 2/050.
21 Cornelius Varley (1781–1873), a founding member of the Old Watercolour Society.
22 William Collingwood (1819–1903), a pupil of Prout.
23 BRP 5/165.
24 A.M. Wood's 'Memoirs'.
25 BRP 5/6.
26 Quoted by Margaret Crompton, 'Prelude to Arcadia': unpublished biography of the early life and friendship of Bessie Parkes, BRP/A 70.
27 See *A Vision of Eden: The Life and Work of Marianne North* ed. Graham Bateman (London, 1980).
28 Ellen Clayton, *English Female Artists* 2 vols (London, 1876) I, 290.
29 Mary Howitt, *An Autobiography*, ed. Margaret Howitt, 2 vols (London, 1889) II, 34–5.
30 BRP 6/52.
31 Letter from MH to ALS 6 October 1882 quoted in Howitt, *An Autobiography*, II, 321.
32 See Morag Shiach, *Discourse on Popular Culture* (Oxford, 1989).
33 Ben Smith knew Fox from the anti-Corn Law campaigns, when his powers of oratory had so impressed Samuel Courtauld that he had given him the property qualification to become MP for Oldham.
34 The seventh edition of a book first published in 1833.
35 Founded by Henry Sass the portrait painter, and continued after his death by Francis Cary.
36 BRP 6/56. Eliza Fox (1825–95). She exhibited at the Society for Women Artists from its inception in 1857 and taught life classes there in 1866–67. In 1858–9 she studied in Rome where she met her first husband, the artist Frederick Bridell. After his death in 1863 she made a prolonged stay with Barbara in Algiers, and her scenes of Arabian life became some of her most widely appreciated works. In 1871 she married her cousin, George Fox, and subsequently exhibited under the name Bridell-Fox.
37 BRP 6/56.
38 AMH to BLS [1848], Beaky.
39 Margaret Gillies (1803–87).
40 Anna Brownell Jameson (1794–1860), author of *The Diary of*

Enuyée (1826) and *Shakespeare's Heroines* (1832). 'Women's Mission and Women's Position' and 'The Relative Position of Mothers and Governesses' were published in *Memoirs and Essays* in 1846.

41 Clara Thomas, *Love and Work Enough: The Life of Anna Jameson* (Toronto, 1967) p. 21.

42 Robert Noel was one of the four children of Revd Thomas Noel, the illegitimate son of Viscount Wentworth. The Revd Thomas would have succeeded to the title and the estate had he been legitimate, so Lady Byron, who was the legitimate heir, always felt it her duty to help provide for her four cousins. On Robert's marriage she had brought him an estate in Bohemia.

43 Gordon S. Haight, *George Eliot: A Biography* (Oxford, 1978) p. 149.

44 Stephen, p. 38.

45 Burton, pp. 14 and 24.

46 In a private collection.

47 Drawings in private collection.

48 BRP 10/46.

49 Tithe survey shows that 'Benjamin Smith esq.' owned Scalands Farm (TD/E 86 County Records, Lewes).

50 Quoted in Norman Longmate, *The Breadstealers* (London, 1984) p. 128.

51 'We saw in the distance the gaunt forms of famine and of disease following in the train of famine [in Ireland, and on the mainland]. The memory of the winters of 1841 and 1842 never can be effaced from my recollection. [We must remove] every impediment to the free circulation of the bounty of the creator.' Quoted ibid., p. 221.

52 Burton, p. 4.

53 *Buchanan*, p. 17.

54 See fragment of a letter from Kossuth to Ben Smith: 7/BMC/F10.

55 Norman Longmate, *The Breadstealers: The Fight Against the Corn Laws 1838–1846* (London, 1984) p. 200.

56 Hcox 2/201. Rebecca was an Irish Quaker who as a young woman had eloped with Robert Moore, but he had deserted her and her young child to run off with yet another young woman, Ada Cogan.

57 Ellen Gibson Wilson, *Thomas Clarkson: A Biography* (York, 1989) p. 183.

58 Harriet Martineau to Lucretia Mott (1793–1880), 24 June 1840: 'It is a comfort to me, in my absence, that two of my best friends, Mrs Reid & Julia Smith, are there to look upon you with eyes of love. I hear of you from them; for, busy as they are, they remember me from day to day & make me a partaker in your proceedings.' 'Lucretia Mott's Diary', ed. Frederick B. Tolles, Supplement 23, *Journal of the Friends' Historical Society* (Pennsylvania, 1952).

59 CSS, 100–1.

CHAPTER 3: THE APPRENTICESHIP YEARS

1 BLSB to Helen Taylor, August 1869; MT 12/50.

2 Roger Sayce, *The History of the Royal Agricultural College Cirencester* (Stroud, 1992) pp. 22 and 54.

3 Ben Smith was a 'donor' of the college, which meant he had a £30 share certificate, necessary to nominate for attendance a boy between the ages of fourteen and sixteen. See Hcox 2/035 and Royal Agricultural Register, Cirencester, which shows that WLS entered in August 1849.

4 *Buchanan*, p. 17.

5 Philip Kingsford (*c*. 1814–54), born at Little Chart, Kent, only son of Edward Kingsford of Knightsbridge, London. Admitted sizar at St John's, 6 July 1837; readmitted as pensioner 12 October 1842. Matriculated Michaelmas 1837, BA 1844. Admitted at the Middle Temple, 25 October 1844. Called to the Bar 19 November 1847. Kingsford gave lectures on political economy and was an examiner in History and

Political Science at the College of Preceptors. He died on 3 September 1854, at Deal. Information from J.A. Venn, *Alumni Cantabrigiensis* (London, 1953).

6 The college had been founded in 1846 to raise the standards and status of the teaching profession. See Richard Aldrich, *School and Society in Victorian Britain* (Epping, 1995) Chapter 4. See also W.A. Munford, *William Ewart MP 1798–1869: Portrait of a Radical* (London, 1960) for Ewart's career as a reforming politician with a special interest in education, free public libraries, opening museums to the public, etc.

7 BRP 5/162.

8 PK, *Two Lectures upon the Study of Political Philosophy* (London, 1848) p. 36.

9 Quoted by Margaret Crompton, 'Prelude to Arcadia', BRP/A, p. 115.

10 BRP 6/51.

11 BRP 6/60.

12 BRP 1/4.

13 Marie Belloc Lowndes, 'Before She Found Arcadia', unpublished ts, BRP/B.

14 BRP 1/4.

15 Quoted by Isaac Kramnick, 'Eighteenth-Century Science and Radical Social Theory', *Journal of British Studies*, 25 (1986) pp. 1–30; p. 8.

16 BRP 5/18.

17 BRP 5/20.

18 Beaky, letter 5.

19 George Eliot's journal, 20 July 1856, quoted in Haight, *George Eliot*.

20 Frederika Bremer, *Hertha*, translated by Mary Howitt (London, 1856) p. 290.

21 BRP 5/165.

22 BRP 5/1.

23 See Kate Flint, *The Woman Reader 1837–1914* (Oxford, 1995).

24 See obituary in *Hastings & St Leonard's Observer*, 28 April 1906.

25 See 'Conformity to Custom' by 'Esculapius', *Hastings & St Leonard News* (7 July 1848); see also Pam

Hirsch, 'Mary Wollstonecraft: a problematic legacy', in *Wollstonecraft's Daughters*, ed. Clarissa Campbell Orr (Manchester, 1996).

26 *Hastings & St Leonards News* 28 July 48.

27 BRP 5/167.

28 In Whitworth Gallery, Manchester.

29 In private collection.

30 BRP 5/21.

31 BRP 5/27.

32 BRP 5/168.

33 Quoted by Victoria Glendinning, *A Suppressed Cry* (London, 1969) p. 19.

34 See Gillian Sutherland, 'The Movement for the Higher Education of Women: its social and intellectual context in England, *c.* 1840–80', in *Politics & Social Change in Modern Britain* (Brighton, 1987).

35 Margaret J. Tuke, *A History of Bedford College For Women* (Oxford, 1939) p. 36.

36 BLS wrote: 'money may be a power to do good', *Women and Work* (London, 1857) p. 48.

37 Quoted by Marie Belloc Lowndes, BRP/B, p. 34.

38 BRP 5/39.

39 BRP 5/38.

40 BRP 6/5.

41 BRP 5/165.

42 BRP 10/10.

43 BPG.

44 *Letters to WA*, p. 86.

45 Lakes Sketchbook, privately owned but on loan to Wordsworth Museum, Dove Cottage, Grasmere, Cumbria.

46 The stanzas Barbara copied were:
The Man
Of virtuous soul commands not, nor obeys,
Power, like a desolating pestilence,
Pollutes whate'r it touches, and obedience,
Bane of all genius, virtue, freedom, truth,
Makes slaves of men, and, of the human frame,
A mechanised automaton.

Man is of soul and body, formed
  for deeds
Of high resolve, on fancy's bold-
  est wing
To soar unwearied, fearlessly to
  turn
The keenest pangs to peaceful-
  ness, and taste
The joys which mingled sense and
spirit yield. (*Queen Mab* canto III,
lines 175–9 and canto IV, lines
153–8).

47 BRP 6/12.

48 AMH to BLS, transcribed in Barbara Stephen's notebook, WS CUL.

49 Anna Jameson's *Visits and Sketches
at Home and Abroad* (1834) had been
influential in drawing Munich to the
attention of British art-lovers.

50 BRP X 75/1.

51 Balmoral boots; see C.W and P.
Cunnington and C. Beard, *The Dic-
tionary of English Costume 900–1900*
(London, 1960).

52 Burton, pp. 32–33.

53 See Annabel Robinson, John Purkis
and Ann Massing, *A Florentine Procession* (Cambridge, 1997).

54 *An Art Student in Munich* (London,
1853) pp. 87–91.

55 CSS ff. 114–15.

56 BRP 6/65.

57 Anna Mary supported herself during
this time by writing articles for the
Athenaeum and for Dickens's journal, *Household Words*. One piece,
'The Sisters of Art', serialised in *The
Illustrated Exhibitor and Magazine of
Art* (July 1852), described heroines
who established a Female Academy
for art training. The women have
fiancés, but they are rather shadowy
figures, seeming rather less substantial than the representation of
vibrant female friendships.

58 Beaky, letter 14.

59 Burton, p. 34.

60 Jane Benham married the artist William Milton Hay, a painter of portraits, genre and biblical scenes, in
October 1851.

61 Asa Briggs *The Nineteenth Century*
(London, 1985) p. 32.

62 Bessie R. Belloc, in *The Englishwoman's Review*, 15 July 1891.

63 Beaky, letter 14.

64 MH, *An Autobiography*, ed. Margaret Howitt, 2 vols (London, 1889)
II, 81.

65 CSS, ff. 102–3.

66 One of the finest PRB paintings,
Ford Madox Brown's *The Last of
England*, was inspired by this depar-
ture.

67 BRP 5/152.

68 A second edition in 1855 included,
under the dedication, a poem she
had written for Barbara in 1850:
  If I in midst of youth should die,
  With thou, beloved, to hold me
    dear,
  And all my strong intents should
    lie
  Like   wither'd   corn-blades,
    brown and sere,
  Blown down in spring-time of
    the year, –
  On baffled hope and vision bro-
    ken
  Were Death's dark pall untimely
    thrown,
  Were my familiar name unspo-
    ken
  By loving voices save thine
    own, –
  In that dark day my greatest
    strength would be
  Casting my soul on God, – *my
    work on thee.*

69 BRP 5/169.

70 Amice Lee, *Laurels & Rosemary:
The Life of William and Mary Howitt*
(London, 1955) p. 216.

71 I thank Jan Marsh for this information.

72 Beaky, letter 15.

73 Pamela Gerrish Nunn, *Canvassing*
(London, 1986) p. 22.

74 BRP 5/172.

75 BRP 5/173.

76 BRP 1/35.

77 BRP 5/180.

78 *Family Letters*, ed. Rossetti, II, 126.

79 BRP 5/174.

80 All three are in the collection of
Mark Samuels Lasner.

81 *The Language of Flowers*, ed. Sheila
Pickles (London, 1990) p. 50.

CHAPTER 4: THE PIONEERS

1 I have largely taken biographical details from Nancy Ann Sahli, 'Elizabeth Blackwell, MD (1821–1910): A biography', PhD dissertation (University of Pennsylvania, 1974). See also Margaret Forster's chapter on Blackwell in *Significant Sisters: The Grassroots of Active Feminism 1839–1939* (New York, 1985).

2 Blackwell, *Pioneer Work in Opening the Medical Profession to Women* (London, 1895) p. 164.

3 Bessie Parkes to BLS, 30 November, 1850. EB Columbia.

4 EB Congress.

5 The Countess de Noailles (1824–1908) was a daughter of Henry Baring, MP, who had married a member of an aristocratic French family. Widowed in 1852 she devoted her life to efforts to improve health and education. Lady Noel Byron (1792–1860) had attended the conference of the British and Foreign Anti-Slavery Society, where she had met Julia Smith, Mrs Reid and her sister, Miss Sturch. Emilia Gurney (1823–96) was a granddaughter of John Venn, the rector of Clapham, who had been one of William Smith's friends, and was well-known for her philanthropic work.

6 Blackwell, *Pioneer Work*, p. 150.

7 Elizabeth's sister, Emily Blackwell, graduated at the Medical College in Cleveland, Ohio, in 1854, and had then 'gained invaluable surgical experience from having been received as assistant by Sir James Simpson' in Edinburgh: *Pioneer Work* p. 161. Elizabeth was also assisted by Marie Zackrzewska, a German woman who had been chief midwife in a Berlin hospital, had emigrated to America and graduated as a doctor at Cleveland.

8 EB Columbia.

9 EB Congress.

10 Jo Manton, *Elizabeth Garrett Anderson* (London, 1966) p. 47.

11 Blackwell, *Pioneer Work*, p. 176.

12 'Health has its science as well as disease and everyday life should be based on its laws', *EWJ*, 5 (May 1860) p. 27.

13 Blackwell, *Pioneer Work*, p. 17.

14 EB Columbia.

15 Ibid.

16 Ibid.

17 EB to BLSB, 25 May 1860, ibid.

18 Dorothy Clarke Wilson, *Lone Woman: The Story of Elizabeth Blackwell the First Woman Doctor* (London, 1970) p. 47.

19 See Paul McHugh, *Prostitution and Victorian Social Reform* (London, 1980).

20 See Chapter 7.

21 *The Leader*, 19 August 1854, p. 783.

22 EB, *Medical Responsibility in Relation to the Contagious Diseases Acts* (London, 1897) p. 4.

23 *Annual Reports* (ref: DC468/2/1), archives of Glasgow University.

24 See Lucy Bland, 'Feminist Vigilantes of Late-Victorian Britain', in *Regulating Womanhood*, ed. Carol Smart (London, 1992).

25 'The Domestic Moloch', *The Leader*, 19 August 1854.

26 There are countless biographies of George Eliot. A useful selection might be Gordon S. Haight, *George Eliot: A Biography* (Oxford, 1968); Jenny Uglow, *George Eliot* (London, 1987); Valerie A. Dodd, *An Intellectual Life* (Basingstoke, 1990); Rosemarie Bodenheimer, *The Real Life of Mary Anne Evans* (Ithaca, NY, 1994).

27 BRP B/230.

28 Rosemary Ashton argues that there is cryptic evidence for this in Chapman's diary; see *George Eliot: A Life* (Harmondsworth, 1996) p. 84.

29 BRP 5/60.

30 29 June 1852: *Selections*, p. 99.

31 Bessie Rayner Parkes, *A Passing World* (London, 1897) p. 21.

32 George Eliot, *Romola* (Harmondsworth, 1980) pp. 93–4.

33 Haight, *George Eliot*, p. 46.

34 *Selections*, p. 110.

35 George Henry Lewes (1817–78). Larken had already funded the plan to translate all George Sand's work into English, a plan which had been undertaken by a friend of Geraldine Jewsbury's, Matilda Hays, but which had to be abandoned halfway through lack of funds.

36 It was a time, not unlike the 1960s, when people were attempting new modes of living. Elizabeth Blackwell's sister Anna, for example, had lived in the Brook Farm Community in America for a time and had translated George Sand's novel *Jacques*, in which a husband allows his wife her freedom once she falls in love with another man.

37 Haight, *George Eliot*, p. 137.

38 Ludwig Feuerbach, translated by Marian Evans (New York, 1957) p. 271.

39 BRP B/279.

40 BRP 5/179.

41 Quoted by Mathilde Blind, *George Eliot* (London, 1884) p. 80.

42 BRP B/274.

43 BRP 2/40.

44 This was typical; everyone knew, for example, that Charles Bray had an illegitimate family, yet no one excluded him from society.

45 ML to Sara Hennell, 21 July 1855, *GEL*, II, 211.

46 BLS to ML, 14 January 1856, Yale.

47 See Haight, *George Eliot*, p. 205, note 2: 'These words are not Barbara's, but are taken from a description of the letter given me by Bessie's daughter Mrs Belloc Lowndes, 31 Aug. 1942, soon after she destroyed it.'

48 Copy of letter BLSB to Florence Davenport Hill, WS/CUL.

49 Ibid.

50 *GEL*, IV, 425.

51 *GEL*, III, 56–7.

52 *The Arabian Nights Entertainments*, translated by Jonathan Scott (London, 1811) p. 352.

53 *GEL*, III, 63–4.

54 Ibid., 102–3.

55 Ibid., 119.

56 Ibid., 105–6.

57 Yale.

58 BLSB to Patty Smith, 29 November [1859] quoted Haight, *George Eliot*, p. 281.

59 Yale.

60 *GEL*, VIII, 238–9.

61 *Arabian Nights*, p. 391.

62 *GEL*, III, 172.

63 Ibid.

64 ALS to ML, November 1859, Yale.

CHAPTER 5: PORTRAIT OF A SCHOOL

1 The traditional route into teaching in boys' schools was attendance at Oxford or Cambridge, followed by ordination into the Anglican Church. Dissenters, of course, could not follow this route, and in 1846 a group of Brighton schoolmasters obtained a charter to establish a College of Preceptors. Its aim was to raise the standards and status of the teaching profession and to validate secular teaching. Kingsford, a Cambridge graduate and barrister-at-law, assisted in writing the college's by-laws, in order to achieve the goal of a self-regulating teaching profession. See Chapter 4 of Richard Aldrich, *School and Society in Victorian Britain:* The College of Preceptors (Epping, 1995) and obituary, *Educational Times*, October 1854.

2 PK, *Two Lectures upon the Study of Political Philosophy* (London, 1848) p. 29.

3 BLS, *Abstract*, BPG.

4 See BLSB's submission to the Commission on Popular Education set up in 1858: *Parliamentary Papers* 21 (1861) p.103–4.

5 T. Southwood Smith to BLS (25 June 1851), BMC F22.

6 BRP 5/164.

7 Copy of letter from BLSB to Alice Bonham Carter, WS/CUL.

8 *Buchanan*, pp. 24–25.

9 PK, *Two Lectures*, Lecture 2, p. 41.

10 Ibid., p. 40.

11 Elizabeth Whitehead Malleson,

Autobiographical Notes and Letters, printed for private circulation, 1926, p. 73.

12 Elizabeth Whitehead Malleson (1828–1916).

13 Malleson, *Autobiographical Notes*, p. 46.

14 Ibid., p. 47.

15 Named in honour of Dr Birkbeck, pioneer of mechanics' institutes.

16 Quoted in W.A.D. Stewart and W.P. McCann, *The Educational Innovators 1750–1880* (London, 1967) I, 335.

17 'The Portrait of a School', *Journal of Education* 1 September 1886, p. 358.

18 Malleson, *Autobiographical Notes*, p. 46.

19 Stewart and McCann, *Educational Innovators*, p. 276.

20 Elizabeth Whitehead to BLS, 7/ BMC/F11.

21 Ibid.

22 Ibid.

23 November 1854: Beaky, letter 23.

24 7/BMC/F12.

25 7/BMC/F11.

26 'The Portrait of a School', p. 358.

27 BLSB's submission to the Commission on Popular Education.

28 EB Columbia.

29 George Combe (1788–1858) after his retirement from the legal profession worked with William Ellis and others to establish secular schools. BLS had studied Combe's philosophy of education treatise, *The Constitution of Man* (1828), when she was seventeen.

30 *Buchanan*, p. 18.

31 EB Columbia.

32 Rosemary Ashton, *Little Germany: German Refugees in Victorian Britain* (Oxford, 1989) p. 180.

33 EB Columbia.

34 Malleson, *Autobiographical Notes*, p. 49.

35 Barbara chronicled the repeated refusals Jessie received from the London teaching hospitals in her pamphlet *Women and Work* (1857) as an example of women being unreasonably excluded from the professions. See also Elizabeth Adams

Daniels, *Jessie White Mario: Risorgimento Revolutionary* (Ohio, 1972) p. 41.

36 Octavia Hill (1838–1912).

37 Ruskin sponsored Octavia's scheme for improving three slum houses, acquiring capital by managing the schemes as a 5 per cent investment. From 1884 Octavia was appointed by the Church Commissioners to manage their property in Southward and elsewhere. She campaigned for the preservation of open space and recreation areas and in 1895 was co-founder of the National Trust.

38 The Ladies' Guild, founded in 1852.

39 Gillian Darley, *Octavia Hill: A Life* (London, 1990) p. 69.

40 Ibid., p. 70.

41 Malleson, *Autobiographical Notes*, p. 51.

42 Yale.

43 ALCF.

44 BRP 5/87.

45 *Letters to WA*, pp. 80–1.

46 Yale.

47 7/BMC/F13.

48 Sir Godfrey Lushington became Permanent Under-Secretary of State for the Home Department.

49 7/BMC/F13.

50 Ibid.

51 Lee Holcombe, *Victorian Ladies at Work: Middle-class Working Women in England and Wales 1850–1914* (Newton Abbot, 1973) p. 21.

52 Malleson, *Autobiographical Notes*, p. 68.

CHAPTER 6: 'ONE ROUND OF A LONG LADDER'

1 PK, *Two Lectures upon the Study of Political Philosophy* (London, 1848), Lecture 1, p. 40.

2 Hcox 2/209.

3 For attributes of leadership see W.J.H. Sprott, *Human Groups* (1958; Harmondsworth, 1967) and Lilian Lewis Shiman, *Women and Leadership in Nineteenth-Century England* (Basingstoke, 1992).

4 See *Tennyson: Poems and Plays*, ed. T. Herbert Warren (1953; Oxford, 1986) p. 225.

5 See Pam Hirsch, 'Mary Wollstonecraft: a problematic legacy', in *Wollstonecraft's Daughters*, ed. Clarissa Campbell Orr (Manchester, 1996).

6 Caroline Norton (1808–77), granddaughter of the playwright, Richard Brinsley Sheridan. See Alan Chedzoy, *A Scandalous Woman* (London, 1992); Margaret Forster, Chapter 1 of *Significant Sisters*; Mary Poovey, Chapter 3 of *Uneven Developments: The Ideological Work of Gender in Mid-Victorian England* (Chicago, 1998).

7 John Jane Smith Wharton, *An Exposition of the Laws relating to the Women of England, showing their rights, remedies and responsibilities* (London, 1853).

8 *The Letters of Mrs Gaskell*, ed J.A.V. Chapple and J.A. Pollard (Manchester, 1966) pp. 606–7.

9 George Eliot, *Middlemarch* (Harmondsworth, 1980) p. 894.

10 '... the almost definitional claim of political discourse is to be a response to a pre-existing need or demand. But in fact the primary motivation is to create and then orchestrate such a demand, to change the self-identification and behaviour of those addressed': Gareth Stedman Jones, *Languages of Class* (Cambridge, 1989) p. 24.

11 Matthew Davenport Hill (1792–1872); see Rosamund and Florence Davenport Hill, *A Memoir of Matthew Davenport Hill* (London, 1878).

12 7/BMC/E2.

13 7/BMC/E3.

14 7/BMC/E4.

15 7/BMC/E5.

16 BLS, *Women and Work*, p. 11.

17 Davenport Hill to BLS, 20 August 1854. 7/BMC/E6.

18 *A Brief Summary* ... (1854; London 1869), 'Remarks'.

19 7/BMC/E10.

20 MH, *An Autobiography*, ed. Margaret Howitt, 2 vols (London, 1889), II, 116.

21 Yale.

22 *GEL*, II, 225.

23 Ibid., 227.

24 Amice Lee, *Laurels & Rosemary* p. 214. One is irresistibly reminded of Alice Walker's comment that 'the real revolution is always concerned with the least glamorous stuff': 'Duties of the Black Revolutionary Artist' paper presented to the Black Students' Association of Sarah Lawrence College, 12 February 1970.

25 Lee, *Laurels & Rosemary*, p. 215.

26 MH, *An Autobiography*, II, 116–17.

27 Burton, p. 63.

28 *Westminster Review*, October 1856, p. 336.

29 Lee Holcombe, *Wives and Property: Reform of the Married Women's Property Law in Nineteenth Century England* (Toronto, 1983) p. 90.

30 Stephen, p. 43.

CHAPTER 7: WILD DESIRES

1 BRP 5/60.

2 Roughly equivalent to taking a first-class degree today.

3 Catherine Spooner was the other witness. See Ben Smith's will; probate describes assets as under £35,000. This does *not* include the property, Public Record Office, Richmond.

4 The solicitors were Meaburn Fatham of 24 Lincoln's Inn Fields, London.

5 Smith records in London Public Record Office.

6 Jane Buss's cousin Kezia Buss (also from Froxfield) appears to have shared the house in Fulham.

7 I have found no trace of the middle child, Alexander, so cannot say whether he died young, or emigrated out of range of censuses.

8 BRP/61*.

9 BLS to Ben LS, 7 December 1852, Hcox 2/011.
10 Hcox 2/010.
11 In Barbara's case, he was the witness to her marriage, and a trustee of her marriage settlement; he remained her trustee all her life.
12 BRP 1/4.
13 Ibid.
14 EB Congress.
15 See Preface to the 3rd edition of *Remarks on the Education of Girls* (London, 1856).
16 BRP 6/66.
17 See reproduction of *View over Snowden with a Stormy Sky* in Scott Wilcox and Christopher Newall, *Victorian Landscape Watercolours* (New York, 1992) p. 90.
18 BRP 24/1.
19 BRP to Elizabeth Parkes, 15 December 1854, BRP 2/4.1.
20 EB Radcliffe.
21 BRP 5/180.
22 BRP 6/137.
23 BRP 9/15.
24 James Joseph Sylvester (1814–97). At the age of sixty-two, because of his groundbreaking work on matrices and linear transformations, Sylvester was offered the Chair of Mathematics at Johns Hopkins University in Baltimore. He returned to England in 1883 when Oxford invited him to become the Savilian Professor of Geometry. See Patricia C. Kenschaft and Kaila Katz, 'Sylvester and Scott', in *The Mathematics Teacher* (Washington, DC, September 1982).
25 BMC/C11.
26 In 1871 after the passage of the University Test Bill, removing the disabilities of both Jews and Dissenters, Sylvester wrote to Benjamin Leigh Smith to ask for his support in 'bringing pressure to bear on the Government from their supporters' in getting his Cambridge BA awarded retrospectively: BMC/C2.
27 7/BMC/E10.
28 Joseph Leach, *Bright Particular Star: The Life and Times of Charlotte Cushman* (New Haven, 1970) p. 210.
29 *Letters & Memories by Harriet Hosmer*, ed. Cornelia Carr (London, 1913) p. 35.
30 30 Burton p. 75.
31 Ibid.
32 Whitney Chadwick, *Women, Art and Society* (London, 1990) p. 198.
33 Burton, p. 77.
34 Bessie Parkes to Emily Blackwell, 1 June 1855. EB Radcliffe.
35 BRP 5/70.
36 Burton, p. 78.
37 *Buchanan*, p. 19.
38 Carlyle seems to have to taken Neuberg's help for granted, referring to him as a 'good and sensible but wearisome and rather heavy man': Simon Heffer in *Moral Desperado, A Life of Thomas Carlyle* (London, 1995) p. 297.
39 See Gordon Haight, *George Eliot and John Chapman* (New Haven, 1940) for details of Chapman's life.
40 Elizabeth Malleson, *Autobiographical Notes* (printed for private circulation, 1926) p. 101.
41 *GEL*, II, 163.
42 All quotations from Chapman's letters are from the collection held in the Beinecke Rare Book and Manuscript Library at Yale University.
43 Jan Marsh and Pamela Gerrish Nunn, *Women Artists and the Pre-Raphaelite Movement* (London, 1989) p. 41.
44 *Munk's Roll: Lives of the Fellows of the Royal College of Physicians of London 1826–1925* (London, 1955).
45 MH, *An Autobiography*, ed. Margaret Howitt, 2 vols (London, 1889) II, 111–12.
46 W.M. Rossetti, in *The Crayon: an American Journal of Art* (August 1856).
47 J.J. Piper, *Robertsbridge and its History* (St Leonards, 1906).
48 Beaky, letter 15.
49 *Athenaeum*, 2 June 1855, p. 648.
50 Beaky, letter 15.
51 See Pam Hirsch, 'Charlotte Brontë and George Sand: the influence of

female Romanticism', in Brontë Society *Transactions*, 21, part 6 (1996).

52 Quoted in Sheila Rosenberg, 'The Financing of Radical Opinion: John Chapman and the *Westminster Review*, in *The Victorian Periodical Press: Samplings and Soundings*, ed. Joan Shattock and Michael Wolff (Leicester, 1982) p. 182.

53 Ibid., p. 185.

54 Beaky, letter 29.

55 24 August 1855: Chapman Letters, Yale.

56 Hcox 2/003.

57 Hcox 2/004.

58 Hcox 2/005.

59 Hcox 2/006.

60 19 March 1856: BRP 5/83.

61 *GEL*, II, 254–5.

62 Gordon S. Haight, *George Eliot* (Oxford, 1968) 205.

63 Hcox 2/008.

64 Quoted by M. Betham-Edwards, *A Winter with the Swallows* (London, 1867) p. 249.

65 Crompton, 'Prelude to Arcadia', p. 130.

CHAPTER 8: BARBARY

1 SPRI ms/640/1/8.

2 Ben attached himself to a mining engineer from Redruth, Cornwall, who was going to Algeria to examine some copper mines in order to advise London speculators on profitability. Gratton decided against investing in Algeria; he judged the lack of coal made it hard to make a profit.

3 *The Times*, 13 October 1854, p. 8.

4 See *Florence Nightingale: Letters from the Crimea 1854–1856*, ed. Sue M. Goldie (New York, 1997).

5 *Buchanan*, p. 20.

6 Yale.

7 SPRI ms 640/1/5.

8 BRP 5/175.

9 Deriving from the Latin word *barbarus* meaning barbarian.

10 See 'The French Take-over of

Algeria', in André Jardin and André-Jean Tudesq, *Restoration and Reaction*, trans. Elborg Forster (Cambridge, 1983).

11 *Algeria considered as a Winter Residence for the English* (1858) quoted in Burton, pp. 83–4.

12 BRP 6/071; quoted in Burton, p. 84.

13 According to the story, when Aeneas sailed out of Africa, Dido had a funeral pyre built in the courtyard of her palace and on it she put the bed she and her lover had slept in, together with the clothes and sword Aeneas had left behind. As Aeneas' ship sailed away from Africa the flames of Dido's funeral pyre lit up the walls of the city.

14 Yale.

15 Charles Theodore Bodichon (1762–1819); Antoinette Le Grand de la Pommeraye (1791–1846).

16 Charles and Antoinette Bodichon had three sons, one of whom died in adolescence and one of whom died in 1843 of consumption. The latter had left a widow, but no children.

17 Isidore Auguste Marie François Xavier Comte, (1798–1857), author of *The Positive Philosophy* (1830–42) and *The Positive Polity* (1851–54).

18 Patricia M. Lorcin, *Imperial Identities: Stereotyping, Prejudice and Race in Colonial Algeria* (London, 1995) pp. 112–13.

19 Bessie Parkes, *A Passing World* (London, 1897) p. 23.

20 Burton, p. 90.

21 *De l'Humanité*, Part 1 (Algiers, 1852); Part 2 (Geneva 1853).

22 After Napoleon III removed the gags with which he had kept liberal opinion silent in France, *De l'Humanité* was published by Lacroix in Brussels in 1866. Carlyle considered that Bodichon's political writings revealed 'an original and independent mind' which proved him 'a thoughtful, true, serious man, one of the few who have not bowed down to Baal'. A short extract in English appeared as 'Napoleon the First' in

Temple Bar (London, November 1873).

23 BLS to ML, Yale. Letter includes a cartoon of Bodichon's head, with hair sticking up.

24 The most useful analysis and contextualisation of Bodichon's work is to be found in Lorcin *Imperial Identities*.

25 Dr Bodichon quoted by BLS, *Women and Work*, p. 6.

26 Algiers, 1851.

27 Quoted in Matilda Betham-Edwards, *In French-Africa* (London, 1912) p. 315.

28 Burton, p. 90.

29 A French hunter called Bonbonnel published the accounts of his hunts in Algeria, in which he described being horrifically mauled by a panther. According to his account, Dr Bodichon had calmly gathered up pieces of torn flesh and patched him up, certainly saving his life. Bonbonnel roundly praised Bodichon's skill as a surgeon. See J.J. Piper, *Robertsbridge and its History* (St Leonards, 1906).

30 See Burton, p. 91.

31 BRP 7/6.

32 BRP 9/143.

33 BRP/B.

34 BRP/B/543.

35 BRP/B/539.

36 Hcox 1/418.

37 GLRO E/LS/1.

38 *GEL*, II, 377.

39 *AD*, p. 156.

40 *Correspondence of Arthur Hugh Clough*, ed. Frederick L. Mulhauser, 2 vols (Oxford, 1957) II, 533.

41 Yale.

42 *Illustrated London News*, 30 July 1859.

43 See Ellen C. Clayton, *English Female Artists*, 2 vols (London, 1876) p.86; portrait sadly lost.

44 See *From Elgin to the Alhambra: The Watercolours of Sophia, Lady Dunbar (1814–1909)* exhibition catalogue (Aberdeen, 1987).

45 François Lauret (1809–68); see E.

Bénézit, *Dictionnaire critique et documentaire des peintres, sculpteurs, graveurs, dessinateurs* (Paris, 1924).

46 *Letters to WA*, p. 84.

47 *GEL*, IV, 118–20.

48 *The Illustrated Times*, 14 March 1857.

49 BRP 6/072.

50 See Chapter 11.

51 *Etudes sur L'Algérie et L'Afrique, Considerations sur L'Algérie* and *Hygiène à suivre en Algérie*.

52 EDFC, p. 159.

53 'Algeria: First Impressions', *EWJ*, September 1860, p. 29.

54 ALCF.

55 Matilda Betham-Edwards, *A Winter with the Swallows* (London, 1867) pp. 21–2.

56 *Letters to WA*, p. 77.

57 Quoted by M. Betham-Edwards in *Friendly Faces of Three Nationalities* (London, 1911) p. 89.

58 BLSB to Anna Jameson 21 April 1859, in *Anna Jameson: Letters and Friendships (1812–1860)*, ed. Mrs. Steuart Erskine (London, 1915) pp. 328, 330, 331.

59 Hcox 2/027.

60 Burton, p. 96.

61 *Women and Work*, p. 6.

62 Yale.

63 The title of the book suggests that Algeria is seen only in terms of its suitability for English visitors; the Arab peoples are not considered in their own right.

64 Vron Ware in *Beyond the Pale: White Women, Racism and History* (London, 1993) pp. 98–102 deals with the limitations of BLSB's views.

65 See Linda Nochlin, 'The Imaginary Orient', in *The Politics of Vision: Essays on Nineteenth-Century Art and Society* (London, 1987) for this argument.

66 See *Women and Work*, pp. 23–32. Deborah Cherry in 'Shuttling and Soul Making' in *The Victorians and Race*, ed. Shearer West (Aldershot, 1996) p. 167 argues that 'the imperial project for feminists is identified

as a concern for the improvement of Muslim women'.

67 BLSB's addendum to Bessie Parkes's *Memoir of Madame Luce of Algiers* (1862); originally *EWJ* May, June, July 1861.

68 *The Art Journal*, February 1865, pp. 45–6.

CHAPTER 9: THE HONEY YEARS

1 BLS, 'The Education of Women', *Hastings & St Leonards News*, (28 July 1848).

2 'Women and Work' first appeared on 7 February 1857 in the *Waverley*. See Chapter 11 for details of Bessie's and Barbara's involvement with the *Waverley* and the founding of the *English Woman's Journal*. A pamphlet version, dated April 1857, *Women and Work*, was published by Bosworth & Harrison in London. Quotations are from this version.

3 *Women and Work* (London, 1857), signed 'Barbara Leigh Smith, Blandford Square, April 1857'.

4 *Aurora Leigh* was published in late 1856, which shows that Barbara was quick to read new feminist works. See also Pam Hirsch, 'Gender Negotiations in Nineteenth Century Women's Autobiographical Writing', in *The Uses of Autobiography*, ed. Julia Swindells (London, 1995).

5 See Chapter 8.

6 Later published as *Sisters of Charity and the Communion of Labour* (London, 1859).

7 This letter is not extant but in the appendix to his *Autobiography* he writes: 'The first step towards civilisation is safety to life and property, and the man only can secure this. He has to fight for it; all government must be based on brute force, and for her share in this kind of government woman by nature is disqualified ... as the weaker vessel, she ought to be under man's special protection, and gain more from his chivalry than from *fighting* for her "rights".' Charles Bray, *Phrases of Opinion and Experience during a Long Life: An Autobiography* (London, 1885).

8 *GEL*, II, 383.

9 'A short black boot lacing up the front', *The Dictionary of English Costume 900–1900*, ed. C.W. and P. Cunnington and C. Beard (London, 1960).

10 The title chosen for the hatchet job is interesting, because the wearing of bloomers was associated with American women's rights agitators, especially Angelina Grimké. The *Saturday Review* was perhaps betraying its alarm at dangerous transatlantic influences.

11 Harriet Grote (1792–1878) was married to the historian and founding member of University College London. She was the author of a 'Memoir of the Life of Ary Scheffer' (1860).

12 Deborah Cherry, *Painting Women: Victorian Women Artists* (Rochdale, 1987) p. 9.

13 W.M. Rossetti, in *Fine Arts Quarterly*, October 1863, p. 340.

14 *AD*, p. 116.

15 Ibid., pp. 57–8.

16 Ibid., pp. 60–1.

17 See Ellen Nickenzie Lawson, *The Three Sarahs: Documents of Antebellum Black College Women* (New York, 1984).

18 *AD*, pp. 63–4.

19 Ibid., pp. 64–5.

20 Ruskin distinguished between three kinds of perception: 'The man who perceives rightly, because he does not feel, and to whom the primrose is very accurately a primrose, because he does not love it. Then, secondly, the man who perceives wrongly, because he feels, and to whom the primrose is anything else but a primrose: a star, or a sun, or a fairy's shield, or a forsaken maiden. And then, lastly, there is the man who perceives rightly in spite of his feelings, and to whom a primrose is for ever nothing else but itself a little flower apprehended in the very plain

and leafy fact of it, whatever and how many soever the associations and passions may be that crowd into it': quoted in Kenneth Clark, *Landscape into Art* (London, 1986) p. 51.

21 *AD*, p. 103.
22 Ibid., p. 71.
23 Ibid., p. 67.
24 Ibid., p. 68.
25 Ibid., pp. 73–4.
26 Ibid., p. 67.
27 Ibid., p. 70.
28 Ibid., pp. 72–3.
29 Ibid., p. 87.
30 Josiah Clark Nott (1804–73) author of *Types of Mankind* (1854) and *Indigenous Races of Mankind* (1857).
31 *AD*, pp. 84–5.
32 Ibid., p. 83.
33 Ibid., pp. 104–5.
34 'A Dull Life', *Macmillan's Magazine*, 74 (May 1867).
35 *AD*, p. 116.
36 Ibid., p. 123.
37 Ibid., p. 124.
38 Ibid., p. 133.
39 Ibid., pp. 136–7.
40 Ibid., p. 141.
41 Founded by Maurice Spring, a New York merchant and philanthropist in 1853 at Perth Amboy, New Jersey – a communal settlement which was the spiritual descendant of Brook Farm and the North American Phalanx.
42 Ibid., pp. 179–89.
43 Ibid., pp. 142–3.
44 Yale.
45 *AD*, p. 147.
46 Ibid., p. 148.
47 Ibid., p. 150.
48 Ibid., p. 153.
49 Ibid., p. 154.
50 CSS, ff. 127–8.
51 *The Crayon*, August, 1856, p. 245.
52 W.M. Rossetti notes made to assist Stillman in promoting the Exhibition of British Art, Beinecke, Yale.
53 AD, p. 159.
54 'An American School', *EWJ*, November 1858, pp. 198–200.
55 'Slavery in America' *EWJ*, October 1858, pp. 94–100.

56 Ibid., p. 27.
57 Ibid., p. 94.
58 'Slavery in the South', *EWJ*, November 1861, p. 182.
59 'Of those who are the property of others, and of the great power that holds them', *EWJ*, February 1863, p. 374.
60 See Joanna de Groot, ' "Sex" and "Race" ', in *Sexuality and Subordination*, ed. Susan Mendus and Jane Rendall (London, 1989) pp. 89–128.
61 'Slavery in the South', *EWJ*, October 1861, p. 112.
62 'Slavery in the South', *EWJ*, December 1861, p. 264.
63 'Slavery in the South', *EWJ*, November 1861, p. 184.
64 'Of those who are the property of others', p. 374.
65 Ibid., p. 372.
66 'Slavery in America', p. 97.
67 *The Letters of Mrs Gaskell*, ed. J.A.V. Chappell and J. A. Pollard (Manchester, 1966) pp. 606–70.

CHAPTER 10: LOVE AND LOSS

1 14 October 1858, Autograph Collection, Girton.
2 *Athenaeum*, June 1856, p. 510.
3 W.M. Rossetti, 'Art News from England', *Crayon*, August 1856, p. 245.
4 Amice Lee, *Laurels & Rosemary*, pp. 216–7.
5 See Germaine Greer's aptly named *The Obstacle Race: the Fortunes of Women Painters and Their Work* (New York, 1979).
6 Stephen ts, WS/CUL.
7 It was not until 1922 that Annie Louise Swynnerton became an associate member, and it was 1936 before Laura Knight was elected to full membership.
8 Tragically, Laura Herford was to die aged thirty-nine in October 1870, from an overdose of chloroform taken for toothache. Her niece, the painter Helen Paterson, later married Barbara's friend, the Irish poet

9 William Allingham, and become her friend too.

9 David Cox (1783–1859), quoted in *Bicentenary Exhibition Catalogue*, Birmingham Museums and Art Gallery, 1983, p. 101.

10 BLSB to Beatrice Shore Smith; ALCF.

11 *GEL*, III, 107–8.

12 Ibid., III, 124.

13 *Illustrated London News*, 30 July 1859, p. 105: 'Madame Bodichon (formerly Miss Barbara L. Smith), who has long been known as a landscapist of great ability and superior purpose, has just opened an exhibition of some of her works. The series is a highly interesting one, the subjects being taken from the fertile, but hitherto inadequately explored, soil of Algeria. Some of the views are of considerable size, and include features of sea, mountain and forest in admirable combination. The figures introduced heighten the effect by the picturesque costume and impressive character. The scene of a funeral is particularly striking. Many of the works – and not in themselves the least interesting of the collection – are studies of the peculiar vegetation, flower, shrub, and tree of the place, some of which are extremely beautiful.'

14 *GEL*, III, 128.

15 BRP 6/12.

16 Anna Jameson, *The Poetry of Sacred and Legendary Art* (London, 1850).

17 Christina Rossetti Letters, Bodleian Library, Oxford.

18 Beaky, letter 34.

19 *The Autobiography and Letters of Mrs Oliphant*, ed. Mrs Mary Coghill (New York, 1899).

20 Beaky., letter 30.

21 Ibid., letter 34.

22 It is possible that she suffered from manic depression (bi-polar disease), which, had she lived today, could be kept under control by prescribed drugs.

23 Hcox 2/007.

24 John Ludlow (1801–82).

25 The genial Colonel Newcome in Thackeray's *The Newcomes* (London, 1853–5) is reputed to be a 'portrait' of Edmund Ludlow.

26 'Lord Hardinge then at Simla, at once caused a notification of this event, coupled with an expression of thanks to Major Ludlow, to be published in the government *Gazette*, September 22, 1846; and, such was the effect of this example, that before Christmas suttee was prohibited by 11 out of the Rajpoot principalities, and by five of the remaining free States of India': obituary in *The Times*, 4 December 1882.

27 Information from the Sutton family (Ludlow descendants) and from the Oriental Club, London.

28 John Malcom Forbes Ludlow (1821–1911).

29 *John Ludlow Christian Socialist: an Autobiography*, ed. A.D. Murray (London, 1981) p. 84.

30 General Ludlow was also a promoter of working men's associations in the early stages of the movement: ibid., p. 170.

31 Beaky, letter 32.

32 GLRO/E/LS/12, 12, 14.

33 The Leigh Smiths' old riding master.

34 Hcox 2/013.

35 Yale.

36 Hcox 2/039.

37 Yale.

38 *GEL*, III, 334.

39 BRP 5/96.

40 Yale. All the Leigh Smiths had inherited packages of stocks and shares as legacies after their father's death; when Ben Smith settled Blandford Square on Barbara, he settled £5,000 each on Bella and Nannie. On her marriage, Ben settled another £5,000 on Bella (GLRO).

41 *GEL*, III, 365–6.

42 *GEL*, IV, 64–5.

43 Among BLSB's books donated to Girton.

44 *GEL*, III, 365-6.

45 Hcox, 2/028.

46 Hcox 2/027.

47 His own brother had been involved in an uprising in 1832, when the Duchesse de Berry, a mortal enemy of Louis-Philippe, had tried to rouse Brittany around the old flag, and had been sent to prison for five months.

48 Quotes from this trip are from the Britanny Letters, BPG.

49 Beaky, letter 35.

50 *Correspondence of A.H. Clough*, ed. Frederick L. Mulhauserm 2 vols (Oxford, 1957) I, 595.

51 *AD*, pp. 92-3.

52 BLSB to Emily Blackwell, 11 and 13 February 1862, EB Radcliffe.

53 Hcox 1/137.

54 AMH to BLSB, November 1864: Beaky, letter 36.

55 BRP 5/131.

CHAPTER 11: THE REFORM FIRM

1 Isa Craig Knox (1831-1903). Isa's first volume of poetry, *Poems by Isa*, was published in 1856.

2 BRP 5/84.

3 Ibid.

4 BRP 5/85.

5 ML to Bessie Parkes, 1 September [1857], *GEL*, II, 379.

6 The *EWJ* published poetry of a high standard by Isa Craig, Adelaide Procter and Christina Rossetti. Marian Lewes was unimpressed by the standard of the literary reviews.

7 BRP, *Essays on Woman's Work* (London, 1865) p. 120.

8 BRP 5/86.

9 BLS in her abstract of Mill's *Principles of Political Economy* had noted that 'the advantages of [such companies] are numerous and important. It is an instance of the folly and jobbery of the rulers of mankind that until lately the joint stock principle as a general resort was interdicted by law': BPG.

10 See Articles of Association of the English Woman's Journal Company Limited, Public Record Office BT 41 227/1274.

11 Widow of the 5th Baron Monson, a Tory peer. Sister-in-law of Lady Monson and the sister of Edmund Larken, she had financed the translation of George Sand's novels into English, which had involved Max Hays.

12 Helen Blackburn, *Women's Suffrage: A Record of the Women's Suffrage Movement* (London, 1902); Appendix C.

13 See Jane Rendall, 'A Moral Engine? Feminism, liberalism and the *English Woman's Journal*, in *Equal or Different: Women's Politics 1800-1914*, ed. Jane Rendall (Oxford, 1987) p. 127.

14 BRP 2/66.1.

15 *GEL*, III, 438-9.

16 *The Oxford Book of Letters*, ed. Frank Kermode and Anita Kermode (Oxford, 1996) pp. 344-5.

17 *GEL*, III, 153.

18 The best analysis of the strengths and weaknesses of the *EWJ* is Jane Rendall's 'A Moral Engine?' op. cit.

19 *GEL*, III, 57.

20 Ibid.

21 Yale.

22 *GEL*, III, 153.

23 BLSB to ML, 27 November 1859, Yale.

24 *GEL*, III, 225-6.

25 Jessie Boucherett (1825-1905) recounted in Blackburn, *Women's Suffrage: A Record of the Women's Suffrage Movement* (London, 1902) p. 50.

26 Emily Faithfull (1835-95).

27 BRP 5/86 and 87.

28 BRP 5/96.

29 See Pauline A. Nestor, 'A New Departure in Women's Publishing', *Victorian Periodicals Review*, 1982.

30 Its full title was the National Association for the Promotion of Social Science (NAPSS).

31 See Lawrence Goldman's excellent analysis, 'The Social Science Association, 1857-1886: a context for mid-

32 Bessie Rayner Parkes, *A Passing World* (London, 1897) p. 20.
33 Ray Strachey, *The Cause* (London, 1928) pp. 93–4.
34 EB Radcliffe.
35 Frances Power Cobbe, quoted in A. James Hammerton, 'Feminism and Female Emigration, 1861–1886', in *A Widening Sphere: Changing Roles of Victorian Women*, ed. Martha Vicinus (London, 1977) p. 58.
36 See Marion Diamond, 'Maria Rye: the primrose path', in *Wollstonecraft's Daughters*, ed. Clarissa Campbell Orr, (Manchester, 1996).
37 *GEL*, III, 64.
38 BRP 5/95.
39 'Prospectus of the Ladies' Institute, 19 Langham Place.'; Blackburn, *Women's Suffrage*, p. 248.
40 BRP 5/95.
41 Ibid.
42 See Bibliography for complete list.
43 BRP 5/104.
44 She worked up this visit into an article, 'Painted Glass Windows Executed by the Carmelite Nuns of Mans', *EWJ*, January 1862.
45 Brittany Letters, BPG.
46 BRP 5/104.
47 BRP 5/126.
48 BRP 5/127.
49 *GEL*, II, 438, note 2.
50 Parkes, *A Passing World*, (London, 1897) p. 32–3.
51 Quoted in Daphne Bennett, *Emily Davies and the Liberation of Women 1830–1921* (London, 1990) p. 42.
52 BRP 8/24.
53 EDFC.
54 Ibid.
55 Quoted in Rendall, 'A Moral Engine?', p. 136.
56 BRP 5/121.
57 BRP 5/108.
58 BRP 5/115.
59 *Dearest Isa: Robert Browning's Letters to Isabella Blagden*, ed. Edward C. McAleer (Austin, Texas, 1951) p. 204.
60 BRP 5/117.

61 BRP 5/159.
62 Public Record Office, J. 77.11, ff. 5–6, parags 2–3.
63 BRP 2/80.
64 BRP 2/79.
65 *Illustrated London News*, 15 June 1895.
66 See details of publishing career in William E. Fredeman, 'Emily Faithfull and the Victoria Press: an experiment in sociological bibliography', in *The Library*, 5th series, 29 (June 1974) and James S. Stone, *Emily Faithfull: Victorian Champion of Women's Rights* (Toronto, 1994) for an account of Faithfull's whole career.
67 MT 12/49.
68 Richard Cobden and Michael Chevalier were both promoters of free trade.
69 *Letters to WA*, pp. 79–80.
70 MT 13/185.

CHAPTER 12: PRACTISING THE ART OF THE POSSIBLE

1 Quoted BRP/A, p. 101.
2 BRP 5/178.
3 *GEL*, IV, 101–2.
4 Bessie Rayner Parkes, *A Passing World* (London, 1897) p. 21.
5 *GEL*, IV, 101–2.
6 Surprisingly little has been written about Procter. See Margaret Mason, 'Queen Victoria's Favourite Poet', *Listener*, 29 April 1965, pp. 636–7.
7 The Procters consented to Max taking charge of the flowers for Adelaide's grave at Kensal Green.
8 BRP 5/127.
9 BRP 5/129.
10 Quoted in BRP/A, p. 192.
11 BRP 5/130.
12 BRP 5/128.
13 BRP 5/131.
14 BRP 2/13.
15 BRP 2/14.1 and Madame Belloc [Bessie Rayner Parkes], *The Flowing Tide* (London, 1900) pp. 68–73.

16 *Letters to WA*, p. 82.
17 See Michael Clarke, *Corot and the Art of Landscape* (London, 1991).
18 See Steven Adams, *The Barbizon School & the Origins of Impressionism* (London, 1994).
19 *AD*, p. 74.
20 *Letters to WA*, p. 86.
21 See autograph letter, BPG; see also Matilda Betham-Edwards, *Reminiscences* (London, 1898) which states that Barbara introduced Daubigny to her beloved Hastings, which he liked so much that he 'settled down with his son at a humble inn in its midst'.
22 Cecil Woodham-Smith, *Florence Nightingale 1820–1910* (Harmondsworth, 1955) p. 330.
23 Burton, pp. 182–3.
24 The *Spectator* 14 June 1862, p. 657.
25 See the *Morning Post*, 9 June 1862, p. 2; the *Daily Telegraph*, 9 June 1862, p. 2; the *Spectator*, 14 June 1862, p. 657
26 Quoted by Burton, p. 143.
27 Ray Strachey, *The Cause*, (London, 1928) p. 103.
28 9 May 1866, MT 12/40.
29 9 May 1866, 7/BMC/B1.
30 11 May, MT 12/42.
31 Ibid., 12/43.
32 7/BMC/B2.
33 7/BMC/B4.
34 BLSB had shortened Helen Taylor's draft petition to the following:
The Humble Petition of the undersigned, sheweth: That it having been expressly laid down by the high authorities that the possession of property in this country carries with it the right to vote in the election of Representatives in Parliament, it is an evident anomaly that some holders of property are allowed to use this right, while others, forming no less a constituent part of the nation, and equally qualified by law to hold property, are not able to exercise this privilege. That the participation of women in the Government is consistent with the principles of the British Constitution, inasmuch as women in these islands have always been held capable of sovereignty, and women are eligible for various public offices. Your Petitioners therefore humbly pray your honourable House to consider the expediency of providing for the representation of all householders, without distinction of sex, who possess such property or rental qualification as your honourable House may determine.
35 7/BMC/B6.
36 MT 12/46.
37 'The Great Unrepresented', *Blackwoods's Edinburgh Magazine*, 100 (September 1866), pp. 367–79.
38 *Objections to the Enfranchisement of Women Considered* (London, 1866).
39 Lydia Becker (1827–90) see Strachey, *The Cause*, p. 106.
40 MT 12/48.
41 Ibid., 12/48.
42 Ibid., 13/188; Ibid., 13/260.
43 Ibid., 12/54.
44 Stephen, p. 115.
45 See Jo Manton, *Elizabeth Garrett Anderson* (London, 1966) p. 182.
46 Helen Blackburn, *Women's Suffrage: A Record of the Women's Suffrage Movement* (London, 1902) p. 60.
47 Stephen, p. 117.
48 Ibid. p. 117–18.
49 Quoted in Burton, p. 153.

CHAPTER 13: LOSING THE HONEY

1 Matilda Betham-Edwards, *In French-Africa* (London, 1912) p. 9.
2 Matilda Betham-Edwards (1836–1919) was the daughter of a Suffolk farmer. The French government made her Officier de l'Instruction Publique de France, the first Englishwoman to receive this honour. She retained her maiden name in honour of her aunt, Mary Betham, a writer and a friend of Mrs Barbauld. Her cousin, Amelia

Blandford Edwards, was a writer and Egyptologist, who at her death left her Egyptian collection and books to University College London, together with a fund to establish the first chair in Egyptology in Britain. The rest of her books she left to Somerville College, the first women's college at Oxford.

3 Betham-Edwards, *In French-Africa*, pp. 34–5.

4 Ibid., p. 139.

5 Betham-Edwards, *A Winter with the Swallows* (London, 1867).

6 Ibid., pp. 192–4.

7 *Mettray: A Letter from the Recorder of Birmingham to Charles Bowyer Alderley, Esq. M.P.*, a pamphlet reprinted from *The Law Review* for February 1855 (London).

8 Yale; as are all following letters on BLSB's journey through France and Spain.

9 *GEL*, IV, 29.

10 See Post Office London Street Directory for 1862. On 27 February 1866, pursuant to Registrar's order, no. 32 became no. 64 (detail from Joseph Gratton's will).

11 Index of inscriptions on memorial stones. My thanks to Mrs Peyton Jones, archivist of St Albans Abbey.

12 The 1841 census describes her as 'housekeeper'; the 1851 census describes her as 'wife'.

13 BRP/A, p. 220.

14 Burton, p. 138.

15 D.J. Frommer, 'The Changing Age of the Menopause', *British Medical Journal*, 8 August 1964.

16 *GEL*, VIII, 358–9.

17 Much later in life, Nannie told her niece, Amy, 'I only bought there in 1866 to please her': Hcox 2/128.

18 See Terri Apter, *Secret Paths: Women in the New Midlife* (New York, 1995) p. 97.

19 Quoted in Betham-Edwards, *In French-Africa*, p. 311.

20 L. Boulos, *Medicinal Plants of North Africa* (Michigan, 1983). Thanks also to Dr James Cullen, director of the Stanley Smith (UK) Horticultural Trust, Cambridge.

21 M. Trottier, *Notes sur l'Eucalyptus et subsidiairement sur la nécessité du reboisement l'Algérie* (Algiers, 1868).

22 V. Shiva, *Staying Alive: Women, Ecology and Development* (London, 1988) p. 170 argues that eucalyptus is destructive to indigenous ecosystems.

23 *Pall Mall Gazette*, 16 May 1868, p. 11.

24 *GEL*, IV, 351–2.

25 See Thomas R. Palfrey 'Louise Swanton Belloc (1796–1881) as an Intermediary between France and America', *Modern Language Forum*, 27 (October 1942), pp. 115–31.

26 A picture of her with her daughter Lily by her husband is in the Louvre. Jean-Hilaire Belloc was a fashionable portrait painter, who became director of the Free School of Design, Architecture and Mathematics in Paris.

27 Margaret Lesser, *Clarkey: A Portrait in Letters of Mary Clarke Mohl 1793–1833* (Oxford, 1984) p. 27.

28 Mrs Belloc-Lowndes, *Where Love and Friendship Dwelt* (London, 1943) p. 25.

29 *GEL*, VIII, 358–60.

30 Jo Manton, *Elizabeth Garrett Anderson* (London, 1966) p. 156.

31 Ibid., p. 181.

32 BRP 5/132.

33 Mrs Belloc Lowndes, *I, too, have lived in Arcadia* (London, 1941) p. 29.

34 Ibid., p. 42.

35 Ibid., p. 52.

36 *GEL*, IV, 362.

37 *Arcadia*, pp. 65–6.

38 Ibid., p. 67.

39 Ibid., p. 70.

40 Ibid., p. 75.

41 CSS.

42 *Letters to WA*, p. 83.

43 Stephen, p. 162.

44 EB Radcliffe.

45 *Arcadia*, p. 81.

46 Ibid., pp. 81–2.

47 EB Radcliffe.

48 This daughter, Marie Belloc-Low-ndes (1868–1947) became a novelist and the biographer of her mother.

49 *Arcadia*, p. 84.

CHAPTER 14: THE HITCHIN YEARS

1 Rita McWilliams-Tullberg, *Women at Cambridge* (London, 1975), p. 36.

2 'Report of the Commissioners Appointed to Inquire into the State of Popular Education in England', *Parliamentary Papers*, 21 (1861), pp. 103–4.

3 'Middle Class Schools for Girls', *EWJ*, November 1860.

4 James Heywood (1810–97) a Uni-tarian, barred from taking a degree from Cambridge, and MP for North Lancashire (1847–57).

5 Louisa, Lady Goldsmid (1819–1901) was the wife of Sir Francis Goldsmid, a barrister and MP.

6 Anne Clough had run a school for children in Ambleside in Cumbria but, after meeting Barbara, had become interested in higher educa-tion for women. In 1867 she had become secretary of the North of England Council for Promoting the Higher Education of Women.

7 Oxford followed in 1870.

8 Burton, p. 163.

9 Stephen, p. 149.

10 Ibid., pp. 150–1. John Westlake spotted that Emily was promising that there would be university examinations of an advanced charac-ter, yet no university had promised them. This was immediately revised. John Westlake (1828–1913) fellow of Trinity College, Cambridge 1851–60; Professor of International Law 1888–1908; member of the International Court of Arbitration 1900–6.

11 EDFC, pp. 538–9.

12 Barbara's name did not appear as a member of the Executive Commit-tee until 16 February 1869.

13 This first committee included Lady Stanley of Alderley, Lady Gold-smid, Lady Hobart, the Dean of Canterbury, James Bryce, Mrs Rus-sell Gurney, James Heywood, G.W. Hastings, Mrs Manning, H.J. Roby, H.R. Tomkinson, Revd Sedley Tay-lor and Emily Davies.

14 See Daphne Bennett, *Emily Davies and the Liberation of Women 1830–1921* (London, 1990) which is so partisan that Barbara's role in the founding of Girton College is unreasonably diminished.

15 EDFC, pp. 540–1.

16 *GEL*, VIII, 409.

17 EDFC, p. 163.

18 Resolution 3 (9 November 1867) quoted in Stephen, p. 164.

19 *GEL*, IV, 401.

20 4 March 1868, GEL, VIII, 414.

21 Quoted in Bennett, *Emily Davies*, p. 90.

22 March 1868, Stephen, p. 169.

23 Burton, p. 170.

24 Girton College Reports, 1891–1905.

25 *GEL*, IV, 401.

26 ML: 'A cluster of great names, both living and dead, rush to our memo-ries in evidence that women can produce novels not only fine, but among the very finest; – novels, too, that have a precious speciality, lying quite apart from masculine aptitudes and experience': 'Silly Novels by Lady Novelists', *Westminster Review*, October 1856.

27 Henry Sidgwick (1838–1900) fellow of Trinity College, Cambridge 1859–69; Knightsbridge Professor of Moral Philosophy 1883–1900.

28 Mary Ewart (1831–1911) Governor of the North London Collegiate School; member of Bedford College Council; left £10,000 to Somerville College, Oxford, to be devoted to scholarships.

29 Bennett, *Emily Davies*, p. 91.

30 Ibid., p. 93.

31 Ibid., p. 105.

32 Stephen, p. 207.

33 Ibid., p. 211.

34 Ibid., p. 215.

35 Ibid., p. 209.

36 MT 12/50.

37 Ibid.

38 ALCF.

39 EB Columbia.

40 MT 12/50.

41 Bennett, *Emily Davies*, p. 110.

42 Stephen, p. 227.

43 *Letters of Dante Gabriel Rossetti*, ed O. Doughty and J.R. Wall, 4 vols (Oxford, 1965–7) II, p. 816.

44 Ibid., p. 819.

45 Julia Wedgwood (1833–1913), was the author of a novel, *Framleigh Hall* 3 vols. (London, 1888) and *John Wesley and the Evangelical Reaction of the 18th Century* (London, 1870). Later she wrote *The Moral Idea* (London, 1888) and *The Message of Israel* (London, 1894).

46 Stephen, p. 229.

47 Sir John Robert Seeley (1834–95), Professor of Modern History at Cambridge.

48 Stephen, p. 240.

49 Ibid., p. 246.

50 Ibid., p. 247.

51 Henry Moore (1831–95).

52 Yale.

53 A Blandford Square insurance policy document of 1879 shows that Barbara owned two paintings by Henry Moore, *Sea – Hastings* and *Sand and Sea*, both valued at £50: GLRO.

54 Reginald Thompson (1834–1912), educated at Trinity College, Cambridge, and trained as a doctor at St George's Hospital, London.

55 A.M.W. Stirling, *William de Morgan and his Wife* (London, 1922) p. 86. In 1874 Reginald was to marry William de Morgan's sister, Annie.

56 EB Congress.

57 Stephen, pp. 47–8.

58 Ibid., p. 239.

59 *Letters to WA*, p. 85.

60 Stephen, p. 243.

61 Ibid., p. 244.

62 8 February 1873; M.C. Bradbrook, *'That Infidel Place': A Short History of Girton College* (London, 1969) p. 31.

63 Stephen, p. 255.

64 15 November 1870; ibid., p. 250.

65 Ibid., p. 260.

66 Yale.

67 Stephen, p. 281.

68 Hcox 1/181.

CHAPTER 15: THE GIRTON YEARS

1 Prudence Waterhouse, *A Victorian Monument: The Buildings of Girton College* (Cambridge, 1990) pp. 12–13.

2 Ibid., p. 4.

3 Burton, p. 164.

4 Waterhouse, *Victorian Monument*, pp. 22–3.

5 Daphne Bennett, *Emily Davies and the Liberation of Women* (London, 1990) p. 146.

6 Stephen, p. 286.

7 Ibid., pp. 290–1.

8 ED to BLSB, 12 June 1874: Stephen, pp. 293–4.

9 Ibid., p. 295.

10 Ibid., p. 295.

11 Norman Moore (1847–1922).

12 Hcox 1/180.

13 Stephen, p. 302.

14 She went on to be the first headmistress of St Leonard's School, St Andrews, and was made a Dame of the British Empire for her service to girls' education.

15 M.C. Bradbrook, *'That Infidel Place': A Short History of Girton College* (London, 1969) p. 31.

16 Ibid., p. 284.

17 Ibid., pp. 301–2.

18 Hcox 2/201; the *Una* was an American feminist journal.

19 Hcox 2/201.

20 Julia Blackburn, *Charles Waterton* (London, 1989).

21 Hcox 2/201.

22 Hcox 1/136 and 1/138.

23 Hcox 1/122.

24 Hcox 1/154.

25 She died at Yotes Court and was buried in the churchyard at Fordcombe Green, Kent.

26 *GEL*, IX, 81.

27 Hcox 1/160.
28 13 September 1875, Hcox 1/176.
29 Hercules Brabazon Brabazon (1821–1906), the son of Hercules Sharpe, a man of considerable means of County Durham, and of Ann Brabazon of County Mayo.
30 In 1891 Wilson Steer proposed him as a member of the New English Art Club, following which it was *de rigueur* to exhibit. His one-man show at the Goupil Gallery in Bond Street in December 1892 led the critics to hail him as Turner's closest successor. His work was much admired by other artists, especially Sickert, Steer and Sargent. See C. Lewis Hind, *Hercules Brabazon Brabazon* (London, 1912) and *Hercules Brabazon Brabazon (1821–1906) and the New English Art Club*, exhibition catalogue (London, 1986).
31 Gertrude Jekyll (1843–92).
32 Hcox 1/159.
33 Ibid.
34 Hcox 1/172.
35 Frederick Walker (1840–76). See Claude Phillips, *Frederick Walker and His Works* (London, 1894).
36 *Life and Letters of Frederick Walker*, ed. John Marks (London, 1896) p. 290.
37 Ibid., p. 288.
38 Marianne North (1830–90).
39 BMC.
40 *A Vision of Eden: The Life and Work of Marianne North*, ed. Graham Bateman (London, 1980).
41 See Gillian Sutherland, 'Emily Davies, the Sidgwicks and the Education of Women in Cambridge', in *Cambridge Minds*, ed. Richard Mason (Cambridge, 1995).
42 Rosemary Ashton, *Little Germany: German Refugees in Victorian Britain* (Oxford, 1989) p. 172. Blind's stepdaughter, Mathilde (1841–96), wrote the first biography of George Eliot in the 'Eminent Women' series (1884).
43 Sharp, pp. 30–1.
44 Ibid., p. 33.
45 CSS.
46 *Letters to WA*, p. 89.
47 Sharp, p. 34.
48 Ibid.
49 Ibid., p. 46.
50 Ibid., p. 45.
51 Ibid.
52 See Pam Hirsch, 'Women and Jews in Daniel Deronda', in *The George Eliot Review* (Coventry, 1994).
53 Eliza Orme to Helen Taylor, MT, vol. 14.
54 *GEL*, VI, 170.
55 Eliza Orme to Helen Taylor, MT, vol. 14.
56 Sharp, p. 38.
57 *GEL*, VI, 235.
58 CSS.
59 Sharp, p. 49.
60 Ibid.
61 Barbara had asked Katie to befriend one of the Hitchin students who lived near to the Scott household in London. The student, Rachel Cook, married Charles Scott in May 1874.
62 Hcox 1/2.
63 This picture is at Girton College.
64 I am grateful to Katherine Heron for supplying me with copies of the deeds to the Poor House.
65 The Poor House (and her Spanish pottery) Barbara left to Gertrude Jekyll, which confirms that the house at Zennor was conceived of, first and foremost, as a house for artists. The tradition has continued. After Jekyll's day, Alice Westlake, Elizabeth Andrews, Alethea Garstin and Delia Heron have all lived and worked there.
66 Sharp, pp. 49–50.
67 Ibid., pp. 57–8.
68 See Philip Gaskell, *Morvern Transformed* (Cambridge, 1996).
69 Hcox 1/194.
70 Marie Belloc-Lowndes (1868–1947) a novelist; Hilaire Belloc (1870–1953) writer of essays, novels and verse.
71 Mrs Belloc-Lowndes, *Where Love and Friendship Dwelt* (London, 1943) p. 2.

72 Hcox 1/272.
73 Hcox 1/236.
74 Hcox 1/209.
75 The birth certificate records the father's name as Shadrach Clements.
76 EB Columbia.
77 Ibid.
78 BLSB to Amy Leigh Smith; Hcox 1/236.
79 CSS.
80 Hcox 1/394.
81 Hcox 1/236.
82 Hcox 1/239.
83 Hcox 1/242.

CHAPTER 16: REDUCED POWERS

1 Hcox 1/225.
2 Sharp, p. 60.
3 Hcox 2/101.
4 Hcox 2/77.
5 Hcox 1/409.
6 Hertha to Amy Leigh Smith, 24 July 1877: Hcox 1/12.
7 Hcox 1/13.
8 GEL, VI, 419–20. In the same letter she noted that Bessie's mother had died aged eighty on 10 October.
9 Sharp, p. 66.
10 31 January 1878: Yale.
11 Unpublished letter, reproduced by kind permission of Catherine Barnes, New York.
12 Minutes of the South Kensington Museum (now the Victoria and Albert Musuem).
13 Plans by Gertrude Jekyll for BLSB are in Documents Collection, College of Environmental Design, University of California, Berkeley.
14 Hcox 1/10.
15 Hcox 1/278.
16 Hcox 1/245.
17 Hcox 1/288.
18 GEL, VII, 71.
19 Ibid., 84.
20 Hcox 1/134.
21 GEL, VI, 93.
22 GEL, VII, 128.
23 The first draft was altered to state that 'Persons of either sex shall be eligible for the election to the Studentship'. Barbara was busily promoting a 'Miss Tomlinson' as a possible candidate. GEL, VII, 183–4.
24 Quoted in Amice Lee, Laurels & Rosemary, p. 301.
25 CSS, ff. 123–4.
26 Stephen, p. 306.
27 Emily Greatorex was a friend of Barbara's latter years. She lived at 1, Cumberland Place, Regent's Park, London, and accompanied Barbara on painting expeditions (Burton, p. 211). She took an interest in Hertha's career (Sharp, p. 92).
28 The 'loan' was largely a gift from Ottilie Blind: GEL, VII, 247–8.
29 Hcox 1/357.
30 GEL, VII, 247–8.
31 Sharp, p. 84.
32 GEL, VII, 247–8.
33 See Carol Gilligan's account of the importance of female role models to secondary schoolgirls: 'If women can stay in the gaze of girls so that girls do not have to look and not see . . . if women can sustain girls' gaze and respond to girls' voices, then perhaps as Woolf envisioned, "the opportunity will come and the dead poet who is Shakespeare's sister will put on the body which she has so often laid down and find it possible to live and write her poetry" (Woolf, 1928)' in the preface to Making Connections: the Relational Worlds of Adolescent Girls at Emma Willard School, ed. Carol Gilligan, Nona P. Lyons and Trudy J. Hanmer (Cambridge, Mass., 1990).
34 GEL, VII, 265.
35 Yale.
36 GEL, VII, 272–3.
37 Ibid., 290–1.
38 Ibid., 287.
39 Hcox 1/346.
40 Hcox 1/347, 1/350. It was engraved in 1880: see Hcox 1/351. This portrait now hangs in Girton dining hall with the Rudolf Lehmann portrait of Emily Davies.
41 Hcox 1/353.

42 *GEL*, VII, 332–3.

43 Gordon S. Haight, *George Eliot* (Oxford, 1967) p. 550.

44 Hcox, 1/92. The other 'great people' BLSB named were Mr Elwin and Gertrude Jekyll.

45 *Inferno* (I, 79–80); it translates as 'that fountain which spreads forth so broad a river of speech'.

46 Sharp, p. 88.

47 Ibid.

48 Bessie Belloc's daughter, Marie, and Elizabeth Garrett Anderson's daughter, Louisa.

49 Although BLSB did not live to see it, Rosalind Shore Smith's younger sister, Barbara (married name Lady Stephen), went up to study history at Girton, from 1891 to 1894, and became the college's historiographer.

50 Hcox 1/332.

51 GLRO: E/LS/10.

52 See Francis Spufford, *I May Be Some Time* (London, 1996).

53 See Arthur G. Credland, 'Benjamin Leigh Smith: a forgotten pioneer', *Polar Record*, 20, no. 125, (1980).

54 Mary Howitt, *An Autobiography*, ed. Margaret Howitt, 2 vols (London, 1889) II, 321.

55 CSS.

56 Fanny Metcalfe, member of Girton College 1872–96, had founded a boarding school for girls in Hendon.

57 London University had opened its degrees to women in 1878.

58 Stephen, p. 301.

59 Ronald Grey and Ernest Frankl, *Cambridge Gardens* (Cambridge, 1984) pp. 24–8.

60 Hcox 1/14.

61 Hcox 1/13.

62 CSS.

63 Hcox 1/130.

64 Hcox 2/203.

65 In a private collection.

66 Emily Osborn (1834–1913); see *Art Journal*, 1864.

67 Girton College Executive Committee Minute Books, IX, 23 October 1885, 85.

68 *English Art in 1884*, illustrated by facsimile sketches by the artists (New York, 1885).

69 Girton College . . . Minutes, IX, 23 October 1885.

70 Howitt, *An Autobiography*, I, xi.

71 Matilda Betham-Edwards, *In French-Africa* (London, 1912) p. 315.

72 Hcox 1/16.

73 Hcox 1/49.

74 Hcox 2/209.

75 Hcox 2/227.

76 Hcox 1/52.

77 Hcox 1/391.

78 Hcox 2/226.

CHAPTER 17: THE LAST YEARS

1 Hcox 2/220.

2 Hcox 1/134.

3 Sharp, pp. 108–9.

4 Matilda Chaplin (1846–71) had married Will Ayrton in 1871 and had gone with him to Japan (1873–8), where she founded a school for midwives. She fought a long sad battle against consumption. She spent the winter of 1877–8 in Hyères, where, by coincidence, she was treated by Elizabeth Blackwell. Matilda recovered sufficiently to qualify as an MD in Paris in 1879, but died of consumption in 1883.

5 By one of those odd quirks of fate, whereas Hertha had married out, her stepdaughter, Edith Ayrton, married *into* the Jewish faith when she married the writer, Israel Zangwill, an impassioned advocate of the need for a Jewish homeland; See Justine Hopkins, *Michael Ayrton: A Biography* (London, 1994).

6 In a second codicil to her will made in November 1885 BLSB left him an annuity of £50. After her death he married Eliza Sanderson (see Ransom's will, Somerset House).

7 Diary, EB Congress.

8 *Munk's Roll: Lives of the Fellows of the Royal College of Physicians of London 1826–1925* (London, 1955).

9 Her father, Frederick William Sellers, was wine merchant in Paddington and her mother a Catholic Frenchwoman who had died in 1871.
10 Sharp, pp. 95–6.
11 Eugénie Sellers (1860–1943) went on to become assistant director of the British School in Rome; see *Girton Review*, Michaelmas Term 1943 and Gladys Scott Thomson, *Mrs Arthur Strong: A Memoir* (London, 1949). Sellers Papers, Girton College.
12 *Punch*, 5 June 1875.
13 Hcox 2/145.
14 Hcox 2/133.
15 CSS, ff. 123–4.
16 Hcox 2/154.
17 Betty Massingham, *Gertrude Jekyll* (Aylesbury, 1987) p. 12.
18 Hcox 1/58.
19 Ibid.
20 Hcox 1/59.
21 Hcox 1/60.
22 Hcox 2/262.
23 Girton College Executive Committee Minute Books.
24 Sharp, p. 126.
25 Eliza Sanderson to EB, 24 July 1891; EB Radcliffe. Elizabeth Blackwell managed his trust fund, which was designed to provide him with sufficient capital to buy a business when he was twenty-one. In 1895 he emigrated to Johannesburg where he worked for Philip Amm & Sons, importers of teas and coffees, and in 1896 he arranged to have his capital sent out. He married Wilhelmina (?) with whom he had four children. After her death in 1832 he married Hilda Kangela. His death certificate records that he was a butcher in Durban, and died in 1936 aged sixty-eight. As he had not left a will, his second wife inherited his estate and put his children into orphanages in Maritzburg: the three boys in a boys' home, and the only girl into a girls' home.
26 Hcox 1/42.
27 Sharp, p. 93.

28 Ibid., p. 126.

CHAPTER 18: THE LEGACY

1 The *Englishwoman's Review*, 15 July 1891.
2 Private collection.
3 She left £10,000 to Girton College and £1,000 to Bedford College; annuities of £40 a year to Elizabeth Blackwell, Hertha Marks and Jessie White Mario; £50 a year to William Ransom and £20 a year to Sarah Lewin as well as sums of £500 to Bessie, £300 to Florence Davenport Hill, £100 to Emily Greatorex, £100 to Henry Moore, £100 to Milly Betham-Edwards, £500 to Reginald Thompson, £300 to John Thornely, £100 to Eliza Sanderson and £200 to Emma Payton.
4 Obituary in *The Times*, 6 January 1913.
5 Thomas Parkin 'Cuttings' at Hastings Museum and Art Gallery.
6 Elizabeth K. Helsinger, Robin Lauterbach Sheets and William Veeder, *The Woman Question in Britain and America 1837 to 1883* 3 vols (Manchester, 1983).
7 Bessie Rayner Parkes, *A Passing World* (London, 1897), p. 22.
8 Deborah Cherry, *Painting Women* (London, 1993). Description of Portraits, 11, no. 40, National Portrait Gallery archives.
9 Letter from ALS to the curator at Hastings Museum and Art Gallery.
10 The picture Milicent Moore removed is now missing; the only reproduction of it is in Helen Blackburn, *Women's Suffrage: A Record of the Women's Suffrage Movement* (London, 1902). Hastings Museum gave 'their' Emily Osborn painting of Barbara Bodichon to Girton in 1963.
11 *Punch* published a cartoon (2 July 1887) showing Mr Punch admitting Agneta to a first-class train carriage marked 'Ladies only'.

12 The University of Oxford admitted women to full membership in 1918.

13 *GEL*, V, 41.

14 Stephen, p. 48.

15 *GEL*, VII, 315.

16 See Joan Mason, 'Hertha Ayrton and the Admission of Women to the Royal Society of London', in *Notes and Records of the Royal Society* (London, 1991) and Marjorie Malley, 'Hertha Ayrton', in the *Dictionary of Scientific Biography* (New York, 1990).

17 Sharp, p. 233.

18 Edith Zangwill, *The Call* (Newcastle, 1924).

BIBLIOGRAPHY

Writings by Barbara Leigh Smith Bodichon

Articles by 'Esculapius' in *Hastings and St Leonard News* (1848).

A Brief Summary in Plain Language, of the Most Important Laws concerning Women (1854; London, 1869).

Women and Work (London, 1857).

'Submission to the Report of the Commissioners Appointed to Inquire into the State of Popular Education' (1858), *Parliamentary Papers*, 21 (London, 1861) pp. 221–7.

'Female Education in the Middle Classes', *English Woman's Journal* (London, June 1858) pp. 217–27.

Algeria Considered as a Winter Residence for the English, with Eugène Bodichon, published at the offices of the *English Woman's Journal* (London, 1858).

'Slavery in America', *English Woman's Journal*, 2 (London, October 1858) pp. 94–100.

'An American School', *English Woman's Journal*, 2 (London, November 1858) pp. 198–200.

'Slave Preaching', *English Woman's Journal* (London, March 1860) pp. 87–94.

'Algiers: first impressions', *English Woman's Journal*, 6 (London, September 1860) pp. 21–32.

'Middle Class Schools for Girls', *English Woman's Journal*, 6 (London, November 1860) pp. 168–77.

'Slavery in the South', *English Woman's Journal*, (London, October, November, December 1861) pp.111–18; 179–87; 261–66.

'Painted Glass Windows Executed by the Carmelite Nuns of Mans', *English Woman's Journal*, (London, January 1862), pp. 316–25.

'Of those who are the property of others, and of the great power that holds others as property', *English Woman's Journal*, 10 (London, February 1863) pp. 370–81.

'Cleopatra's Daughter, St Marciana, Mama Marabout and Other

Algerian Women', *English Woman's Journal*, 10 (London, February 1863) pp. 404–16.
'Six Weeks in la Chère Petite Bretagne', *English Woman's Journal*, 11 (London, May 1863) pp. 188–97.
'Accomplices', *English Woman's Journal*, 12 (London, February 1864) pp. 394–400.
'Kabyle Pottery', *The Art Journal* (London, February, 1865) pp. 45–6.
'Reasons for the Enfranchisement of Women', paper presented at the Social Science Association, London, 1866.
Objections to the Enfranchisement of Women Considered (London, 1866)
'A Dull Life', *Macmillan's Magazine*, 74 (London, May 1867) pp. 47–53.
Reasons for and against the Enfranchisement of Women (London, 1869).
'An Easy Railway Journey in Spain, *Temple Bar*, 25 (London, January 1869), pp. 240–49.

Select Bibliography of Works Consulted

Ackerman, Gerald M., *Les Orientalistes de l'Ecole Britannique* (Paris, 1991).
Adams, Steven, *The Barbizon School and the Origins of Impressionism* (London, 1994).
Allingham, William, *A Diary* (Harmondsworth, 1985).
Annan, Noel, 'The Intellectual Aristocracy', in *Studies in Social History*, ed. J.H. Plumb (London, New York and Toronto, 1955).
The Arabian Nights Entertainments, trans. Jonathan Scott, 6 vols (London, 1811).
Ashton, Rosemary *The German Idea: Four English Writers and the Reception of German Thought 1800–1860* (Cambridge, 1980); *G.H. Lewes: A Life* (Oxford, 1991); *Little Germany: German Refugees in Victorian Britain* (Oxford, 1986); *George Eliot: A Life* (Harmondsworth, 1996).
Barrett, Dorothea, *Vocation and Desire: George Eliot's Heroines* (London, 1989).
Beer, Gillian, *Darwin's Plots: Evolutionary Narrative in Darwin, George Eliot and Nineteenth Century Fiction* (1983; London, 1985); *George Eliot* (Brighton, 1986).
Belloc-Lowndes, Mrs: *'I Too Have Lived in Arcadia': a Record of Love and Childhood* (London, 1941); *Where Love and Friendship Dwelt* (London, 1943).
Bénézit, E., *Dictionnaire critique et documentaire des peintres, sculpteurs, graveurs, dessinateurs* (Paris, 1924).

Bennett, Daphne, *Emily Davies and the Liberation of Women 1830–1921* (London, 1990).

Betham-Edwards, Matilda: *A Winter with the Swallows* (London, 1867); *Reminiscences* (London, 1898); *Friendly Faces of Three Nationalities* (London, 1911); *In French-Africa* (London, 1912); *Mid-Victorian Memories* (London, 1919).

Blackburn, Helen, *Women's Suffrage: A Record of the Women's Suffrage Movement* (London, 1902).

Blackburn, Julia, *Charles Waterton* (London, 1989).

Blackwell, Elizabeth: *Medical Responsibility in Relation to the Contagious Diseases Acts* (London 1897); *Opening the Medical Profession to Women* (New York, 1977).

Blake, William, *Blake: Complete Writings*, ed. Geoffrey Keynes (1966; Oxford, 1976).

Bodichon, Eugène, *Considerations sur L'Algérie* (Paris, 1845); *Etudes sur l'Algérie et l'Afrique* (privately printed, Algiers, 1847); *De l'Humanité*, Part 1 (Algiers, 1852), Part 2 (Geneva 1853); *De l'Humanité* (Brussels: Lacroix, 1866); *Of Humanity*, an abridged translation (London, 1859); 'Napoleon the First', extract printed in *Temple Bar*, November 1873.

Brabazon, Hercules, 'Madame Bodichon's Pictures at the Museum', *Hastings Observer*, 13 August 1892.

Bray, Charles, *Phases of Opinion and Experience during a Long Life: An Autobiography* (London, 1885).

Bremer, Frederika, *Hertha*, trans. by Mary Howitt (1846; London, 1856).

Browning, Elizabeth Barrett, *Aurora Leigh* (1857; London, 1978).

Buckley, Jessie K., *Joseph Parkes of Birmingham* (London, 1926).

Burstyn, Joan N., *Victorian Education and the Ideal of Womanhood* (1980; New Brunswick, NJ, 1984).

Burton, Hester, *Barbara Bodichon 1827–1891* (London, 1949).

Callen, Anthea, *Angel in the Studio: Women in the Arts and Crafts Movement 1870–1914* (London, 1879).

Chadwick, Whitney, *Women, Art and Society* (London, 1990).

Cherry, Deborah, *Painting Women: Victorian Women Artists*, art gallery catalogue (Rochdale, 1987); *Painting Women* (London, 1993).

Clark, Kenneth, *Landscape into Art* (1949; London, 1986).

Clarke, Michael, *Corot and the Art of Landscape* (London, 1991).

Clayton, Ellen C., *English Female Artists*, 2 vols (London, 1876).

Clough, Arthur, *Correspondence of Arthur Hugh Clough*, ed. Frederick L. Mulhauser, 2 vols. (Oxford, 1957).

Clough, Blanche Athena, *A Memoir of Anne Jemima Clough* (London, 1897).

Collini, Stefan, *Public Moralists: Political Thought and Intellectual Life in Britain 1850–1930* (Oxford, 1991).

Cookson, J.E., *The Friends of Peace: Anti-war Liberalism in England 1793–1815* (Cambridge, 1982).

Crabbe, John: 'An Artist Divided: the forgotten talent of Barbara Bodichon, a very remarkable Victorian', *Apollo*, May 1981; 'Feminist with a Paintbrush: Barbara Leigh Smith Bodichon 1827–91', *Women Artists Slide Library Journal*, 22 (April/May 1988); 'Wild Weather in Watercolour', *Country Life*, 2 March, 1989; 'Hidden by History: Barbara Bodichon, an artist obscured for a century by her feminist image', *Watercolours, Drawings and Prints*, spring 1991.

Crompton, Margaret, *George Eliot: The Woman* (New York, 1960).

Daly, Gay, *Pre-Raphaelites in Love* (Glasgow, 1990).

Daniels, Elizabeth Adams, *Jessie White Mario: Risorgimento Revolutionary* (Athens, Ohio, 1972).

Davies, Emily, *The Higher Education of Women* (1866; London, 1988).

Davis, R.W., 'The Strategy of "Dissent" in the Repeal Campaign, 1820–1828', *Journal of Modern History*, 38, no. 4 (December 1966); *Dissent in Politics* (London, 1971).

Darley, Gillian, *Octavia Hill: A Life* (London, 1990).

David, Deirdre, *Intellectual Women and Victorian Patriarchy* (Ithaca, NY, 1987).

Davidoff, Leonore, *The Best Circles* (1973; London, 1986); Davidoff and Catherine Hall, *Family Fortunes: Men and Women of the English Middle Class 1780–1850* (London, 1987).

Dodd, Valerie A., *George Eliot: An Intellectual Life* (Basingstoke, 1990).

Eliot, George, *Adam Bede* (1859; London, 1962); *The Mill on the Floss* (1860; Harmondsworth, 1979); *Romola* (1863; Harmondsworth, 1980); *Middlemarch* (1871–2); *Daniel Deronda* (1876; Harmondsworth, 1967); *Essays of George Eliot*, ed. Thomas Pinney (London, 1968); *Collected Poems*, ed. Lucien Jenkins (London, 1989).

Faderman, Lillian, *Surpassing the Love of Men* (London, 1977).

Festing, Sally, *Gertrude Jekyll* (Harmondsworth, 1991).

Flint, Kate, *The Woman Reader 1837–1914* (Oxford, 1995).

Forster, Margaret, *Significant Sisters: The Grassroots of Active Feminism 1839–1939* (New York, 1985).

Fredeman, William E., 'Emily Faithfull and the Victoria Press: an experiment in sociological bibliography', *The Library*, 5th series, 29 (June 1974).

Gandy, *Barbara Bodichon 1827–1891*, centenary exhibition catalogue ed.

Frances Gandy, Kate Perry and Peter Sparks (Girton College, Cambridge, 1991).

Gaskell, Elizabeth, *The Letters of Mrs Gaskell*, ed. J.A.V. Chapple and J.A. Pollard, (Manchester, 1966).

Gaze, Delia (ed.) *Dictionary of Women Artists* (London and Chicago, 1997).

Gifford, Zerbanoo, *Thomas Clarkson and the Campaign against Slavery* (Fakenham, Norfolk, 1996).

Gillett, Paula, *The Victorian Painter's World* (Gloucester, 1990).

Gilligan, Carol, *In a Different Voice: Psychological Theory and Women's Development* (Cambridge, Mass. and London, 1982).

Glendinning, Victoria, *A Suppressed Cry* (London, 1969).

Goethe, Johann Wolfgang von, *Wilhelm Meister's Years of Apprenticeship*, trans. H.M. Waidson (London, 1977).

Goldman, Lawrence, 'The Social Science Association, 1857–1886: a context for mid-Victorian Liberalism', *English Historical Review*, 101, (1986).

Goodwin, Albert, *The Friends of Liberty: the English Democratic Movement in the Age of the French Revolution* (London, 1979).

Greer, Germaine, *The Obstacle Race: The Fortunes of Women Painters and Their Work* (New York, 1979).

Haight, G.S., *George Eliot and John Chapman: with Chapman's Diaries* (New Haven, 1940); *George Eliot: A Biography* (Oxford, 1968).

Hanson, Lawrence and Elizabeth, *Marian Evans and George Eliot* (Oxford, 1952).

Helsinger: Elizabeth K., 'Robin Lauterbach Sheets and William Veeder', in *The Woman Question in Britain and America 1837 to 1883*, 3 vols. (Manchester, 1983).

Hemming, Charles, *British Landscape Painters* (London, 1989).

Herstein, Sheila, *A Mid-Victorian Feminist – Barbara Leigh Smith Bodichon* (New Haven and London, 1985).

Hind, C. Lewis, *Hercules Brabazon Brabazon* (London, 1912).

Hirsch, Pam, 'Barbara Leigh Smith Bodichon and George Eliot: an examination of their work and friendship'. Unpublished dissertation, Anglia Polytechnic University in collaboration with the University of Essex, 1992; 'Women and Jews in Daniel Deronda', in *The George Eliot Review* (Coventry, 1994); 'Barbara Leigh Smith Bodichon: artist and activist', in *Women in the Victorian Art World*, ed. Clarissa Campbell Orr (Manchester, 1995); 'Gender Negotiations in Nineteenth Century Women's Autobiographical Writing', in *The Uses of Autobiography*, ed. Julia Swindells (London, 1995); 'Mary Wollstonecraft: a problematic legacy', in *Wollstonecraft's Daughters*, ed. Clarissa Campbell Orr (Manchester, 1996); 'Charlotte Brontë and George Sand: the influence of female Romanticism', in Brontë Society *Transactions*, 21, part 6 (1996).

Holcombe, Lee, *Victorian Ladies at Work: Middle-class Working Women in England and Wales 1850–1914* (Newton Abbot, 1973); *Wives and Property: Reform of the Married Women's Property Law in Nineteenth Century England* (Oxford, 1983).

Holt, Raymond V., *The Unitarian Contribution to Social Progress* (1938; London, 1952).

Hopkins, Justine, *Michael Ayrton: A Biography* (London, 1994).

Howitt, Anna Mary, 'The Sisters in Art', *Illustrated Exhibitor and Magazine of Art* in seven sections, July 1852; *An Art-Student in Munich*, 2 vols (London, 1853).

Howitt, Mary, *An Autobiography*, ed. Margaret Howitt, 2 vols (London, 1889).

Hudson, Derek, *Munby: Man of Two Worlds. The Life and Diaries of Arthur J. Munby* (London, 1972).

Hunt, Felicity (ed.), *Lessons for Life: The Schooling of Girls and Women 1850–1950* (Oxford, 1987).

Jackson, Margaret, *The Real Facts of Life* (London, 1994).

Jameson, Anna, *Shakespeare's Heroines* (1832; London, 1897); *The Poetry of Sacred and Legendary Art* (London, 1850); *Legends of the Madonna* (London, 1857); *Sisters of Charity and the Communion of Labour* (London, 1859).

Jardin, André and Tudesq, André-Jean, *Restoration and Reaction 1815–1848*, trans. Elborg Forster (Cambridge, 1988).

Jones, E.E.C., *As I Remember* (London, 1922).

Jordan, Elaine, *Alfred Tennyson* (Cambridge, 1988).

Jordanova, Ludmilla, *Sexual Visions: Images of Gender in Science and Medicine between the Eighteenth and Twentieth Centuries* (Madison, Wisconsin, 1989).

Kamm, Josephine, *John Stuart Mill in Love* (London, 1977).

Kingsley Kent, Susan, *Sex and Suffrage in Britain 1860–1914* (London, 1990).

Lacey, Candida Ann (ed.), *Barbara Leigh Smith Bodichon and the Langham Place Group* (New York and London, 1987).

Leach, Joseph, *Bright Particular Star: The Life and Times of Charlotte Cushman* (New Haven, 1970).

Lerner, Gerda, *The Majority Finds Its Past: Placing Women in History* (Oxford, 1981).

Levine, Philippa, *Victorian Feminism 1850–1900* (London, 1987).

Lewes, George Henry, *The Life and Works of Goethe*, 3 vols (New York, 1855); *The Biographical History of Philosophy: from its Origins in Greece down to the Present Day* (London, 1857).

Lorcin, Patricia M., *Imperial Identities: Stereotyping, Prejudice and Race in Colonial Algeria* (London, 1995).

Maas, Jeremy, *Gambart, Prince of the Victorian Art World* (London, 1975).

McAleer, Edward C. (ed.), *Dearest Isa: Robert Browning's Letters to Isabella Blagdon* (Austin Texas, 1951).

McCobb, A., *George Eliot's Knowledge of German Life and Letters* (Salzburg, 1982).

McWilliams-Tullberg, Rita, *Women at Cambridge: A Men's University – Though of a Mixed Type* (London, 1975).

Malleson, Elizabeth, *Autobiographical Notes* (printed for private circulation, 1926).

Manton, Jo, *Elizabeth Garrett Anderson* (London, 1966).

Marsh, Jan, *Pre-Raphaelite Sisterhood* (London, 1985); *Jane and May Morris* (London, 1986); *The Legend of Elizabeth Siddal* (London, 1989); Jan Marsh and Pamela Gerrish Nunn, *Women Artists and the Pre-Raphaelite Movement* (London, 1989); *The Pre-Raphaelites: Their Lives in Letters and Diaries* (London, 1996).

Martineau, Harriet, *Society in America* (New York, 1837); *Deerbrook* (1839; London, 1983); *Household Education* (London, 1849); *The Positive Philosophy*, freely translated and condensed by Harriet Martineau (New York, 1855); 'Female Industry', *Edinburgh Review*, 109 (April 1859) pp. 293–336; 'Middle-class Education in England: Girls', *Cornhill Magazine*, 10 (1864).

Mason, Joan, 'Hertha Ayrton and the Admission of Women to the Royal Society of London', *Notes and Records of the Royal Society*, London, 1991.

Massingham, Betty, *Gertrude Jekyll* (Aylesbury, 1987).

Matthews, Jacquie, 'Barbara Bodichon: integrity in diversity (1827–1891)', in *Feminist Theorists*, ed. Dale Spender (London, 1983).

Mill, John Stuart, *Autobiography* (1873; New York, 1964); *Dissertations and Discussions, Political, Philosophical and Historical*, 4 vols (1859; London, 1875); *The Subjection of Women* (1859; London, 1906).

Moore, Andrew W., *The Norwich School of Artists* (Norwich, 1985).

Morgan, A.D.F., 'A Fine Art in Gardening: context, influences and realisation in the life and work of Miss Jekyll', RIBA thesis, School of Architecture, Portsmouth Polytechnic, 1974.

Morley, John, Review of *The Social and Political Dependence of Women* (London, 1867), *Fortnightly Review*, June 1867.

Munford, W.A., *William Ewart 1798–1869: Portrait of a Radical* (London, 1960).

Newall, Christopher, *Victorian Watercolours* (Oxford, 1987).

Niccol, John, *Dante Gabriel Rossetti* (New York, 1976).

Nightingale, Florence, *Ever Yours, Florence Nightingale: Selected Letters*, ed. M. Vicinus and B. Nergaard (London, 1989); *Florence Nightingale: Letters from the Crimea 1854–1856*, ed. Sue M. Goldie (New York, 1997).

Nisbet, Robert A., *The Sociological Tradition* (London, 1967).

North, Marianne, *A Vision of Eden: The Life and Work of Marianne North*, ed. Graham Bateman (London, 1980).

Nunn, Pamela Gerrish, *Canvassing* (London, 1986); *Victorian Women Artists* (London, 1987).

Oliphant, Margaret, 'The Great Unrepresented', *Blackwood's Edinburgh Magazine*, 100 (September 1866), pp. 367–79.

Parkes, Bessie Rayner, *Poems* (London, 1852; repr. with extra poems London, 1855); *Summer Sketches and Other Poems* (London, 1855); *Remarks on the Education of Girls, with Reference to the Social, Legal and Industrial Position of Women in the Present Day* (London, 1856); *Essays on Women's Work* (London, 1865); 'A Review of the Last Six Years', *English Woman's Journal*, 12 (February 1864); 'The Use of a Special Periodical', *Alexandra Magazine and English Woman's Journal*, 1 (September 1865); 'A Year's Experience in Women's Work', *English Woman's Journal*, 6 (October 1860); 'Dorothea Casaubon and George Eliot', *Contemporary Review*, 65 (February 1894); *A Passing World* (London, 1897).

Patmore, Coventry, *The Angel in the House* (London, 1854).

Peterson, Karen and Wilson, J.J., *Women Artists: Recognition and Reappraisal from the Early Middle Ages to the Twentieth Century* (London, 1978).

Phillips, Claude, *Frederick Walker and His Works* (London, 1894).

Pollock, Griselda, *Vision and Difference: Femininity, Feminism and the Histories of Art* (London, 1988).

Pollock, John, *Wilberforce* (Berkhamsted, 1977).

Procter, Adelaide, *The Complete Works of Adelaide A. Procter* (London, 1905).

Rendall, Jane, *The Origins of Modern Feminism* (Basingstoke, 1985); Rendall (ed.), *Equal or Different: Women's Politics 1800–1914* (Oxford,

1987); Rendall and Susan Mendus (eds) *Sexuality and Subordination*, (London, 1989).

Reynolds, Graham, *English Watercolours* (1950; London, 1988).

Robinson, Annabel, Purkis, John and Massing, Ann, *A Florentine Procession* (Cambridge, 1997).

Rosen, Charles and Zerner, Henri, *Romanticism and Realism: the Mythology of Nineteenth Century Art* (London, 1984).

Rosenberg, Sheila, 'The Financing of Radical Opinion: John Chapman and the *Westminster Review*', in *The Victorian Periodical Press: Samplings and Soundings*, ed. Joan Shattock and Michael Wolff (Leicester, 1982).

Rossetti, D.G., *Dante Gabriel Rossetti: His Family Letters*, ed. W.M. Rossetti, 2 vols (London, 1895); *Letters of Dante Gabriel Rossetti*, ed. O. Doughty and J.R. Wall, 4 vols (Oxford, 1965–7).

Rossetti, William Michael, 'Art News from England', *The Crayon: an American Journal of Art*, August 1856, pp. 244–46; *Some Reminiscences* (London, 1906).

Rossi, Alice S., *Essays on Sex Equality: John Stuart Mill and Harriet Taylor Mill* (Chicago, 1970).

Rousseau, Jean-Jacques, *Emile or On Education*, trans. Allan Bloom (New York, 1979).

Ruskin, John, *Modern Painters*, 3 vols (1834–60; London, 1898); *Sesame and Lilies* (1865; London, 1917).

Russett, Cynthia Eagle, *Sexual Science: The Victorian Construction of Womanhood* (1989; Cambridge, Mass. and London, 1991).

Sahli, Nancy Ann, 'Elizabeth Blackwell, MD (1821–1910): a biography', PhD dissertation, University of Pennsylvania, 1974.

Said, Edward W., *Orientalism: Western Conceptions of the Orient* (1978; Harmondsworth, 1991).

Sand, George, *Jacques*, trans. Anna Blackwell (New York, 1847); *Mauprat*, trans. Matilda M. Hays (London, 1847); *The Miller of Angibault*, trans. Revd Larken (London, 1847); *The Story of My Life*, trans. and ed. D. Hofstadter (London, 1984); *Story of My Life* (a group translation), ed. Thelma Jurgrau (Albany, NY, 1991).

Sellar, E.M., *Recollections and Impressions* (Edinburgh, 1907).

Shanley, Mary Lyndon, *Feminism, Marriage and the Law in Victorian England 1850–1895* (London, 1989).

Shiman, Lilian Lewis, *Women and Leadership in Nineteenth-Century England* (Basingstoke, 1992).

Showalter, Elaine, *The Female Malady* (London, 1978); *Hystories: Hysterical Epidemics and Modern Culture* (New York, 1997).

Spender, Dale, *Women of Ideas and What Men Have Done to Them* (London, 1982); Spender (ed.), *Feminist Theorists* (London, 1983).

Spencer, Herbert, 'The Rights of Women', in *Social Statics* (London, 1892) pp. 173–91; *The Principles of Biology*, 2 vols (London, 1864–7); *An Autobiography*, 2 vols (London, 1904).

Sprott, W.J.H., *Human Groups* (1958; Harmondsworth, 1967).

Spufford, Francis, *I May Be Some Time* (London, 1996).

Stedman Jones, Gareth, *Languages of Class: Studies in English Working-Class History 1832–1982* (1983; Cambridge, 1989).

Stephen, Barbara, *Emily Davies and Girton College* (London, 1927).

Stewart, W.A.D. and McCann W.P., *The Educational Innovators 1750–1880* (London, 1967).

Stirling, A.M.W., *William de Morgan and his Wife* (London, 1922).

Stone, James S., *Emily Faithfull: Victorian Champion of Women's Rights* (Toronto, 1994).

Strachey, Ray, *The Cause: A Short History of the Women's Movement in Great Britain* (London, 1928).

Sue, Eugène, *The Wandering Jew*, 6 vols (Boston, 1900).

Sutherland, Gillian, 'The Movement for the Higher Education of Women: its social and intellectual context in England, *c.* 1840–80', in *Politics and Social Change in Modern Britain* (Brighton, 1987); 'Emily Davies, the Sidgwicks and the Education of Women in Cambridge', in *Cambridge Minds*, ed. Richard Mason (Cambridge, 1995).

Taylor, Barbara, *Eve and the New Jerusalem: Socialism and Feminism in the Nineteenth Century* (1983; London, 1984).

Taylor, Charles, *Sources of the Self: The Making of the Modern Identity* (Cambridge, 1989).

Taylor, Ina, *George Eliot: Woman of Contradictions* (London, 1989); *Helen Allingham's England* (Exeter, 1991).

Tennyson, Alfred, *Tennyson: Poems & Plays*, ed. T. Herbert Warren (1953; Oxford, 1986).

Thomas, Clara, *Love and Work Enough: The Life of Anna Jameson* (Toronto and London, 1967).

Thompson, Dorothy, 'Women and Nineteenth Century Radical Politics: a lost dimension', in *The Rights and Wrongs of Women*, ed. Juliet Mitchell and Ann Oakley (Harmondsworth, 1986).

Todd, Margaret, *The Life of Sophia Jex-Blake* (London, 1918).

Tuke, Margaret J., *A History of Bedford College for Women* (Oxford, 1939).

Turner, James, *The Politics of Landscape: Rural Scenery and Society in English Poetry 1630–1660* (Cambridge, Mass., 1979).

Tuttle, Lisa (ed.), *Encyclopedia of Feminism* (London, 1986).

Uglow, Jenny, *George Eliot* (London, 1987); *Elizabeth Gaskell* (London, 1993).

Vaughan, William, *Romantic Art* (London, 1988).

Vicinus, M. (ed.), *Suffer and Be Still – Women in the Victorian Age* (London, 1980); *A Widening Sphere: Changing Roles of Victorian Women* (London, 1977).

Wharton, J.J.S., *An Exposition of the Laws Relating to the Women of England, showing their rights, remedies and responsibilities* (London, 1853).

Williamson, Tom and Bellamy, Liz, *Property and Landscape: A Social History of Land Ownership and the English Countryside* (London, 1987).

Wilson, Dorothy Clarke, *Lone Woman: The Story of Elizabeth Blackwell the First Woman Doctor* (London, 1970).

Wilson, Ellen Gibson, *Thomas Clarkson: A Biography* (York, 1989).

Wollaston, William, *The Religion of Nature Delineated* (London, 1759).

Wollstonecraft, Mary, *A Vindication of the Rights of Women* (1792; Harmondsworth, 1986); *Mary* and *The Wrongs of Woman* (1788 & 1798; Oxford, 1987).

Woodham-Smith, Cecil, *Florence Nightingale 1820–1910* (Harmondsworth, 1951).

Woolf, Virginia, *A Room of One's Own* (1929; St Albans, 1979); *Women and Writing* (London, 1979).

Wordsworth, William, *The Prelude*, 1805 text edited by Ernest de Selincourt and revised by Stephen Gill (Oxford, 1970).

Wright Mary, *Elizabeth Blackwell of Bristol: the First Woman Doctor* (Bristol, 1995).

Yeazell, Ruth Bernard (ed.), *Sex, Politics, and Science in the Nineteenth-Century Novel*, (1986; Baltimore and London, 1990).

ACKNOWLEDGEMENTS

My most enormous thank you is to Jenny Uglow for recognising the significance of Barbara Leigh Smith Bodichon to the nineteenth century women's movement and for believing that I should be her biographer. I would also like to thank Caz Hildebrand for her work on the dustcover of the book and Beth Humphries for her expert copy-editing.

I am grateful to Homerton College, Cambridge, for awarding me a personal research grant to help with travelling and other costs and to all those colleagues and students who have borne patiently with my obsession.

I am indebted to the following individuals whose interest, friendship or support have enabled me to complete the project: Richard Aldrich, Bonnie Anderson, Terri Apter, Gillian Beer, Hester Burton, Carrol Cooper, John Crabbe, Elizabeth Crawford, Alma Cullen, Dawn Dixon, Juliet Emerson, Elizabeth Ermath, Allen Freer, Nancy Fresella, Carol Gilligan, Felicia Gordon, Jenny Graham, Sarah Greaves, Mary Hamer, Katherine Heron, Andrew von Hirsch, Mary Jacobus, Mary Joannou, Elaine Jordan, Valerie Kent, Peter Lee, Dawn McClochlan, Jane Marcus, Jan Marsh, Joan Mason, Jacquie Matthews, Ann Moore, Charlotte Moore, Richard Nunn, Clarissa Campbell Orr, Janet Reibstein, Jane Rendall, Jennifer Rubin, Morag Schiach, Vera Schuster-Beesley, Julia and Graham Smith, Janet Soskice, Michelle Stanworth, Marilyn Strathern, Gillian Sutherland, Oliver and Virginia Sutton, Julia Swindells, Barbara Valentine and Louis Dodd, Rachel and Graeme Walker, Simon and Katherine Weston Smith.

I would also like to thank the following librarians, archivists and curators at the following institutions for their help. First and foremost I wish to express my gratitude to Kate Perry, the archivist, and to Frances Gandy, the Librarian, at Girton College, Cambridge. Secondly, I thank the staff at Cambridge University Library too numerous to mention individually, although I must acknowledge the expertise of the photographic team. I would also like to thank Marriott's Photo Stores in Hastings for their prompt response to commissions.

Thanks are also due to: Lynne Amidon of the Royal Free Hospital Archives in London; Catherine Barnes of 'Autographs and Signed Books', Philadelphia; Paul Burgin and Judy Stock at the University of California; Cambridgeshire County Records Office; Alison Cresswell, Centre for Kentish Studies, Maidstone; Bernard R. Crystal of Butler Library, Columbia University; Roger Davey, Philip Bye and Christopher Whittick of East Sussex County Council; David Doughan at the Fawcett Library, Guildhall University, London; Anne Wheeldon, Archivist of Hammersmith & Fulham; Family Heritage Centre, Cherry Hinton, Cambridge; Bob Henderson at the British Library; staff at the Public Record Office, Kew; Philippa Hogg of Scott Polar Research Institute, Cambridge; Susan North of the Victoria and Albert Museum; Brian Scott, Team Librarian, Hastings Reference Library; Una O' Sullivan of the Royal Commission on Historical Manuscripts, London; H.L. Mallalieu of *Country Life*; Vincent Giroud, Danielle C. McClellan and Kevin L. Glick at the Beinecke Rare Book and Manuscript Library, Yale University Library; Huw Jones, Herbert Art Gallery and Museum, Coventry; Jerome Farrell and Elizabeth Cory, City of Westminster Archives Centre, London; David and Barbara Martin of the Rape of Hastings Architectural Survey; Wendy Thomas of the Schlesinger Library, Radcliffe; Victoria Williams at Hastings Museum and Art Gallery; M.E. Gibson and Dr G. C. Cook at London School of Hygiene and Tropical Medicine; Lesley Richmond at the University of Glasgow; Angela Raspin at the British Library of Political and Economic Science, London School of Economics; Claire Skinner and Mrs N. Roche at Hampshire Record Office; Sophie H. Badham at Royal Holloway, University of London; Maria Twist, Central Library, Birmingham; Sarah Wimbush at the Courtauld Insitute, London; Marilyn Ward, Illustrations Curator, Royal Botanic Gardens, Kew.

Closer to home, the first friend of this book has been my husband, Desmond Hirsch, who has been computer help-desk, research assistant, photographer and French translator all rolled into one. Thanks to Stephanie who has typed up transcriptions from 'pencil only' archives, to Sophie for being the quickest off the mark finding names on gravestones in churchyards all over the country and to Sarah and Charlotte for cheering me on.

1. *William Smith MP* by Henry Thomson (1773–1843), oil on canvas 241 x 149.5 cm (courtesy of Norfolk Museums Service, Norwich Castle Museum).
2. Frances Coape Smith and her elder son, probably by John Opie (1761–1807) (courtesy of Hampshire Record Office; ref. 94M72/F691/23)
3. Photo of Ben Smith (courtesy of private collection).
4. Photograph of Ben Smith's and Anne Longden's grave at St Edmund's church, Wootton, Isle of Wight (photo by Desmond Hirsch).
5. Silhouettes of the five Leigh Smith children (courtesy of private collection; photographed by Marriott's Photo Stores).
6. Engraving of Pelham Crescent, Hastings (reproduced with kind permission of the Mistress and Fellows of Girton College).
7. BLS drawing of herself as Olivia, Bella as Maria, Ben as Malvolio in *Twelfth Night* (courtesy of private collection).
8. Drawing of Julia Smith by Hilary Bonham Carter (courtesy of Hampshire Record Office; ref 94M72/F552)
9. Photograph of James Buchanan reproduced from Robert R. Rusk's *A History of Infant Education* (London University Press, 1933). I have tried and failed to contact the picture's owner.
10. *William and Mary Howitt* by Margaret Gillies (1803–87), watercolour on ivory (courtesy of City of Nottingham Museums: Castle Museum and Art Gallery).
11. Photograph of Anna Brownell Jameson by Hill and Adamson, *circa* 1845 (with kind permission of the Scottish National Portrait Gallery).
12. BLS, *Ireland – 1846* watercolour & bodycolour with varnish (with kind permission of the Whitworth Art Gallery, University of Manchester).
13. BLS, *Trieste – Vienna Road*, 1850, sepia wash with white highlights (courtesy of private collection).

14a. BLS, cartoon of Bessie Parkes (reproduced with kind permission of the Mistress and Fellows of Girton College.

14b. BLS, cartoon of 'Barbara Leigh Smith in the Pursuit of Art unconscious of small humanity' (reproduced with kind permission of the Mistress and Fellows of Girton College.)

15. BLS, *Ye Newe Generation* ink on paper (reproduced with kind permission of the Mistress and Fellows of Girton College).

16. BLS pencil drawing of Lizzie Siddal, 8 May 1854 (collection of Mark Samuels Lasner).

17. *Eruption of Vesuvius from Naples, May 1855* (courtesy of private collection).

18. Carte de visite of BLSB on honeymoon by Holmes of New York (courtesy of the National Portrait Gallery, London).

19. BLSB, *Louisiana Swamp*, reproduction in *The Illustrated London News*, 23 October 1858.

20. Photo of Bessie Parkes (with kind permission of the Mistress and Fellows of Girton College).

21. Drawing of Elizabeth Blackwell by the Comtesse de Charnacée (courtesy of the archives of the Royal Free Hospital, London).

22. Drawing of George Eliot by Samuel Laurence, 1857 (with kind permission of the Mistress and Fellows of Girton College).

23. Jessie White Mario (with kind permission of Istituto par la Storia del Risorgimento Italiano).

24. Adelaide Procter, reproduced from an engraving of a painting by E. Gaggiotti Richards, the frontispiece of *The Complete Works* (London, George Bell and Sons, 1905). I have tried and failed to contact the owner of the picture.

25. Florence Davenport Hill (with kind permission of the Mistress and Fellows of Girton College).

26. Jessie Boucherett (with kind permission of the Mistress and Fellows of Girton College).

27. Drawing of Mathilda Hays, believed to be by Bessie Parkes (with kind permission of the Mistress and Fellows of Girton College).

28. Photograph of Eugène Bodichon, reproduced from Matilda Betham-Edwards, *In French-Africa* (Chapman & Hall, 1912).

29. Campagne du Pavillon, Mustapha Supérieure, Algiers (ref. 94M72/F648, courtesy of Hampshire Record Office).

30. BLS *Arab draught players* in *Illustrated Times* 14 March 1857; p, 164 (courtesy of the British Library).

31. BLSB with Hamet (with kind permission of the Mistress and Fellows of Girton College).

32. Samuel Laurence crayon drawing on buff paper of BLSB, 1861 (with kind permission of the Mistress and Fellows of Girton College).

33. Campagne du Pavillon, Mauves, France (photo by Desmond Hirsch).

34. Exterior of Scalands Gate, Robertsbridge, Sussex (with kind permission of Hastings Museum and Art Gallery).

35. Scalands Gate Dining Room (with kind permission of Hastings Museum and Art Gallery).

36. BLSB, 'Solitude' (courtesy of private collection).

37. BLSB, frontispiece to Matilda Betham-Edwards *A Winter with the Swallows* (Hurst & Blackett, 1867).

38. Photograph of the first College building at Girton 1873 (with kind permission of the Mistress and Fellows of Girton College).

39. Photograph of Girton College Fire Brigade 1880 (with kind permission of the Mistress and Fellows of Girton College).

40. Rudolf Lehmann portrait of Emily Davies (with kind permission of the Mistress and Fellows of Girton College).

41. Samuel Laurence, BLSB, portrait in oils (with kind permission of the Mistress and Fellows of Girton College).

42. BLSB pencil & ink sketch of Segovia (courtesy of private collection).

43. BLSB, *Chateau Gaillard on the Seine* 1870 watercolour over graphite (with kind permission of the Mistress and Fellows of Girton College); photo by Mike Clifford.

44. BLSB, *Near the Land's End,* watercolour and bodycolour 1875 (with kind permission of the Mistress and Fellows of Girton College); photo by Mike Clifford.

45. Photo of Gertrude Jekyll about 1880 (reproduced with kind permission of the Jekyll Estate).

46. Portrait of Hercules Brabazon Brabazon by John Singer Sargent (courtesy of the National Portrait Gallery, London).

47. Photograph of Mary Ewart (with kind permission of the Mistress and Fellows of Newnham College).

48. Photograph of Marianne North by Elliot & Fry, first seen as the frontispiece to *Some Further Recollections of a Happy Life* (Macmillan, 1893) (reproduced with kind permission of the Royal Botanic Gardens, Kew).

49. Milly Betham-Edwards, reproduced from Helen C. Black, *Notable Women Authors of the Day* (Glasgow, 1893). I have tried and failed to trace the copyright holder.
50. Photo of Norman Moore (courtesy of family collection).
51. Photo of Amy Leigh Smith (courtesy of family collection).
52. Benjamin Leigh Smith on the *Hope* 1882 (courtesy of Scott Polar Research Institute, Cambridge University).
53. Emily Osborn's missing portrait of BLSB reproduced from photo in Helen Blackburn, *Record of Women's Suffrage* (London, 1902) (with kind permission of the Syndics of Cambridge University Library.)
54. Portrait of BLSB by Emily Osborn, oil on canvas (reproduced with kind permission of the Mistress and Fellows of Girton College).
55. The Poor House at Zennor (photo by Desmond Hirsch).
56. Photograph of Madame Bodichon with Nurse Hornsby from the Gertrude Jekyll Collection (courtesy of College of Environmental Design, Documents Collection of the University of California, Berkeley).

Dates

1827   Born in Whatlington, Robertsbridge, Sussex

1834   Death of mother, Anne Longden

1836   Move to Pelham Crescent, Hastings, Sussex

1848   Financial independence at the age of twenty-one; starts to publish under pen-name 'Esculapius'

1849   Attends art classes by Francis Cary at Bedford College

1850   Travels to Munich with Bessie Parkes to visit Anna Mary Howitt and Jane Benham Hays

1852   Start of lifetime friendship with George Eliot

1853   Leaves Pelham Crescent

1854   *A Brief Summary of the Most Important Laws Concerning Women* published. Founds Portman Hall School; painting expedition to Italy

1855   Petition to Parliament to change the Married Women's Property laws

1856   First trip to Algiers

1857   *Women and Work* published; founds the Society of Female Artists, marries Dr Eugène Bodichon, tour of America with her husband

1858   Founds the *English Woman's Journal* with Bessie Parkes and Max Hays as editors

1859   Petition to the Royal Academy Schools for the admission of women students; buys Campagne du Pavillon, Algiers

1860   Death of father, Ben Smith

1863   Builds Scalands Gate on the Glottenham estate, East Sussex

1864   Studies with Corot in Paris; friendship with Daubigny

1865   Start of women-only Kensington Society

1866   Petitions Parliament for the enfranchisement of women property holders, publishes *Reasons for the*

Enfranchisement of Women

1867	Contracts typhoid, stays in England for winter and starts planning college with Emily Davies
1868	Death of Aunt Dolly Longden
1869	Leasing of Benslow House, Hitchin. Barbara donates the first £1,000
1872	Land bought at Girton for permanent college
1875	Buys Poor House in Zennor, Cornwall
1877	Suffers first stroke
1878	Gertrude Jekyll designs a room to be attached to Scalands Gate to serve as a reading room and night school
1882	Sells 5 Blandford Square, London
1883	Death of Aunt Julia Smith
1884	Gives another £5,000 to Girton College
1885	Death of Dr Bodichon; Barbara suffers another stroke
1891	Dies at Scalands Gate. Leaves Girton £10,000

Principal Exhibitions

1850–72	Royal Academy, London (seven appearances)
1851–74	Royal Society of British Artists, London (five appearances)
1855/63	British Institution, London
1856–78	Crystal Palace, London (four appearances)
1857–58	Touring exhibition of British Art; New York, Philadelphia, Boston, Washington D.C.
1858–59, 1866–77, 1880–81	Society of Female (later 'Lady') Artists, London (sixteen appearances)
1862/65	Liverpool Academy Exhibitions
1858/65/66	French Gallery, Pall Mall, London
1859, 1861, 1864	French Gallery, Pall Mall, London (solo exhibitions)
1863–81	Birmingham Society of Artists (eight appearances)
1865–6, 1869–73, 1875–81	Dudley Gallery, London (fourteen appearances)
1871–5	Liverpool Autumn Exhibition
1872	International Exhibition, London

INDEX

Entries under Bodichon, Barbara are those which cannot be readily found elsewhere. In sub-headings she is merely referred to as Barbara.

INDEX

INDEX